DISCARD

DATE DUE

MAR 2 3 2012	

D1195095

THE BOURGEOIS FRONTIER

RECENT TITLES

War of a Thousand Deserts: Indian Raids and the U.S.– Mexican War, by Brian DeLay
"Liberty to the Downtrodden": Thomas L. Kane, Romantic Reformer, by Matthew J. Grow
The Comanche Empire, by Pekka Hämäläinen
Frontiers: A Short History of the American West, by Robert V. Hine and John Mack Faragher
Bordertown: The Odyssey of an American Place, by Benjamin Heber Johnson and Jeffrey Gusky
Emerald City: An Environmental History of Seattle, by Matthew Klingle
Making Indian Law: The Hualapai Land Case and the Birth of Ethnohistory, by Christian W. McMillen
The American Far West in the Twentieth Century, by Earl Pomeroy
Borderlines in Borderlands: James Madison and the Spanish-American Frontier, 1776–1821, by J. C. A. Stagg
The Spanish Frontier in North America, The Brief Edition, by David J. Weber

FORTHCOMING TITLES

Defying the Odds: One California Tribe's Struggle for Sovereignty in Three Centuries, by Carole Goldberg and Gelya Frank
Under the Tonto Rim: Honor, Conscience, and Culture in the West, 1880–1930, by Daniel Herman
William Clark's World: Describing America in an Age of Unknowns, by Peter Kastor
Geronimo, by Robert Utley

THE BOURGEOIS FRONTIER

French Towns, French Traders, and American Expansion

Jay Gitlin

Yale University Press
New Haven & London

Published with the assistance of the Frederick W. Hilles Publication Fund of
Yale University, and with assistance from the Annie Burr Lewis Fund and the
income of the Frederick John Kingsbury Memorial Fund.

Maps by Adrian Kitzinger.

Set in Electra type by Tseng Information Systems, Inc., Durham, North Carolina.
Printed in the United States of America by Sheridan Books, Ann Arbor, Michigan.

Library of Congress Cataloging-in-Publication Data
Gitlin, Jay.
The bourgeois frontier : French towns, French traders,
and American expansion / Jay Gitlin.
p. cm. (Lamar series in Western history)
Includes bibliographical references and index.
ISBN 978-0-300-10118-8 (cloth : alk. paper) 1. French—West (U.S.)—History
2. French Americans—West (U.S.)—History. 3. West (U.S.)—Ethnic relations.
4. Frontier and pioneer life—West (U.S.) 5. West (U.S.)—History. I. Title.
F596.3.F8G585 2009
978′.01—dc22   2009015230

A catalogue record for this book is available from the British Library.

This paper meets the requirements of ANSI/NISO Z39.48-1992 (Permanence of Paper).

10 9 8 7 6 5 4 3 2 1

For Ginny and Basie
And for Howard

And in memory of my wonderful parents:
Benjamin Gitlin and Libby Graff Gitlin

CONTENTS

ACKNOWLEDGMENTS

I used to marvel at the long lists of people's names in the acknowledgments of scholarly books. Little did I realize how many people would be helping me over the course of so many years. Only two have been there from the very beginning when this book was born as an undergraduate senior essay for the history major at Yale College: my advisor Howard Lamar and my roommate Jim Babst, who introduced me to New Orleans. Over the years, Jim and his wife, Cindy, have sent books and provided a place for me to stay, even after Hurricane Katrina dislodged them from their own home. Now their children, Morgan and Beau, whom I saw first as newborns, have both graduated from Yale. I thank them all for years of friendship, great meals, and much conversation. Beau has written his own senior essay on the history of francophone Louisiana, and I hope he will someday publish his work. Don't take as long as I did, kiddo. I also thank several other classmates for their support and encouragement: Glenn Murphy, Jim Steele, and Max Addison.

We all follow our own paths. Some of us follow more than one. I could never stop playing music, and for countless years my fellow band-mates have endured my occasional scholarly ramblings during breaks on gigs. Their artistry, companionship, and support deserve a special shout out: Chris Coulter, Don Wallace, Bob D'Angelo, Gaetan Veilleux, Joe Belanger, Gray Fowler, Bob Semanchik, Tod Baharian, Pete Hohmeister, Sal Ranniello, Steve Taylor, and others. Thanks for the good times and see you next weekend. Above all, Vincent Oneppo has been there throughout music school, club dates, and concerts. Our families have grown up together. He has seen me through endless computer-related meltdowns. (As one of my cousins once jokingly said as the twenty-first century arrived, "Jay is now ready to enter the twentieth century.") So thanks for everything Vin. I needed the help, and you've always been there.

The world of my history day-gig has expanded greatly over the years. I'm indebted to colleagues, students, and friends at Yale. Former undergraduate students Ranie Hotis, Stephen Butler, and Heath Ackley wrote wonderful essays
that I acknowledge in the footnotes of this book. Current student Mara Harwel
helped with research on John R. Williams of Detroit. All of my students have
been a great source of inspiration and enthusiasm. In the graduate school, Bob
Morrissey, Karen Marrero, and Adam Arenson have all sharpened my thinking
and found material that I missed. I look forward to their own published books
and am grateful for their help and friendship. It has been an honor and a pleasure to be a part of the special family of scholars gathered by Howard Lamar.
Ann Fabian was the first to read a part of this manuscript. As anyone who knows
her will attest, Ann is one of the most generous and perceptive of colleagues.
Clyde Milner, Carol O'Connor, Kathy Morrissey, and Marni Sandweiss have
been wonderful and supportive friends for years. There are others, but George
Miles and Bill Cronon have earned special recognition. George, consummate
gentleman and conference roommate, always inspires me with his incisive comments. Bill has been a second mentor and constant friend, and his clear thinking has provided a guiding light. The late Robin Winks led me into the field of
Canadian history and, as department chair, encouraged my work as a teacher
and a scholar. Another department chair, Jon Butler, gave me the push I needed
to finish my long-delayed dissertation and has been a strong supporter. Florence
Thomas, long-time graduate registrar, has faith in all her graduate students, and
her faith in me never wavered. The fellows and students of Davenport College
at Yale have provided an ideal environment for years. I owe special thanks to
Barbara Munck, Rhonda Vegliante, former master Gerald Thomas, and current
master and classmate Richard Schottenfeld for their support. Sandy Isenstadt,
co-teacher and friend, has shared ideas and enthusiasm.

I never expected to receive so much assistance and encouragement from historians and archivists in places beyond New Haven, but I was naive. The late John
Francis McDermott, whose work provided the initial inspiration for my own
journey of discovery, welcomed me into his St. Louis home when I first started
this project. The late Abe Nasatir did the same in San Diego. Dan Usner and I
had our first conference panel experience together and have been friends ever
since. We have shared the joys and tribulations of working in this now growing
field of French colonial history or francophone North American studies. Dan's
work has been a model for others. His reading of this manuscript has saved me
from various errors and strengthened the final product. Bill Foley has provided
constant encouragement and enthusiastic support. I am grateful for his help as
a reader, a colleague, and a friend. His work on the Chouteaus remains the gold

standard, and I have borrowed shamelessly from it. Fred Fausz has graciously shared his research on and ideas about early St. Louis while preparing a new edition of the Chouteau manuscript on the founding of the city. My younger colleague and now old friend Peter Kastor has enriched my own thinking and become an important member of the circle of scholars we all gather in the course of our work. That circle began to expand for me when I first joined the French Colonial Historical Society. I don't get to see the members of this group as often as I would like, but the work of historians such as Carl Ekberg, Pat Galloway, Dale Miquelon, and many others has guided my own humble efforts. One whom I met years ago at a meeting of the society, Carl Brasseaux, has become a close friend, and we have shared the richness of Louisiana history over pastrami sandwiches at Katz's deli in New York and crawfish and macque choux at Prejean's in Lafayette. Who knew that history could be so delicious? With his son Ryan Brasseaux and family now at Yale, our worlds happily coincide. Ryan's own work on francophone North America will mark the entry of an important new voice in the field.

Several successive cohorts of archivists and historians at the Missouri Historical Society in St. Louis have provided generous assistance and guidance, from Kathy Corbett, Peter Michel, Ken Winn, and Eric Sandweiss to Duane Sneddeker, Ellen Thomasson, and Carolyn Gilman. Eric's book on St. Louis has been an invaluable guide to the city's growth, and Carolyn's work as a historian and her guided tours of the treasures of the collections have been great gifts. John Hoover at the Mercantile Library in St. Louis has also been a constant friend and helper. We share a deep admiration for the work of John F. McDermott. I have been fortunate to have such boon companions. I thank John Hoover and Louis Gerteis at the University of Missouri–St. Louis for inviting me to give the James Neal Primm Lecture in 2007, a great experience made all the more memorable by sharing drinks and conversation with Professor Primm himself afterwards. St. Louis is lucky to have such excellent historians and to have so many citizens who care deeply about the city's past. Elizabeth Gentry Sayad and *Les Amis* and Bob and Jeanette St. Vrain have been gracious hosts and shared their enthusiasm and knowledge during visits to St. Louis. (Thanks also to my friends down in Old Mines.) St. Louis has become a second home to me, and I am deeply in the debt of all who have welcomed me and encouraged my work.

Many other archivists in various cities have provided critical assistance. The folks at the Historic New Orleans Collection deserve special mention. I also thank Rebecca Mayne, archivist at the Grand Rapids Public Library. Research and writing can be a lonely business, which is why university departments and centers have been organizing workshops with increasing frequency to promote the sociable exchange of ideas and provide critical feedback for works in progress. I was very fortunate to have such an opportunity at an early and critical point when Steve Aron invited me to participate in a colloquium at the Shelby Cullom Davis Center for Historical Studies at Princeton University. I have always been a big fan of Steve's work and am grateful for the generous support and feedback he has supplied. He is one of the good guys in our profession. At that colloquium I met Gerry Friesen of the University of Manitoba. We later had an opportunity to invite Gerry to Yale as the Visiting Professor of Canadian Studies. It was a delight to have him and his spouse, Jean, at Yale. The Friesens and Nicole Neatby, the visiting professor the following year, have remained good friends and important correspondents, sharing thoughts about Canadian history and francophone North America. The chance to extend the scholarly community at Yale to include such brilliant historians from Canada has been provided by the Yale Canadian Studies Committee, of which I am a proud member. The chairs of that committee, the late Robin Winks and Professor Harvey Goldblatt, master of Pierson College, have been quick to support Canadian activities and studies. Thanks also to the WHINERS (Western Historians in the New England Region) for their friendship and enlightening conversation.

Of all the many scholars and friends I have been lucky enough to gather, no one has been more important than John Mack Faragher. It was Johnny's idea to establish the Howard R. Lamar Center for the Study of Frontiers and Borders at Yale, and that institution has been my primary home since its inception. Under Johnny's leadership, we have together guided the growth of the center, and he has personally been a constant source of scholarly feedback and practical guidance. The latter can be a rare commodity in academia. Johnny's many students are lucky to have him as a mentor. As a supportive colleague and as a historian, Johnny has been a great role model. My wife, Ginny, and I are grateful for the long friendship we have enjoyed with Johnny and Michele and lucky to have been together for so many family celebrations.

Roland and Lois Betts have supported the Lamar Center from the beginning. I am very pleased to have the opportunity to thank them in print for their dedication to Yale and to the field of western history. Jeremy Kinney and Holly Arnold Kinney have also supported the center and graciously welcomed Ginny and me into their beautiful Denver home. They took the time to take us to Taos, New Mexico, and continue to share their enthusiasm for the history and cuisine of the West. Waugh! I am also grateful to Edith Rotkopf for managing the center with a sure hand and a friendly face. I appreciate her intellectual engagement with all our activities.

The Lamar Center has provided many opportunities for intellectual exchange and amiable conversation. Our postdocs—Sheila McManus, Mark Brilliant, Barbara Berglund, Alyssa Mt. Pleasant, and Honor Sachs—have brought enthusiasm and the joy of historical discovery to our westerners' lunches. I thank them all for their ideas and perspectives and take great pleasure in seeing their work being published. Visiting scholars such as Bob Utley, Melody Webb, Sue Armitage, David Wrobel, Jim Ronda, Colin Calloway, Ned Blackhawk, and Elliott West have inspired me more than they can know. Our most recent Beinecke Senior Research Fellow, David Weber, took the time, in the midst of a health crisis, to read a chapter of this book. His encouraging and critical reading saved me from making a number of mistakes and reassured me at an important juncture.

None of this, of course, would be possible without the wisdom, infinite patience, and familial guidance of Howard Lamar. Howard has been the other person who has seen this project from the very beginning. Howard's undergraduate lectures on the international West and the fur trade inspired me. I used to sit outside his office waiting to see him, thinking that I hadn't an idea in my brain. I would leave much later with renewed confidence, full of thoughts. I have always suspected that the ideas came from him; yet he made me feel that they were my own. When I handed in my dissertation, Howard—with his usual smile—unveiled a present he had been saving for the occasion: a large and beautiful flag of Quebec. Sometimes I think the most important aspect of a book is to honor those who have taught us, to provide thanks, and, at least in some small way, to justify their confidence in us. That is certainly the case here. Johnny Faragher and I took Howard's graduate seminar together many years ago. We have always wanted to perpetuate the environment of genial exchange, broad thinking, and generosity of spirit that Howard created for us. I hope we have succeeded. Howard and Shirley: I cannot adequately express my gratitude, so just thanks for everything.

I am the most fortunate person. In addition to having such wonderful friends and colleagues, I am blessed with the best of families. My parents were incredibly loving and supportive. My father was strong, gentle, kind, and intellectually curious; my mother was fun-loving and instinctive and had a discerning eye for people and things. My aunts and uncles have always been there for me, and my cousins are like brothers and sisters. My brother Bruce has been a great friend and a fun interlocutor since the day he was born. I love you all. My parents-in-law, Don and Julie, have been equally supportive. I know they will actually read this book. Last—and first in my heart—are my wife, Ginny Bales, and my son, Basie Bales Gitlin. Ginny is truly my soulmate. I could not ask for a better partner in life. We have been playing music together for thirty years, and every day has been a song. She has read every page of this manuscript, helped with typing, and pushed me forward. Our son is now writing his own history papers as a Yale undergraduate. He has been and continues to be the best of companions as we hunt down used bookstores in every place we visit. This book is for them.

"Constructing the House of Chouteau: St. Louis" first appeared in a special issue titled "Early Cities of the Americas" of *Common-Place* (3:4 [July 2003]). I thank the editors of that superb journal and the American Antiquarian Society for permission to reprint the article in this book. I am also grateful to the Whitney Humanities Center and the Frederick W. Hilles Publication Fund of Yale University for providing a grant to reduce the publication costs of this book. Special thanks go to Professor Jay Winter, chair of the Hilles Publication Fund Committee. Finally, I thank the people at Yale University Press. I have always been a firm believer in the value of professionalism. Nothing gets produced without the skill, expertise, and experience of many, many individuals. My thanks to Lara Heimert, who accepted this manuscript, and Laura Davulis, who answered my many questions. Annie Imbornoni guided me through the copyediting stage with great patience and collegiality. Above all, I am grateful to Chris Rogers for pushing me to make this a much better and more coherent book. I take full responsibility for the imperfections that remain—but hey, *you* try writing history in between choruses of the "Electric Slide."

French World of Mid-America

Quebec

Montreal

L. Superior

Ft. Michilimackinac

St. Paul

La Baie Verte/
Green Bay

L. Michigan

L. Huron

L. Ontario

Prairie
du Chien

Milwaukee/
Juneau Town

Grand Rapids

Detroit

L. Erie

Dubuque

Chicago

Ft. St. Joseph
/Niles

St. Joseph R.

Maumee R.

Davenport

South Bend

Logansport

Fort Wayne/Kekionga/Miamitown

Peoria

Ft. Ouiatenon

Wabash R.

Terre Haute

Portage des
Sioux

St. Ferdinand de
Florissant

Vincennes

Missouri R.

St. Charles

St. Louis

Cahokia

Fort de Chartres

Prairie du Rocher

Ohio R.

Ste. Genevieve

Kaskaskia

Apple Creek

Cape Girardeau

New Madrid

Cumberland R.

Tennessee R.

APPALACHIAN MOUNTAINS

ATLANTIC OCEAN

Mississippi R.

Natchitoches

Natchez

Mobile

N

W   E

S

New Orleans

Gulf of Mexico

MILES

0   100   200   300   400   500   600   700   800

Kilometers

0   200   400   600   800

Modern state boundaries indicated for reference.

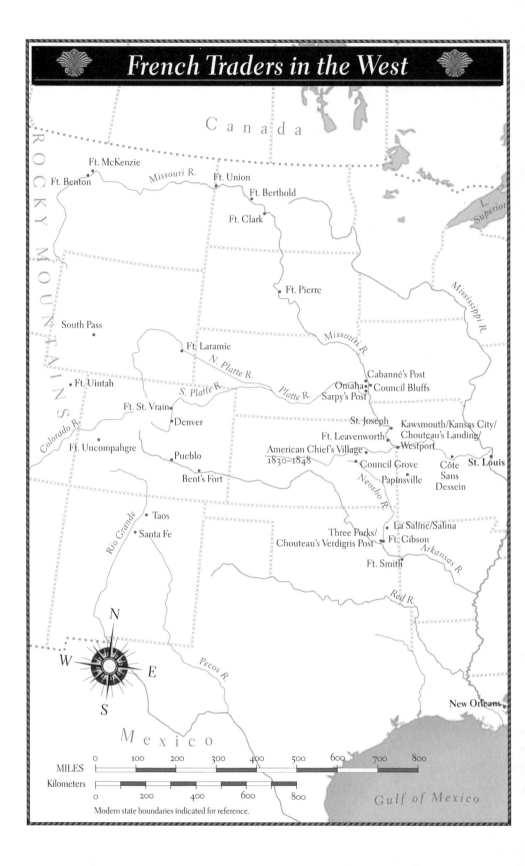

French Traders in the West

Canada

ROCKY MOUNTAINS

Ft. McKenzie

Ft. Benton

Missouri R.

Ft. Union

Ft. Berthold

Ft. Clark

L. Superior

Mississippi R.

Ft. Pierre

South Pass

Ft. Laramie

N. Platte R.

Missouri R.

Ft. Uintah

S. Platte R.

Platte R.

Cabanné's Post

Omaha

Council Bluffs

Sarpy's Post

Ft. St. Vrain

Denver

St. Joseph

Kawsmouth/Kansas City/

Ft. Leavenworth

Chouteau's Landing/

Westport

Colorado R.

Ft. Uncompahgre

Pueblo

American Chief's Village

1830–1848

Council Grove

Côte
Sans
Dessein

St. Louis

Bent's Fort

Papinsville

Neosho R.

Rio Grande

Taos

Santa Fe

La Saline/Salina

Three Forks/

Ft. Gibson

Chouteau's Verdigris Post

Arkansas R.

Ft. Smith

Red R.

N

W

E

S

Pecos R.

New Orleans

M e x i c o

| MILES | 0 | 100 | 200 | 300 | 400 | 500 | 600 | 700 | 800 |

| Kilometers | 0 | 200 | 400 | 600 | 800 |

Gulf of Mexico

Modern state boundaries indicated for reference.

Introduction: The Vanquished and the Vanishing

First-time visitors to the western settlements of the United States were often shocked to discover that English was not the language of the majority of the inhabitants. The initial reaction was often one of dismay, displayed perfectly in the words of William H. Keating, a member of Stephen Long's expedition to the Upper Mississippi in 1823. Passing from the state of Ohio to the state of Indiana and arriving in Fort Wayne, Keating wrote: "Not being previously aware of the diversity in the character of the inhabitants, the sudden change from an American to a French population, has a surprising, and to say the least, an unpleasant effect; for the first twenty-four hours, the traveller fancies himself in a real Babel. . . . The business of a town of this kind differs so materially from that carried on in our cities, that it is almost impossible to fancy ourselves still within the same territorial limits."[1] Keating's sense that he had passed into a new and rather foreign country had a firm basis in reality. The French language or a patois derived from it could be heard in an enormous region stretching from Detroit to St. Louis to New Orleans. The entire western fringe of the young republic had a French or Creole flavor.[2] French cultural hegemony only gradually receded during the decade of the 1830s, retaining pockets of influence in the larger cities and their suburbs and in frontier villages such as Kansas City. By the end of the nineteenth century, French was spoken only in isolated areas of Louisiana and Missouri and in the parlor rooms of certain neighborhoods of New Orleans, Detroit, and St. Louis.[3] It is not the ultimate demise of French hegemony that should surprise us, but rather its persistence over so large a region for so many decades after the incorporation of that region into the United States.

Who were these French-speaking Americans? Where did they come from? The French empire in North America had fallen in 1763 when France ceded the east bank and Canada to Great Britain. Why was French still the predominant language in areas that had belonged to England or Spain before becoming a part of the United States? Sadly, we are still asking the same questions today that uninformed travelers asked during the 1820s. We are ignorant because the story of this French corridor, this crescent-shaped francophone world, has never found a place in American history textbooks. It has never found a place for three related reasons: the dramatis personae have never been correctly identified; the geographical setting of the story lies upon a north-south axis and therefore lies counter to the traditional east-west presentation of U.S. history; and the story has been dismissed as being irrelevant to the general themes of American history. In short, the story of the French has been seen as nothing more than a quaint interlude in the dynamic drama of national expansion. Much of the blame for this can be laid at the doorstep of nineteenth-century historian Francis Parkman. As James Axtell has noted, most textbooks "continue to pattern the French story after the dusty scenarios of Francis Parkman."[4] To situate the story that unfolds in the following chapters, we should begin with a closer look at the historiographical trajectories that have obscured it.

It was the misfortune of the French to have their story told by one of the nineteenth century's great amateur historians. Parkman, born in Boston in 1823, was the son of a Unitarian minister, and in all respects, was truly a Boston Brahmin. He attended Harvard, was financially independent, and counted members of the city's best families as his friends. He wrote nine volumes during his life: *The Oregon Trail* (1849); *The Conspiracy of Pontiac* (1851); and his seven-volume magnum opus, *France and England in North America* (1865–1892). He was a great storyteller, but as modern critics of his work have pointed out, he was not a great historian. His interpretations were often simplistic; he was not above distorting his sources; and above all, he was one of the foremost proponents of scientific racism and often substituted pseudo-biological attribution for historical explanation. As Francis Jennings has noted, Parkman "created the grand new epic myth. . . . Invoking Providence, race, spirit, and the inevitability of progress, he sang the glories of his people and their most splendid prototypes, centered, not by chance, in Boston."[5] The French never had a chance.

The competition for empire in North America between the French and the English was Parkman's grand story, which ended with the triumph of the English—read Anglo-Saxon race—on the Plains of Abraham in 1760. With the death of both Louis Joseph Montcalm de Saint-Véran and James Wolfe on that battlefield, we are led to the ultimate victory of self-government and civilization on the continent, the emergence of the American republic. So, in essence, Parkman's task throughout his histories is to explain why the French and their Indian allies must fail. In Parkman, the dangers of teleological reasoning are magnified by his faith in Social Darwinism. To explain the failure of the French and the Indians, Parkman returns again and again to their "national" or racial characteristics. Indeed, the Indians rarely even receive national attributes from Parkman. Most often they are simply likened to wild animals. As savage brutes, incapable of becoming civilized, they must disappear as the wilderness gives way to progress. Voilà, the vanishing red man.

Parkman's French were more complex, although they were to share the same fate as their "uncivilized" allies. According to Parkman, the French were brave and courageous, yet simple. They were capable of rational behavior but were ultimately done in by their emotions. Whereas the Anglo-Saxon was "peculiarly masculine" and "fitted for self-government," the "French Celt" was bound by "his own impulses and passions." In short, Parkman stereotyped the French in much the same manner as he stereotyped women. They were capable of reason but seldom exercised it. They were capable of noble acts but were best left to simple lives. In the New World, the French in Canada showed signs of developing into a hardy race, but they were shackled by royal absolutism and the Catholic Church. And so Parkman concluded that "a happier calamity never befell a people than the conquest of Canada by the British arms."[6]

Parkman's legacy to future historians had two components. The first was a narrative influence. Because Parkman linked the fate of empire to national or racial characteristics, it followed that when the French empire fell, the French people in North America ceased to be historical actors of any importance or with any power. Parkman felt no need to take the story of the French in North America any further than 1763. Their tale was told. This from a man who in 1846 placed his life in the hands of his French guide, Henri Chatillon of Carondelet, Missouri, and accepted a safe-conduct and a line of credit from the powerful French Creole firm of Pierre Chouteau Jr. and Company.[7]

The second part of Parkman's bequest consisted of the stereotypes he employed. His descriptions, inaccurate yet appropriate for the story he wished to tell, had a lasting influence on later historians. Here is Parkman: "The Creole of the Illinois, contented, lighthearted, and thriftless, by no means fulfilled the injunction to increase and multiply; and the colony languished in spite of the fertile soil."[8] At the turn of the twentieth century, historians of such stature as C. W. Alvord of Illinois and Reuben G. Thwaites of Wisconsin were still using such phrases. Indeed, Parkman's adjectives threatened to become permanent fixtures. In an article written in 1938, Nelson Vance Russell, after granting that several French families in Illinois and Michigan had risen to prominence during the British regime "by industry, astuteness, and good fortune," went on, immediately thereafter, to state: "Gay they were, and light-hearted, yet pious; honest beyond comparison, generous to a fault, hospitable, free, and laughter-loving, with no cares from 'ambition or science.'"[9]

Although interest in the history of the French in the Great Lakes and Mississippi Valley regions has consistently been shown, most authors, until recently, have been unable to escape the narrative and descriptive straitjacket that Parkman provided. Many books have focused on explorers during the French regime and have been filled with romantic portraits of "cavaliers" and black-eyed Creole "damsels." Those historical works, both fiction and nonfiction, that have extended their coverage of the French beyond 1763 have generally chosen as their finale the capture of Vincennes by George Rogers Clark in 1779. In essence, the "simple, freedom-loving French" of the Old Northwest are redeemed by the actions of the Virginians. Reduced to being passive spectators in this historical tableau, the French shout "Vive Zhorzh Vasinton!"[10]

After Parkman, the historian who has wielded the most influence in shaping our interpretation of this French corridor in time and space has been Frederick Jackson Turner. Unfortunately, Turner's influence has also been largely negative. In his famous essay of 1893, Turner proposed a narrative paradigm for historians that still, with many refinements offered by generations of critics, exerts its power. Elegant and seductive in its simplicity, Turner's frontier thesis suggests that the process of settlement itself is the central drama of North American history. According to Turner, that drama was repeated numerous times as settlers, expanding from east to west, encountered the land. Turner also proposed a series of "stages" in that drama running from simpler to more complex socioeconomic activities. Like Parkman, he felt that the Indian peoples of North America were basically irrelevant to the process of economic and political development on the frontier. It was his view, developed in his doctoral dissertation, that the fur trade disrupted traditional Indian socioeconomic patterns and led to the disintegration of tribal integrity and independence. Fur traders, therefore, paved the way for European herders and farmers.[11]

Although Turner recognized that the fur trade had an effect on later economic development—primarily in the form of information, avenues of commerce (blazed trails and portages), and future sites for cities (trading posts)—he did not believe that the fur traders themselves had any future in this American frontier story. He felt that the traders, tied to the interests of the Indian trade, were bound to conflict with the Anglo-American frontier settlers who were looking to dispossess the Indians and claim their land. There was, of course, some truth to this point of view; however, Turner underestimated the ability of the fur merchants to diversify their economic activities.

Why did Turner fail to see that these early merchants did, in fact, often play an important role in facilitating the development of an urban civilization in frontier regions? In part, it was because he generally overemphasized the rural, isolated nature of the early frontier. Eager to demonstrate that the frontier was responsible for the evolution of the "national character," an ill-defined assortment of "agrarian" virtues and democratic political inclinations, Turner tended to downplay the role of financiers, speculators, and other citizens of the metropolis. He was certainly not the first American to locate the source of democracy in the yeomanry, but in so doing, he weakened his historical analysis. Frontier development was always tied to metropolitan investment, and pioneer farmers and merchants themselves understood, even if they did not always appreciate, their interdependence.[12]

Also evident in Turner's analysis, though not as blatant as in Parkman's, was a reliance on national or racial stereotyping. Turner recognized that the majority of fur traders in the frontier regions of the United States were French. Indeed, he even noted that "in parts of the Great Lake basin the old French life went on until the end of the first third of the present [nineteenth] century."[13] But Turner, like Parkman, felt that the French could play no important role in the development of American republican culture. In an article titled "The Rise and Fall of New France," he stated his case: "The English farmers and seamen stood for the ideals of political freedom and local self-government. They were implacable foes to the Indian and to the wilderness—a solid, substantial people, hewing out homes for their race. They lacked in picturesque elements, but what they took they held and reduced for the purposes of civilization."[14] The French, on the other hand, were "boon companions of the Indians, they ate and drank and sang and fought side by side with their savage brothers, married with them and took up their life. The gay, adaptable Frenchman was no wilderness conqueror."[15] Later in the article, Turner praises various republican leaders of Huguenot descent in the United States. It would seem, therefore, that the French traders of mid-America were insignificant actors in the drama of national expansion because of both their Roman Catholic religion and their relations with the various Indian groups.

This Parkman-Turner interpretation of the French presence in the American Midwest has been reinforced recently and ironically by historians investigating the métis people of the region. In trying to reconstruct the complex social and cultural worlds of the "people in-between," scholars such as Jacqueline Peterson perhaps have overemphasized the extent to which French and métis traders identified themselves as nonwhite or non-European. For example, in her article on the Great Lakes métis, Peterson makes it clear that the métis distanced themselves from their native cousins. At the same time, she notes that "early 19th-century

Americans, in general, were contemptuous of these suspiciously Indian-like folk who had lost their sense of private property and its full exploitation." Elsewhere Peterson describes métis villages as "practicing a subsistence-barter economy."[16] Yet here is Augustin Grignon, a member of one of the families described in her study, remarking on a certain chief of the Menominee nation: "He is among a very few Menomonees who contract debts, and pay them as they promise."[17] This remark and many others would seem to indicate that the Grignons of Wisconsin and many of their associates had not forgotten how to be businesspeople. Peterson herself points out in her article that competition from the powerful American Fur Company proved disastrous to many of the French traders in the Great Lakes region. Surely competition along with the lack of opportunities to accumulate land grants and political power in Wisconsin during the British regime must be acknowledged when one tries to account for the relative lack of success of the French in that area under American rule.

In another article on the métis traders of early Chicago, Peterson paints a vivid portrait of Mark Beaubien and his nephew Madore (Medard) Beaubien. She suggests that these "golden youngsters," possessing many advantages, in the end were unable to thrive in their own community when they came up against Yankee prejudice and economic ambition. Noting that Mark Beaubien disposed of his lots in an unprofitable manner and, in his words, "didn't expect no town," Peterson leads us to conclude that the métis generally were ambivalent capitalists who found it impossible to achieve status and recognition in the new Anglo-American order. It may be that Mark Beaubien was simply reflecting on the established urban hierarchy of the day when he made his remarks about Chicago. Chicago, after all, was no more than a minor post during the heyday of the fur trade. The more ambitious and important French merchants were located in St. Louis and Detroit. It may also be that the Beaubiens of Chicago were not very good businesspeople. And, of course, it may be that Peterson is right.[18]

But it would be wrong to conclude that all métis traders were like the Beaubiens. Antoine LeClaire, a French-Potawatomi man, grew up in a number of different French/métis communities: St. Joseph, Michigan; Peoria, Illinois; and Portage des Sioux, Missouri. During the 1830s, he established the town of Davenport, Iowa, and spent the next thirty years acquiring land, building hotels, and securing emigrants, capital, and railroad lines for his new city. He was the prototypical town booster.[19] Then there was Jean-Baptiste Richardville, the métis chief of the Miami tribe. Unlike LeClaire, Richardville obtained prestige and power primarily by virtue of his tribal position. He capitalized on the fur trade and the federal policy of removal. At his death, he was reported to be the richest man in the state of Indiana.[20]

The point is that not all métis traders were ambivalent capitalists unable to adjust to a new regime. It is almost as if defeat and withdrawal in the face of American expansion provides the only proof of métis distinctiveness. There is also a tendency to exaggerate the hegemony of métis culture by blurring the boundaries between French and métis society. It is true that the French were influenced by Native American customs and techniques, but the reverse is also true. However, the borrowing of cultural traits did not necessarily signal, in this case, the abandonment of a French or Creole identity or even the beginning of a métis identity. After all, bridges can mark boundaries just as effectively as moats. As one historian, borrowing from the insights of anthropologist Fredrik Barth, has observed, "distance and antagonism are not necessary to maintain distinctions between peoples. Frequently relations may be close and friendly; cultural elements as well as individuals may pass relatively freely among communities. Yet practices are maintained that perpetuate distinctions."[21]

It does indeed seem that an incipient métis culture existed throughout this French corridor. Peterson and others have already gone a long way toward reconstructing this complex world. Despite the brilliance of their work, however, three points have not been made clearly. First, some of the métis were able to thrive in the new republican and capitalist order. Indeed, some profited from the very policies that forced their kin to remove across the Mississippi. And failure should not necessarily be attributed to biological or cultural inclinations. Powerlessness and racism played an important role. We need to put Parkman behind us. Second, we must remember that métis nationalism was not a factor in the Midwest. When forced to choose between a native or a nonnative future, some chose the former, some the latter, and still others continued to occupy the periphery on reservations in the West. Any attempt to analyze the decision-making process that occurred and explain the structural basis underlying social classification must await further research.

Third, and most important in our attempt to clear the historiographical dust from our eyes, we must use travelers' accounts of métis and French groups with an extremely critical eye. In an article by R. David Edmunds on the métis of the Old Northwest, the author, following his sources, tends to lump the two groups together, in one case inserting the term "métis" in brackets after "Frenchmen" in the text.[22] But we need to examine further the observers Edmunds quotes most often: William Hull, William Keating, Judge J. B. C. Lucas, and Lewis Cass. Hull, the first governor of the Territory of Michigan, alienated the French residents of Detroit and its environs almost as soon as he arrived. In 1809, four years after Hull assumed his office, the inhabitants sent a petition to President James Madison requesting Hull's removal. Not surprisingly, Hull's letters to Secretary of War William Eustis in 1810, which Edmunds quotes, were full of invective against the French and tried to portray them as being friendly with and similar to the Indians.[23] Lucas and Cass began their careers as Jeffersonian appointees. Although both were intelligent men with principles, they were also zealous in the pursuit of frontier fortunes and acquired land as fast as they could. Like many other Jeffersonian bureaucrats, Lucas and Cass endeavored to pry real estate out of the hands of Indian and French holders and into the open market where they could engross it themselves. Both were quite successful, but in the process, they ran into resistance from French merchants. Lucas, whose 1807 letter Edmunds quotes, was not a favorite of the French Creole faction in Missouri, especially during the years he sat on the Board of Land Commissioners for Missouri (1805–1812). Lucas, Hull, and Cass all knew the difference between a relatively poor métis laborer and an unambivalent French capitalist. None of them was above insinuating to officials back in Washington, D.C., that the French in the West were an indolent people whose claims to the land were generally without merit—like their Indian friends, an impediment to progress.[24] Edmunds does note in his conclusion that métis ties to French, not English, culture made them "doubly undesirable" to American observers, but he fails to acknowledge the role of frontier politics in producing descriptions that deliberately blurred the very real class distinctions in fur-trade society.

Some travelers, like Keating, were simply ethnocentric observers who were genuinely "disgusted" (Keating's word) by the sight of Frenchmen wearing native dress.[25] And without a doubt, many of the French were influenced by their Indian neighbors. Keating, however, spent no time in St. Louis, Detroit, or New Orleans and never met members of the French middling and upper classes. To obtain an accurate picture of francophone society during this period, one must consult the accounts of those who were in contact with the bourgeois elite as well as those who saw only the *engagés*. And the French themselves left many documents for the use of historians. Although they were no match for the self-conscious New Englanders, who kept diaries and reminiscences, memoirs, and autobiographies, they kept careful records of their business transactions and were dutiful letter writers.

The picture that does emerge from the various sources is very different from the one Parkman drew. First of all, the communities of this French corridor were not simple or homogeneous. The assumption that the French in this region were primarily transplanted Canadians had some basis in reality for Detroit but much less so for St. Louis and New Orleans. The French came from a variety of provinces and colonies in the Old World and the New. Other ethnic backgrounds or "nationalities" were quite in evidence. In the major urban centers and even in the villages, a traveler could encounter French-speaking inhabitants born in the cities of Italy or Holland.²⁶ The Native American contribution to French culture has often been observed, but the diversity of Indian cultures having an effect is rarely noted. The task of tracing the influence of individual Indian societies would be formidable, but not impossible. And no picture of French culture in this region would be complete without the men, women, and children of African descent. Nonwhite Francophones, slaves and free, were to be found in every settlement. Their effect on the culture-at-large was possibly as great as that of native people, yet except for Lower Louisiana, their presence has seldom been acknowledged.²⁷ In addition to being ethnically and racially mixed, francophone society admitted and perpetuated distinctions of class. Although not rigidly hierarchical, French society in the western towns was certainly deferential and acknowledged the prerogatives of occupational rank even at distant fur-trading posts, much to the annoyance of the more egalitarian Anglo-Americans who might be present.²⁸

If the French communities in this region were generally more heterogeneous than has been acknowledged, they were also more cosmopolitan. They were cosmopolitan in two ways: the towns themselves were centers of cross-cultural contact and exchange, and the leading merchants of the towns were aware of prices and conditions in the major metropolitan centers of North America and Europe, often making long journeys to transact business and reconnect with creditors and suppliers.²⁹

In the towns, a high percentage of the inhabitants derived at least a part of their income from commerce or support services adjunct to trade. A knowledge of or familiarity with the languages and customs of other cultures, usually native, was a necessity. It was not uncommon for French traders to know at least one, if not several languages in addition to their own.³⁰ Keating was not the only traveler to be struck by the profusion of languages and dialects being spoken in the streets.

The French mercantile families, bourgeois to the core, were by necessity in touch with the world. Business concerns came first, but literature, art, and fashion were not ignored. Anglo-American travelers were quite surprised at the elegance and sophistication they found in towns they assumed to be out of touch with civilization. Captain Amos Stoddard, who took possession of St. Louis for the United States in 1804, wrote in a letter to his mother back home in Connecticut that "the people are rich and hospitable; they live in a style equal to those in the large sea-port towns." After being entertained by the St. Louis elite, Stoddard politely threw a party in return and had to borrow four hundred dollars from Pierre Chouteau Sr., a local merchant, to pay the bills.³¹

It has long been my sense that the French world in this western borderland was primarily an urban one. Following the lead of historians such as W. J. Eccles and John Francis McDermott, I took an interest in the core group of merchants in towns and incipient cities such as Vincennes, Detroit, St. Louis, and New Orleans and was struck by how little they resembled the happy-go-lucky premodern stereotypes. Infantilized and trivialized as children of empire and associates of the Indians, these utterly bourgeois families have been written out of our histories. To create both local and national stories that celebrated the Anglo-American basis of moral, political, cultural, and economic progress, historians and novelists bypassed these francophone merchants and the messy world of race and class they presided over. The French, like the Indians, occupy, at best, that telling introductory chapter of colorful exploration and mythical foundings—irrelevant to the course of American empire.

Historians such as Jacqueline Peterson, Tanis Thorne, and Richard White have turned our attention back to the French, in part, to search for stories of interaction and accommodation less disheartening than the stories with which we grew up—in White's words, "the shared meanings and practices of the middle ground."[32] Though the middle ground signifies a shared world, the French are not at the heart of his history. Above all, he has tried to rediscover Indian meanings and agendas on a frontier where they had to be taken seriously. Similarly, métis histories for Thorne and Peterson force us to reconsider the importance of race and gender, inclusion and exclusion, in the story of American expansion. All of this is praiseworthy; however, a key group of actors has continued to occupy the periphery of these stories—the French merchants themselves. Balkanized by local historians of the Midwest, ignored by French colonial historians interested primarily in imperial policymaking, and out of view from Canadian historians who tend to focus either on the colonial St. Lawrence Valley or modern Quebec, these French merchants from Detroit to New Orleans have not been seen as a coherent or a relevant group.

Living in Louisiana, the Illinois Country, and the Great Lakes basin, the French had, by 1763, already established a landscape of villages and urban places alongside Indian communities. On this frontier, Europeans and natives did indeed live side by side. As Richard White has observed, "Their knowledge of each other's customs and their ability to live together . . . had no equivalent among the British."[33] But there is no need to essentialize the French. As White points out throughout his book, this knowledge had been achieved over decades of experiences—pleasant and unpleasant. Although we may view cross-cultural partners and métis men and women as inhabitants of a literal middle ground, French and Indian places remained distinct. But they were connected by a variety of bridges—primarily economic and linguistic, but also religious and social. For me, the idea of bridges comes closer to capturing the essence of this French and Indian world.

Marie-Anne Cerré—later to become the wife of Pierre-Louis Panet—was born into this world in the French village of Kaskaskia in 1769. In 1847 her niece wrote down the following family story about her:

> Little Manon [her nickname] was very pretty and a favorite of her father, her mother and Madam de Renom. The Indians of the area, who used to crowd into her father's store, would overwhelm her with affection. Early one day at Kaskaskias, a chief, well esteemed by my grandfather, and who had camped with his band across the river from the white village, saw little Manon alone in her father's garden. He went up to her, took her by the hand and asked her if she wanted to go with him to the other side. The child, who knew the Indian well and was fond of him, consented; the man of the woods, without bothering about anything else, took her up on his shoulders and, entering the river Kaskaskias, crossed it, swimming upright with his feet, with [the child] astride his neck and holding on to her with his hands. He put her down safely on his side of the water and she spent the day at the chief's hut, playing with the children and being much petted by the whole camp. Meanwhile, her poor parents were desperate, not knowing what had become of her, searching at all the neighbors' homes, in this direction and that, without success, never once imagining that she could be on the other side. They were relieved of their extreme anxiety that same evening when the chief brought her home the same way he had carried her off that morning.[34]

This charming story illustrates the everyday cross-cultural familiarity of this rather unique frontier. But the ending is even more telling: aroused by this playful incident, Manon's father, Gabriel Cerré, realized that he would have to send his daughter away before too long, and several years later, he took her to board at a convent school in Montreal. Friendly neighbors though they might often be, the French and the Indians envisioned different pathways through life.

The chapters that follow, then, are about the actions and pathways of this core group of French bourgeois families. My primary focus is on the Chouteau clan of St. Louis, but I also discuss merchants in other French communities to reinforce the interpretation and to provide some sense for the reader that a broader francophone world existed throughout this period, from the 1760s to at least the 1840s.

If Parkman's picture of simple and irrelevant French people is truly to be dismantled once and for all, one more critical characteristic must be reemphasized. This francophone world was not a static one; rather, it was dynamic. The French communities in this western borderland were ready to confront and adjust to changing conditions. Those adjustments are at the heart of this narrative.

In the end, the French world of this borderland that so surprised and dismayed William Keating became increasingly invisible. It is my hope to write it back into our historical memory and show that the French merchants who went from being frontier brokers to brokers of frontiers played a significant role in the history of American western expansion. Moreover, as town founders and urban elites, they shaped the local histories of their native cities—a fact I have been continually reminded of by their descendants during my visits to Detroit, St. Louis, and New Orleans.

Constructing the House of Chouteau:
St. Louis

Cities, like people, are conceived, then born. St. Louis was the brainchild of imperial officials and two ambitious merchants. In 1763, Jean Jacques Blaise d'Abbadie, the last governor of French Louisiana, granted to Gilbert Antoine Maxent an exclusive privilege to trade with the Indian tribes west of the Upper Mississippi and along the Missouri for six years. Such monopolies followed a certain colonial logic: granted a privileged track in the pursuit of American wealth, private parties would do the costly work of breaking ground, building posts, and pursuing alliances with local tribes. D'Abbadie, faced with a depleted treasury, inflation, shortages, and trade disruptions, all consequences of the disastrous French and Indian War, hoped to jumpstart the colony's fortunes and secure the ties that bound the southern and northern parts of this vast region.[1]

Maxent, long involved with this Illinois Country commerce, seized the opportunity. (He would work closely in the future with Spanish governors of the colony, two of whom would become his sons-in-law.) A quarter share in the venture would go to Pierre de Laclède Liguest (known as Laclède), who had come to New Orleans in 1755, for serving as the new company's field partner.[2] Laclède's conception was clear. We know exactly what he had in mind and how he proceeded because his clerk and stepson, Auguste Chouteau, wrote a "Narrative of the Settlement of St. Louis." (The fourteen-page manuscript is a fragment of a longer narrative account that Chouteau had been writing decades after the actual events. It may have been based on a journal or diary. Neither a complete draft nor a journal exists. It is our most reliable firsthand account.[3]) The party left New Orleans in August and arrived in Illinois three months later on November 3, 1763. Storing their trade goods on the eastern bank of the Mississippi at the administrative center of French Illinois, Fort de Chartres, Laclède and Chouteau (thirteen or fourteen years old at the time) surveyed the western bank between the small mining and farming village of Ste. Genevieve and the mouth of the Missouri, selecting the site of St. Louis for its beauty, its elevation (relatively immune from the very real dangers of flooding), and its easy access to the Mississippi, Missouri, and Illinois rivers. In retrospect, it seems an obvious choice. And so, as Chouteau recalled, "We set out immediately afterwards, to return to Fort de Chartres, where he [Laclède] said, with enthusiasm, to Monsieur de Neyon [Neyon de Villiers, the commandant], and to his officers that he had found a situation where he was going to form a settlement, which might become, hereafter, one of the finest cities of America—so many advantages were embraced in this site, by its locality and its central position."[4]

Chouteau's "Narrative" is an astonishing document. To be present in this way at the birth of a great city is a historian's dream. (It is, of course, a gift to be used with some caution.) St. Louis, like many colonial American cities, was an intentional creation—a planned birth, not an accidental one. The moment of its birth recorded, St. Louis resembles so many American children, videotaped and well documented upon arrival. The sense of purpose that guided settlers, that covered the distance from old to new, created a most bourgeois environment of great expectations, of possibilities, even of entitlement. The act of self-shaping seems to lie at the heart of the American experience. Laclède directed young Chouteau and thirty workers to clear the land and build cabins and a large shed in February after the winter thaw. He returned in April with a design for the town and christened the newborn city, naming it St. Louis after King Louis XV's patron saint, Louis IX.

Having made the obligatory nod toward royal patrons and the church, Laclède revealed his priorities and the incipient city's raison d'être. A towpath for boats separated the river from the limestone ledges. On the ridge, workers laid out three streets parallel to the river: Grande Rue, Rue de l'Eglise, and Rue des Granges. The public market was front and center, followed by Laclède's own house. Behind that would be the church. In the back were the barns. Commerce lay at the heart of this place; farming was an afterthought. St. Louis soon acquired the nickname *Paincourt* or "short of bread," for food supplies were occasionally brought in from neighboring villages such as Ste. Genevieve, which was in turn dubbed *Misère*. Within decades, the Creole citizens of St. Louis would poke fun at the rustic manners of their rural neighbors.[5] The riverfront of the city today would most probably surprise the founders. The dense and bustling antebellum city with goods and people crowding the space between steamboats and Front

Street: that was what Laclède envisioned. Today, all remnants of the original city have disappeared. Only the old cathedral and a national park stand on the site. Busy storefronts would have been more appropriate as historical markers.

The first place established during the French regime in North America, Samuel de Champlain's Quebec, and the last, St. Louis, carried the same birth-mark: the *comptoir*—the fortified warehouse and counting house. Other economic activities would fill the landscape, but the driving force of this frontier was commerce—specifically, the fur trade. As W. J. Eccles wrote more than thirty years ago, French North America "can hardly be said to have had a frontier at all. Rather, it can be said to have been a metropolis, dominating the hinterland around it."[6] Establishing trading posts and other urban enclaves, the French plugged Indian producers and consumers into an international market economy. Merchants such as Laclède and the Chouteaus facilitated exchange and encouraged regional development from a pioneering urban base. And so the French left a legacy of cities across North America from Montreal to New Orleans, Detroit to St. Paul. And native peoples were hardly passive participants in this enterprise. It was the Mi'kmaqs who insisted that Jacques Cartier forget about a passage to China and trade for furs.

The conception of St. Louis likewise owed a huge debt to native groups. An Indian metropolis, Cahokia, had once existed across the river. More than simply a confluence of river systems, this location encompassed a primary crossroads of native peoples. Indian groups from the Upper Mississippi, the Great Lakes, the Missouri, the Wabash, and the Illinois rivers all frequented the area. A network of small-scale traders, French and métis, already blanketed the region. Above all, it would be the increasingly powerful Osages living to the west of the new city that determined the success of this enterprise. As J. Frederick Fausz has observed, "the fur trade represented a mutually beneficial convergence of French and Indian interests." Providing more than half of all "Indian-supplied furs between 1764 and 1803, [the Osages] greatly influenced the development of early St. Louis, which they called 'Chouteau's Town,' then the gateway to *their* West."[7]

With so many parents watching over the birth, it is not surprising that St. Louis prospered immediately. Imperial contingencies favored the growth of the settlement. Laclède arrived in the fall of 1763, and the news of France's cession to Great Britain of the Illinois Country east of the Mississippi and Canada had already preceded him. He persuaded forty families from the east-bank villages to move across the river to the new settlement. More families followed when the British formally took control in present-day Illinois in October 1765. News that France had secretly ceded New Orleans and Louisiana west of the Mississippi in the Treaty of Fontainebleau in 1762 finally reached St. Louis in December 1764. The first Spanish officials did not arrive until 1767. By then, St. Louis had passed through its infancy. It grew up speaking French, and its new imperial guardian made no attempt to change it. The Mississippi River had now become an international boundary. Spanish lieutenant governors, palms well greased, usually winked at contraband trade, and furs, skins, and trade goods would flow across borders with relative ease.

The trade exceeded Laclède's expectations. Sir William Johnson, back in New York, wrote to the Lords of Trade in November 1765 that a Frenchman established near the mouth of the Missouri "carries on a vast Extensive Trade, and is acquiring a great influence over all the Indian Nations."[8] The following summer, a visiting British officer noted that Laclède "takes so good Measures, that the whole Trade of the Missouri, That of the Mississippi Northwards, and that of the Nations near la Baye, Lake Michigan, and St. Joseph's, by the Illinois River, is entirely brought to him. He appears to be sensible, clever, and has been very well educated; is very active, and will give us some Trouble before we get the Parts of this Trade that belong to us out of his hands."[9] That year, 1766, Laclède wrote to his brother Jean, a lawyer in France, that his business was worth more than two hundred thousand livres.[10]

To be a successful merchant on this frontier, one needed good judgment, careful calculations, and connections. Procuring goods on credit in anticipation of the next year's production of furs, skins, and robes meant establishing a reputation for reliability and integrity. Trust was critical, but information was the key. Knowing about the conditions that would affect the market for all the goods being exported and imported required a network of correspondents in a dazzling array of places, from tribal villages to American, Canadian, and European cities. The fur trade was a global business. Letters and ledgers were as important as pelts. Good relations sustained trade, literally and figuratively. The objective of a merchant was to create a successful house—*la maison*—through the gradual accumulation of capital of all kinds. There was no separate commercial district in early St. Louis; business was conducted out of one's house. The private sector was just that, and, more often than not, partnerships were family affairs.

Literacy and a cosmopolitan outlook were a merchant's tools. So it should not surprise us that Maxent had a library of almost five thousand volumes.[11] The Laclèdes of Béarn had been *notaires* and *avocats* for generations. Pierre's Uncle Jean was a man of letters and science, known by Voltaire. Pierre's library in St. Louis included practical business guides, histories, a volume by Mirabeau on the theory of taxation, essays on electricity and physics, and books by Sir Francis

Bacon, John Locke, and René Descartes. Jean Jacques Rousseau's *La Nouvelle Héloïse*, published in 1767, could be found in Pierre's room in St. Louis.[12] Some of these volumes were later purchased at the estate sale by his stepson Auguste, who would amass his own impressive library. An affinity for Voltaire seems to have been passed down; Auguste owned a clock adorned with a figure of the great French philosophe.[13] Not surprisingly, freemasonry would attract French merchants in St. Louis, Detroit, and New Orleans. The first generation of merchants who migrated to St. Louis was, indeed, a cosmopolitan group. The majority came from western and southern France; northern Italy and Spain provided four each; and others came from Canada, the West Indies, Swiss cities, Holland, and Germany. In short, colonial St. Louis, although a muddy, village-sized enclave in the middle of Indian country, was not a sleepy and isolated frontier town. It could not afford to be.

Nor could it afford to be inhospitable to Indian clients who hunted and processed the animal skins that would become luxury goods in distant markets. Their productivity, their taste as consumers, and their goodwill were all key elements. Knowing your customers in this business often meant having connections within Indian settlements. Kinship ties, real and fictive, were maintained. The most important merchants in St. Louis had métis allies in the field. (Some also had more direct relationships with Indian women.) Historian Tanis Thorne described the family of one trader, André Roy, a client of the Chouteau family. After Roy's death, a woman of the Ioway tribe, Angelique, with whom he had two children, moved with her family from their village on the Des Moines River to St. Charles, a suburb of St. Louis. There, Roy's Ioway family lived near his French widow and children. Both women remarried, the children shared in the inheritance, and apparently, the "siblings enjoyed a close relationship."[14]

St. Charles, a village some twenty miles northwest of St. Louis on the north bank of the Missouri River, was founded in 1768 by a hunter named Louis Blanchette. Other suburbs were settled within the metropolitan orbit of St. Louis during this first generation of the city: Carondelet or *Vide Poche* ("empty pocket") in 1767, St. Ferdinand de Florissant in 1785, Portage des Sioux in 1799. The Deshetres, a family of Indian interpreters, went to Florissant. The Antoine LeClaires, father and son, the latter achieving some fame as Black Hawk's interpreter and the métis founder of Davenport, Iowa, lived in Portage des Sioux. By 1800, more than half of the 2,447 people living in the St. Louis metropolitan district actually lived in these satellite villages. This suburban population included many of those who filled the lower rungs of the fur trade's occupational ladder. Closer to Indian country, these villages provided convenient jumping-off sites and, for older workers, a place to retire and do a little farming. Land there being cheaper and more available than in St. Louis, these villages also attracted full-time farmers. Florissant contained the summer homes of some of St. Louis's wealthier merchants.[15] Viewing the metropolitan district of St. Louis in its entirety, one can say that the place included a rather diverse population. To call it a middle-ground city would be both redundant and a little misleading. It was, simply, a city, a crossroads, a place where people from different cultures met and products were exchanged.

As the surrounding suburbs drew off the métis portion of the population, the core became increasingly French. But the city proper was, from the beginning, a French home. When a group of 150 Missouri Indians arrived in 1764 while Chouteau and Laclède's workers were first laying out the town, Laclède hurried back to the site and carefully explained to the Indians why they must leave, disabusing them of their notion of settling in the heart of the new post. (Before they left, the women and children were engaged to dig a cellar for the company's main building.) Never intended to be an Indian home, St. Louis nevertheless quickly became a place of both interest and influence within Indian country. Coeur qui Brule, a Kansas chief, wrote to the lieutenant governor in 1800, "Depuis longtemps je désire voir la ville [for a long time I have wanted to see the town]." Understanding that St. Louis was a place of French manners and values, he added that he did not want to visit, like some chiefs, to seek presents. On the contrary, he said, "J'ai le coeur d'un français [I have the heart of a Frenchman]."[16]

Exchange and curiosity did not always produce harmony. The proximity of disparate cultures with unequal resources and power could easily produce tense situations. In one telling incident in December 1778, an Indian man named Louis Mahas announced that "he had dressed long enough as a Frenchman, he would now dress as an Indian warrior and go and take scalps." He was quickly arrested.[17] Early French St. Louis was a compact settlement, and lots were enclosed with palisades. When Auguste Chouteau purchased Laclède's old stone headquarters in 1789, he enclosed the entire lot with a "solid stone wall two feet thick and ten feet high, with portholes about every ten feet apart, through which to shoot Indians in case of an attack."[18]

The vulnerability of St. Louis was exposed only once during its early period. In 1780, a force of around 950 British soldiers and Indian allies, with some Canadian traders, attacked the town. The invaders were repelled, but not before more than ninety inhabitants, free and slave, were killed, wounded, or captured. The losses were deeply felt in a town with a population of some seven hundred souls.[19]

But the challenge of this first generation was not how to defend the place; rather, the primary task was that of constructing a city, a family, and a business from scratch. Consider the story of its founding mother, Marie Thérèse Bourgeois Chouteau.[20] Madame Chouteau, born in New Orleans in 1733 to a French immigrant, Nicholas Bourgeois, and his Spanish wife, Marie Tarare, did not have an easy early life. Her father died when she was six; her mother remarried. Family tradition has it that Marie Thérèse was placed in the Ursuline convent, but more likely, she lived with her mother and stepfather. She married René Chouteau, a baker and innkeeper, at age fifteen. By all accounts, her husband was contentious and physically abusive. He abandoned his wife and young son, Auguste, possibly as early as 1753 and returned to France. She must have met Pierre de Laclède fairly soon after his arrival in New Orleans in 1755. They remained together until his death in 1778. According to the laws of the Roman Catholic Church and France, the couple could not marry. Therefore, when their four children arrived—Jean Pierre (1758), Marie Pelagie (1760), Marie Louise (1762), and Victoire (1764)—they were given the name Chouteau. When Laclède and Auguste Chouteau, Marie Thérèse's only child by her legal husband, left on their founding journey, she was pregnant with Victoire. Sometime soon after the baby's baptism, she left New Orleans to make the seven-hundred-mile journey upriver with her three young children and infant in tow. In short, Marie Thérèse and her children, alone in the world with few resources, left a fragile past for a most uncertain future.

Arriving at Fort de Chartres, Madame Chouteau and the children then traveled to Cahokia in a bumpy, two-wheeled *charrette* and crossed the river in a *pirogue*. The family began their new life in the newly built stone headquarters. Four years later, they moved to a new house down the street. Laclède deeded this residence to Madame Chouteau, along with the lot, an additional piece of land in the common fields, three black slaves, and two Indian slaves, Manon and Thérèse, both in their teens. These gifts Pierre gave to his partner in consideration of his clerk Auguste's "faithful service" and "the affection" he bore the other four children of "dame Marie Thérèse Bourgeois and of Sieur René Choutaud."[21]

By this time, the missing husband had reemerged. Boarding a ship at La Rochelle in 1767, he returned to Louisiana. He spent some time in jail in New Orleans in 1771 for slandering a rival baker, and then in 1774, he initiated legal action to force his wife to return. Governor Luis de Unzaga directed the lieutenant governor in St. Louis to send Madame Chouteau back to New Orleans to be "under the authority of her husband."[22] Although another set of letters followed, this time with a promise to keep Marie Thérèse and Laclède apart, no further action was taken. Laclède continued to live in a room in the house he had given to Madame Chouteau. His children could never acknowledge their true father in public. All of this caused some consternation among the many socially prominent descendants as late as 1921 when one published a tract titled *Madame Chouteau Vindicated.*[23] What the story suggests is that St. Louis provided not only an economic opportunity, but a domestic one. In this distant place, the family could be secure, beyond the reach of legal propriety. Their stake in the city's survival represented an unusual risk.

To their relief, René Chouteau died in 1776. Thereafter, Marie Thérèse signed herself as Veuve (Widow) Chouteau. Laclède and Madame Chouteau never married, very possibly because he was heavily in debt to his former business partner, Maxent. The two had terminated their arrangement back in 1769, several years after their trade privileges had been discontinued. Laclède bought Maxent out but was never able to cover the notes he had signed. When Laclède died in 1778, the governor appointed his stepson Auguste to settle the estate at the request of Maxent.[24] The results of the sale suggest that Maxent allowed the widow to acquire enough property cheaply to provide a good future income.

Auguste purchased Laclède's gristmill (the only one in the region), a dam, a lake (known thereafter as Chouteau's Pond), and more than eight hundred arpents (1 arpent equals about 0.85 acre) of land for two thousand livres.[25] By this time, both Chouteau brothers, Auguste and Pierre, were trading on their own account quite successfully. All three daughters married well, bringing well-educated men (from France, Canada, and Switzerland) with capital and connections into the family and its city. It was Marie Thérèse Bourgeois Chouteau who gave the family its sense of direction and purpose. She set the tone in this bourgeois enclave in Indian country. By the turn of the nineteenth century, a new generation of family firms had begun to form. New relations, the building blocks of the urban community and the interconnected family businesses, arrived from Gascony, from Laclède's home province of Béarn, even from Italy.[26]

At her death in 1814, Veuve Chouteau was mourned by close to one hundred children, grandchildren, and great-grandchildren. Given her experiences, it is not surprising that she acquired a reputation for being thrifty, but family stories also describe her as a woman who loved clothes and jewelry. She conducted her own business affairs, with help from her Indian slave woman, Thérèse, whom she taught to manage her household. The town and family the widow constructed retained its French character during her lifetime. As one visitor described it in 1816: "St. Louis, as you approach it, shows like all the other French towns in this region. . . . The French mode of building, and the white coat of lime applied to the mud or rough stone walls, give them a beauty at a distance, which gives place to their native meanness when you inspect them from a nearer point of view. . . . The site is naturally a beautiful one, rising gradually from the shore to the summit of the bluff, like an amphitheatre. It contains many handsome, and a few splendid buildings."[27]

The city changed quickly after Madame Chouteau's death: new commercial and industrial enterprises, banks, Protestant churches, a new cathedral, civic institutions. Even some of the muddy streets would be paved. Above all, the first steamboat arrived in 1817, an impressive tool for conquering the tyranny of distance and reinforcing the city's position as a center of navigable rivers within a regional and national economic network. Madame's grandson, Pierre Chouteau Jr., would use steamboats to consolidate the family firm's dominant position in the fur trade, eventually superseding and even acquiring John Jacob Astor's American Fur Company. Chouteau would become the most famous name in the West during the antebellum period, appearing on Indian medals and flying from the flagpoles of company vessels. Controlling the flow of people, information, and goods, the Chouteau company would continue to serve both their private interests and those of an expanding American empire — in that order.[28] Within a new diversified portfolio that included railroads, railroad iron, and real estate, the fur trade would become an Indian business that drew profits from the dispossession of native people. But St. Louis had been from the beginning a place that took advantage of its proximity to Indian communities. It was not a home for native people, and Indian residents of the city during this early period were more likely to be slaves, outnumbered by the sizable population of African slaves.

The family remained open ended. Veuve Chouteau's grandson General Charles Gratiot Jr., a graduate of West Point, would spend much time in Washington, D.C., as a company lobbyist. His daughter Marie Victoire would marry a Frenchman and become "one of the most brilliant ornaments of the court of the Empress Eugénie."[29] Another grandson, Frederick Chouteau, would spend most of his adult life in Kansas and Oklahoma. His son William would marry a Shawnee woman, Mary Silverheels. That couple's great-granddaughter, Yvonne Chouteau, would celebrate both her Chouteau ancestry and her Indian ancestry and achieve fame during the 1940s and 1950s as the prima ballerina of the Ballets Russes de Monte Carlo.

It was a curious and fascinating circle that Laclède and Chouteau created when they first arranged the pattern of people and buildings named St. Louis. Perhaps the most representative sight in the city's first generation was that of the two Thérèses, one French, one Indian, walking down its streets. The Indian Thérèse served as Madame Chouteau's personal secretary and close companion for almost fifty years. If only we could have recorded their conversations. They were said to have been a "formidable combination."[30] In her will, Madame Chouteau gave the Indian woman her freedom and a small amount of cash and goods. During her lifetime, the French Thérèse, surmounting a rough start, became the mother of a city and a family dynasty. The Indian Thérèse, we should remember, was her slave.

These four watercolors, painted by Anna Maria von Phul (1786–1823), capture the air and style of the growing Creole American town of St. Louis in 1818. Von Phul produced them while visiting the city, where her brother Henry and his wife Rosalie Saugrain belonged to the elite circle of francophone families. At this time, one might see both moccasins and the latest Paris fashions in St. Louis. Both the Indian and Creole women Von Phul painted clearly had a fondness for jewelry and reddened their cheeks with either rouge or vermillion. Missouri History Museum, St. Louis.

French colonial armoire, circa 1800, bequeathed to the Missouri Historical Society by Mary Mitchell, a descendant of Pierre Chouteau Sr. It passed through several generations of daughters, beginning with Pelagie Chouteau Berthold. Made primarily of cherry wood (with walnut and tulip poplar), this beautifully crafted piece is made in the Louis XVI style. Once thought to have been made by Antoine Roux of Vincennes, it is possible that it was made by a craftsman trained in France. One of the finest surviving examples of French colonial furniture in mid-America, the armoire is evidence of the polished and refined tone of life in early St. Louis. Photograph by Cary Horton. Missouri History Museum, St. Louis.

Early métis baby shoe used by the Sarpy or Peugnet family. According to historian Carolyn Gilman, the shoe is "made like a European slipper rather than an Indian moccasin." The style of the floral quillwork was associated with the Red River métis, but researchers have argued that the style was more widespread than Red River because it is associated with many of the major fur-trading posts of the nineteenth century. This blend of cultural repertoires shaped everyday objects and life on such posts and affected the material culture of French frontier towns such as St. Louis. From the Amedee A. Peugnet estate. Photograph by Cary Horton. Missouri History Museum, St. Louis.

"We are well off that there are no Virginians in this Quarter": The Two Wests from 1763 to 1803

As a new French settlement, St. Louis quickly became a boomtown,[1] but it had started just as the French empire in North America ended. This is an irony that deserves closer examination. The French and Indian world in mid-America — which has been described variously as a "middle ground," an "empire of trade," or simply as the *pays d'en haut* — had from its earliest years existed both within and beyond constantly shifting imperial policy directives and agendas emanating from France and the colonial centers of Canada and Louisiana. As historian Colin Calloway puts it, "The collapse of the French empire in North America . . . did not mean the end of French presence and influence. Long after the Peace of Paris removed the French nation from North America, French, French Creole, and French-Indian populations, social systems, and cultures survived across large swaths of Canada, the Great Lakes, and the Mississippi Valley."[2]

That the so-called "interior French" not only endured, but prospered after 1763 suggests that Francis Parkman misunderstood the French colonial enterprise in North America. Writes J. F. Bosher: "The Parkmanian image of the French colonial government, as a leviathan hampering the development of private enterprise, no longer appears in the writings of our best historians. The converse might now be shown . . . because there is evidence that rampant private enterprise prevented the proper functioning of the government."[3] Under the French regime, commercial competition shaped colonialism as many of the most lucrative fur-trading posts were sold for fairly exorbitant fees. In addition, illegal trading had long been a fact of life in the French colonial West. With regime change, the entrepreneurial pattern remained, only the fees disappeared and "these Frenchmen prospered by the change in government."[4] During the Seven Years War and afterwards, young Frenchmen were leaving the war-torn St. Lawrence Valley to seek opportunities in the western Great Lakes and the Illinois Country.

The establishment of St. Louis provided a new center of gravity for a region whose economic importance was on the rise. This western entrepôt now provided an alternate market for furs and a new source of goods through New Orleans. With two viable avenues of trade—the Great Lakes route linking Michilimackinac (in present-day Michigan), La Baye (Green Bay, Wisconsin), Detroit, Montreal, and Quebec and the Mississippi route through St. Louis and New Orleans—goods, capital, and enterprising merchants began to flow into what we might call a new Creole Corridor.[5]

One place that grew and prospered during the tumultuous decades of the 1760s and 1770s was Prairie du Chien at the junction of the Mississippi and Wisconsin rivers in present-day Wisconsin. New Englander Jonathan Carver visited the place in 1766 and described it as a "large town," a "great mart where the adjacent tribes, and even those who inhabited the remote branches of the Mississippi, annually assembled, about the latter end of May, bringing with them their furs and peltries, to dispose of to the traders."[6] Seven years later, another New Englander, Peter Pond of Milford, Connecticut, came to Prairie du Chien to trade and described a colorful scene with merchandise and traders arriving from both ends of the Creole Corridor. Hams, cheeses, and wine came in boatloads from New Orleans. Local and distant Indian groups came to trade, camping out and playing fierce but peaceful games of lacrosse. The French, according to Pond, practiced billiards.[7] Several times a year, the place became a gigantic trading fair with amusements in addition to a significant exchange of valuable commodities. The permanent population, a mix of French and métis trading families, grew slowly as homes exhibiting a blend of French and native characteristics were built along the river on typical narrow French longlots to fully utilize the frontage. What mattered most about Prairie du Chien was that it provided, as Lucy Murphy has noted, "a safe haven, a place of refuge and peace for the purposes of trade."[8] It was a location where rival Indian communities agreed to put aside their differences, even if temporarily, and a trading zone beyond the reach of imperial soldiers and officials. The French or Creole Corridor was shaped by the calculus of commerce. As General Thomas Gage, the British commander in chief in North America, noted in frustration in 1766, "the Traders, particularly those upon the Lakes, shew little Regard to the Regulations that have been made to oblige them to traffick only at the Forts, which they avoid, and rove at Pleasure."[9] Rather, as Gage observed to the British governor in Canada, Guy Carleton, a year later, the French from Detroit, the Illinois Country, and Canada "all ramble over the Country without restraint, holding Conferences with each other, planning mischief by exciting Savages against us, and carrying on illicit trade."[10] In short, the Creole Corridor that emerged after 1763 was a new West, a West "beyond the frontier." Built upon the foundation of the old French and Indian *pays d'en haut*—but with a critical new anchor in St. Louis—this far western region drew the fur trade from all directions, defying the attempts of two great empires to establish their sovereignty over areas that had previously been part of the French empire. Nevertheless, this francophone zone did not exist in a vacuum, and the four decades between the end of the Seven Years War and the Louisiana Purchase were tumultuous ones that would ultimately change the context, if not the calculus, of western commerce.

Let us quickly review the imperial boundaries that emerged as a result of the Seven Years War. The Spanish now had jurisdiction over Louisiana—in essence, three subregions: Lower Louisiana, including the great port of New Orleans; the Arkansas country; and Upper Louisiana—also known as Spanish Illinois—which included the towns of Ste. Genevieve and St. Louis and a number of smaller settlements. The British gained jurisdiction over Canada, which, of course, contained the cities of Quebec and Montreal. Canada also included the former *pays d'en haut*, the Great Lakes region anchored by the settlements and forts at Detroit and Michilimackinac. Finally, the British had jurisdiction over the French villages in the present-day states of Illinois and Indiana. The villages in this last region—including Vincennes, Peoria, Kaskaskia, and Cahokia—were the weakest links in the imperial chain, being removed from the centers of power yet connected by ties of trade and family to both Spanish Illinois and New Orleans to the west and south and the Great Lakes and Montreal to the north and east.

The great show of imperial, and later republican, plans and agents notwithstanding, the reality was this: the West beyond the old military fault line in western Pennsylvania that had been the focus of the imperial struggle between France and Great Britain was dominated by Indian people who controlled the land, raised the crops, and gathered fish and furs. The tribal majority cast a long shadow over the pretensions of non-Indian politicians. In between Indian communities were French villages and incipient cities such as Detroit, St. Louis, Natchez, and New Orleans, inhabited by fur traders and merchants who managed the commerce between Indian North America and Europe. Although a plantation economy—mostly sugar, tobacco, and cotton—had emerged in Lower Louisiana, and the French in Illinois with the help of African labor raised a significant amount of wheat and maize, this vast area was best described as a trading-post frontier—a region of colonial towns within Indian country. French was the lingua franca that tied together this complex polyglot, multicultural area of mid-America.

All the subregions within the former boundaries of French North America had much in common, and the leading merchants in towns from New Orleans to St. Louis to Vincennes to Montreal often corresponded—primarily about business matters, but also about the political events that affected trade. Children might be sent to Montreal, to New Orleans, or to France to be educated. In the end, neither the Spanish nor the British were successful in controlling their new acquisitions. The Spanish retreated to Texas, the British to Canada. In the middle of this period, of course, a new player emerged—the republic of the United States. The French, in the meantime, went about their business.

Spain accepted the port of New Orleans and the trans-Mississippi portion of Louisiana by the Treaty of Fontainebleau in November 1762. Louis XIV ceded this territory to Charles III as compensation for the loss of Florida to Great Britain. France thus avoided British domination of the entire mid-continent of North America and gave itself the possibility of a colonial comeback at a later date. Although Spain eventually played a constructive role in the growth of Louisiana, the province was always considered a defensive buffer zone between the British colonies and New Spain. Only that rationale allowed Spanish officials to justify the annual subsidy of four hundred thousand pesos that the Crown spent to administer Louisiana. Even this amount proved insufficient. Officials in Louisiana were constantly facing budget deficits. One distraught official, Juan Ventura Morales, intendant at New Orleans, harassed Charles Dehault Delassus, the lieutenant governor of Upper Louisiana, over the price of peas and barrel staves in 1798.[11] Spanish Louisiana was neither a profitable nor essential part of the empire. Few Spaniards ever visited the colony; fewer settled there.

Spain, after years of procrastination, finally sent Antonio de Ulloa to Louisiana in 1766 to serve as the colony's governor. After further delays to the formal transfer of sovereignty, Ulloa was essentially booted out by the French inhabitants, who feared Spanish trading restrictions and were in the midst of a currency crisis. This Louisiana Revolt of 1768 anticipated the American Revolution by seven years. Several leaders of the revolt even suggested setting up a republic and hoped France would back them up. (French ministers briefly considered this course, thinking that a Louisiana republic would encourage English colonists to follow suit.) The following year, however, Spain sent an Irish officer in the Spanish service, Alejandro O'Reilly, to put down the revolt and establish Spanish rule once and for all. Five of the French rebels were executed.

Despite the brief flirtation with republican ideas, the French in both Upper and Lower Louisiana soon realized that the Spanish regime would essentially be benign. As historian Stuart Banner has noted, "Spanish officials responded to [the] gap between their theoretical and actual power by allowing the French residents of Upper Louisiana to retain the institutions of self-government they possessed before they lived under Spanish sovereignty." What mattered most in a colony that depended on the Indian trade was that civil disputes could be swiftly resolved—and here Spanish procedures "mirrored earlier French colonial practice"—and that the maintenance of friendly relations with tribal neighbors be guided by the counsel of leading merchants well-versed in the practices of the middle ground.[12] The inability to do the latter would plague Spain's imperial counterparts east of the Mississippi.

The British accepted Canada and the trans-Allegheny portion of French Louisiana in 1763 with none of Spain's initial reluctance. Indeed, they entered the West with confidence. The departing French governor of Louisiana, D'Abbadie, described the British as "men drunk with success, and who regard themselves as masters of the world."[13] The outbreak of Pontiac's War in the summer of 1763 destroyed those illusions. An Ottawa warrior named Pontiac coordinated the pan-tribal attack on the British garrison at Detroit. His actions inspired other Indians in the West, and many posts fell thereafter, including the important post of Michilimackinac. Smaller posts such as Green Bay were abandoned at this time, never to be reoccupied by the British.

The British quickly realized that defeating the French empire did not mean that they had won the West. One British detachment under a Major Loftus, attempting to occupy the Illinois Country by sailing up the Mississippi, was turned back by a group of Tunicas in Pointe Coupé in Louisiana in March 1764. Captain Thomas Morris, sent by General John Bradstreet to take possession of Fort de Chartres in Illinois by traveling overland through present-day Indiana, was held prisoner by the Miamis at their town of Kekionga (Fort Wayne). Only the intervention of a French trader named Godfroy saved him from being killed.[14] The British finally occupied Fort de Chartres in 1765—two years after the Treaty of Paris.

The British faced three dilemmas. First, they quickly realized that they could not wrest control of the western fur trade from the French. Second, they could not reconcile the conflicting agendas that informed British policy: the desire to maintain good relations and trade with Indian communities and still create new areas for settlement that would satisfy both the demands of backcountry colonials and the speculative dreams of various elite groups that often included the policymakers themselves. Third, they inherited a moving frontier that already carried with it the historical burden of decades of mistrust and ethnic hatred. Partially obscured by the military struggle between European powers during the

Seven Years War, the strong undercurrent of settler-native violence emerged full-blown toward the end of Pontiac's War with the murder of Christian Indians by the Paxton Boys in Pennsylvania in December 1763.[15] This episode "politicized Indian-hating in Pennsylvania." Thereafter, "opportunistic squatters from Pennsylvania and Virginia once again pressed, remarkably quickly, onto Indian lands. This time they came as Indian-haters, hardened by the experience of war and organized for self-defense." Leaders might lament the situation—Benjamin Franklin wrote, "It grieves me to hear that our Frontier People are yet greater Barbarians than the Indians, and continue to murder them in time of Peace"—but British policymakers could not find a way out of the morass.[16] In the end, the first two dilemmas fed on each other, and the third overwhelmed them both. "Faced with a huge new territorial empire in North America in 1763, the British tried to defend it, administer it, and finance it. Instead they lost it."[17]

In essence, there were two Wests, and each carried a different legacy. In the trans-Appalachian backcountry, two "village worlds," to use Richard White's phrase, with much in common—a history of multiple dislocations, violence, alcoholism, evangelical visions, political fragmentation, and small-scale economies dependent on a similar mix of grazing, hunting, and agriculture—increasingly found themselves on either side of a dividing line with no ground for cooperation. Beyond this polarized "dark and bloody ground" bordering the Ohio River, the Creole Corridor continued to privilege trade relations and respect Indian sovereignty. With the piece-by-piece collapse of British policy during the decade between Pontiac's War in 1763 and Lord Dunmore's War in 1774, the British found themselves unable to avoid the vortex of violence and wound up on one side of what amounted to state-sanctioned ethnic cleansing from 1777 to 1782. In the Creole Corridor, the Spanish provided a measure of security and authority that helped Indian and French communities to distance themselves from the Ohio country. The two Wests had this essential difference. In the Creole Corridor, commerce and kinship relations sustained complementary French and Indian worlds. The bridges of exchange held because there were, as yet, no demands being placed on Indian homelands. In the British-Indian West farther east, the bridge of commerce—which did exist on a smaller scale—could not resist the pressure of competition over land and animals. The settlers' need to create more and more property stiffened Indian resistance, and countless episodes of brutality deepened patterns of racial violence. When Major Arent DePeyster, the British commandant at Detroit in 1782, tried to explain to his superiors why the western Indians were "fickle allies" in the war against the colonials, he reported the natives as saying simply that "we are well off that there are no Virginians in this quarter."[18]

To explain how the French fit into the events that brought these two Wests together from 1763 to 1803, let us return to Pontiac's War. British officers in the field were convinced that French traders in the West were partly responsible for the hostilities.[19] Major Henry Gladwin, commandant at Detroit; General Jeffrey Amherst, the commander in chief; and General Gage, the man who replaced Amherst at Montreal in 1763, all accused the French of mischief and perfidy. Governor James Murray at Quebec recommended to Lord Halifax, the new secretary of state for the southern department, that the French inhabitants of the interior be removed. This recommendation would be reiterated many times over the course of the next ten years. Halifax needed little convincing. He and Lord Hillsborough, the new president of the Board of Trade, desired a program of strict imperial control that would achieve their vision of orderly Protestant settlement. Expansion would be limited by Indian reserves in the interior. To that end they issued the Royal Proclamation of October 1763. Neither minister had much use for the French Catholic population that Britain had acquired by conquest. Halifax hoped Quebec would become another Nova Scotia. It was hard enough to know how to deal with the French in Quebec. Those living in the interior were even more problematic, and Hillsborough kept hoping they would somehow disappear. Legally they did. The Proclamation of 1763 left the interior outside the jurisdiction of any civil government. Even commanding officers at the western posts could not exercise legal jurisdiction until passage of the Mutiny Act of 1765. By the time Detroit was fully included within a civil jurisdiction in 1788, it was de jure no longer a part of the empire.[20]

British officials might ignore the need for civil government in the interior, but they could not ignore the need to regulate the fur trade and maintain relations with western Indian groups. Indeed, they suffered the presence of the French in large measure because they realized that—in the words of one British officer in 1762—"The french Inhabitants and Indians are soe much connected that if you disoblige one of them, the other takes Part."[21] At first, the British tried to control the fur trade through a plan formulated by Sir William Johnson, the northern superintendent of Indian affairs. Influenced by Dutch practices in New York, Johnson's plan called for a line of posts with commissaries, interpreters, and blacksmiths, strictly controlled by the superintendent. Indians would have to come to these posts to trade, and fur traders would not be allowed to operate in Indian villages. A similar system would be tried by the U.S. government later on with a strikingly similar lack of success. Johnson's plan, issued in July 1764 but not fully implemented until 1766, also called for the licensing of all traders in Indian country. By 1765, sixty-five Montreal fur traders and merchants were petitioning British officials to abandon this plan, claiming that the Indians of the

Great Lakes region were simply carrying their furs and skins to French traders operating under Spanish protection.[22]

In short, British officers and policymakers were stymied. Pontiac's War showed them that the French were there to stay—the Indians insisted on that. Yet the British could hardly rely on the French. When one trader, Alexander Henry, asked his neighbor, Charles de Langlade, to hide him during the attack on Michilimackinac, Langlade coolly replied, "Que voudriez-vous que j'en ferias?" (What do you want me to do about it?).[23] The French understood that they, too, were in Indian country. Johnson's restrictive fur-trade policy only put British traders at a further disadvantage—which they hardly needed. As a British officer noted, "the Indians here will never be in our Intrest, for although our Merchants sell them a Stroud for 3 Beaver, they will rather give six to a Frenchman."[24] Confined to their posts, British traders watched the furs flow to French traders who continued to visit or even lived among their Indian customers. The British commander at Fort de Chartres in the Illinois Country wrote in 1768: "As I am very Sensible of the great Expence this Country is to the Crown, and the little advantage the Publick has hitherto reaped by the Trade with the Savages; And the reason is that the Inhabitants have continued to Send their Peltry to New Orleans, which is shipped from thence for old France, and all the Money that is laid out for the Troops and Savages, is immediately sent to New Orleans, for which Our Subjects get French Manufactures."[25] The officer, Captain Gordon Forbes, hit the nail on the head. The inability to control the fur trade led to further cost-cutting measures, which further weakened British authority. One short example will show how this worked.

Baynton, Wharton, and Morgan of Philadelphia had entered the Illinois Country with great enthusiasm and an investment in trade goods of seventy-five thousand pounds sterling in 1766. After alienating his French customers, failing to capture an expected number of furs, and losing a bid to supply provisions to the troops stationed at Fort de Chartres, George Morgan—the company's resident trader in Illinois—had to rely on supplying the commissary at the fort with Indian goods, but the commissary was removed in March 1769 to reduce the mounting costs of empire. The firm had failed by 1770 and sold its stock of goods to a rival company. The principals of the company now relied even more on a land scheme, the Illinois Company, to recoup their losses.[26]

And so it went. In 1768, the architect of the disastrous fur-trade plan, Sir William Johnson, negotiated the rather cynical Treaty of Fort Stanwix. This treaty extended the line of colonial settlement, set aside a tract for the "suffering traders," and alienated the Indians of the Ohio country both by opening their hunting grounds to settlement and by ignoring them in the negotiations as Johnson allowed the Iroquois to speak for the native parties who were directly affected by the deal. The treaty nicely summarized the bankruptcy of British policy and its conflicting agendas. By 1768 the British had admitted their weaknesses—and once again, a flurry of schemes to deport the French surfaced. (As Keith Widder has observed, such schemes "amounted to no more than hallucinations brought about by a desire to wish away a group of people whom they [the British] neither liked nor trusted but could not live without."[27]) That same year, regulation of the fur trade was given back to the individual colonies.

Several years of costly mismanagement later, the British were ready to dismantle many western posts in the backcountry. In December 1771, the decision was made to abandon Fort Pitt and Fort de Chartres. In 1770, General Gage had written Lord Hillsborough about the British dilemma in the West. Acknowledging that the French had secured both communications and "the Affections of the Savages," he concluded that the British would not be able to match their success at such a "small Expence."[28] Hillsborough's response was to suggest, once again, that the French inhabitants simply be removed. Aware that such a policy would be difficult to implement at Kaskaskia and merely result in a further removal to the Spanish side of the Mississippi, the policymakers agreed that Vincennes posed no such difficulties; therefore, a proclamation ordering the inhabitants on the Wabash to "quit those countries instantly and without delay" was issued on April 8, 1772. This Acadian solution—what historian John Mack Faragher has described as a form of frontier ethnic cleansing—drew an immediate response from those inhabitants.[29] Claiming that they were indeed settlers with legitimate land titles, not "vagabonds" as they had been described, the French of Vincennes declared their fidelity to the king. In language remarkably like that of the French Canadians asked to support the British empire during the Boer War and World War I, the Vincennes French noted that they would be more than willing to sacrifice their lives and property for the King—but only when "his service shall in reality require it."[30] (The French in Vincennes were saved from deportation by a timely change in administration from Lord Hillsborough to Lord Dartmouth.[31]) In the meantime, the French at Kaskaskia, frustrated with the arbitrary and oppressive acts of their British commandants, John Reed and John Wilkins, sent a memorial to General Gage in 1772 that outlined a plan for a republican form of government modeled after the colony of Connecticut.[32]

Gage returned to England, and his reports and advice contributed to yet another change in British policy. The Quebec Act of 1774 restored the civil law in Quebec and guaranteed toleration of the Catholic Church. Indeed, this act—which infuriated Protestant Anglo-Americans—even granted certain key legal

and political privileges to French Catholics in North America that were not extended to Irish Catholics in Great Britain—a fact that did not go unnoticed in
Ireland. The Quebec Act also extended Quebec's boundaries to include Indian
country between the Ohio and Mississippi rivers. In short, the commercial logic
of the pre-1763 era had been restored, but British officials continued to ignore
the need for civil government in the interior. For that matter, the competing
interests of trade and land continued to prevent the execution of any consistent
vision for the western borderlands. Imperial bureaucrats and colonial lobbyists
squabbled with each other and among themselves over prerogatives, responsibilities, and expenses. Serious political considerations obstructed practical solu-
tions. The growth of the British national debt cast a long shadow over the proceedings. Like their counterparts in Spanish Louisiana, officials at Detroit and
Michilimackinac were constantly upbraided by their superiors in Quebec for ex-
ceeding their budgets. With one eye on the expenses of the Indian Department
and the other on the latest trade reports, British officials gradually abandoned
their Indian allies south of the Great Lakes. They beat a slow, but steady retreat
from the region.[33]

In the Creole Corridor, the consequences of this retreat were at first negligible.
Both Great Britain and Spain had experienced difficulty fitting these costly new
territories into their imperial systems. The two countries also faced each other,
with intermittent hostility, across uncertain and awkward boundaries. The Mississippi River had once been the central, unifying artery of Louisiana. It functioned
considerably less well as a dividing line. Spanish and British officials complained
constantly that trade was being siphoned off to the other side. Contraband was a
fact of life. As one British official had noted, "Smuggling with them [the French]
. . . amounts to so considerable a Sum annually as to become a National Ob-
ject."[34] It could hardly have been otherwise. The road that connected the two
main settlements of Spanish Illinois, St. Louis and Ste. Genevieve, ran along the
coast of British Illinois.[35]

In the Ohio country, the consequences of this "vacuum of authority" were
disastrous. Eric Hinderaker, in his book *Elusive Empires*, has summarized the
situation perfectly: "A confusing jumble of ventures arose during the intermi-
nable period of ministerial indecision. Old and now invalid Indian grants to individual colonists were converted into real estate and sold off in lots; the governor
of Virginia defied royal authority to pursue the interests of speculators (including himself); eager to establish their own claims to the land without having to
buy it from self-appointed proprietors, squatters pushed ever farther into the
valley. The Ohio Indians were infuriated by all the activity, but the collapse of

British authority left them no diplomatic recourse."[36] An "unprecedented burst of immigration" in precisely those years that witnessed the collapse of British authority compounded the problem as European colonists joined the western land rush. British general Frederick Haldimand predicted the outcome in 1773: the emigrants would provoke the Indians, and "settlements . . . so far remote from all influence of the laws, will soon be the asylum of the lawless."[37] There were comic moments in what followed. Dr. John Connolly, an agent of Virginia governor Lord Dunmore, appeared in Pittsburgh on January 1, 1774, claimed the place for Virginia, and promptly called for a militia. He was then arrested by Pennsylvania magistrate Arthur St. Clair.[38] The humor faded quickly. By March, Connolly had returned with a militia to fight the Indians. Lord Dunmore's War and the Battle of Point Pleasant in October of that year kicked off what would become the American Revolution in the West: eight years—the bloodiest being the year after the British surrender at Yorktown—of brutal raids and massacres. We might charitably call it "petite guerre" in the West, but realistically, it amounted to state-sanctioned ethnic cleansing on either side of the Ohio.

The Creole Corridor or francophone West experienced little of this. In 1779, Spain joined with France and the American rebels and declared war on Great Britain. The Revolution crippled Spanish attempts to benefit from the fur trade of Upper Louisiana. The Quebec Act had already encouraged British, primarily Scottish, merchants to increase their activities and investments in the western fur trade. Armed with more capital, a greater supply of cheaper merchandise, access to better markets for selling furs, and a cooler climate in which to store the perishable bundles of fine pelts, British firms operating out of the Great Lakes "redirected the export of furs from the Mississippi Valley to London via Montreal . . . a condition that lasted until . . . the War of 1812."[39] Spanish officials now complained that the Upper Mississippi trade was controlled by merchants operating out of Michilimackinac, Detroit, and Prairie du Chien. To make matters worse, a partial British blockade of the Gulf of Mexico disrupted the flow of goods in and out of New Orleans, and gangs of mostly Anglo pirates were plundering boats traveling along the Lower Mississippi. Until the 1790s, Spanish officials in Upper Louisiana were forced to look the other way while the merchants under their jurisdiction traded illegally with British companies.

Despite their economic advantage, British officials knew that the (British) Illinois Country could never be secure while New Orleans was in Spanish hands. They looked upon war with Spain in 1779 as a golden opportunity to seize control of the Lower Mississippi Valley.[40] In short, as the Revolution progressed, neither the British nor the Spanish felt very secure. Could either power rely on the allegiance of the Indian and French inhabitants of this vast area? Such grand diplomatic questions were complicated by the entry of a new group, stage right: George Rogers Clark and his motley band of frontiersmen.

In a theatrical series of events that had all the aspects of grand opera—comic, tragic, and gruesome—Clark and his small force of Virginians and Kentuckians, 178 men in all, "conquered" the French Illinois villages of Kaskaskia, Cahokia, and Vincennes in July 1778. (There was no conquest. The last small group of British troops stationed at Kaskaskia had withdrawn two years earlier. Clark announced to the local French settlers that France and the United States were now allies, and dinners and balls were held in Clark's honor.[41]) Later in the year, Lieutenant Governor Henry Hamilton of Detroit and his British army retook Vincennes. Then in February 1779, Clark and the Americans—after a march of some 180 miles in the dead of winter—recaptured Vincennes, brutally executed several captured Indians, and took Hamilton prisoner, sending him in irons to a jail in Williamsburg, Virginia. It is a "heroic" episode that has been told and retold many times by historians and writers of historical fiction. In reality, half of Clark's army that retook Vincennes consisted of local French villagers, and the majority of men commanded by Hamilton were also local Frenchmen. It seems that the French settlers of Vincennes had become old hands at taking oaths of allegiance during the course of this campaign. When Lieutenant Michel Brouillett, a French rebel, was captured by the British in the vicinity of Vincennes, British captain Normand MacLeod commented on the fellow's misfortune. It seems Brouillett had that very day received his commission as an American officer. He already held one in the British army. Captain MacLeod also reported in his journal that when his superior, Major Jehu Hay, entered Vincennes, "he not only gave his hand to Major LaGran, Captain Bosseron and some others [leading pro-American Frenchmen] but kissed them and received them with every mark of friendship."[42]

How should we read these events? Why was Clark there? After all, the Indians in that quarter were not the same ones raiding the Kentucky settlements. Although his motives and goals are hard to pin down, they seem to include opening lines of communication with Spanish officials in St. Louis, receiving credit for needed supplies from French merchants (they would rue that decision), distracting British officials in Detroit, and ultimately detaching a piece of the British empire—a piece that had already been abandoned for all practical purposes. (Virginia could never seem to extend its claims to land and sovereignty quite enough. Virginia governor Patrick Henry, who approved of Clark's mission, incorporated the Illinois Country as a Virginia county in December 1778.) It was certainly a successful expedition. Clark managed to capture the hated Henry Hamilton, who had been sponsoring raids by the Ohio Indians since June 1777.

(The orders for this, of course, came from above, and the raids continued until 1782.[43]) Certainly, the boundaries of the final settlement at the Treaty of Paris in 1783 reflected Clark's bold achievement.

What of the French? What did they think about all of this, and what was their opinion of these armed backcountry invaders? Most French traders in this contested region probably had little love for Clark's Virginians and even less affection for the British. Captain Richard Lernoult, a Swiss-born British career officer in command at Detroit since 1777, wrote the following in March 1779: "The [French] Canadians are exceedingly amused on our bad success and weakness. . . . Not one of them will lend a hand. . . . All the Canadians are Rebels to a man"[44] (and Lernoult was apparently well liked by the local inhabitants). Pro-American French traders at Prairie du Chien such as Daniel Linctot led native groups from that area to a pan-Indian conference Clark held at Cahokia to try to win the tribes to the American side.[45]

If the British thought them rebels, then George Rogers Clark was ready to put his own spin on the situation, calling the people of Vincennes "true citizens." But Richard White surely has it right when he observes that after the fighting, "the dualities broke down." Back to being local Frenchmen, not Americans or Brits, two members of Hamilton's force were saved by a father who had marched with Clark and a sister who happened to live in Vincennes. Another trader who had accompanied Clark saved Pontiac's son because Pontiac had once saved him.[46] "What decided the outcome of Vincennes was not the fighting, of which there was relatively little," White writes, "but the decisions of the French and the Indians. The Vincennes militia, resentful of Hamilton, immediately deserted to Clark . . . and 'said it was hard they should fight against their own Friends and relations who they could see had joined the Americans.'"[47] Clark's actions had, "largely unwittingly," "buttressed the de facto republican independence of the French villages."[48]

Independent they surely were. British officer Captain Donald Campbell described the French in Detroit this way in 1760: "The Women surpasses our expectations, like the rest of America the men very Independent."[49] And if we connect their pro-American stance in the Clark episode to their revolt in New Orleans in 1768 and their Illinois pamphlet in 1772, then we can, at the very least, suggest that the French in the Creole Corridor were familiar with republican ideas and certainly were not merely the simple, passive peasants they were later depicted to be in novels such as *Alice of Old Vincennes*. Independence mattered to the French. It was contextualized by the need to maintain market connections and ensure civil order to protect life and property.

One trader who left the richest documentation of a French perspective during this period was Charles Gratiot. Swiss by birth, Gratiot had established a permanent residence in Cahokia only in December 1777. Having been sent to London as a youth to receive an English education, he was one of the few residents in the village who could actually converse with Clark and his men. Although he apparently became friends with Clark, Gratiot was not entirely enchanted with the course of events. In 1778, he wrote to his father David back in Lausanne: "The English side of this country is taken by the Americans since July last, I much fear that Canada will experience the same fate in the course of the winter." A year later he wrote to American colonel John Montgomery "that if business continues any longer on this footing, I shall be obliged in spite of my inclinations to become a Spaniard, so as to be able to participate in all the advantages of the trade of both sides—Seeing that it will be impossible to carry on any business here, without running the risk of ruin."⁵⁰ And so Gratiot did indeed move across the river to St. Louis in 1781, where he married into the prosperous Chouteau family. When Americans proved, quite quickly, to be as ineffective as the British in restricting the markets on their side of the river to the merchants under their jurisdiction, the French crossed over. If it was liberty they desired, it was a businessman's definition of it: free trade for all and government intervention when it is good for business. Those who seemed most inclined to support the American cause—Gratiot, Gabriel Cerré in Kaskaskia, and Francesco Vigo in Vincennes (an Italian born in Sardinia in 1747 who came to New Orleans in the Spanish service in 1774 and then moved to Vincennes)—already had correspondents in American towns and anticipated the growth of an American trade. Merchants who happened to live in the West of the Creole Corridor, they were used to focusing on many places and potential markets at once. Their perspective was international—and that outlook, from the beginning, has always been part of the western experience.

It stands to reason then that the American Revolution played out in very different ways in the two Wests. The racial violence that prevailed in the Ohio country simply was not a significant factor in the Creole Corridor. Indeed, there were few violent episodes, and those that did occur—beyond Clark's famous adventure— were shaped in part by trade rivalries, not by a competition for land.

The attack on St. Louis and Cahokia in May 1780, although part of a mostly unsuccessful three-pronged British counteroffensive, was inspired locally, to some measure, by several French traders such as Jean Marie Ducharme, who bore a grudge for having been cut out of the lucrative Osage trade by Spanish officials in 1773. Patrick Sinclair, the British lieutenant governor at Michilimackinac, admitted as much in a letter to General Haldimand, observing that "the reduction of Pencour" [St. Louis] would gather "the rich furr Trade of the

Missouri River" and redress "the injuries done to the Traders who formerly attempted to partake of it."[51] The two French-Spanish raids on St. Joseph (Niles, Michigan) were largely shaped by the loyalties and trade competitions revolving around the Chevalier kinship group, as Susan Sleeper-Smith has shown. In 1765, in an effort to placate the Potawatomi Indians at St. Joseph, the British appointed French trader Louis Chevalier the "king's man" at that post. Fifteen years later, the uneasy British had less tolerance for subjects whose loyalties were unknown, and in 1780, the same Patrick Sinclair evicted Chevalier. In December 1780, a party of Illinois Frenchmen looted the post but were later killed or captured by Potawatomi defenders led by a "British" Frenchman, Lieutenant Louis Fontenoy de Quindre of Detroit. Two months later, a party of "Spanish" Frenchmen led by Eugene Pourée of St. Louis seized the village and flew the Spanish flag—for a day. The "Spanish" party included Louis Chevalier Jr.[52]

Like their distant relatives the Acadians, the French throughout this vast region tried to maintain a position of neutrality. They were not averse to exploiting British and Spanish connections when they could, but in times of conflict, they usually sang a familiar refrain. They were simply local residents with long-standing ties to the region. Empires and republics came and went. This position of neutrality was mostly driven by the necessity of maintaining economic and social connections to local Indian communities—native groups that continued to assert their own sovereignty over the land. Moreover, the French used their ties to native groups to enhance their own identity as indigenous residents. And so during Pontiac's War, the French addressed an Indian assembly with the following words: "My brothers . . . we have come here only to renew the ancient alliance which our fathers made with you, and which you are today destroying by bringing death upon us. When you began your attack upon the English you gave us to understand that you would do us no wrong."[53] When the Indians attacked the Kentucky militia at River Raisin during the War of 1812, the French uttered remarkably similar words, proclaiming their neutrality to all who would listen.

But just who were these French residents? Were they, in fact, the ancient inhabitants of the region? Many of the French "were not the same people with whom the British had been waging war for decades."[54] The Creole Corridor was not simply the old *pays d'en haut*. There were, as we have noted, new places and new connections. There were also new people. Although the French had indeed inhabited parts of this vast region since the late seventeenth century, a surprising number of prominent merchants were recent arrivals. Gabriel Cerré, born in Côte-Saint-Paul near Montreal in 1734, had volunteered to fight in the Seven Years War. Having seen the Ohio country, he determined not to return to Canada and life as a farmer, opting instead to test his abilities as a trader. He married into an old French Illinois family in 1764. Cerré himself became one of the most prosperous merchants in the region. His daughter Marie-Anne, schooled in Montreal, eventually married one of the most prominent French Canadians of the period, Pierre-Louis Panet, a supporter of the British regime and a member of the Governor's Executive Council. Panet kept the Chouteau clan well acquainted with events in Canada.

François Vallé, like Cerré a native of Canada, arrived in the Illinois Country sometime during the 1740s. He married well, moved across the river to Ste. Genevieve, and built a fortune from slave-based agricultural production, lead, and real estate. Though he died under the Spanish regime, his children and grandchildren continued to build the family's wealth and prestige after the sale of Louisiana to the United States. Louis Bolduc followed a path similar to Vallé's. His native village of St. Joachim near Quebec City was burnt to the ground by the British in 1759. Bolduc fled to the Mississippi Valley and settled in Ste. Genevieve, ultimately becoming a member of that town's elite with wealth accumulated in the same manner as Vallé.[55]

Other Canadians arrived later. Joseph Marie Papin, whose father had been the royal commissary at Fort Frontenac, entered the area in the 1770s, marrying Marie Louise Chouteau in 1778. Both Papin and Cerré had connections to Huguenot merchants, though both died in the fold of the Catholic Church. Pierre Menard, born in Montreal in 1766, found his way to Vincennes in 1786, serving there as a clerk for Francesco Vigo. Menard ultimately settled in Kaskaskia and became the most important citizen and merchant in that community. He was perhaps the only Frenchman in the area with a true love of the young republic: his father had raised a company of volunteers in Canada to support the American cause, and Menard himself would serve as the first lieutenant governor of the new state of Illinois.[56] None of these Canadians were themselves natives of the western country, though they married into families with deeper roots. All three were clearly ambitious self-made men. Canadian historians have long debated the fate of the francophone merchant class in Canada after the conquest. However, they have not looked at the many traders who left Canada to take up positions and pursue opportunities in places such as St. Louis and Detroit. They would find many success stories south of the border.[57]

Others came to these French-American villages and towns directly from France. In early St. Louis, which we must remember was a new town, more of those who described themselves as merchants were born in France (twenty-three) than in Canada (eleven), the Illinois Country (three), or New Orleans (three)— the majority of those coming from the provinces of Aunis, Saintonge, Béarn, Gascony, and Provence in the southern and western portions of the country.

Two other merchants came from Huguenot families in Switzerland, four from northern Italy, four from Spain, and one each from Holland and Germany.[58]

In Detroit, many newly arrived British merchants married into older French families. John Askin married Marie-Archange Barthe in 1772. Her sister Thérèse Barthe married Commodore Alexander Grant. William Park and his partner George Meldrum married, respectively, Thérèse Gouin and Marie Chapoton. Though British in name, Detroit remained a French town—linguistically and socially. At the same time, it is obvious that the French and British merchants of this small city expanded their cultural horizons as well as their circles of connection.

In short, the idea that these communities were ancient is problematic. Throughout this chaotic period before the Louisiana Purchase, these French towns and villages were works in progress. Many clearly viewed this borderland region as a zone of opportunity, attracting a surprising number of ambitious francophone newcomers from a variety of places. In the absence of French state interests, these new arrivals, as individuals, reinforced the existing francophone cultural and economic patterns of the region, even as British and Anglo-American settlers began to move into the area. The economic opportunities were abundant. Although the Great Lakes fur trade declined toward the end of the century because of an overabundance of merchants, a slow market in Europe, and Indian wars, the trans-Mississippi trade showed great promise.[59] The prize in that area was the Osage trade, secured by the Chouteau clan, who profited from their connections to both important members of the tribe and Spanish bureaucrats.[60] The fertile farmlands of the region were beginning to attract Anglo-Americans, but French farmers were already raising a substantial amount of grain, often with the help of slave labor. The port of New Orleans was also prospering during the late Spanish period as new staples—cotton, sugar, and grains—broadened the export base. As Spain relaxed its trade policies, an increasing number of ships from both France and American seaports visited the city.[61] But the region was also plagued by political instability, and the entry of the United States seemed, at first, to make matters worse.

The first French region to become part of the United States was, of course, the British Illinois Country. After George Rogers Clark conquered the area— "occupied" is probably a more appropriate term—the Virginia assembly established the county of Illinois in December 1778. Virginia, following the precedent of the British empire, allowed civil government in the Illinois Country to lapse in 1781. A French military officer in the area in 1780, Augustin Mottin de la Balme, observed firsthand the anarchy that reigned: the Virginians "randomly entered French houses, absconding with food that they believed they needed."

De la Balme was shocked by what he witnessed and noted the "anger among the French Creoles."[62] In November 1781, a prominent merchant at Cahokia, Antoine Girardin, wrote to British official Patrick Sinclair at Michilimackinac, suggesting the possibility that the disgruntled French might welcome the return of British rule. Shortly thereafter, news of the British surrender at Yorktown reached the Illinois Country.[63] Virginia ceded the entire area to the United States in 1784. The United States in turn neglected the area, failing to send a civil representative to Illinois until 1790. Ignored by Congress, the French in Illinois suffered through the tyranny of a local bully, John Dodge, from 1783 to 1787. Frustrated by the debased currency of Virginia and that state's inability to honor its debts, Kaskaskia's most prominent merchants fled across the river to Spanish St. Louis.

This was not a performance calculated to impress the French inhabitants of the region. The two Wests were beginning to converge. The world of the Ohio country, a frontier forged during the violent experiences of the revolutionary period, was moving west. The "empire of liberty," as Eric Hinderaker has dubbed it, was "pushed forward by the activities of thousands of land-hungry western settlers; revolutionary governments at both the state and the confederation level, for reasons of strategy as well as theory, chose to follow their lead and support their efforts." The positive side of this was balanced by the absence of effective authority and a strong sense of racial divide and animosity.[64] Vincennes, once securely a part of the Creole Corridor, was by 1786 increasingly engulfed by this other frontier. As Americans moved in, murders, robberies, race hatred, and alcoholism increased dramatically. Local Indians began to retaliate, and local French magistrates found themselves increasingly unable to control the situation. Their native friends warned the French that they would not always be able to distinguish between them and these frontier Americans.[65] Some of the French decided to move. Louis Lorimier, a French trader from the Ohio country who had served as a British partisan because of his dependence on British supply contracts and his commercial and kinship ties to the Shawnees, moved to Spanish Louisiana in 1787. He brought with him a substantial number of his Shawnee and Delaware friends. Lorimier received a Spanish land grant, was made the commandant of the Cape Girardeau district, and lived a comfortable life there until his death in 1812.[66] Lorimier, in short, moved to that part of the Creole Corridor that remained safely beyond the American frontier. Those who stayed played a careful juggling act. To protect their land from the incoming Kentuckians, the French in Vincennes in 1787 petitioned Congress to survey and distribute their lands.[67] Keeping one hand in the Indian trade, French merchants used their other to start dabbling in real estate. Over the next several years, the most substantial French merchants in Vincennes began to speculate rather furiously in land, anticipating an influx of Anglo-American farmers.

During the 1790s, the British and Spanish regimes in the other parts of this French-speaking region began to unravel. The British at Detroit found themselves increasingly burdened with Indian requests for support in their wars with the Americans. British officials still relied on French militia support, but that support was lukewarm at best. When Colonel Richard England, the last British commandant at Detroit, charged Jean Baptiste Chapoton with encouraging disaffection among the militia, a jury promptly found Chapoton not guilty. When Father Burke, a Tory priest sent to Detroit in 1794 at the request of Lord Dorchester, arrived, he found Colonel England's situation most hopeless: "His soldiers were deserting, the militia was worse than useless, civil officers were faithless to their king, and even his personal friends, among many others, were so eager to add to their landholdings that they were sending emissaries to General Wayne [Mad Anthony] to beg that huge grants recently acquired from the Indians be confirmed."[68] When Burke tried to influence the Potawatomis before they met with General Wayne at Greenville in 1795, two Frenchmen intercepted his letter and appended the following postscript: "[this man is] neither a Frenchman nor a Priest but a rascal who is chosen by the English to deceive you and blind you."[69] Throughout 1795 and 1796, the French inhabitants of Detroit prepared for the arrival of American sovereignty by making private land purchases from Indian friends and relations.

In Spanish Louisiana during the 1790s, Governor Carondelet spent five years of anxiety worrying about rumors of slave rebellions, French revolutionaries, and Indian depredations. In 1795, Spain signed Pinckney's Treaty, which granted Americans the right to navigate the Mississippi and deposit goods at New Orleans. The following year, with Spain and Great Britain at war, Carondelet began encouraging the immigration of American settlers into Spanish territory to provide some measure of defense against the possibility of a British invasion. By 1804, three-fifths of the ten thousand inhabitants of Upper Louisiana were Americans.

The winds of change were in the air, and the French merchants of St. Louis anticipated the change in sovereignty that occurred formally in 1804. As in Detroit during the years right before the American transfer (1796), the French elite in Upper Louisiana began to accumulate land claims from friendly Spanish officials.[70] In this endeavor, French merchants living under Spanish rule had a distinct advantage over their counterparts in places held by the British or the Virginians. Although French—and British—merchants in places such as Detroit might, and indeed did, purchase Indian lands, regulations prohibited them from doing so. Spanish officials were, on the other hand, quite liberal in the dispensation of land grants. The Chouteau clan was predictably fortunate to have their brother-in-law, Antoine Soulard, be appointed the royal surveyor in 1795. There can be little doubt that French merchants in this Spanish-held Creole Corridor had a vision of the future. In 1796, Charles Gratiot wrote to a friend in London about the effect of Pinckney's Treaty: "By the advantages of this treaty the americans can consider themselves the masters of the trade of this colony, under their Flag they can enter all parts of the world, and the neighboring territory on the west will become the empire, more and more flourishing, of the American Union."[71] He went on to predict that New Orleans would quickly become one of the most powerful cities in the universe—and so it did, especially during the first half of the nineteenth century.

The French did not disappear when the British and Spanish regimes in the region ended. For that matter, they did not disappear when the fur trade became a less dominant part of the local economy or when Native Americans were forced by the United States to remove farther west. French entrepreneurs were busy doing what entrepreneurs do: they were identifying advantageous crossroads and establishing relationships with Indian clients. They were trying to maintain lines of credit with suppliers in Montreal, New Orleans, and London. They were building stores and homes in the region. In other words, they were both developing a network of commercial exchange and engaging in the process of community formation. And they were learning valuable lessons in the fine art of managing the transition from imperial sovereignty to republican sovereignty, one West to the other.

Pierre-Louis Panet of Montreal wrote a letter to his brother-in-law Auguste Chouteau of St. Louis on May 18, 1804. "Vous êtes actuellement citoyens [des États-Unis]. Je souhaite que vous vous trouviez bien de le changement inattendu. [You are now citizens of the United States. I hope that you like this unexpected change.]"[72] In this same letter, Panet reported that Chouteau's son, in school at Montreal, had learned to read and speak English fairly well. The change may have been unexpected, but the French were not unprepared.

Auguste Chouteau (1749–1829). Born in New Orleans, the son of René Auguste
Chouteau and Marie Thérèse Bourgeois, Auguste helped his stepfather, Pierre de
Laclède, establish the new settlement and future city of St. Louis in the winter of 1763–
1764. Chouteau, trading on his own account and with various family partnerships,
eventually accumulated a fortune in the fur trade. His ties to the Osage Indians and his
good relations with Spanish and later American officials cemented his position as the
"first citizen" of the region. After 1816, he focused his attention on banking, a flour mill
and distillery, and a vast estate of more than fifty thousand acres. Known far and wide
as a man of intellect and curiosity, Chouteau received a host of distinguished visitors in
his home. From the St. Louis Globe–Democrat Archives of the St. Louis Mercantile
Library at the University of Missouri–St. Louis.

3

SURVIVING THE TRANSITION
TO AMERICAN RULE

In 1796, Auguste Chouteau, forty-six-year-old merchant of St. Louis, wrote the following letter to the Spanish governor of Louisiana, the Baron de Carondelet:

> Monseigneur . . .
>
> I take this occasion to renew the assurances of my respect and of my sincere devotion. . . . I see with pleasure that you will be the Governor for at least another year, and that this space of time will furnish you the possibility of giving consistence to the wise views you have conceived for the happiness and the growth of this vast and immense country, which is as yet not well enough known. . . . I beg you, monseigneur, to accept a little gift of apples that I hope will reach you safely. I would have sent you more if they had not been so scarce this year. These are all I have and I am happy that they have a destination so satisfactory to me.[1]

This obsequious letter was followed the next year by one similar in tone, this time addressed to Carondelet's successor, Governor Manuel Gayoso de Lemos:

> Monseigneur
>
> I have the honor of offering you my sincere congratulations on your promotion to the place of Governor of the Province of Louisiana; no one could better than you replace M. Le Baron . . .[2]

The objective behind both letters was the continued patronage by Spanish officials of Chouteau's monopoly of the Osage Indian trade and an annual stipend of two thousand pesos for maintaining a fort in Osage territory. Chouteau's successful efforts to link his private interests with the welfare of the Spanish empire, as one historian has noted, were well within the "established mercantilist tradition."[3] The language and tone of both letters will certainly sound familiar to any student of the *ancien regime*.

Let us switch now to the year 1819. The *Missouri Gazette* for July 14 reported that Colonel Auguste Chouteau, now almost sixty-nine, had presided over an Independence Day celebration at Pierre Didier's orchard. The festivities featured a full-length portrait of General George Washington surmounted by a live eagle. After many toasts and a sumptuous dinner, the crowd sang a rousing chorus of "Yankee Doodle."[4] We may assume that Chouteau sang "Yankee Doodle" in French, for he died without bothering to learn English.

Had Auguste become an ardent republican during his declining years? Certainly the lessons of citizenship were not wasted on his nephew Pierre. Following in his uncle's footsteps, Pierre arranged a timely loan for Senator Thomas Hart Benton in 1843 just when Benton's support for confirmation of an Indian treaty highly profitable to Pierre Chouteau and Company seemed to be wavering.[5] This was not the first or the last incident of its kind. Senator Benton seems to have been as much an employee of Chouteau and Company as a representative of the people of Missouri. *Plus ça change, plus c'est la même chose.*

The consistent vision of merchants like the Chouteaus, that is, the development and exploitation of the resources of their regional base—the Creole Corridor—was eventually pursued with great success in the context of national expansion even farther west. Francophone entrepreneurs in the West played a critical role in ushering in a new regime of private property and market relations, forging transportation links and connections of capital and personal influence with national centers of commerce and power in New York, New Orleans, and Washington, D.C. Let us begin by disabusing ourselves of the notion that our story was bound to unfold as it did.

With the purchase of Louisiana in 1803, the United States cleared its imperial rivals out of an immense area and secured the main trade route of the interior for its western citizens. The port of New Orleans, long coveted by British policymakers, was now in the hands of the young republic. The upriver town of St. Louis provided a gateway to the West and the promise of a limitless trade in furs. The vision of a republican empire was beginning to take shape. The glorious dreams of commerce and territory were tempered, however, by one potential nightmare. There was a human reality on this vast and fertile ground. Anglo-Americans were not the first people of European descent to stake their claim in Louisiana. Far from it. Shrewd and observant French merchants called this land home and were following events closely.

Two new areas that formerly had been part of the French empire became part of the United States during the 1790s: the Detroit region in 1796 and Mississippi Territory in 1798. The French in Spanish Louisiana looked on with growing interest. Both in the Illinois Country and in the Detroit region during its first decade of American rule from 1796 to 1805, the United States did little to reassure the French inhabitants that the new regime would be either responsive or responsible. In both Vincennes and Detroit, only one American officer—John Francis Hamtramck, a native of Quebec and a Roman Catholic—managed to command respect and create a bond between the francophone citizens and their new government. If one were to survey French opinion about Americans during the decade before the Louisiana Purchase, the results would not, in general, seem very promising. Zenon Trudeau, the French lieutenant governor of Upper Louisiana under the Spanish regime, wrote to François Vallé at Ste. Genevieve in 1792 that the Americans were "un peuple sans loix ni discipline [a people without law or discipline]."[6] The following excerpt from a letter written by Bartholomew Tardiveau to Charles Gratiot in St. Louis sheds some light on French stereotypes: "Major Dunn blew out his brains in 1790 after having discovered the infidelity of his wife. He was an extremely fine man although Irish by birth and American for many years."[7] One Frenchman referred to the newcomers simply as *américoquins*. French sentiments were perhaps best summed up in a limerick written by an anonymous Creole from Ste. Genevieve in 1796:

> Soyez 'y' ci les Bien venu cher enfant de sodome
> Soyez 'y' ci les Bien venu homme au milieux de rome
> Et vous detestable putain don le con nous degoute
> Allez chez les ameriquien cherchez gens qui vous foute[8]

In general, it may be said that the French who lived west of the Mississippi realized that the Americans were "determined to transplant their institutions and culture into the territory."[9] This was in stark contrast to the Spanish, who viewed Upper Louisiana as a defensive borderland, a barrier between the expansive American republic and New Spain. Realizing that they did not have the manpower or expertise in local Indian affairs to do otherwise, the Spanish were content to let the French Creoles run their own show in their own language. Moreover, the Spanish spent great sums of money on defense and public improvements and asked for little in return in the form of taxes. Despite a welter of official restrictions on trade, Spanish officials in Missouri generally allowed French merchants to buy goods from wholesalers in Michilimackinac, Montreal, and London.[10] The French were clearly afraid that the U.S. government, on both local and national levels, would provide little in terms of defense and require much support in the form of duties and taxes. Closer to home, the French merchants of St. Louis were not impressed by the rowdy Americans who had settled in the lead-mining district near Ste. Genevieve.

If the French had already begun to form their stereotypes of the Americans, the reverse was even more strikingly the case—and the prejudices of Americans writing from the centers of power on the Atlantic coast were rarely informed by personal encounters. The incorporation of Louisiana into the republic was not the first instance of French inhabitants in the West becoming American citizens, but the magnitude of this addition forced a systematic discussion for the first time. Jeffersonians and Federalists alike wondered out loud how to make good Americans out of the French inhabitants of the Mississippi Valley.

Although cultural conflicts soon surfaced over seemingly inconsequential issues such as whether the French quadrille or the Virginia reel would take precedence at a public celebration of the transfer, most American concerns were political in nature.[11] Thomas Jefferson himself, writing to John Breckinridge in 1803, worried that "the Constitution had made no provision for our holding foreign territory, still less for incorporating foreign nations into our union."[12] The Constitution had clearly authorized the admission of new states into the Union and also implied that the country might expand territorially, but the status of the inhabitants acquired by such expansion was open to judicial interpretation.[13] Behind such constitutional concerns lay the assumption that U.S. citizenship, like divine grace, properly belonged to those individuals who had made a conscious decision to deserve it. The common stereotype held by many American political leaders was that the French of the Mississippi Valley were at best indifferent to the rights and responsibilities of free men. Simply put, they were French (strike one); they were ignorant of the principles of self-governance, being the "children" of empire (strike two); and they were Roman Catholic and therefore spiritual servants of the Pope (strike three).[14] This last bias against Catholicism was rarely expressed in public, but it certainly existed in the minds of many. Frederick Bates, a young Virginian and Jeffersonian bureaucrat who held appointive offices in Detroit and St. Louis, described the French in Missouri in a letter to his brother:

> The very name of *liberty* deranges their intellects. . . . If their Commandant spurned them from his presence: deprived them of half their Estate or ordered them to the black Hole, they received the doom as the dispensation of Heaven, and met their fate with all that resignation with which they are accustomed to submit indifferently. . . . Surrounded with wretchedness they dance and sing; and if they have their relations and friends within the sound of their violin, they have nothing more to ask of the Virgin; Provided her viceregent the Priest, will design to forgive those sins which perhaps they never committed.[15]

Bates clearly had a rather low opinion of Catholicism, but the point here is that his religious bias informed his assessment of the French Catholic's fitness as a potential citizen of the republic. He assumed that they were in the habit of being submissive, spiritually and politically. Albert Gallatin, Jefferson's secretary of the treasury, was a native French speaker but was from Geneva, the Calvinist heart of Europe. His opinion of the French in the Mississippi Valley, expressed in a letter to Jefferson, was that they were "but one degree above the French West Indians, than whom a more ignorant and depraved race of civilized men did not exist."[16]

Many American politicians would have agreed with Josiah Quincy, the Massachusetts Federalist, when he proclaimed that the people of Louisiana "may be girt upon us for a moment, but no real cement can grow from such an association."[17] Congressman William Eustis from Boston declared: "I am not one of those who believe that the principles of liberty can be grafted suddenly upon a people accustomed to a regimen of a directly opposite hue. I consider them standing in the same relation as if they were a conquered nation."[18] Indeed, it is not too much of a stretch to assume that many Anglo-Americans, like the British before them, secretly hoped that the French would either disappear or, at the very least, be outnumbered as soon as possible so that the republic might progress unimpeded. One Anglo-American newcomer suggested at a dinner that it would take many French funerals to improve St. Louis.[19] It is worth noting here that some Jeffersonian territorial appointees were not above discrediting those French merchants who had priority in the western territories as a way of advancing their own interests in the race for political office and land.

American politicians were not only pessimistic about the essential political fitness of the French, they were also troubled by what they perceived to be their historic inclinations. When Pierre Chouteau, Auguste's younger half-brother, suggested to Albert Gallatin in 1804 an arrangement in the Osage country similar to that which had prevailed under the Spanish regime, Gallatin's response, detailed in a letter to Jefferson, was as follows:

> I had two conversations with Chotteau [*sic*]. He seems well disposed, but what he wants is power and money. He proposed that he should have a negative on all the Indian trading licenses, and the direction and all the profits of the trade carried on by the government with all the Indians of Louisiana, replacing only the capital. I told him this was inadmissible; and his last demand was the exclusive trade with the Osages. . . . As he may be either useful or dangerous, I gave no flat denial to his last request, but told him to modify it in the least objectionable shape. . . . As to the government of Upper Louisiana, he is decidedly in favor of a military one, and appears much afraid of civil law and lawyers; in

some respects he may be right, but, as regular laws and courts protect the poor and the ignorant, we may mistrust the predilection of him who is comparatively rich and intelligent in favor of other systems.[20]

The Chouteaus soon realized that the "privileges" of the old regime must be reduced in the American system to a more private peddling of interests.

As Gallatin's letter implies, officials in Washington were concerned with the loyalty of the French as well as with their character. As events in the West had already shown and were to show again during the Burr Conspiracy, even the affections of Anglo-American settlers in the West for the new nation were prone to be fickle. It was natural for Jeffersonian bureaucrats to assume that the French might prefer different masters, even though the French in Kaskaskia and Vincennes had lent their support to George Rogers Clark and the American cause during the Revolution.

Perhaps more troubling to American officials than the specter of European intrigue were the French traders' ties to various Indian groups, especially those in the Old Northwest who viewed American claims to sovereignty and the land hunger of investors and squatters alike with increasing dread and anger. At least up until 1804, French traders had shown themselves to be sympathetic to Indian jurisdictional claims. It took the Treaty of Greenville in 1795, which officially spelled out the boundaries between Indian and American jurisdiction in Illinois and the rest of the Northwest Territory, to explain to Governor St. Clair why the French inhabitants of Cahokia had consistently refused his offer of four-hundred-acre donation grants in the high ground beyond their village.[21] The relative harmony that existed between French settlers and their Indian neighbors went beyond mere economic partnership. Kinship ties and mutual respect of political boundaries supported the bridges between the two cultures. Time and time again, the French would show a willingness to let Indian ground rules govern situations that would surprise and annoy American settlers and politicians.

But just how well did the Americans understand the inhabitants of Louisiana? How valid were their preconceptions? And how well do we understand those francophone inhabitants two centuries later, given the relative absence of historical scholarship directed at this Creole society?

The first American misconception was geographical. It is worth reiterating that this region, as a social and cultural zone, stretched beyond the boundaries of the Louisiana Purchase to include places such as Vincennes and Detroit. French customs and language predominated in the region. English gradually eclipsed French as a public language in St. Louis and Detroit by the 1830s, but it would take the Civil War to finally determine that struggle in New Orleans. The linguistic battle was complicated by racial boundaries as people of African descent, both free and slave, might belong to either linguistic group. Add to this mix an incredible array of immigrants and Indian groups and one can appreciate the disorientation of American travelers.

This was also a region that flowed, literally, from north to south, not east to west. And it was a region dominated by towns. Detroit and St. Louis were still small in numbers in 1803, neither place containing much more than one thousand inhabitants, although both functioned as urban centers, connecting the paths of goods and people. Farther down the Mississippi River, one encountered another urban center, Natchez. Similar in numbers and culture to the other Creole towns, Natchez possessed a diverse citizenry. Underneath the patina of French customs, one could discover merchants who had come from as far away as Majorca and Genoa. And then there was *la ville*, New Orleans. At the time of the transfer, New Orleans was already one of the largest urban centers in the young nation. By 1820, it was the largest city south of Baltimore and the fifth largest in the United States. By 1850, it had a population of more than one hundred thousand. In 1835, the city's exports exceeded those of New York City—though the latter would take back the lead by 1850. New Orleans had also eclipsed Montreal in population by 1820. Given that Montreal had a British majority from 1830 to 1860, one could argue that New Orleans, with its flourishing French-language schools, newspapers, and opera companies, was the preeminent French city in North America before the Civil War.

Who were these thousands of French residents? We have already seen that many had arrived in the region after the fall of the French empire. Emigrants from France continued to arrive in the region both right before and for some time after the Louisiana Purchase. Frenchman Nicolas Jarrot arrived in the Illinois Country in the 1790s. A tireless land speculator, he died a wealthy man, and his wife, Julie Beauvais Jarrot, pursued the family business interests with great success after his death. Joseph Sire, born in 1799 in La Rochelle, arrived in St. Louis in 1821, served as a master of various American Fur Company steamboats, and became an important partner in Pierre Chouteau Jr. and Company in 1838.

Exiles from successive regimes in France sought asylum and opportunity in French America. Royalist Louis Philippe Joseph de Roffignac arrived in New Orleans in 1800 and served several terms as mayor during the 1820s. Exiles from the Bonapartist regime included the famous New Orleans lawyer Etienne Mazureau. After Waterloo, the architect Benjamin Buisson arrived in New Orleans. Ange Palms, a former officer under Napoleon, settled in Detroit where his daughter Marie-Françoise married the son of Joseph Campau, the richest man in the territory. Statesman-politician Pierre Soulé, destined to achieve national prominence in the Democratic Party, fled Restoration France in 1825. The stream of emigrants from France to Louisiana actually increased from the 1830s to the Civil War.[22]

French people from the French colony of St. Domingue (present-day Haiti) arrived in both St. Louis and New Orleans in significant numbers from 1793 to 1804. Then in 1809 and 1810, the largest wave of francophone refugees from St. Domingue arrived in Louisiana, deported by officials in Cuba in response to Bonapartist schemes in Spain. More than ten thousand arrived in less than a year. Many of these stayed in New Orleans, but others found homes in French towns upriver. René Paul from Cap François married a daughter of Auguste Chouteau. Educated at the École Polytechnique in Paris, he served as the official surveyor of St. Louis from 1823 to 1838, a critical period of urban expansion of great value to his new family. One Anglo-American resident of New Orleans, James Brown, was so frustrated by the stream of Gallic refugees who poured into that city from St. Domingue via Cuba in 1809 that he suggested to Henry Clay in 1810 that the French simply not be allowed to vote.

Then there were those who defied categorization. Pierre Derbigny, born into the nobility in Laon, France, fled the French Revolution for St. Domingue in 1793. He married the daughter of a prominent French Illinois family and settled in Louisiana in 1797, ultimately becoming governor of the state. The powerful *bon papa* of Bayou Lafourche, Henry Schuyler Thibodaux, was born in Albany, New York, in 1769 of French Canadian and Dutch New Yorker parents. He landed in Louisiana in 1794 after "a youth spent in Scotland."[23]

In every town and city in the region, these newcomers reinforced the linguistic, cultural, economic, and political staying power of the French community. Indeed, in New Orleans, the so-called Foreign French were so numerous as to constitute a distinct group within the city's ethnic and cultural politics. If these French towns were indeed experiencing social and demographic changes, were the values of the inhabitants nevertheless rather traditional? Were they prepared for the influx of—as they have so often been described—"enterprising and progressive" Anglo-Americans?

The Catholicism of the French was often taken as one measure of their traditional character. Putting aside the fairness of such an unwarranted interpretation, have we overlooked some interesting complications? Historian Melvin Holli has described Joseph Campau, from one of the oldest families in Detroit, as conservative and feudal—unable to adjust to the more modern values of incoming Yankees.[24] Yet in 1800, Campau became the first Frenchman in Detroit to join the Zion Lodge, Number 10, of Ancient Free and Accepted Masons. Following his lead, Gabriel Godfroy and six other Frenchmen had joined by 1805. Freemasonry, of course, was frowned upon by the church as being both anti-Catholic and dangerously liberal. Indeed, when Campau, in ill health in 1802, asked Detroit's Father Richard for spiritual aid, the priest made him promise, among other things, to withdraw from the lodge. That year Campau went to confession and took a more active part in church affairs, even being chosen a *marguillier* or churchwarden. Campau, apparently feeling much better—he died at the age of ninety-five—did not withdraw from the lodge and was reelected treasurer by his freemason brethren before the year was over. He would later lead the struggle of the most prosperous portion of the parish over the control of church property.[25]

Campau was not the only French Catholic in this region to become a freemason. Pierre Chouteau Jr. was also one. French Catholic freemasons dominated the board of church trustees or *fabrique* controlling St. Louis Cathedral in New Orleans, resulting in a serious church schism in 1805. We may perhaps attribute such progressive or liberal tendencies to Americanization, but the freemasons in New Orleans were resisting attempts by the church hierarchy to appoint priests sympathetic to the American cause and the needs of English-speaking Catholics.[26] Disputes between middle-class Francophones and church officials over liberal ideas and the control of church property were also becoming more common in Quebec during this period.

It is hard to gauge the political sentiments of the French, given the relative absence of letters or published materials that address such concerns directly. The documents generated by the revolt of 1768 provide some intriguing early hints that the French were not necessarily inclined to be submissive or traditional. The memoir composed in his own defense by Pierre Caresse, a leader of the rebellion and a New Orleans merchant, is noteworthy. Defending free trade he exclaimed: "One would have to be an unzealous citizen not to applaud these principles. M. Ulloa, however, never permitted us to put them to his review. We had to suppress even the cry of pain. The admission of our slavery was a potentially explosive challenge to authority. We were expected to shout 'I am free,' imitating the galley-slaves of Venice, whose chains bear the engraving 'Liberty.'"[27] Given such strong words, it should not surprise us that Alejandro O'Reilly had Caresse executed. Professing his devotion to the French king, Caresse refers consistently to himself and his fellow Creoles as *citoyens* (citizens), not *sujets* (subjects). The language of the Enlightenment had certainly penetrated this distant colony.

British agents of empire, like their Spanish counterparts, were surprised by the French resistance they encountered in Canada. With American forces threatening Montreal and Quebec in 1775, Chief Justice William Hey wrote the following to Colonial Secretary Dartmouth: "Every day furnishes too many instances of it, and gives me an Idea of the real character of the Canadians very different from what I used to entertain. . . . Your Lordship will remember how much has been said by us all of their Loyalty, obedience & Gratitude, of their habitual submission to Government . . . but time and accident have evinced that they were obedient only because they were afraid to be otherwise."[28] Governor Carleton noted that a bust of King George III in Montreal had been "smeared with soot and decorated with a collar of potatoes and a wooden cross with the inscription: 'Voilà le pape du Canada et le sot anglais' [Behold the Pope of Canada and the English fool]."[29]

Often pictured as infantilized and backward peasants and fur traders, quite literally the children of empire, the French have appeared in many a historical novel as passive spectators to the noble exploits of Anglo-American liberators such as George Rogers Clark and Andrew Jackson. It was a misperception at the time, and American politicians quickly learned that it was not correct. Any perceived American attempt to deprive the French of their political voice or their property drew an immediate response. One can read numerous petitions sent by the inhabitants of Indiana, Illinois, and Michigan during the 1780s and 1790s. The Governance Act of 1804 prompted lengthy memorials from the leading francophone citizens of Lower and Upper Louisiana and delegations to deliver the documents to Washington, D.C., from both New Orleans and St. Louis. Loathing the prospect of a dictatorship of Jeffersonian bureaucrats and the imposition of anglophone institutions, the memorialists chided Congress for not extending the essential privileges of a free people, including, of course, any form of representative government. Speaking a language eastern politicians could easily recognize, the French sounded much like other groups of disenfranchised westerners chafing at the territorial bit. There were, of course, special concerns, noted in the memorial sent from St. Louis with a fair measure of sarcasm: "the records of each county, and the proceedings of the courts of Justice in the District of Louisiana, should be kept and had in both the English and French languages as it is the case in a neighboring country under a monarchial Government and acquired by conquest."[30]

The French, I would argue, were more than ready to play the game of republican politics, as their subsequent actions in Louisiana and elsewhere amply demonstrate. In Detroit, the alienated French majority grew so exasperated with territorial Governor William Hull that in 1809 they sent a petition to President Madison requesting Hull's removal.[31] In that city, Joseph Campau's nephew wrote to François Navarre in 1819 about an upcoming election and observed with great passion that the "natives of the country" must guard against the "strangers" who would "insolently ravish our rights and our natural privileges."[32] Though presented to some degree as an ethnic struggle, the contest was framed as a political one, a struggle of our *concitoyens* (fellow citizens) in defense of their status as free members of the republic.

Bernard Marigny, perhaps the most ardent defender of the status of French Creoles in Lower Louisiana, understood quite clearly what the change from an imperial regime to a republican regime implied. Chiding the former French aristocrat Mayor Roffignac of New Orleans for his obsequious behavior during a formal visit of Andrew Jackson to the city, Marigny observed that "servile flattery" was unbecoming in a republican nation. In Marigny's words: "the compliments of our Mayor are of the kind, called, in good French *de l'eau bénite de cour* [holy water of the court]."[33] Times had changed, and the French in this region, especially those from the dominant commercial class, had heard the news.

When the delegations from St. Louis and New Orleans arrived in Washington with their memorials in 1804, Senator William Plumer of New Hampshire described the petitioners from Lower Louisiana (Derbigny, Pierre Sauvé, and Jean Noël Destrehan): "They are all Frenchmen. Two of them [Derbigny and Sauvé] speak our language fluently. They are all gentlemen of the first respectability in that country—men of talent, literature and general information, men of business and acquainted with the world. I was much gratified with their company. They had little of French flippancy about them. They [more] resembled New Englanders than Virginians"[34] (the ultimate compliment!). The French complaints were well thought out and wide ranging. The petitioners from both cities demanded guarantees on their property—their land claims and their slaves. Slavery was on the minds of the St. Louisans, who were to be included within the jurisdiction of Indiana, created under the conditions of the Northwest Ordinance (which included a ban on slavery). The French also demanded some form of representative government. And, of course, they requested French and English schools and judges and officials fluent in both languages.

If American concerns were mostly political in nature, French concerns were primarily economic and legal, for it was to the law these merchants looked to protect their rights and property. French merchants were to fight court battles over land grants and slaves that dragged on for decades. The French were also more generally worried that Anglo-American jurisprudence would bring with it prolonged trials by jury that would impede the smooth flow of commerce.[35] As Louis Nicholas Fortin, a merchant near Baton Rouge, wrote to his brother-in-law Antoine Marechal of Vincennes: "they will bring with them, in a free and peaceful country, the discord and disunion of families through lawsuits and taxation. Lawyers, sheriffs, and constables will come crowding in here. I do not despair . . . of seeing a few of these idle worthless fellows, that carry a little green satchel filled with useless old papers, come here and seek their fortune in their shabby motheaten black suits, and their Blackstone under their arms! They won't be the most welcome."[36] Such concerns had a basis in reality. Even a newly arrived American judge, John Coburn, had to admit that by the "local standards" to which the French in St. Louis were accustomed, "the administration of Justice is dilatory." The fact that trial by jury was mandated in civil and criminal cases by the Governance Act of 1804 meant that cases concerning property would take longer and have greater restrictions regarding evidence. Nor were the French at all pleased with the very idea of juries. As historian Stuart Banner has observed: "the leading French inhabitants of St. Louis protested [that juries] were made up of 'whatever individuals may happen to be present, without regard to character, standing or property' . . . [they] thus endangered 'the liberty, property or even life of the citizens by entrusting the most material interests of criminal justice, to Agents who having no stake in the community, have no interest to protect it.'"[37]

There was also a substantive difference between common law and the civil law the French were used to. As historian George Dargo has noted, "the civil law worked to put property in the hands and under the control of the living. It promoted the commercialism of all property, including land." Common law, on the other hand, "still wrestled with more fragmented notions of property—the relativity of title, the competing claims of present and future property holders, and the differences between legal and equitable ownership."[38]

In Lower Louisiana, where sheer numbers and a professional class of francophone lawyers, mostly immigrants, supported the effort, the French managed to hold on to their civilian legal tradition in the sphere of private substantive law. Criminal law and criminal procedure, on the other hand, followed common-law traditions. The Quebec Act of 1774 had erected a similar compromise in Canada, much to the dismay of British merchants in Quebec. A contemporary Canadian political cartoon viewed the result of this unholy alliance of French and English legal traditions as producing an illegitimate child. In Louisiana, francophone planter Julien Poydras used the phrase "mongrel offspring of injustice and chicane." Nevertheless, the Louisiana French could look back with some satisfaction after civil codes were adopted in 1808 and 1825. Codification of the civil law in Quebec did not occur until 1866, and the final product was less progressive than Louisiana's earlier efforts.[39]

For the French in the Upper Mississippi valley, the protection of their property in land and slaves and the future of the fur trade mattered most. To that end, the French in Upper Louisiana would gather Anglo-American allies, mostly lawyers, such as Edward Hempstead from Connecticut, John Hay of Cahokia—the son of Jehu Hay who served briefly as a British lieutenant governor of Detroit—and Thomas Hart Benton. In St. Louis and French Illinois, francophone lawyers were unavailable, and, in truth, Anglo-Americans were probably more useful for the concerns of merchants pursuing congressional favors regarding Indian affairs and western lands.

When their investments were threatened by the Governance Act of 1804, which nullified Spanish land grants awarded after October 1, 1800 (the date of Spain's cession of Louisiana to France), and prohibited the foreign slave trade, the francophone elite were quick to point out that these provisions violated the Louisiana Purchase agreement which guaranteed that "the inhabitants shall be maintained in the full enjoyment of their property."[40]

It was property in land above all else that initially tied French merchants throughout the emerging Midwest to the interests of an expanding American republic. The French in Indiana and Illinois had begun to assert themselves in 1788, addressing numerous petitions to Congress to settle the issue of land titles and to confirm that their property in slaves would be upheld under Article 2 of the Northwest Ordinance.[41] At least one important pro-American French merchant, François Bosseron of Vincennes, went to an early grave, "bankrupt and disillusioned" with his new country.[42] But in the 1790s the economic situation brightened for other French merchants, who began at last to derive some benefits from their American connection. The rush for land in southern Indiana and Illinois was certainly fueled by the acts of Congress passed in 1788 and 1791 that provided for donation grants of four hundred and one hundred acres. Beginning in 1791, Francesco Vigo of Vincennes began supplying goods to new American customers. The following year, Vigo made his first recorded trip to Philadelphia; for ten years, he or one of his agents made the trip east to buy a stock of goods from importers and manufacturers. Although he continued to maintain business relations with merchants in Detroit, St. Louis, New Orleans, and Kaskaskia, Vigo expanded the range of his activities and apparently expanded his profits, for he entered a period of frenzied land speculation that eventually backfired.[43]

Not all French settlers had the resources to speculate in land, and some sold their claims for a fraction of their eventual worth. But those French merchants who had the resources, and there were many, speculated extensively in land and welcomed the newcomers despite their misgivings. Meriwether Lewis and William Clark, waiting across the river from St. Louis in the winter of 1804 for the formal transfer of Upper Louisiana to the United States, were wined and dined by the Chouteau family. An examination of the expedition's financial records reveals that the Chouteaus provided blankets, gunpowder and bullets, Indian goods, and most of the other material needs for this famous journey—at a profit, of course. They also extended credit to the Americans for paying wages to workers and soldiers. As historian William Foley has noted, "the expedition's departure symbolized the true beginning of a long and successful partnership uniting the old French inhabitants and the American newcomers in a common effort to develop the trans-Mississippi frontier."[44]

That same year, in another gesture of alliance, President Jefferson appointed six young men, all scions of leading Missouri French families, to the national military school at West Point. Among the young men were Pierre Chouteau's oldest son, Auguste Pierre (A.P.), Charles Gratiot Jr., and two sons of Louis Lorimier, the former commandant at Cape Girardeau who had led a large contingent of Shawnees and Delawares from the Ohio Valley to Missouri in the 1780s. (Of the six, only Gratiot pursued a career in the army.)[45]

In July 1804, Pierre Chouteau Sr.—in Washington with a visiting delegation of Osage chiefs—was appointed Upper Louisiana's first U.S. Indian agent. A few months later, the departing Spanish lieutenant governor of Upper Louisiana—on his way down the Mississippi to New Orleans—encountered Chouteau in the company of William Henry Harrison, the new U.S. territorial governor, on their way up to St. Louis. It would be interesting to know the Spanish official's innermost thoughts on that occasion given the fact that the Chouteaus had recently extended credit to the U.S. government but insisted on cash in helping the Spanish in their evacuation.[46]

In November 1804, Harrison, assisted by the Chouteau brothers, Auguste and Pierre, and Charles Gratiot, negotiated a treaty with the Sac and Foxes on the Rock River in Illinois. A special provision, added after the treaty had been negotiated, acknowledged the validity of the Spanish grant to Julien Dubuque in which Auguste Chouteau had recently purchased a half interest.[47]

So far, so good, but the coming years brought increasing problems. In March 1805, Congress changed the status of Upper Louisiana and created the Territory of Louisiana (Missouri). (Lower Louisiana was named Orleans Territory.) Under this act, General James Wilkinson was appointed governor of the territory; Joseph Browne, a brother-in-law of Aaron Burr, was named secretary; and Jean Baptiste Charles Lucas, John Coburn, and Rufus Easton were named judges of the superior court. Although pleased with the selection of Wilkinson, the Creoles of St. Louis were undoubtedly suspicious of the others. Judge Lucas, born in Normandy in 1758, was a friend of Albert Gallatin, and like his friend, Lucas disliked what he viewed as the corrupt old-regime machinations of merchants such as the Chouteaus. Browne and Coburn were transient Republican office-seekers. Easton, a native of Connecticut, was an ambitious and ardent Jeffersonian, determined to find his fortune in his new home. These men were to exercise legislative authority over the francophone natives of the town. Furthermore, the 1805 act confirmed the provision for jury trial, though it did relax, though not yet repeal, the laws invalidating post-1800 land grants and prohibiting the slave trade.[48]

That same month Congress enacted a separate bill that provided strict regulations for determining the validity of Spanish land titles and created a board of land commissioners consisting of a recorder of titles and two other members to make sometimes quite arbitrary decisions regarding claims. The first members of the board appointed by Jefferson were Judge Lucas, Clement Biddle Penrose from Philadelphia, and James Lowry Donaldson from Baltimore. Lucas, in particular, was a thorn in the side of the Creole merchants. He held that all land claims should meet the requirements of Spanish law to the letter. The merchants protested that the Spanish regime had never been that exacting in granting and sustaining title—and bearing the burden of proof in these proceedings would be difficult and costly at best. They were also irritated that the land in question would continue to be assessed for taxes, yet they were unable to mortgage, subdivide, or sell their property.

At first the board was lenient. Penrose and Donaldson were sympathetic to the Creoles and politically aligned with Wilkinson. There were apparently attempts to circumvent Lucas by not telling him where meetings were to be held. Wilkinson did his best to support the interests of the French, who had found his number soon after his arrival. He appointed Antoine Soulard to the post of surveyor general, the position he had held under the Spanish. Marie Philippe LeDuc, formerly the secretary to the Spanish lieutenant governor, was appointed translator for the board. (Soulard and LeDuc were both related by marriage to the Chouteaus.) Charles Gratiot was made clerk of the board. The stakes were high. The claims of the Chouteau brothers alone came to 234,000 arpents (about 198,000 acres).

Just as the board began to take action, events broke down this Creole coalition. Wilkinson, amidst rumors of the Burr Conspiracy, was ordered to New Orleans. For a few months, Secretary Browne was acting governor until Burr's arrest persuaded the Creoles to join in the move for his ouster. The following year, Donaldson—having been attacked by a drunken Rufus Easton—returned to Baltimore, and Jefferson appointed Frederick Bates to replace both Browne and Donaldson and Meriwether Lewis to replace Wilkinson. Bates, a native of Virginia, an anti-Catholic, and a former officeholder in Michigan Territory—where he had been snubbed by French belles—joined forces with Lucas and Easton in opposing the interests of the Creole elite on the land board and on the legislative council.[49]

It is fairly obvious that many of the French merchants, informed early on by

Spanish officials and other correspondents of the possibility of the Louisiana Purchase, had secured, even antedated, substantial land claims. They naturally assumed that the arrival of the Americans would bring a rise in land values. Their hopes for a quick killing were frustrated by the obstinacy of the land board. The opposition—Easton, Lucas, and Bates—had already experienced the American settlement frontier and hoped to make fortunes of their own in speculation. (Lucas eventually did.) Unfortunately for these Jeffersonian bureaucrats, they found, upon their arrival in St. Louis, that much of the best land was already tied up. Their hopes for success rested upon the freeing of as much land as possible for the public domain. (Easton established an agency next to the surveyor's office in St. Louis to buy and sell land.[50]) To reinforce their efforts, they appealed to democratic sentiments and cultural prejudices.

Matters concerning Indian affairs also deteriorated after the initial successes of 1804. In 1805 Pierre Chouteau quarreled with Major James Bruff, the region's ranking military officer, over the appropriate punishment for several Sac warriors who had killed three Americans north of St. Louis. Chouteau argued that the warriors should be punished according to tribal law; Bruff ordered the Sacs to surrender the accused to U.S. authorities. The squabble led Bruff into the anti-Wilkinson camp in the territory, for he felt that Wilkinson had sided with the Chouteaus on this and other matters. Wilkinson himself proved less accommodating than Harrison had been in supporting Chouteau's ways of handling Indian affairs. He wrote to Secretary of War Henry Dearborn that Chouteau was "ambitious in the extreme" and steeped in "Spanish habits."[51] Chouteau, hoping to escort a new Indian delegation to the capital that year, was told by the War Department to remain in St. Louis and allow someone else to do the honors. Dearborn also admonished Chouteau to keep expenses down. Chouteau had let out government contracts to many relatives and friends, including Bernard Pratte—who would later become Chouteau's son's partner in the fur trade—and John Mullanphy. The following year, 1806, Lieutenant Zebulon Pike leveled charges against Pierre Chouteau, apparently resenting Chouteau's influence with the Osage. In 1807 the controversy came to a head, and Chouteau was replaced by William Clark as the head of Indian affairs for the region. Chouteau had obviously been demoted; however, he retained his position as Osage agent because of his influence and connections within that tribe.

Three years of American-style politics taught the francophone elite a few lessons. One obvious lesson was that Americans much preferred private combinations of special interests to public displays of authority. And hitching their interests to Wilkinson's star had been a costly mistake. His high-handedness had antagonized many of the recently arrived American fortune-seekers, who then banded together to oppose both him and the French. The lawyer Edward Hempstead, who had come to St. Louis in 1805, captured this sentiment in a letter written that year: "With the principles of civil liberty in which I have happily been bred, and the patriotic examples of my father before me, I can not bow the knee to any political Baal, nor give my approbation to conduct that I am fully conscious is despotic. With a Governor who holds the office of Brigadier General, and in addition is vested with a strange combination of powers, you cannot imagine to what a degree I wish for a change of times. From a rank Federalist to a suspected Republican he became a Burrite and is now a petty Tyrant."[52] Wilkinson's removal gave the French a chance to regroup. Auguste Chouteau led the attack that culminated in a grand jury indictment of Rufus Easton for land fraud. Jefferson removed Easton from office shortly thereafter.[53] Major Bruff's aspirations to influence were neutralized by the appointment of Lewis to the governor's office in 1807. This much accomplished, the French began to forge new alliances.

A second lesson in American civics was the realization that lawyers were a necessary evil. One of the first they turned to was Edward Hempstead. In 1808 Hempstead married Clarissa Dubreuil, a member of the francophone elite. In 1813 Hempstead's sister Susan married Charles Gratiot's son Henry.[54] Americans, even lawyers, were not so bad if they were members of the family. Hempstead, a brilliant student of Spanish law, became the territorial attorney general and an advocate of a liberal land claims policy. Another new ally came in the person of Silas Bent, son of a leader of the Boston Tea Party and an assistant surveyor for Rufus Putnam in Ohio. Bent became the justice of the Court of Common Pleas in 1807 with Auguste Chouteau, Bernard Pratte, and Louis Labeaume serving as his associates. Bent's sons were later associated with the Chouteaus and Ceran St. Vrain in the Santa Fe trade and fur trade of the southern Rockies.

Creoles with capital could also make friends in other ways. From 1810 on, the documents indicate that the French elite were showing greater interest in retailing and renting land to settlers of moderate means. Joseph Charless, the publisher of the *Missouri Gazette*—a paper usually opposed to French interests—wrote the following to Pierre Chouteau in 1810: "Since I had the pleasure of speaking to you on the subject of the two arpens [*sic*] of land adjoining Mr. Carr's tract, I had a conversation with Mr. Bradbury [who] has declined the purchase. Could you make the payments easy I would be glad to have it."[55] Auguste Chouteau and his son Henri became heavily involved in this side of the family business. Henri toured the agricultural hinterlands of the region with regularity. By the early 1820s, the Chouteaus had their own agents and rent collectors and were receiving payments in corn and beef from many modest American farmers.[56] At least in good times, when they were not repossessing homes and farms, Creole capitalists who could provide for easy payments were increasingly seen as friends of democracy and the common citizen.

The chief concerns of most French merchants north of New Orleans, however, centered on the fur trade and national and international markets and developments. As early as 1807, the Creole merchants of St. Louis were receiving reports from their network of informants on the likelihood of war between England and the United States. In November of that year, John Mullanphy, on business in Philadelphia, wrote to Auguste Chouteau that the talk in that city was all of war. He suggested to Chouteau that the time was ripe for buying out Dubuque's lead-mining operations in present-day Iowa and for exchanging furs for lead whenever possible.[57] In 1810 Pierre Chouteau Jr. was sent to Dubuque to oversee the family interests. He remained there until the outbreak of hostilities.[58] In 1809 Jean Nicolas de Maclot, a native of Metz in France who had arrived in St. Louis in 1804 and married Marie Thérèse Gratiot in 1806, built the first lead shot tower west of the Alleghenies in Herculaneum, Missouri. Another Gratiot friend, Moses Austin, built his own shot tower nearby the following year.[59] (In 1825, Henry and Jean Pierre Bugnion Gratiot would move to Galena, Illinois, and establish a center for lead mining and smelting just north of the border known as Gratiot's Grove, Wisconsin.[60])

Cornering the regional lead market for the manufacture of lead shot was only one aspect of the Creole agenda and response to the growing likelihood of war. A Chouteau informant at Prairie du Chien in Wisconsin, Nicholas Boilvin, and Pierre Chouteau Sr.'s father-in-law, François Saucier, at Portage des Sioux, an Indian crossroads, reported the disposition of the Potawatomis, Sioux, Ioways, and Sac and Foxes in 1809 and 1811.[61] Given their access to information and their intimacy with the decision-making process going on in various Indian communities, it is not surprising that the French again assumed a position of importance in the eyes of local and national officials. In the coming war, it would be critically important to prevent the Indian tribes of the region from siding with the British. If the French had begun to distinguish between their friends and enemies among the Americans, the Americans would now learn that not all French were alike in their allegiance to the United States. The War of 1812 was both a crisis and an opportunity for French communities in the West.

French support for the American cause during the war varied across a predictable fault line. The French communities at Green Bay and Mackinac were still tied to Montreal and were utterly dependent on the fur trade. Support for their British suppliers was almost mandatory. Indeed, competition for the Great Lakes trade had increased in recent years, and declining profits during the Napoleonic

Wars placed French merchants in that region in a weak position for commercial expansion after 1815. Those communities would offer little resistance to the take-over of Astor's American Fur Company and Anglo-American bureaucrats after the war.

French merchants in St. Louis, on the other hand, had everything to gain and almost nothing to lose by supporting the Americans. They could market their goods through New Orleans and New York. (The colony of Louisiana, after all, had been founded by traders motivated in part by a desire to bypass government officials and creditors in Canada.) There were some attempts to smuggle furs into Canada in violation of the Embargo and Non-Intercourse acts. Chouteau kins-man Jean Pierre Cabanné was arrested in 1812 by an American official and had six hundred packs of furs confiscated.[62] Nevertheless, St. Louis Francophones were holding large land claims that would only increase in value when the de-mand from American settlers grew. And though they were heavily invested in the trade with local tribes who would be pressured to leave the area when those very settlers arrived in the decades after the war, French traders would still have a vast Indian country to their west to exploit.

French merchants in Indiana, Illinois, and Michigan were also inclined to sup-port the American cause. They had begun to see the potential in the commodi-tization of land and the merchandizing of agricultural products. Commercial relations with the American cities of Albany, New York City, Baltimore, Phila-delphia, Pittsburgh, and Louisville had already been established. Their Montreal connection had not been severed, but it was now one alternative among many.

When war began in the West in 1811, the question of French loyalty—to the British or the Americans—became critical. American control of this region was, after all, tenuous, and francophone citizens composed a key component of those with property and standing. Indeed, the war provoked something of a "French scare." In St. Louis, where Auguste and Pierre Chouteau had been commis-sioned as colonel and major, respectively, in the militia, animosity toward the French may have reached a peak. Silas Bent in 1813 warned Auguste not to resign his office as judge in the Court of Common Pleas because "those Americans who declare the most inveterate hatred to the french and manifest a disposition to govern law and be governed themselves by the opinions of the Executive will be the most likely to be appointed to office by Mr. Bates."[63] The Chouteaus' nephew, Charles Gratiot Jr., was in command of the U.S. troops at Fort Malden in 1814. This Frenchman from St. Louis, now stationed in the Detroit area, must have flinched when he read a letter from a subordinate describing the "worthless French who come only to beg or steal."[64]

Throughout the West, the war forced the French to declare themselves. In

Lower Louisiana, a number of French immigrants faced legal restrictions or persecution as aliens. In two significant cases, *Debois' Case* and *United States v. Laverty*, the courts decreed that bona fide inhabitants of a territory gained the rights and privileges of citizenship when Louisiana became a state in 1812.[65]

Perhaps the most telling case of anti-French behavior occurred in November 1812 when a band of Kentucky militiamen on their way to join with Illinois troops under Governor Ninian Edwards attacked, pillaged, and burned down the French village of Peoria. The inhabitants were left with only the clothes on their backs to make their way in the cold down the river to St. Louis. Among those robbed were Antoine LeClaire, the future founder of Davenport, Iowa; Marguerite La Croix, the future wife of Governor John Reynolds of Illinois; and Thomas Forsyth, an official of the U.S. government whose anger over the incident manifested itself for years afterwards.[66]

American hostility toward the French sprang in part from the perception that the French and the Indians were partners in crime. This opinion became widespread after the massacre of James Winchester's Kentucky militiamen at Frenchtown on the River Raisin south of Detroit on January 23, 1813. Although many French citizens later swore that they were unable to intervene, the fact that a number of the American soldiers were butchered or burnt alive in French houses and that the Indians generally regarded the French as their friends led to much ill will. Prominent French citizens such as François Lasselle were denounced as traitors. That Lasselle had been a member of the grand jury that investigated territorial governor Hull in 1809 made him seem all the more suspicious.[67] In fact, the Indians involved were Wyandots, who were not closely connected with the local French, and those same Wyandots did shoot a number of French citizens. Nevertheless, the perception that the French were allied with the British against the Americans remained, and in some parts of the French Midwest, there was some truth to it. In Green Bay, Charles Réaume and Jacques Porlier fought with the British although both had served as U.S. justices of the peace, appointed by Governor Harrison of Indiana.[68]

And so it went. French support bolstered the American war effort in certain areas. It does not appear to have been a critical element overall. Yet had the French in the Midwest been opposed to the American cause, the outcome might well have been different. The importance of the war to the French and to all groups in the West was that it cleared the air. Those French who had supported the American cause found themselves on the winning side. Clearly, their stock rose in the eyes of their American neighbors, and their access to power and influence was often enhanced. Charles Gratiot Jr., whom we left at Detroit in 1814, was a major in the army by the war's end. In 1828 he was made chief of the Army

Corps of Engineers, and in 1838 he retired with the rank of brigadier general. Thereafter, he served the extended Chouteau family interests as a lobbyist in Washington, D.C. At St. Louis, Auguste Chouteau had served as both the commander of the militia and the chairman of the town's Committee of Safety. Five sons of Auguste and Pierre had served in the territorial forces. Pierre had served as a reporter from Indian country and organized a small contingent of Osages to fight on the American side. Both brothers were instrumental in concluding peace treaties with an array of Indian groups from the Yanktons and Tetons to the Miamis and Delawares at Portage des Sioux in 1815 and 1816. The Chouteau children would reap the benefits of their fathers' influence.[69]

More to the point, those who supported the American side usually did so because their vision of future prosperity coincided with the policies and activities of their fellow citizens. Excluded from that vision were the Indians of the Old Northwest. The fur trade in this region had declined substantially from 1808 to 1815. The European market had bottomed out, and the Indians were in no position to hunt. As one trader noted: "fear keeps the Indians from hunting. They continually imagine that the Americans are coming upon them."[70] Immigration to the Old Northwest and to Missouri boomed during the postwar years, and the pressure for Indian cessions began immediately. French merchants were in a unique position to profit from the government's need to dispossess the Indians. Those who were willing and able to persuade their Indian clients and relatives to cede lands, and later to move to Iowa, Kansas, and the like, stood to profit in three ways: (1) by having land set aside for themselves in treaty negotiations, (2) by providing annuity goods promised by the government to the various tribes as specified in treaties, and (3) by receiving money directly from the government in payment of individual Indian debts, such money being subtracted from the amount the government was obligated by treaty to pay into the tribal fund.[71] As one might suspect, by means such as these, the fur trade gradually became an Indian business with government money supplanting furs in importance. As one merchant put it: "Indian money . . . treaty . . . lands and lastly their skins . . . must be our motto."[72]

4

HOW THE WEST WAS SOLD

During the decade after the War of 1812, with settlers rushing into the Old Northwest, St. Louis became both a regional emporium and the central headquarters of the national quest for empire. Put another way, St. Louis became a clearinghouse for regional settlement, a jumping-off place for new pathways to the Far West—especially New Mexico and the Upper Missouri—and the center of the nation's defense business. The city occupied a central position on western transportation routes, and the city's merchants controlled the western fur trade. The military frontier and the trading frontier were bound together as both soldiers and fur traders served as the primary intermediaries between native peoples and the republic after the war. The dream of an American empire envisioned by Charles Gratiot back in 1796 was about to become a reality.

The fur trade remained the central enterprise of the Chouteaus until the 1840s, but the nature of the business would change profoundly after the war. One change was internal. Two powerful companies, heavily capitalized, drove out or absorbed smaller enterprises and exercised an ever-increasing amount of control over the business. The two companies were John Jacob Astor's American Fur Company, incorporated in New York City in 1808, and a succession of Chouteau-family firms, eventually operating as Pierre Chouteau Jr. and Company in St. Louis. In the end, there was one: Chouteau bought out the American Fur Company. Capital and organization were two keys to growth. Another was the ability to incorporate a new technology—steamboats—that further tightened and centralized the control of the trade. The final factor was the ability to influence government policy. This last factor would become increasingly important as the other change in the fur trade—this one external—became more apparent.

As the settlement frontier reached the Mississippi and new states joined the

Union—twelve between 1816 and 1848—the chorus of voices demanding Indian removal grew louder and louder. Even as the debate in Congress over policy was playing out, treaties providing for immediate or gradual removal were being signed. In 1830, Andrew Jackson ended the debate and pushed through the Indian Removal Act. As negotiators began the process of forcefully persuading tribes to move to new lands west of the Mississippi, it became clear that they would need the services of those who knew the native communities best, the traders. At the same time, traders recognized that there was as much money to be made in supplying annuity goods as there was in furs. Moreover, the Chouteaus had realized that treaties provided the perfect occasion to extinguish Indian debts. This practice they put into place with the Osage treaty of 1825. (The 1825 Osage treaty marked the true beginning of this practice, which expanded and "had become a fixed policy at Indian treaty negotiations by 1831."[1]). This new way of handling debts stabilized their profits as importers and retailers to the Indians; the federal government now became, in effect, the guarantor of this end of the business, and it paid in cash. At the same time, the fur merchants continued to extract profits from the wholesale marketing of furs, primarily in Europe. The fur trade then became, in part, the Indian business.

Success in such a business depended on having friends at court in Washington, D.C., to secure confirmation of costly treaties; friends at the local level of government bureaucracy, that is, Indian agents, treaty commissioners, governors and the like; and friends within the Indian tribes themselves. Although many merchants prospered from such dealings, it was the Chouteau family in St. Louis that blazed the trail, if you will, to New York and Washington. Their primary friend at court was Thomas Hart Benton. Benton, a young lawyer from Tennessee, had arrived in St. Louis in 1815. The first person he met in the city was Charles Gratiot, who was so impressed with the young man that he invited him to stay at his home. A few days later, Benton was employed as a land claims attorney in the office of the Chouteaus' primary counsel, Edward Hempstead. The Chouteaus and their relatives and friends sponsored Benton's rapid rise to political prominence. In 1819 Benton assumed the editorship of the *St. Louis Enquirer*, a paper friendly to the Chouteau interests. He was elected to the Senate in 1820 and never failed his patrons.[2] In 1824, he pushed through a bill that provided for the reexamination of Spanish land claims by the district court of Missouri. This approach failed when a local judge named Peck proved obstinate. (The Chouteau interests had him impeached.) Benton, meanwhile, persuaded Congress to appoint a new Board of Land Commissioners. That board eventually submitted its final report in 1835, and its liberal treatment of Missouri claimants drew howls from some in Washington; nevertheless, Benton pushed it through to confirmation.[3] As Benton noted in an 1824 letter to Bernard Pratte, another member of the Chouteau extended clan, "It will give me a pleasure, in the discharge of my public duties, to oblige at the same time my individual friends."[4]

Benton was most valuable to the Chouteaus as an advocate of their fur-trading and Indian business interests. He pushed through countless favorable Indian treaties. When he took a stand against the confirmation of a Sioux treaty in 1843, a timely loan of one thousand dollars from Pierre Chouteau Jr. induced him to change his position.[5] Benton's first important service to the Chouteaus occurred in 1822 when he succeeded in having Congress abolish the government factory system, a thorn in the side of private fur-trading companies. With one stroke, the government withdrew from this important aspect of Indian relations, allowing the private sector to dominate the field. The federal government thereafter became increasingly dependent on the traders.

Out in the field, in Indian country, the supervision of Indian relations—in essence, the coordination of private interests and government policy—was handled by federal Indian agents. That same year, 1822, Congress created the Superintendency of Indian Affairs at St. Louis. William Clark, the former territorial governor of Missouri and a fast friend of the Chouteaus since his expedition days, held this critical post from 1822 to 1837.[6] Clark reported directly to the secretary of war until 1824 when then Secretary of War John C. Calhoun established the Bureau of Indian Affairs. Acts of Congress periodically created new superintendencies, but the office in St. Louis remained the only "full" superintendency in the field throughout the antebellum period. In St. Louis and Washington, the Chouteau family "supervised" the appointment of Indian agents by the government. When the Whigs of Clay County in western Missouri—staunch opponents of both Benton and Chouteau—tried in 1840 to get the Indian Office to move the St. Louis superintendency farther west and out of the clutches of the Chouteaus, their efforts came to naught. They had sensed an opportunity with the election of William Henry Harrison, but they were wrong.[7] The Democrat Benton was only one friend at court. The company had many Whig friends as well, among them Daniel Webster, who served the Chouteaus as a legal adviser before the Supreme Court on several occasions. The Chouteaus also had permanent lobbyists in Washington. The most important was Brigadier General Charles Gratiot, Pierre's brother-in-law, who had served as the head of the Army Corps of Engineers.

Political influence, of course, was only one piece of the strategy of the Chouteau enterprise. It was the Chouteaus' presence in the field that commanded attention and deference. Chapter 6 details the growth of the family business, from

Bvt. Brig. Gen. Charles Gratiot (1788–1855), oil on canvas (1830), by Thomas Sully (1783–1872), 30 by 25 inches. Gratiot, the eldest son of Charles Gratiot and Victoire Chouteau, was one of four young men from leading French Creole families appointed to West Point by President Thomas Jefferson in 1804. Gratiot graduated with honors in 1806, became a captain in the Army Corps of Engineers in 1808, and served as the chief engineer from 1828 to 1838. Stationed in Washington, D.C., Gratiot also served as the point man for the family company's interests in land claims and Indian treaties.

This portrait, and the companion piece of Gratiot's wife Ann Belin, both by Sully, captures the sense of an emerging aristocracy in the United States. The couple's two daughters married well. Marie Victoire married the Marquis de Montholon, a member of the French legation in Washington, D.C. She became a lady of honor to the Empress Carlotta in Mexico. Julia married Charles P. Chouteau, son of Pierre Jr. West Point Museum Art Collection, United States Military Academy, West Point, New York.

a family perspective, but we can offer a brief sketch of it here. In 1822 — clearly a significant year — several smaller St. Louis firms (and relatives) combined to form Berthold, Chouteau & Pratte. That same year, the St. Louis group signed its first agreement with Astor's American Fur Company. The St. Louisans agreed to import all their trade goods through Astor, and Astor in turn would buy their furs at a guaranteed price. At this point, the St. Louis family consortium was strictly a regional business with important connections to Missouri River tribes such as the Osages, Omahas, Poncas, and Arikaras relatively close to home. Over the next few years, they would begin to specialize and expand their operations. Jean Pierre Cabanné took charge at Council Bluffs to manage the Lower Missouri trade; Bartholomew Berthold supervised the Upper Missouri posts; Jean Sarpy handled the books in St. Louis; Bernard Pratte took charge of external affairs; and Pierre Chouteau Jr. oversaw the entire operation.

The French partners learned their lessons from Astor. Astor understood that fur trade profits could be maximized only by reducing competition in the field—thereby stabilizing the prices paid for furs—and increasing market share—thereby obtaining the ability to respond to world fur markets. Ruthless in the field, Astor and his first lieutenant, Ramsay Crooks, absorbed a host of smaller enterprises in the Great Lakes region. At the same time, Astor and his son William supervised the marketing end, holding particular pelts in storage in their New York warehouse, to be released when prices rose in London and Leipzig.[8] Through a series of partnerships and an overall rationalization of coverage and information, Astor brought a form of corporate control to the seemingly chaotic trade. At its height, the American Fur Company had more than twelve regional operations, called outfits, at least seven hundred employees, and agents in three continents.

The Chouteau-managed St. Louis company followed Astor's lead in integrating and rationalizing the business. Beginning in the 1820s, Chouteau's company either built or purchased trading posts that served a variety of Indian customers all over the West. After the marriage of Ramsay Crooks to Bernard Pratte's daughter Emilie in 1825, the St. Louis firm—which remained a family partnership—signed an agreement with Astor in December 1826 to share the Western Department of the American Fur Company. In alliance with the nation's largest monopoly, the Chouteau clan took over the Columbia Fur Company in 1827 and renamed its operation the Upper Missouri Outfit. They converted the Columbia Fur Company's shabby Fort Tecumseh in the heart of Dakota country to Fort Pierre in 1832. They built Fort Union in 1829 at the mouth of the Yellowstone River, thereby linking the trade of the northern Rockies with that of the Missouri River system. In the 1830s they built Fort Clark in Mandan country and acquired Fort Laramie in present-day Wyoming on the northern fork of the Platte River.

In 1834, when Astor retired, the Chouteau company bought out the Western Department of the American Fur Company. By this point, the Creole family company had achieved what economic geographers call a highly articulated system. They had extended the reach of their commerce and integrated the various links of the chain. When the company's steamboat, the *Yellowstone*, reached Fort Union in 1832, the picture was complete. Thereafter, the company sent several company-owned or -chartered steamboats up the Missouri every year until 1865. With hundreds of employees; a host of trading posts large and small; and provisions, lumber supplies, and trade goods on hand at every establishment, the company had consolidated its control over the western fur trade. Chouteau was arguably the most famous name in the West during the antebellum period. Even today one can find a town named Chouteau in Oklahoma and a Chouteau County in Montana. By controlling the flow of information and goods, indeed, by holding the keys to survival for any traveler or government agent, the Chouteau company was in a perfect position to profit from both commerce and expansion.[9]

When the American Fur Company failed in New York in 1842, Pierre Chouteau Jr. and Company bought its Upper Mississippi Outfit, thereby gaining hegemony over the Minnesota trade. It also opened an office in New York City to handle the export-import end of the business with Europe. In 1851, Chouteau would send his son-in-law John F. A. Sanford to London to control the flow of furs going to the annual fair at Leipzig, bypassing the former marketing agent, Curtis Lampson of London.[10] From the company's New York city office at No. 40 Broadway and from its headquarters in St. Louis, Chouteau controlled the flow of furs going to London and Leipzig on a scale that surpassed his predecessor, John Jacob Astor. Even when the market for beaver and muskrat crashed in 1841, the Chouteaus floated along—the value of the trade's exports continued to rise mostly because of the increasing importance of buffalo robes. (The Chouteaus had pioneered this market back in the 1820s.[11]) And during the depression years that followed the Panic of 1837, the Chouteaus capitalized mightily on the government's need to secure Indian lands and remove remnant tribal groups west.

During the Spanish regime, the Chouteaus had persuaded client Osage leaders such as White Hair and Big Track to relocate for purposes of trade. They continued to manipulate and negotiate tribal politics and movements throughout the antebellum period. For example, the Sac and Fox Indian agency in Iowa distributed $40,000 in annuities every year, most of which went to the Chouteaus. When a rival band influenced by a rival trader threatened to decrease profits, Keokuk, the most highly regarded chief, urged his people to purchase goods from "their friend Chouteau."[12] On May 25, 1837, as the country suffered from financial anxiety, Pierre sat in a hotel room in New York City smoking cigars and drinking sherry. Perhaps he was anticipating the bill he was about to present to Congress for claims on the Sac and Fox Indians to the tune of $89,697.65.[13] In 1842 the Sac and Foxes signed a new land-cession treaty, and the Chouteaus were allowed more than $100,000 in compensation for past debts.[14] The Chouteau Indian business that began with the Osages in 1825 gradually included a long list of tribes: the Sioux, Cheyenne, Ponca, Potawatomi, Seneca, Sac and Fox, Miami, Osage, and Cherokee, among others.[15] In 1851, the Santee Sioux of Minnesota signed the Treaty of Traverse des Sioux in which they ceded much of their homeland. Through the machinations of Chouteau's son-in-law Sanford and Chouteau allies Henry Sibley and Governor Alexander Ramsey, the treaty provided $210,000 to pay traders' debts. It was ratified the following year, and the Chouteaus and their partisans received the entire sum. Eleven years later, Congress appropriated more than $100,000 to remove these same Santee Sioux, who had gone to war with newly arrived settlers in Minnesota the previous year, and a group of Winnebago people. Chouteau received the contract to transport them to south-central Dakota Territory and charged the government twenty-five dollars per passenger and ten cents per person per day for provisions. Baggage was free up to one hundred pounds, and Indian agents traveled free. The company moved a total of 3,251 Santee Sioux and Winnebago people to their new reservation at Crow Creek.[16]

In this tragic story of removal, powerful merchants such as Pierre Chouteau were certainly complicit. It was a complicated story, however, and the brokering of French fur traders and métis chiefs such as Jean-Baptiste Richardville of the Miamis may have mitigated, to some degree, the potential for genocidal violence that occurred in other frontier areas.[17] Native people, of course, had limited options. On the other hand, the rapid pace of expansion played into the hands of those powerful merchants who controlled the interaction. They knew what native people needed and wanted, and they spoke their language. They knew that the Crows were taller than their neighbors and needed larger clothes. They knew that the Kansas Indians preferred green blankets.[18] They had provisions on hand and were often the only ones able to prevent starvation during lean months. They also spread the terrors of alcoholism. From an Indian standpoint, credit was a necessity because native economies had been disrupted by non-Indian settlement. As one trader noted: "[We were] forced into the credit system by government policy. The average tribesman receives less than $10 per annum from annuities, not enough for survival as tribal resources have declined."[19] What had begun as an adjunct to the fur trade during the 1820s became a business in its own right by the 1840s. By 1842, the federal government was paying out more than two million dollars a year in cash to satisfy traders' claims.[20] Many tribes were forced to move three or four times in the space of two decades. As Spotted Tail observed, "Why does not the Great Father put his red children on wheels, so he can move them as he will?"[21]

By the 1840s, Pierre Chouteau Jr. had indeed become the master of movement. As early as 1835, he began to turn his attention to profiting from the transportation needs of incoming settlers and a growing industrial nation. Like the Astors, the Chouteaus and their relatives diversified their investments, taking money earned in the fur and Indian business and applying it to future-oriented enterprises. In 1849, Chouteau established a new firm in New York to market railroad iron. His son-in-law John F. A. Sanford, a native Virginian who wed

Emilie Chouteau in 1832, became a partner in this venture. Sanford had begun his career as a clerk in the superintendent's office of William Clark in 1825. He worked for the Indian Service until 1834, at which point he joined the Chouteau family firm, becoming a partner in the fur-trading operation in 1839. By 1852, Sanford had withdrawn from the St. Louis branch of what was by now an investment company. Living in New York City, he managed the Chouteau interests in railroads and railroad iron. The Chouteaus had substantial holdings in the Illinois Central and Ohio and Mississippi railroads. Sanford served as the director of the Illinois Central from 1851 to 1857. (He was also the defendant in the *Dred Scott* case.) Like the Janus-faced Genoese merchants, the Chouteau clan now faced both east and west. Dealing in railroad bonds, Pierre Chouteau acquired a substantial share in the Cincinnati, Logansport, and Chicago line sold by disgruntled British bondholders in 1860.[22] England also provided a market for furs and railroad iron. In 1849, Chouteau, along with James Harrison and François Vallé, founded the American Iron Mountain Company to produce the ore he was brokering in New York. (Their silent partners included Samuel Ward, William Astor's wealthy son-in-law, and August Belmont, the American agent for the House of Rothschild.[23]) In 1851, that company completed a plank road to transport the ore, replacing that road with a branch of the Illinois Central seven years later. By the late 1850s, the company owned several blast furnaces and the Laclede Rolling Mill in St. Louis.[24]

At the same time, the family firm continued its stranglehold on western development and capitalized on the position of St. Louis as the headquarters of western defense. When the army needed a post along the Oregon Trail from which to protect emigrants, they purchased Fort Laramie in 1849 from Chouteau for four thousand dollars.[25] Six years later the army purchased Fort Pierre from the company for the inflated price of forty-five thousand dollars. One company official had warned the army quartermaster of St. Louis that the fort was rather worn out, but Chouteau himself pressured the quartermaster general in Washington to complete the transaction.[26] Troops stationed in the rickety fort that first winter reportedly sang the following verse:

> Oh, we don't mind the marching, nor the fight do we fear,
> But we'll never forgive old Harney
> for bringing us to Pierre.
> They say old Shotto built it,
> but we know it is not so;
> For the man who built this bloody ranche
> is reigning down below.[27]

As late as 1861, we find John Mullan contracting with Charles Chouteau, Pierre's son, for the construction of a military road in Montana.[28] The Chouteaus finally sold their fur-trading business in 1865. Before they did, however, gold was discovered in Montana, and the Chouteau outpost in that territory, Fort Benton, became the center of a new mining frontier. The last company boat on the Upper Missouri returned to St. Louis in 1865 with twenty-nine hundred bales of buffalo robes, seventy passengers from the mines, and more than $250,000 in gold dust.[29]

The Chouteaus, of course, were exceptional in their wealth, power, business acumen, and good fortune. Can we draw any conclusions about francophone merchants in general from their story alone? To help us answer this question, let us look briefly at the careers of several francophone merchants in Indiana.

The situation in Indiana after the War of 1812 was comparable to that in Missouri, and the career of Senator John Tipton in many ways paralleled that of Senator Benton. Both men consistently supported the cause of expansion and development. To encourage commerce and the availability of land was to encourage the vision of merchant and settler alike. In Indiana, no single French merchant or family had the resources and connections of the Chouteaus. Indeed, if there was one family that compared, it was the Anglo-American Ewings.[30] However, without the presence of numerous French merchants in Indiana, the process of Indian dispossession and removal would not have been nearly as smooth nor as prolonged and lucrative for all involved. It was the Lasselles, the Lafontaines, the Chandonnais, Navarres, Godfroys, and Bertrands who persuaded their Miami, Potawatomi, and Shawnee friends and relatives to sign treaty after treaty from 1818 to 1833.[31] The money acquired from such treaties capitalized the construction of canals, roads, ferries, and bridges during the 1830s.[32] Prime real estate, located near canal and road sites, was of course reserved by the merchants.

From 1833 to 1855, when most native people in Indiana were removed to Kansas and the final scramble for treaty payments and Indian land occurred, another Frenchman emerged as a key figure, Alexis Coquillard. Coquillard used his removal profits to develop South Bend, Indiana, and endow a new college, Notre Dame. Considered the most capable leader of Indian emigration parties by government officials, Coquillard was also respected by the Indians, who hoped to avoid the various calamities that could and did occur on some of these unhappy journeys.[33] Indian sentiment is hard to document, but Father Benjamin Petit, escorting a band of Potawatomis in 1838 on the infamous "march of death," did record two incidents that seem revealing:

> When the Indians arrived at Quincy, the inhabitants . . . could not help expressing their surprise at the modesty of our Christians. . . . A Catholic lady,

accompanied by a Protestant friend, made the sign of the cross, symbolizing religious fraternity. Immediately the Indian women came up to shake their hands cordially; the savages never fail to do this when they encounter Catholics. The Protestant lady wanted to do as much and tried the sign of the cross, but, betrayed by her lack of practice, she could not succeed. At once an Indian, who knew some English, went up to her and said, "You nothing."

One day Judge Polke, our principal officer, introduced one of his friends, a Baptist minister. I was in my tent, surrounded as usual by Indians. He wanted to shake hands with the Indians, and I told them to approach—that he called himself their friend. Then, as if he must make a sensation, this minister, with that commanding enthusiasm in which his kind are never lacking, cried: "Ah, they are the bone of my bone, flesh of my flesh! I truly feel here [putting his hand on his heart] that I love humankind. Young man, may God bless your labors among them—make them better than they are." When he had gone, I told my Indians that he was a Protestant minister. At this all who had shaken hands with him replied with a grimace.[34]

The French traders continued to be trusted by their Indian clients. The Winnebago Prophet is reported to have said to one trader, a Gratiot, that if he "came as a 'Chouteau' . . . [he] welcome[d] him to his village; but he if came as a white man he must consider him, like all whites, an enemy."[35]

If the Indians of the state trusted the French, one might well wonder why the French did not try to prevent their removal. This is a complex question to which we could not begin to do justice here. Some of the French did, in fact, remove to Kansas with their Indian clients and relatives.[36] Others, especially certain members of the clergy, did intercede on the Indians' behalf.[37] Most French traders, however, were actively involved in the treaty-making process and complicit in the hardships Indian communities experienced during removal. Some traders may have felt that they represented a mediating force between American settlers and native communities, justifying their own actions as facilitators of removal with the same logic employed by the advocates of this policy—that is, native groups would be better off in some distant place out of the path of settlers and "progress."[38] It is also possible that powerful business leaders such as Pierre Chouteau Jr., who spent most of his time in St. Louis and New York City and much less time than his father and brothers cultivating personal relationships out in Indian country, were physically and emotionally more removed from the consequences of their actions on native clients.

The correspondence of such merchants reveals little. Pierre Chouteau Jr.'s letters focused on financial matters and the details of the trade. Apart from inquiries and comments about the health and activities of family members, he kept his opinions and reflections to himself. He was notoriously tight-lipped. Here and there in the letters we may catch an oblique glimpse of the sympathy some traders may have felt for their native customers. For example, in a letter from one of Chouteau's former agents in Detroit, Frederick Buhl, to trader Antoine Campau in Grand Rapids, Buhl admonishes Campau for paying too high a price for furs and having high collection costs: "We are sorry the amount in the hands of the Indians is so large. You wish us to send you $87.84 the balance due you as per statement. We would much rather you would collect this amount from some of the Indians, and think you might easily do so and collect much more of them. At the rate you have been managing with them you will never get the Indians out of your debt."[39] Antoine and Louis Campau, the founder of Grand Rapids, were said to be friends of the Indians. Perhaps such a letter indicates some sympathy on their part. On the other hand, as a newspaper article on the early days of Grand Rapids written in the 1970s observed, the Campaus also sold alcohol to local native communities and were deeply involved in various Michigan treaties that resulted in the loss of Indian land and substantial profits for the traders. Pierre Chouteau Jr. had an "English made Gold Watch" engraved and presented to Antoine Campau as "an acknowledgement of services rendered" several years after the Treaty of Detroit in 1855 with the Ottawas and Chippewas. The expensive present was not given to reward humanitarian endeavors.[40] A sense of connection to and sympathy for long-time native neighbors and clients must have existed, yet I think it is safe to conclude that such feelings for most French traders were balanced if not outweighed by the bottom line.

Several generations of French traders observed the transition from Indian country to settlement frontier in a variety of places. For the most part, the French merchants of Indiana and elsewhere in the Creole Corridor behaved in a rather consistent manner. When land showed signs of becoming a valuable commodity, those French merchants with the resources to do so were not about to lose out to the newcomers from the East. They used their priority to gather land at important geographical sites and platted towns. Although the fur trade had overshadowed all other business pursuits during the eighteenth century, even before the War of 1812 most French merchants seemed quite ready and eager to lessen their dependence on this one volatile international market. When the smoke cleared and American settlement began in earnest, the French were in the forefront of the new economic activities. St. Louis, we should remember, was conceived as a French city. Indians were neighbors, not residents.

The post–War of 1812 careers of most French merchants in Indiana followed predictable paths. The career of Hyacinthe Lasselle Sr. was typical. Born at Kekionga or Fort Wayne in 1777, the youngest son of Jacques Lasselle and Thérèse

Portraits of Louis Campau (1791–1871) and Sophie de Marsac
Campau (1807–1869) painted by Charles Moore in 1852. Louis began
his career in the fur trade at an early age, working for his Uncle Joseph and his
father, Louis Sr. He fought in the War of 1812 on the American side and was an
active participant in the Treaty of Saginaw in 1819. A shrewd purchaser of lands
at key locations, he filed plats of two future Michigan cities, Saginaw (1822) and Grand
Rapids (1833), and is considered the founder of both. He built a permanent home
in Grand Rapids in 1827, and a number of brothers and nephews followed him
there from Detroit. Grand Rapids History & Special Collections, Archives,
Grand Rapids Public Library, Grand Rapids, Michigan.

Berthelet, Hyacinth was baptized in Detroit later that year. After schooling in
Montreal, he returned to Indiana to work for his older brothers Jacques and
François. Hyacinthe moved to Vincennes in 1804 and the following year married Julie Bosseron, daughter of the unfortunate Captain Bosseron already mentioned. Two other Bosseron daughters married merchants who had been born
in France and immigrated to Vincennes at the turn of the century. Like other
centers of French settlement in the United States, Indiana attracted immigrants
from France and refugees from St. Domingue who contributed to the survival of
French culture in those locations.[41]

Hyacinthe Lasselle served as a lieutenant of the Indiana Rangers during the
War of 1812. He was apparently of great use as an interpreter and Indian scout.[42]
He had operated an inn as early as 1810,[43] and by war's end, this newly refurbished

inn was the principal public gathering place in Vincennes. Lasselle's Ball Room, as it was called, was the site of many patriotic bashes, and Lasselle was on his way to becoming an honored American patriot and pioneer.[44] In 1816, Lasselle and a number of other merchants, French and Anglo-American, formed the Terre Haute Land Company, surely a convincing sign of dedication to the American future.

Lasselle had always maintained cordial relationships in the Potawatomi and Miami Indian communities. The Miamis called him Kekiah and celebrated his athletic abilities. Those friendships paid off. He served as administrator of the estate of John Old Owl or Ma-son-pe-con-gah in 1817. He arranged for deed transfers from various Potawatomi Indians at the treaty negotiations of 1826 and 1832.[45] In 1833, he purchased shares in the Wabash and Erie Canal and moved his family to Logansport, the county seat of newly created Cass County. This appropriately named county became the focal point of the Indian-related business in 1828 when John Tipton moved the Indian Agency to Logansport.[46]

Lasselle died in 1843. He was not the most famous or successful of Indiana's French merchants; the brothers-in-law François Comparet and Alexis Coquillard are perhaps better known for their civic and economic contributions to the cities of Fort Wayne and South Bend, respectively. The history of the Lasselle family, however, makes a number of points most clearly. Hyacinthe's Uncle Antoine was almost shot in 1794 as a British spy. His older brother François was accused of treason during the War of 1812. Yet Hyacinthe was elected major general of the militia in 1820 by his fellow citizens, many of them Anglo-Americans.[47] Were the Lasselle brothers that different? Had their goals and values changed? I think not. The year of Hyacinthe's election, the Indiana Supreme Court declared in *The State v. Lasselle* that the institution of slavery was incompatible with the new state constitution.[48] (Lasselle was defending his property rights.) What changed was simply Hyacinthe's decision to invest in the new order.

During the 1820s and 1830s, the Indiana French were still a distinct and different community. Political appeals were still made in the French language. In Michigan, Father Gabriel Richard was elected to Congress.[49] As Lasselle and others of his generation increasingly moved in non-French circles, their interest in cementing their ties to French culture and supporting their distinct institutions seems to have increased as well. Lasselle began a subscription to a new national newspaper, *Le Courier des États Unis*, in 1830.[50] French merchants sponsored Catholic churches and schools in every part of the French Midwest during the 1830s and 1840s.[51] Although the French character of these institutions was soon lost, the institutions themselves survived and prospered. Their endurance ensured the existence of a pluralistic society in the Midwest.

French traders were in the right place at the right time. Most of them had little use for noble sentiments about democracy and did not share the political values of their Anglo-American neighbors. By 1815, however, they had taken the measure of republican government and made the transition from old-regime clientage to American-style backroom deals. Unlike their Anglo counterparts, they drank brandy and wine, not whiskey. And they had a different outlook on and relationship with the Indians. It was critical that they did. Although the transition from Indian country to settlement frontier was not the only source of their wealth, many certainly made a killing on that transition.

Some diversified their investments and entered the world of industrial capitalism with enthusiasm. A substantial number held stock in canal companies, steamboats, and railroads. They were, if we may generalize, uninterested in carving out country estates. They were town founders and urban residents. Country acres were for them a source of income, not status. What mattered most to the Chouteaus, for example, was *la maison*, the prosperity of their house—by which they meant both the family and the family business. Ironically, millionaire Pierre Chouteau Jr. felt that the business class of New York City was too obsessed with profits. In short, the francophone merchants of this western borderland constituted a significant bourgeois elite who were flexible though cautious in their investment strategy, crafty and discreet in their political maneuvering, and utterly tenacious in their pursuit of social and economic capital.

As a group, these merchants are most interesting and most visible to historians during this dramatic period of American expansion—from Lewis and Clark to the opening of the Far West. If we try to assess the big picture, several tentative conclusions come to mind. First, the transition period in this region is perhaps best characterized not as a conquest, but as a series of negotiations between groups with unequal amounts of power. And a significant number of francophone merchants (*négociants* in French)—rooted in places that antedated Anglo-American settlement—assumed important roles in these negotiations.

A second conclusion flows from the first. Beyond the Mississippi River, the federal government had few resources before the Civil War. When the army needed a post, it turned to Pierre Chouteau Jr. Chouteau steamboats were used to transport soldiers as well as Indians. If native peoples were unprepared for the invasion and transformation of their homelands, then so was the federal government. In this sense, French merchants—veterans of the middle ground—served as the middlemen of American expansion in a surprising number of cases. When Stephen W. Kearny's Army of the West entered New Mexico in 1846, it found a number of well-established francophone traders, some of whom they relied on for support. (This is the story of Chapter 5.) Indeed, French and métis traders seemed to bring the middle ground with them. In the late nineteenth century in the Jocko and Mission valleys of Montana, one can find a French town and a host of successful French and métis ranchers and traders named Allard, Rivais, Morigeau, Courville, and the like.[52] In a sense, the middle ground became the "negotiable instrument" of American expansion. Frontier brokers became brokers of frontiers.

When you gaze at the portrait of Pierre Chouteau Jr. at the Missouri Historical Society, his shrewd expression smiles down on you and he seems to be saying— in French, of course—keep your log cabin, I have a mansion in town. Like so many bourgeois Napoleons of the American West, these francophone merchants helped negotiate the course of empire. Their collective story suggests not how the West was won or lost, but how it was sold.

BEYOND ST. LOUIS:
NEGOTIATING THE COURSE OF EMPIRE

In the previous chapters I have tried to show that the French in a variety of places in mid-America, in what I have dubbed the Creole Corridor, were not only able to survive the transition to American sovereignty and avoid marginalization under the new regime, but many were able to profit by brokering the transition from Indian country to a settlement frontier. In Indiana and Missouri, Illinois and Michigan, French traders with the means to do so accumulated parcels of land that they assumed would rise in value as droves of American immigrants headed west. They also held political capital as their connections to a variety of Indian tribes ensured their usefulness in the decades after the War of 1812 that saw local and federal officials desperate to sign treaties and obtain one land cession after another. Many of the French continued to pursue the fur trade, but as forests gave way to farms, those with means began purchasing town lots and shares in canals, steamboats, and railroads. Because their collective story has never been told, but rather lies in the fragments of midwestern local history, the pattern has eluded our textbooks. The successful métis businessman Antoine LeClaire, the same man who recorded Black Hawk's autobiography, developed Davenport, Iowa; Louis Campau played the same role for Grand Rapids, Michigan. They are well-known in the cities they founded, but their actions have not been seen as part of a larger narrative.

It seems clear that the French in St. Louis, above all the Chouteaus and their many relations, followed a similar trajectory on a grand scale and with spectacular success. Above and beyond their skill as entrepreneurs and their political acumen, they occupied a most fortunate position in time and space. Decades of Spanish rule had allowed them to accumulate connections and land claims.

And, of course, their geographical position in Missouri allowed them to squeeze the profits out of frontiers in transition even as they were consolidating their hold over the fur trade on the Upper Missouri and elsewhere in the vastness of the new American Far West. Chapter 4 provided an overview of that dramatic example of private empire-building, shaped by company consolidation and control and the needs of the federal government pursuing a policy of westward expansion. Chapter 6 will examine the ways in which family formation and generational succession shaped business interests, for the Chouteau companies, unlike Astor's American Fur Company and the Hudson's Bay Company, remained, throughout this period, family businesses.[1] But this chapter will pursue not the grand strategy from the perspective of French merchants stationed in St. Louis, co-ordinating operations and connections in Indian country and eastern centers of power, but the actions of the French on the ground in the various Wests beyond St. Louis—specifically, the role of the French as brokers of frontiers in western Missouri; in the present-day states of Kansas, Nebraska, and Oklahoma; and also in a Hispanic region on the international border between two young republics, Mexico and the United States. Here and elsewhere in the Far West, the French were often the first in the field, the advance guard of U.S. expansion pursuing a variety of economic opportunities though often starting with furs. In following the activities of the French and their role in this story of western expansion, I hope at the same time to provide a case study not only of the dispersion of the French, but also the French in the process of middle-grounding, of occupying a cultural and social space of accommodation while pursuing an economic agenda of development and change.

So let us return briefly to 1803 and St. Louis, the capital of the American fur trade in the newly acquired territory, the place Jefferson called "the center of our western operations."[2] No group had a keener appreciation of the resources of this new American empire than the French Creoles of the city that would soon become known as the Gateway to the West. The timing of the Lewis and Clark expedition was in many ways perfect for the French Creole elite of St. Louis. A new generation of Chouteaus and their many cousins would reach their maturity in the following two decades, and the new American West would provide a host of opportunities for them to test their abilities as frontier entrepreneurs. During the 1820s, established French families such as the Chouteaus, the Menards, the Papins, the Sarpys, and the St. Vrains sent sons and daughters to establish western branches of family enterprises up and down the Missouri River, into the Rocky Mountains, and into Texas and New Mexico. Others ventured out from Lower Louisiana, especially from the border town of Natchitoches.

It was also time, from a business standpoint, for a new regime. The Chouteaus had mastered the system of Spanish imperial patronage and had enjoyed a six-year monopoly on the lucrative Osage trade from 1794 to 1800. Although the French already had a long history of trading in western Missouri and present-day Kansas, they had been unable to establish a strong presence there and faced competitors supplied with British goods at Michilimackinac in the Great Lakes region. A number of attempts to reach tribal peoples living on the Upper Missouri in the 1790s had failed to get beyond the Mandan villages in west-central North Dakota. The Chouteaus and other French traders were ready to cast their lot with the new American regime. The Spanish had viewed Missouri as a defensive borderland; the French Creoles, like the Anglo-Americans, were ready to expand.

The Lewis and Clark expedition seemed to break the ice. After their return to St. Louis, reports of a wealth of fur-bearing animals in the Rocky Mountains prompted Manuel Lisa to lead a party to the Upper Missouri in 1807. That venture enjoyed limited success, enough to prompt Pierre Chouteau Sr. to join a new venture with Lisa, the Missouri Fur Company, in 1809. Over the next decade and a half, the scramble to exploit the Upper Missouri trade would see a variety of individuals and companies establish posts with varying results. The Chouteaus focused their interests on consolidating their position in the central portion of the valley from the mouth of the Kansas River to the area north of the Platte around Council Bluffs near present-day Omaha.[3]

In 1808, with war looming between Great Britain and the United States, many of the Indian nations were threatening to join forces in a pro-British alliance directed against American settlers. Pierre Chouteau Sr., acting in his capacity as the U.S. government's agent for the Osages, negotiated a treaty with that nation that secured the cession of a huge tract of land between the Missouri and Arkansas rivers. Many of the Osages agreed to move to the west and southwest in search of better hunting grounds. The treaty thus moved this potentially dangerous group safely away from the pro-British tribes and opened central Missouri for white settlement. At the same time, the treaty included a provision confirming the Chouteaus' title to thirty thousand arpents of land in the ceded area.[4] This was not the first time, nor would it be the last, that the Chouteaus would show themselves to be masters of combining their personal interests with the diplomatic agenda of their new government. That same year, the first town in central Missouri, Côte Sans Dessein, was settled. The residents of the town—mostly métis families who worked as interpreters, hunters, and voyageurs in the fur business—were partisans of the Chouteaus.[5] They included people like the Philiberts. One Philibert daughter, Constantine, would later marry Daniel Boone's grandson and move to the new Chouteau town of Kansas City. Their daughters,

Elizabeth and Eulalie Boone, were baptized in the Catholic Church and presumably spoke French.[6]

Most of the families at Côte Sans Dessein had come from the St. Louis suburb of St. Charles, Missouri. At one point, St. Charles had been the place where fur-trade workers lived, the center of a French-Indian kinship network that facilitated commercial relations. Some forty years after the founding of St. Louis, the center of gravity in the fur trade was shifting westward.[7] But it was not simply the lure of pelts, and later buffalo robes, that pulled French traders west, it was also the push of American settlement driving their customers and producers out of their homes.

Additional land-cession treaties negotiated in 1818 and 1825 with the Osages, 1823 with the Ioways, 1824 with the Sac and Foxes, and 1825 with the Kansa Indians removed all those peoples who were indigenous to the area from the boundaries of what became the state of Missouri in 1821. To further complicate matters, Indians who had immigrated into the region, having been driven from homeplaces farther east, were also removed from Missouri. The Shawnees and Delawares had lived in southeastern Missouri since the 1780s and received a Spanish land grant in 1793. In 1815, more than twelve hundred Shawnees occupied comfortable cabins along Apple Creek (north of Cape Girardeau) with flourishing fields, land rich in game, and livestock and slaves, but white squatters had begun to make life miserable for these immigrant Indians. Robberies and beatings increased in frequency, and the Shawnees and Delawares began to seek new lands farther west. Despite protests from French traders such as Pierre Menard and Auguste Chouteau[8] and attempts by territorial governor William Clark to create a new reservation for the Shawnees and Delawares in western Missouri, the majority of Missourians would have none of it. Clark's attempts to protect native rights secured his defeat in the first gubernatorial election of 1820. A final land-cession treaty in 1825 forced the Shawnees to exchange their lands in Missouri for fourteen thousand dollars and a tract of land beyond the western border of the state near the junction of the Kansas and Missouri rivers. And while Congress debated, but failed to pass, a measure to create an Indian Territory in 1825, more Indians were on their way west. The potential for hostilities between tribes on the move and under pressure was palpable, and only a few gave voice to any humanitarian concern for the refugees: Pierre Menard warned officials that Shawnees from Ohio heading west "are naked and starving and will be unable to join their friends in time to raise a crop, if they are not assisted."[9]

As Indians moved west, traders followed. In short, during the decades after Lewis and Clark, and especially during the 1820s and 1830s, traders in pursuit of furs expanded into vast new territories—up the Missouri to the edge of present-day Montana, into the northern and southern Rockies—acquiring new groups of Indian clients such as the Assiniboines and the Crees. Traders also established new posts among familiar groups such as the Osages along a new and tenuous border separating Indian country from an expansionist republic of land-hungry settlers. In these new borderlands from the Three Forks of the Arkansas to the mouth of the Platte River, the fur trade would become as much a business of providing annuity goods for cash—or providing goods on credit in hopes that debts might be paid later, often through the medium of an additional land-cession treaty—as a gathering of skins and pelts. This somewhat tedious business of keeping retail accounts for increasingly impoverished customers might be supplemented by providing goods and services for the army posts that began to be established to keep the peace between hostile Indian groups (Fort Smith in 1817 in western Arkansas, Fort Gibson in eastern Oklahoma in 1824) and to ensure the safe passage of traders heading up the Missouri or southwest along the Santa Fe Trail (Fort Atkinson at Council Bluffs in 1820, Fort Leavenworth in Kansas in 1827).

The fur trade had always combined aspects of wholesaling and retailing, opening new markets and linking western resources with the rest of the world while serving local retail customers, Indian and non-Indian. The bourgeois who ran a trading post was at once a shopkeeper and a link in a larger wholesale network. As the new western edge of trade from eastern Oklahoma to the far reaches of the Upper Missouri took shape during the 1820s and 1830s, it would become clear that the potential profits from furs were greater farther north, in trading regions that would remain distant and isolated from overland trails and the pressures of American settlers until after the Civil War.[10] On the eve of selling the Astor interests in the western fur trade to Pierre Chouteau Jr. and his associates—the two companies had been working in tandem since 1827—William Astor noted in 1833 that the Upper Missouri Outfit had recently been credited with sales of furs amounting to $20,322.63. The Kanzas [*sic*] Outfit account, by way of contrast, had amounted to $2,288.77.[11] (Such figures do not provide an annual summary of profits but do indicate the relative value of the outfits.)

Furs, however, were only part of the story. There was, of course, a great potential for profit in brokering the transition from Indian country to a settlement frontier—profits derived from the payment of accumulated Indian debts, transportation services, wholesaling, and land speculation—but to gather such profits, traders had to be on the ground both before and after the transition. Frederick Jackson Turner, in his dissertation on the fur trade, had noted that the French trading posts had pioneered the sites of future American cities, but he thought that the traders themselves and the French-Indian world in which they operated were essentially washed away by the tide of American settlement.[12] He was wrong. French traders not only broke the cake of custom, they often began the process of baking the new cake.

But we are getting ahead of ourselves. The decade following the end of the War of 1812 saw an enormous increase in the population of the Old Northwest and Missouri—the latter rose from 19,783 in 1810 to 66,586 in 1820 to 140,455 in 1830. The westering line of settlement drove a corresponding line of Indian resettlement. And the second generation of Chouteaus and their various cousins followed. As the youngest of Pierre Chouteau Sr.'s sons, Frederick, observed later in his life: "In 1830 I made my house on the American Chief creek, on the south side of the Kansas river, about fifteen or twenty miles above [present-day] Topeka. American Chief had a small band living there, twenty lodges. . . . They remained there until 1845. I remained there till that time; then I went with them to Council Grove." But if the traders followed the Indians, it was also true that native customers were influenced by the location of traders. Frederick Chouteau wrote: "Hard Chief had his village, in 1830, about a mile above the American Chief, away from the creek, and nearer the Kaw [Kansas] river, on the highland. . . . These two bands built their villages there because I was going there to trade, as I told them." Chouteau later added: "I was up at the trading-post most of the time. The [government] agent never lived there, or at any of the other Indian villages. He only went there once a year, to make the payment—about Christmas—when the Indians returned from their hunt. All the Indians of the tribe of all the villages traded with me. I was the only trader."[13]

Frederick first arrived in Indian country in the fall of 1825 at the age of fifteen. He states that he landed at the trading post of his brothers, François and Cyprien, at Randolph Bluffs in Clay County, Missouri, "about two miles below Kansas City, on the opposite side of the Missouri river."[14] The first of this second French Creole generation to arrive had been Paul Liguest Chouteau, the third son of Pierre Sr. Liguest, as he was known to his family, set up shop with the Osages, the people most well-known by the Chouteaus and the source of the first generation's fur-trade wealth. Liguest's first post was established in 1816 on the Marais des Cygnes, a tributary of the Osage River. A Frenchman traveling through the United States in 1840, Victor Tixier, left us a description of Liguest, referred to as Major Chouteau: "The Major is one of those men whose faces show natural kindness. For a long time he lived the life of the Osage on the prairie. . . . 'now that old age is approaching,' he said, 'I am resting from my hardships; formerly I wasted little of my time at school, and I completed my education at the Osage academy.'"[15] Liguest maintained the post on the Marais des Cygnes until 1823. At this post, he apparently schooled his half-brother François and his cousin Gabriel Sylvestre Chouteau—known as Cerré, after his mother's maiden name—in the fur-trade business. Cerré was the second son of Auguste. Cerré and François apparently arrived at Liguest's post as early as 1816. By 1819, they were ready to strike out on their own and set up a post known as Four Houses twenty miles above the mouth of the Kansas River. They also had a post at Randolph Bluffs. Two more brothers arrived to work under François. Cyprien came in 1822 or 1823 and by 1828 was operating a trading post for the Shawnees and Delawares near present-day Turner, Kansas, slightly west of Kansas City. Frederick arrived for his apprenticeship in 1825 and set up his own post for the Kansa Indians in 1829.

In the meantime, Liguest had moved with the Osages to the Neosho River in Kansas. Here he was joined by yet another cousin, Pierre Melicourt Papin, who ran a trading post linked to White Hair's band. Liguest received the government appointment as subagent, then agent, for the Osages. Papin had been at the Marais des Cygnes post, which became known as Papin's Town then Papinsville in western Missouri. Married to Sophie Mongraine, whose family had close relations with White Hair (Pawhuska), Papin had settled down at the Neosho post in Kansas by the fall of 1825 and remained there for most of his life, though he died in St. Louis in 1849.

As if there weren't enough brothers and cousins in what was becoming a busy crossroads region bounded by the Kansas, Arkansas, and Missouri rivers, the oldest son of Pierre Chouteau Sr., A. P. Chouteau, would arrive, probably in 1822, having taken out a license to trade with the Osages with his brother Liguest in July of that year. A.P., a graduate of West Point, is—with his younger brother, Pierre Jr.—the most famous of the second-generation Chouteaus, primarily because of the description by Washington Irving of him and his "frontier plantation" at La Saline, "a big salt spring some thirty-five miles up the Neosho from its mouth in eastern Oklahoma."[16] A.P. and Jules de Mun, another family relation, had led an unsuccessful trading venture to New Mexico from 1815 to 1817 (more on that later) and upon their return to St. Louis had borrowed money from Berthold & Chouteau (Bartholomew Berthold and Pierre Chouteau Jr.) to open a store in St. Louis. At this time, A.P. also built a two-story frame house in town. In short, it would appear that he had opted for a more permanent place in the city of his birth. The business had failed by 1821. As historian Janet Lecompte observed in her biographical sketch of A.P., the debt to Berthold & Chouteau "amounted with interest to $66,000 fifteen years later . . . a veritable fortune requiring a lifetime of work or a windfall of good luck to repay. A.P. was a failure unprecedented among the vigorous and ambitious Chouteaus."[17] A.P. already had much knowledge of and experience with the Osages so relocating to Osage country was a logical next move. In 1822, he arrived in eastern Oklahoma and bought a house recently constructed at La Saline by Joseph Revoir. (Revoir had traded in partnership with Liguest, but he was killed by the Cherokees in 1821.)

The field, however, was becoming rather too crowded for so many relatives. Pierre Chouteau Jr. wrote from St. Louis to "mon cher cousin" Cerré on July 19, 1822, that Gesseau (the family usually referred to François by his middle name) "wanted to take the merchandise for his own account, because he alleges, with reason, that the profits are so limited that it is not worth the trouble to increase the number of partners in a small operation; we are leaving it to you and to him to settle it." Pierre offered Cerré his choice of other posts, suggesting that he spend the winter with the "Otos or the Mahas" farther north.[18] Cerré took his cousin up on the offer and spent the next seven years upriver. When his father, Auguste, died in 1829, Cerré returned to St. Louis and took over the operation of the Chouteau flour mill until Chouteau's Pond, one of the city's landmark places, was drained in 1852 for health reasons and rail yards. Far from Indian country, he became known as "the miller" and died, unmarried, in 1887.[19]

A new sense of structure and permanence emerged in 1822. As we have seen, it was a pivotal year: a new consolidated family firm, known as the French Fur Company,[20] signed a marketing agreement with John Jacob Astor's American Fur Company, and the Chouteaus' political ally, Senator Benton, pushed Congress to abolish the government factory system, thus abandoning the federal government's most direct connection to the tribes and leaving the field to private companies, most notably those run by Astor and the Chouteaus. The Chouteaus' privileged position was reinforced that year by the creation of the Superintendency of Indian Affairs at St. Louis, directed by their fast friend William Clark. And that same year, the new family firm, in one of its first acts, put François Chouteau in control of the family operations at the junction of the Kansas and Missouri rivers in what would become a second Chouteau's Town, Kansas City.[21]

Let us try to make some sense of all the Chouteaus and their cousins. In 1822, François brought his wife, Berenice Menard Chouteau—a cousin by marriage— their two young sons, several slaves, and a number of employees to the Randolph Bluffs post. After a flood in 1826, he built a large warehouse and several other buildings in a place on the south side of the Missouri first known as Chouteau's Landing—the nucleus of Kansas City. This complex would become the clearinghouse for the family's activities in the West, midway between the trade in New Mexico and the Upper Missouri posts on the one hand and the eastern terminus of St. Louis on the other. A supply center and a place for receiving bales of furs, Kansas City began its urban life in a manner quite similar to its parent city.

François supervised the operations centered around this region that, by the end of the 1820s, included the warehouse in Kansas City, the Kansa Post managed by Frederick Chouteau, the Shawnee Post managed by Cyprien, and several smaller posts serving the Wea and Kickapoo emigrants. For supervising this area, François received a salary from the home office in St. Louis; in effect, he was a branch manager. But he was also a shareholder in the Kansas Outfit. In addition, he "bought and sold real estate, and served as a one-man banking system on the frontier."[22] Likewise, the brothers who managed the various posts—the bourgeois or head traders of those posts—were both managers of the company's interests, keeping track of inventory at all times, and semiautonomous entrepreneurs, ready to invest on their own accounts. To complicate matters, François also looked after the interests of his father-in-law. The marriage of François and Berenice not only created the social and cultural foundation for a new city, it united the business interests of the Chouteau family and their long-time associate, Pierre Menard of Kaskaskia. Menard, who served as the first lieutenant governor of the state of Illinois, had been a "key figure in the relocation of the Shawnees and Delawares" to Kansas.[23]

The trading assignments of the various head traders and supervisors were both human and geographical in scope. Investments in client bands and tribes were especially mobile during a period characterized by multiple land cessions and relocations. For example, in a letter written to Pierre Chouteau Jr. in August 1829, François noted that "the chiefs of the Shawnee came to see me upon my arrival to ask me if I had brought their annuities. I told them 'no.' Captain Vashon [their agent] took two thousand dollars to them. They have taken a thousand of them. They took a thousand and a thousand was reserved for Mr. Menard."[24] The money for Menard was likely intended to pay off past debts. Menard's interest in the Shawnees, both humane and financial, continued over time and was maintained—in this case by his son-in-law—over long distances. The increasing importance of annuity payments only reinforced the need, in this complex phenomenon we tend to oversimplify by using the phrase "fur trade," for capital reserves as goods were often sold on credit. In a similar vein, Victor Tixier noted in 1840 that a recent treaty with the Osages (concluded in 1839) had promised a sum of eighteen thousand dollars annually for twenty years in exchange for a further land cession. Though he was slightly off with that figure, his remarks were telling: "This annuity comes back to the Fur Company almost in its entirety; in 1840, $16,000 went into Mr. [Pierre Melicourt] Papin's coffers."[25]

To the south of these operations centered in Kansas City was the territory known as the Osage Outfit supervised by A. P. Chouteau. This trading turf included the old post at Marais des Cygnes, Papin's post on the Neosho in Kansas near White Hair's village, the home at La Saline where his cousin Auguste Aristide Chouteau (Auguste Sr.'s oldest son) helped out, and a post near the Three Forks on the Verdigris River where another brother (half-brother), Louis Pharamond Chouteau, came to work as a clerk. Later on, Edward Chouteau, a son of Liguest, built an additional post at Flat Rock Creek and traded with the Beaver band of the Osages, a group connected to his métis wife, Rosalie Capitaine.[26] Tixier noted that Edward "was the only white man who spoke [the Osage language] like an Osage."[27]

The post on the Verdigris near the Three Forks was the business center and contained a warehouse, a boat landing, and fields of wheat and corn. This post served Clermont's Osages and increasing numbers of Cherokees, Creeks, Choctaws, and white settlers, all—in the words of historian Janet Lecompte—"pushing the frontier west from Arkansas."[28]

It should be clear by now that the various Chouteau relatives were in a perfect position to dominate the trade in both furs and annuity goods in this region by the mid-1820s. But were they successful economically? Socially? What constituted success in this new frontier zone? The first generation of French Creoles in St. Louis had not only achieved success in the volatile fur business, they had also positioned themselves perfectly for the transition to American rule, accumulating Spanish land grants in anticipation of American settlers and serving as valuable go-betweens in the negotiations with Indian tribes in the path of settlement. On less of a grand scale, French merchants such as Hyacinthe Lasselle and Alexis Coquillard in Indiana and the Campaus in Michigan played a role similar to that of the Chouteaus in St. Louis. One rather significant complication of life on this new frontier, this new middle ground, was that St. Louis remained the financial epicenter of the business, and also the center of the French Creole social world. Many of these Chouteau traders had not only left brothers, sisters, and parents behind, they also, in a number of cases, had wives and children in St. Louis. The first generation of French fur traders in St. Louis often had marriages or partnerships *à la façon du pays* with Indian women. Such alliances cemented trade relations and built trust between communities.[29] But the distance between Indian communities and St. Louis in the 1790s was much shorter, and the separation less severe. There was simply no question that the *maison* that mattered was in St. Louis, and for businessmen such as Auguste and Pierre Chouteau and their various brothers-in-law, the children of their marriages with French Creole women were the future. But now many of those children had traveled to a new Indian country far from home. What would the future beyond St. Louis look like?

Tanis Thorne, in her book *The Many Hands of My Relations*, has done a wonderful job of tracking the construction of a métis world in this frontier region and the history of a number of mixed-blood communities after the decline of the fur trade. Here we are more concerned with French Creole traders themselves and their outcomes. Indeed, Thorne suggests that many of these second-generation Creoles left St. Louis because the French population there was being "rapidly overshadowed by the Anglo-American population. . . . [that many sons of the] leading families chose a life in the Indian country, rather than struggle for social position in St. Louis."[30] This, I would suggest, was not the case, but it is a point worth addressing. It can be argued more successfully that a number of French and métis people who lived in places like St. Charles, a place where those we might describe as the proletariat of the fur trade lived, were, to some degree, pushed out by rising land values and competition from incoming Anglo-American farm families.[31] But what of the leading families?

Thorne uses the example of A. P. Chouteau's store in St. Louis to illustrate her case. No doubt, A.P. seems to have been a rather poor businessman, and he certainly removed to Indian country after his mercantile establishment in St. Louis failed. His hard luck would continue in eastern Oklahoma. A flood on the Verdigris in June 1833 destroyed his central business buildings, causing losses of more than ten thousand dollars. It also swept away most of a local Creek village, further impoverishing his customers.[32] But beyond mere luck or lack of business acumen, A.P. was in a tough place to make a profit. The nearby Osage villages were pressed by incoming groups of Creeks, Choctaws, and Cherokees; Comanches and Pawnees to the west did their best to keep all of these groups away from their hunting grounds; and white squatters were an added annoyance. The 1820s and 1830s were years of constant, if intermittent, bloodshed. A.P. was called upon to act as a peacemaker on numerous occasions. The establishment of Fort Gibson at the Three Forks in 1824 provided some measure of assistance, and additional customers, but no respite from the violence. To make matters worse, the arrival of newcomers to the area had made game scarce. And when a group of Creek emigrants arrived in 1828 and 1829, A.P. found that the government had failed to provide them with the goods and money promised. He supplied them with food, clothing, and other items to the tune of more than five thousand dollars. He was not reimbursed during his lifetime. Heading east in 1835, he formed a new partnership to trade with the Cherokees, the only native group in the area with money, purchasing thirty thousand dollars worth of goods on credit from a firm in Philadelphia and taking an additional loan of ten thousand dollars. (At this point, he was already deeply in debt to the family company in St. Louis.) Back in Oklahoma, he found that the Cherokee agent would not let him rent a store on the Cherokee reserve. The goods remained unsold, and in January 1838, the Philadelphia firm, Siter, Price & Company, sued him to recover the forty thousand dollars. This forced his brother Pierre Jr. to bring suit for the older and larger debt of sixty-six thousand dollars, and A.P.'s property in St. Louis was attached. A.P. died on Christmas Day of that year.[33] By the standards of St. Louis and his family, he was utterly unsuccessful, but the context of his business actions was a most difficult one. By way of contrast, his brother Pierre Jr., who spent most of his life in St. Louis and New York City, died leaving a fortune estimated to be worth "several millions," including more than four hundred thousand dollars worth of railroad bonds.[34]

The oldest son of Auguste Chouteau, Auguste Aristide, a rather helpless soul, went to Indian country in hopes of finding some useful employment. He had been a disappointment, a problem child, from the start.[35] He fared no better out west. Working as a farmer on La Saline, he wrote to his father the year before the latter's death in 1829:

Dear Papa,

   This is to inform you of the unfortunate situation I have been in for three years. I work on a farm and by my work and the diligence which I devote to it I flatter myself to see the moment arrive when I could meet my engagements, but the treaty the Government has just made with the Cherokees has taken away all means. I have made a quantity of corn, for which I can get nothing because the settlers have been obliged to leave the country. . . . I do not know what to do; I hope that you will tell me.[36]

The son died in 1835. The last Spanish lieutenant governor of Upper Louisiana, Charles Dehault Delassus, went to visit his mother that year in St. Louis and observed in his diary: "She is at the moment in sorrow, having learned of the death of her eldest son—a sorry person, who had abandoned wife and children here to live with the Osages in the greatest disorder, but he was her son!"[37] Again, by way of contrast, the three other brothers spent most of their lives in St. Louis. Cerré ran the family flour mill. Henry or Henri served as the county clerk and recorder and was a very successful businessman. Henri and two of his sisters married members of an elite Paris-educated family from St. Domingue and settled down to comfortable lives as well-respected citizens of St. Louis.

To cite one other example, the Papin family, cousins of the Chouteaus, had eleven children who lived into adulthood. Of the seven sons, three spent most of their lives engaged in the fur trade (we have already encountered Pierre Melicourt Papin). The other four stayed in St. Louis and had successful careers in real estate and wholesale groceries. One brother-in-law worked in the fur trade. Another, Marie Philippe LeDuc, born in Paris and the former secretary for Spanish lieutenant governor Delassus, became the presiding judge of the St. Louis County Court.

This is a limited survey, to be sure, but the evidence seems to suggest that the elite French Creole families retained their status in the city they had established. Most second-generation sons and daughters stayed in St. Louis, and many made fortunes in real estate as the city grew and prospered. We may, however, suggest that the fur trade continued to provide opportunities—for adventure, if not always for great fortune—for some. It was, after all, the original family business. Notably, the one member of the first generation who spent the most time in Indian country, Pierre Chouteau Sr., seems to have had the highest percentage of sons who lived most of their lives in Indian country—seven of eight. The eighth was Pierre Jr., and under his guidance in St. Louis, the family firm reached its pinnacle of power and profit. It is also noticeable that Indian country provided an outlet, a place to send those few who were not very capable. Not surprisingly, they had little financial success away from home.

If St. Louis remained the home base for French Creole society and business, then how did those who worked in the field deal with the separation? Pierre Melicourt Papin, stationed on the Neosho River in Kansas near White Hair's Osages, seems to have had a stable relationship with his métis wife, Sophie Mongraine. They had a son, Edward, and their household—described by Tixier in 1840— included Sophie, "a rather pretty half-breed," their son, Sophie's mother (who herself had been married to a Frenchman and then an Osage man), Sophie's half-sister, and several slaves. Papin later had another child by a different Osage woman.[38] French traders rarely put into words their thoughts about their circumstances, but Tixier recorded, how faithfully we cannot know, a conversation with Papin about how he came to acquire a glass eye. In telling the story, Papin observed that "all my friends in Saint Louis insisted upon my going to the city, where since my mother's death [1817] I had decided never to return, because I like living in Nion-Chou [Neosho] and because I would have found sorrowful memories there, everywhere. In short, I had not been there for nine years when one day Major Chouteau [Paul Liguest] came and took me back with him. After spending two months with my family, I came back with two eyes which moved almost in the same manner, with the difference, however, that the glass eye is somewhat lazy."[39] Papin, unlike many of the other French traders in the region, never married a French Creole woman. He seems to have been content, in a wistful way, with his life in Indian country. He kept in contact with his family in St. Louis and regularly received letters full of family news. A letter to Coucours (apparently the family nickname for Pierre Melicourt) from his brother

Theodore Dartigny Papin in 1833 described the ravages of a cholera epidemic, but quickly—since all had recovered—moved on to family news and gossip. Describing a recent visit by brother Laforce (Alexander Laforce Papin), who was a trader for the Chouteau company around Council Bluffs, Theodore observed: "Laforce left with some worries that his son caused before his departure. This young man, dear friend, I am afraid will cause him much anxiety. His disposition is that of a young man chained to dissipations. Unfortunately his father, because always absent, could not guide his early steps, and that his mother, like other mothers, was a little too weak towards him."[40] The son in question, Alexander, eventually died while serving as a captain during the Mexican War. The separation dictated by the business of the fur trade during this era clearly had a cost. Laforce, in the meantime, transferred some property to one of his sons-in-law. (Laforce and his Creole wife, Julie Brazeau, had three adult daughters and one son.) Another son-in-law, Dr. Henri Masuré, born in Belgium, was, according to Theodore, "still in Mexico [on business] and we are pleased to hear that he is doing well." Laforce also had six children in Indian country with Pawnee, Otoe, and Omaha women but did not pay much attention to their futures.[41] It was undoubtedly easier for the four brothers who remained in St. Louis to watch over their children. Theodore noted in his letter that Sylvestre and Timothy, sons of brother Sylvestre Vilray Papin, were in college and doing well. Timothy ultimately studied medicine in St. Louis and Paris and became a professor of clinical gynecology.[42] Theodore closed his letter by saying: "I beg you to write us and give us more details of your affairs, which can only interest us. I am not saying that you should come down next spring. If you have the misfortune of giving excuses we will quickly declare war against you."[43]

Pierre Melicourt Papin left a substantial estate in Bates County, Missouri, to his son by Sophie Mongraine, Edward.[44] Having no other children in St. Louis, his choice may have been a relatively easy one. A. P. Chouteau, on the other hand, had a wife, Sophie Labbadie, back in St. Louis and seven children who survived into adulthood. He also had at least seven children with five Osage women in Indian country.[45] Perhaps because of his financial difficulties, A.P. seems to have become increasingly estranged from his St. Louis family by the 1830s. When his property was attached in 1838, the year of his death, his wife and children were apparently put out of their home. But in 1851, the United States paid the claims of its citizens against Mexico, and A.P.'s losses from his 1815–1817 trading expedition were indemnified to the tune of $81,772, 10 percent of which went to Thomas Hart Benton for his services and the rest to his brother and creditor Pierre Jr. and to A.P.'s St. Louis heirs. His wife Sophie also inherited property from her family. We know that she clearly landed on her feet for in the late 1840s she built a lavish mansion in the genteel Frenchtown district of St. Louis. There she was said to have held court as the "acknowledged matriarch of the town."[46] Daughter Emilie Sophie married an eminent doctor from France, Nicolas De-Menil, and they built their own mansion nearby. (The DeMenil mansion still stands, one of the only places left in St. Louis where one can get some sense of the rather elegant and gracious manner of elite Creole life during this period.)

A.P.'s efforts on behalf of his St. Louis family were negligent at best. On a trip east in 1835, he enrolled his son Pierre Sylvestre at a school in West Chester, Pennsylvania. He left him there for three years without any correspondence to the schoolmaster and let his brother Pierre Jr. pay the bills.[47] But in Indian country, where he apparently enjoyed a strong relationship with his métis wife, Rosalie Lambert, he made careful efforts to provide for her future and that of his métis children and relations. The Osage Treaty of 1825—negotiated by Pierre Chouteau Sr.—had set aside two reserves for people of mixed blood, one at Marais des Cygnes and the other at the Three Forks near A.P.'s post. A.P.'s métis family members were listed by name as the recipients of the Three Forks reserve, and he was appointed to be their guardian. Ten years later, in a treaty negotiated by John F. Schermerhorn to secure a place for emigrant Cherokees, A.P. exchanged the eight sections of land held by his métis family for fifteen thousand dollars. A.P., in his capacity as "agent and guardian," not to mention paterfamilias, bought thirty-two slaves with the money as an investment, but after his death, most of the slaves returned to their former owners, the Creeks, who would not give them up.[48] A government agent, Montford Stokes, recognizing the legitimacy of A.P.'s métis family, helped them to recover their losses, which were secured by an act of Congress.[49]

If the experiences of Pierre Melicourt Papin, his brother Laforce, A. P. Chouteau, and his cousin Auguste Aristide Chouteau—whose St. Louis wife divorced him in 1830—show some of the strains of maintaining connections to St. Louis, then the experience of François Chouteau illustrates an alternative, which was to start a new French Creole town in the West. In essence, this is what he did when he brought his French wife with him to the settlement that would become Kansas City. This act of bringing his wife was not simply symbolic; it meant that all of his resources could be applied to the construction of one family, one *maison*. It also meant that Berenice would work to build a cultural environment appropriate for a French family. Though she was no doubt comfortable with Indian practices and a métis society—she was, after all, the daughter of Pierre Menard—she was a bourgeois Frenchwoman who expected her children to have a usable education and a Catholic upbringing. But the Chouteau settlement at Kawsmouth, as it was called early on, was also distinctive in two other ways. Because it was adjacent to Indian country, but located in Missouri, it would be possible to accumulate property there in anticipation of a settlement frontier. This is precisely what François did, purchasing and patenting large tracts of land amounting to some twelve hundred acres at government sales.[50] Moreover, François's warehouse was a central place, its permanence underwritten by the operations of the family firm back in St. Louis, rather than being subjected to the movements or actions of any Indian community. It was on the water route, a satellite community with direct access to St. Louis. And when the family company began operating regular steamboat service to the Upper Missouri in 1831, travel, communication, and commerce became much easier. The travel time between Kansas and St. Louis was reduced from several weeks or more to fewer than ten days.[51]

François and Berenice played the roles of urban pioneers with great success. Berenice returned to St. Louis for the birth of three of her children; the last four were born in the West. They had nine all together, but four died in childhood.[52] The younger family members remained connected culturally, socially, and economically to their home base in St. Louis. Several of the boys were sent to St. Mary's of the Barrens for schooling, an institution some eighty-seven miles south of St. Louis run by the Vincentian fathers. Berenice sent her sons several pairs of Indian moccasins to wear, which suggests that they had acquired frontier habits and were comfortable in an environment informed by both French and native cultures.[53] The first resident priest in Kansas City, Father Benedict Roux, arrived in 1833. François Chouteau wrote his father-in-law on the occasion, observing that "the thing cannot be anything but advantageous. We will then later on certainly have a small group of fine people. The riffraff perhaps will improve as this will be a cause of betterment for the area."[54] Chouteau's Church, as it was first known, was constructed in 1835; on that same site today stands the Catholic Cathedral of the Immaculate Conception.[55] Father Roux turned out to be a mixed blessing as he criticized the small community's fondness for dancing. Berenice ignored him and continued organizing balls, importing the settlement's first piano to augment the Rivard brothers' fiddles.[56] In short, François and Berenice, as their parents had done a generation earlier, laid the foundations for a new French Creole city on the frontier. They gathered capital and relatives, built a church, and provided leadership for the new settlement's social life.

François Chouteau died in 1838, and a flood swept away the family home in 1844. Berenice built a new two-story house with long verandas and French windows in a location known as Quality Hill. One pioneer observer described it as "a place where hospitality was dealt with a lavish hand. Inherent French politeness and wealth characterized the entertainment."[57] Their son, Pierre Menard Chouteau, known as Mack, inherited his father's business, was a member of the committee that drew up a charter for the town in 1850, and became an owner of steamboats.[58]

After the death of François, his brother Cyprien took over many of his responsibilities from his Shawnee post not far from the Kawsmouth area. Rather late in life, in 1855, Cyprien married Nancy Francis, a Shawnee woman who had been orphaned at the age of seven and educated at a Quaker mission. The couple had three children. Cyprien retired from the fur trade in 1857 and sold his land in the Shawnee area. He bought a farm closer to town (Kansas City) in 1859 and moved to the city proper in 1862. His sons settled in Oklahoma, but his daughter Mary Francis or Mamie married Joseph Karl Guinotte, the son of a Belgian civil engineer, Joseph Guinotte, who had bought more than five hundred acres of land from Berenice Menard Chouteau in 1853 and formed a colonization company to bring settlers to his new subdivision known as the Guinotte Addition. Joseph Karl Guinotte became a well-known architect in the city. Cyprien Chouteau died in Kansas City in 1879 and was buried in Mount St. Mary's Catholic Cemetery.

Cyprien's brother Frederick had a similar trajectory. He married a Shawnee woman, Elizabeth Tooley, in 1830. The couple had three children. Frederick outlived Elizabeth; in fact, he outlived his next two wives as well. He operated a ferry and bought and sold land after the creation of Kansas Territory in 1854 and the negotiation of several land-cession treaties that same year that opened up the new territory to white settlement. He moved to Westport in 1874 and had sold his land in Shawnee County by 1877.[59] He is said to have become one of the wealthiest men in the area before his death in 1891 at the age of eighty-two. Like his brother Cyprien, Frederick was buried in Mount St. Mary's Catholic Cemetery. His descendants remained in Oklahoma although his son William Meyer Chouteau, who married another Shawnee woman, Mary Silverheel, also moved back to Kansas City. William's sons, John and Edmond, stayed in the town of their childhood, Vinita, Oklahoma. John was a storekeeper, and Edmond, who was blind, was a respected violin and piano teacher for thirty years. Edmond's son Corbett became an oilman in Oklahoma City, and Corbett's daughter, Yvonne Chouteau, achieved fame as the prima ballerina of the Ballets Russes de Monte Carlo. Yvonne Chouteau, the founding director of Ballet Oklahoma, served as artist in residence at the University of Oklahoma for more than twenty-five years. In a sense, she completed the circle, returning to the francophone world of the first Chouteaus; yet today she is celebrated—along with Maria and Marjorie Tallchief and Rosella Hightower—as a great Native American dancer and artist. Chouteau herself has, appropriately, celebrated both sides of her ancestry.

But how do we make sense of these various outcomes? How do we take the measure of these lives? The social and familial relationships of these Chouteau brothers and cousins seem to fall along a rather broad spectrum of plot lines. A. P. Chouteau and his cousin Auguste Aristide opted for Indian country for many reasons and were estranged from their Creole families in St. Louis. Alexander Laforce Papin felt the strain of trying to maintain relationships in two places simultaneously. Pierre Melicourt Papin and Paul Liguest Chouteau's Creole son Edward had longstanding, stable relationships with their native wives, yet Pierre Melicourt died in St. Louis, possibly of cholera, in 1849. Edward ultimately returned to St. Louis as well and married a white woman. He left an annuity to each of his métis children that paid them $133 yearly for life.[60] One of the children, Sophie, became a trader and a leader in her Osage community. She was interviewed later in her life and remarked: "I have never been to St. Louis, but I may go during the 'World's Fair.' The Chouteau kindred live in St. Louis, but it has been a long, long time since I have seen any of them."[61]

Aunt Sophie, as she was known, may have captured an important point. The variety of accommodations that these different French traders made regarding their familial arrangements cannot obscure one central conclusion: Indian communities in Kansas and Oklahoma and American towns of French origin such as St. Louis and early Kansas City during this antebellum period belonged to two distinct worlds, yet their social and economic connections suggest just how complex the American frontier experience was.

A. P. Chouteau, after years of operating in the red, years spent helping to negotiate settlements between competing native groups in eastern Oklahoma, turned to the West. During the last three years of his life (1835–1838), he spent much of his time around Camp Holmes, one hundred miles west of Fort Gibson, mediating peace treaties with the Kiowas and the Comanches. He built several posts and began to trade with these groups. After A.P.'s death, in the spring of 1839, Santa Fe trader Josiah Gregg encountered a group of Comanches and told them the news. Gregg recorded their reaction: "Great was their grief when we informed then that their favorite trader had died at Fort Gibson, the previous winter."[62] Back at Three Forks, A.P.'s partner, Rosalie Lambert, ultimately married a Cherokee man. Lewis Ross, brother of Cherokee leader John Ross, bought A.P.'s frontier mansion at La Saline. After Ross's death, the Cherokee Nation bought the place, and it served as the National Orphans' Home for Cherokee children for more than thirty years until it was destroyed by fire in 1903.[63] In short, everything A. P. Chouteau built was reframed, recontextualized, by Indian agency. The small towns of Chouteau and Salina (La Saline) in Mayes County, Oklahoma, are part of Cherokee country.

François Chouteau's establishment, on the other hand, evolved into Kansas City, an urban link to the social and economic world of St. Louis. Not surprisingly, his brothers Frederick and Cyprien retired there later in life, acquired property, and were buried in the Catholic cemetery. Land values began to rise during the 1830s, and the city experienced a boom during the mid-1840s. In short, the fur trade, and the middle ground it generated, had been a phase, albeit one with human consequences. When the transition to a primarily Anglo-American settlement frontier began, the French Creole merchants were once again in a position to profit from it.

Farther north, nine hundred miles upriver from St. Louis, the same pattern unfolded. The area around Council Bluffs, the present-day Omaha–Council Bluffs metropolitan region, had emerged as another fur trade crossroads by the 1810s. There were Otoe-Missouri villages around the mouth of the Platte River, Omaha and Ponca villages to the north, and a Pawnee homeland to the west along the Platte and its tributaries. Ioway and Sac and Fox peoples to the east were also drawn to trade in the area. Like the Kansas area to the south, the Council Bluffs area was a jumping-off place for trails farther west. Traders and trappers seeking to tap the furs of the Rocky Mountains followed the Platte River. Located between the rich trade of the Upper Missouri and the administrative station of Kawsmouth, the Council Bluffs area was a key stop, and Fort Atkinson was built there during the winter of 1819–1820 to protect trading parties traveling north along the Missouri.

The area around Council Bluffs during the 1810s and 1820s was not as close—in time or space—to being a site of native resettlement and white immigration as the Kansas-Osage area farther south. In this sense, from a business standpoint, it was still a place primarily for gathering furs. And unlike the Kansas-Osage trading area, the Chouteaus did not monopolize the region around Council Bluffs. The result was a fierce competition that would frustrate the traders and have dire consequences for the native peoples of the area. Manuel Lisa had established a foothold there in 1817 at Bellevue, below the bluffs and near the mouth of the Platte. After an attempt to combine forces and capital with several French Creole partnerships ended in failure in 1819, Lisa formed a new Missouri Fur Company, which continued its operations after his death in 1820. Another trader, Joseph Robidoux, set up shop in the area, apparently with some backing from the St. Louis firm of Berthold & Chouteau. When the Creole family firm reorganized in 1822, bringing in Bernard Pratte as a partner, it may have established a more stable relationship with Robidoux to trade on its behalf in that area. The following year, however, Robidoux was replaced by Jean Pierre Cabanné, who had recently joined the family firm as a partner.[64]

Cabanné entered a rough situation in 1823, and he was probably not the right man for the job.[65] Born in 1773 in Pau, France, the same birthplace as St. Louis's founder, Pierre de Laclède, Cabanné had lived in Charleston and New Orleans before coming to St. Louis in 1798 and marrying the oldest daughter of Charles Gratiot, Julie, in 1799. Roughly the same age as his first business partner, Gregoire Sarpy, and Bernard Pratte, Cabanné was sixteen years older than his brother-in-law, Pierre Chouteau Jr. One of Sarpy's sons, Jean B., would become Pierre Jr.'s closest business associate. Another, Peter A. Sarpy, would replace Cabanné at Council Bluffs. Cabanné was fifty years old when he took over the post, and it showed.

One of Cabanné's daughters, Adèle—who had married Jean B. Sarpy in 1820—wrote a loving letter to Cabanné after his arrival at Council Bluffs:

Dear Papa,
    It is with great pleasure that I would like to express my love and my respect for you, but the lack of habit of letter writing and especially my ignorance take from me the power to trace with a pen what my heart thinks. . . . All the children are fine except little Isabelle who is teething, I shall leave it to Sarpy to tell you the news . . . Good-bye dear papa, believe that I shall be your sincere and devoted daughter as long as I live.[66]

Cabanné hardly needed such letters from his daughter to reinforce his longing for home. He wrote to Pierre Chouteau Jr. in 1825: "my wife wants to come up here, alas! can I contemplate her leaving the children after our recent loss? [the death of Isabelle, mentioned above, the last child born to Cabanné and his wife Julie] If it were possible, I would doubtless wish it; she must be crushed with grief. Guide her, my friend, and do what you think best."[67] Of all the French traders out in the field, Cabanné was perhaps the least ambivalent about his feelings of separation. Indeed, he was often a bit too expressive for the tight-lipped partners back in St. Louis. He wrote to Pierre Jr. in February 1831:

Your house, Mr. Sainfort [John F. A. Sanford, Pierre's son-in-law] tells me, is a house of pleasure, where good society assembles. The young people find there amusement suitable to their age, and those of middle age play Wisik [*Le Wisik*—perhaps whist] etc . . . It is without contradiction a way to pass one's time agreeably; life is short and if you do not profit by it now, at what happier time will you be able to enjoy it? As for me, my time is past; my feelings now are only ephemeral—provided I have enough food and slumber on a chair, it is all I need.[68]

Later that month he wrote to Pierre Jr. again—this time in a more whimsical, if rather indiscreet, state of mind:

If you can come here and if I am here, you can count in advance on the hearty reception you will receive, a good cup of coffee, some crêpes, some nymphs [une bonne tasse de café, des crêpes, des nymphes], etc. This last word is superfluous—I forgot that you had become chaste and I forgot myself. . . . I am here in pretty good company, Laforce [Papin], Abadie [Peter Sarpy], Charles [possibly Pierre's son] and Sinford [Sanford]. Food is abundant; I am in good enough health, except for some regressions, my intestines are still not perfectly right. I have the smokehouse full of deer-legs; perhaps, I will keep some to send down. If I only had the talent of a magician, I would quickly metamorphose them into so many packs of beaver.[69]

Although Cabanné's offer of "some nymphs" would suggest that he had most probably had sexual relations with Indian women, it does not seem that he had any long-term or useful partnerships. This may explain why he did not seem to ever have a good hold on the trade of the area and why he seemed to be dependent on personnel he could not trust. His letters are full of complaints about the men under his command; indeed, he complained about partners and relatives in the field as well—which could not have endeared him to the partners back in St. Louis.[70] But Cabanné's problems were mostly generated by competition. William Ashley had begun sending an annual brigade of trappers out to the Rocky Mountains in 1822. The success of his rendezvous system surprised the Chouteau company partners, and Pierre Jr. worked out an arrangement with Ashley in 1827. The Missouri Fur Company put up fierce opposition, but the company finally folded in 1828.[71] Then there was Joseph Robidoux. His relationship with the Chouteau company was a rocky one. After being replaced at Council Bluffs in 1822, Robidoux persuaded the partners to partially back a trading venture to Santa Fe and the southern Rockies in 1824. Cabanné pleaded with Chouteau in April 1825: "I ask you in the name of the friendship that is between us, no more Robidoux! This man will bring about our ruin! His competition is no more to be feared than any other's; disabuse yourself, my friend, it is buying him at too high a price."[72] Robidoux was back on the Missouri with Jean Baptiste Roy by 1826. Cabanné complained that Robidoux and Roy were using whiskey to trade with the Indians and were "hurrying on to their own destruction."[73] Increasingly exasperated, Cabanné wrote in January 1828 that "Robidoux is always in competition with us."[74] That same year, Pierre Chouteau bought out—or at least tried to temporarily muzzle—Robidoux, who was given a salary of one thousand dollars per year for two years in exchange for restraining from direct or indirect competition. Cabanné, who had suggested the idea in the first place, also expressed reservations: "It is better to have Robidoux against us than for us because he is always making new demands upon us for family, etc."[75]

Personalities aside, the fierce competition had resulted in serious game depletion. Intertribal warfare had become endemic by the late 1820s, especially
between tribes such as the Omahas, who lived on the western side of the Missouri, and tribes such as the Ioways and Sac and Foxes, who were being pushed
from their hunting grounds on the eastern side. To make matters much worse,
the trade in alcohol was increasing as the supply of furs declined. Despite an official restriction on the liquor trade, smuggling was easy, and companies and the
government itself brought substantial quantities of whiskey upriver for the use
of their own men. Drunken binges became commonplace among Indians and
fur-trade personnel.[76] Congress passed a bill in 1832 banning liquor from Indian
country, whether intended for Indians or fur traders. That year, Cabanné took it
upon himself to seize the cargo—which included alcohol—of a rival trader, Nar-
cisse Leclerc. Leclerc had eluded the authorities at Fort Leavenworth, which infuriated Cabanné. Leclerc returned to St. Louis to report the illegal seizure and
sued the Chouteau company, which settled with Leclerc for ninety-two hundred
dollars. Cabanné was banned from Indian country for a year, although the alcohol trade, after a brief pause, continued unabated.[77] Cabanné remained a partner in the firm until the reorganization of the company in 1839 and died at his
home in St. Louis in 1841. He may never have been well-suited for his position
as a field partner. Unlike the second-generation traders of the Chouteau clan, he
had grown up in France, not in the cross-cultural world of St. Louis and its environs. Yet as he noted in 1825: "None of you can replace me here and it would be
with greater difficulty that I could fulfill my task at St. Louis. What I do is simple
and easy and demands only attention, and your part, on the contrary demands a
knowledge of business and a greater soundness in transactions that present themselves."[78]

Cabanné's younger assistant, Peter Sarpy, would assume responsibilities at the
company's post. Sarpy seems to have been much more successful at Bellevue,
the new location of the company's post, than Cabanné had been at Council
Bluffs. This may have been partly due to his marriage to Nicomi, the multilingual
daughter of an Ioway chief and an elite woman of Otoe-Omaha lineage. Their relationship was long-lasting, if occasionally stormy. On one occasion, Sarpy tried
to limit his household spending and had apparently refused Nicomi some blankets and calico. According to one eyewitness: "Madame Nekoma marched into
the store, with that look on her face that bade the clerks stand aside, and grab-
bing several bolts of calico, she made for the Missouri river and heaved them in,
declaring, in Indian, she would clear the store out in the same way. Before she
got her second load to the bank Sarpy gave in and told Englemann [the clerk] to
let her have anything she wanted."[79] Unlike Cabanné, Sarpy was unambivalent

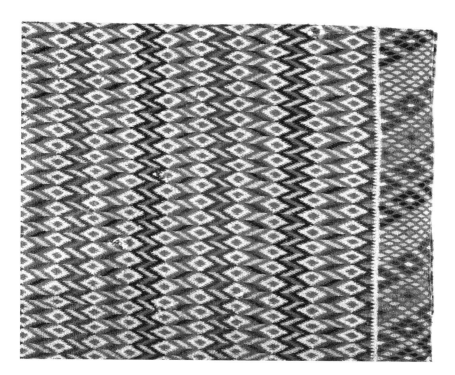

Multicolored serape (wearing blanket) from Saltillo, the capital of the Mexican state of Coahuila, presented to Peter Sarpy, circa 1840. Sarpy, stationed at a Chouteau post near present-day Omaha, was also involved in the trade of the southern Rockies. The blanket exemplifies the cross-cultural, border-crossing nature of the fur trade. Photograph by Cary Horton. Missouri History Museum, St. Louis.

about being in Indian country, though he remained connected to his kin in St. Louis. His letter to his niece, Virginia "Mimi" Sarpy, in 1847 on the occasion of her marriage to Frederick Berthold was affectionate and, perhaps surprisingly, religious. He ended with a profound wish that God would bless her union.[80] In his will, Sarpy left the bulk of his estate to his brother Jean B. Sarpy. Peter and Nicomi had no children, but he provided for her with an annuity that would pay two hundred dollars per year "for and during the term of her natural life." He added that "if the said 'Nicomy' should ever wish to live in the said city of Saint Louis, it is my will and desire that my said Executor . . . shall provide her with suitable lodgings and pay the rent for the same out of my Estate."[81]

Though he remained connected to St. Louis, Sarpy stayed in the West. From 1836 to 1838, he actively pursued the fur trade in the area between present-day Denver and Fort Laramie. This joint venture between Sarpy and his partner,

Henry Fraeb, and the company (known as Pratte, Chouteau and Company at this time) enjoyed success, but it ended when the partners in St. Louis decided to join forces with Bent, St. Vrain and Company, a competitor in the region.[82] Meanwhile, conditions around Council Bluffs had worsened for native people. With Indian communities suffering and the fur trade in decline, alcoholism became a growing concern, and Sarpy asked for government assistance in controlling the flow of whiskey.[83] Even the mountain fur trade had passed its peak years. By the late 1840s, the Upper Missouri and Minnesota would supply most of the furs and robes for the company back in St. Louis.[84] The 1840s and 1850s in the Council Bluffs region brought on the full force of what Tanis Thorne has described as a "parasitic economy." The Indian land base shrank, liquor sales continued, and the traders began to rely on annuity payments.[85] Sarpy's accounts in the St. Louis records for 1851 show collections of debts from the U.S. Indian Department ($58.27), the Sac and Fox Indians ($7,048.75), and the Potawatomi Nation ($11,106.26).[86] The emigrant Potawatomis had arrived in the area in 1837. Mary Gale, Sarpy's stepdaughter, remembered that the trade was now "not for pelts . . . but for specie." The Potawatomis had received fifty dollars per capita in gold in exchange for a land cession. It quickly fell into the traders' hands.[87]

Sarpy, as his cousins had done downriver, began to profit from the transition. He laid out new towns for settlement at Bellevue, Tekamah, and Decatur in Nebraska and St. Mary across the river in Iowa.[88] At the latter, he founded a newspaper, the St. Mary *Gazette*. He also began a highly profitable ferry service across the Missouri for immigrants and travelers. It was Sarpy who sold supplies to Brigham Young's Mormons in 1846 and 1847 when that group began the famous trek that would land them in the valley of the Great Salt Lake in present-day Utah.[89] And in 1854, he helped negotiate land-cession treaties with the Omahas and the Otoes. Though Sarpy and his cousins such as Frederick and A. P. Chouteau were often the only people available with the resources to help Indian communities during difficult times, and though they themselves might have had strong personal ties to those communities — bonds that would be remembered generations later — in the end, there was always a bill to pay. At the moment the Omahas were ceding much of their land in Nebraska in 1854, Sarpy used his influence to try to collect on a claim for ten thousand dollars.[90] At a similar point of desperation for the Kansa Indians in 1846, Fool Chief expressed his concern that their debt of fifteen hundred dollars to Frederick Chouteau would have to be paid from their last annuity payment under the terms of an 1825 treaty. They signed a new treaty that year ceding more land.[91] Even A.P.'s bill came due, though after his death, as Gabriel Franchere secured an acknowledgment of a debt of $18,231.68 owed by the Cherokee Nation to the firm of Pierre Chouteau Jr. and Company in January

1847.[92] This painful transition phase for native groups produced a windfall for French traders. In grateful recognition of Peter Sarpy's role, the Nebraska legislature named Sarpy County for him in 1857.[93]

Perhaps no single French Creole trader embodied the moral ambiguities and extreme changes that occurred during this period of frontier transition more than Joseph Robidoux. Robidoux, Cabanné's nemesis, was the oldest of six sons of Joseph Sr.—a baker and fur trader in St. Louis. Robidoux gave the Chouteaus fits for decades. He was independent and somewhat unsavory, but he was obviously a capable trader. Despite their intermittent hostilities, Robidoux and Pierre Chouteau Jr. continued to do business together for most of their lives. In truth, it was hard to avoid Pierre Chouteau Jr. as he had a reliable source of capital. Chouteau remained the proper bourgeois merchant in St. Louis. Robidoux was hardly proper. He had many casual relationships with Indian women; Thorne estimates that he had fourteen children by different Indian and white women before 1830. Later reports had the total as high as sixty.[94] One Indian agent identified Robidoux in 1832 as having engaged in sales of Indian girls to traders.[95] Robidoux also liked to gamble and drink, and his trading activities with Jean Baptiste Roy during the 1820s had contributed to the rise of alcoholism in the region. But Robidoux protested in a letter to Pierre Chouteau Jr. in 1833 that he had "a horror" of whiskey and its effects. Essentially blaming Roy for the use of liquor in the trade, Robidoux pleaded his case: "You will tell me that I have not always thought thus—but I assure you that for many years I have known the consequences and how little profit there is in it."[96] Perhaps he had always thought this way. More likely, his changing views were a reflection of the changing conditions of his life.

Despite his period of contractual inactivity from 1829 to 1831, Robidoux had remained active. By 1831 he had resurfaced at Blacksnake Hills, a post between Kawsmouth and Council Bluffs. A post had certainly existed there earlier.[97] Between 1829 and 1834, Robidoux and his French Creole wife, Angelique Vaudry,[98] were selling off their assets in St. Louis—mostly real estate. In 1834 they signed a deed with Pratte, Chouteau and Company, mortgaging their property in St. Louis in exchange for a loan of $16,500. Although much of this money probably went to underwrite different trading ventures on the Missouri and in New Mexico, it seems clear in retrospect that Robidoux was also building up his post at Blacksnake Hills.[99]

In 1836 Missouri's two senators pushed through a bill to attach a large tract of land—more than three thousand square miles bordering the river—to the state of Missouri. This area, known as the Platte Purchase, had been given by treaty to the immigrant Prairie Potawatomis. It was also a homeland for the Ioways and Sac and Foxes. Efforts to remove white squatters failed, and a few land-cession deals later, the Indians were pushed north and west of the area. It was opened to white settlement, and by 1844, the area contained thirty-seven thousand people.[100]

Robidoux was ready. In the summer of 1836, he borrowed $2,019 from another St. Louis merchant, Henry Shaw.[101] In September of that year, William Clark signed the land-cession treaties. Robidoux, according to one source, had tried to get a donation of land to himself by the Indians inserted in the treaty. When that failed, he bought two quarter sections at a public sale.[102] The idea of platting the town and building a future city may not have occurred to him right away, but when several other speculators proposed buying his land to lay out a town in the fall of 1839, Robidoux decided to do it himself. He considered two different town plans—one designed by Simeon Kemper with wide streets and parks, the other designed by Frederick W. Smith, who had grown up in Germany in places with narrow streets. Robidoux apparently liked the Smith plan and was reported to have said, "I want to sell my land in lots, not give it away in streets." He filed his plan in St. Louis in 1843, had it lithographed, and began selling lots.[103] By 1845, the town had several hotels and boarding houses, a newspaper, blacksmith shops, and more than a dozen stores.[104] St. Joseph was incorporated that year with Joseph as the president of the board of trustees. His son, Julius C. Robidoux, began to take over more of his business at that point. Julius had been serving as the first postmaster since 1840 and also kept a ferry on the Missouri at Robidoux Landing.[105] The town became one of the principal jumping-off points during the California Gold Rush, and the railroad arrived in 1859, assuring the future importance of the city. Joseph Robidoux died a prosperous man in 1868. Several of his buildings, known as Robidoux Row, are still standing.[106]

St. Joseph became the new gathering place for the Robidoux family. Joseph and Angelique had seven children, Julius C. being the oldest. Angelique may have moved the family there as early as 1831, since her youngest son was born in Blacksnake Hills in 1831.[107] Angelique's sister, Suzanne Vaudry, was married to Joseph's youngest brother Michel. Suzanne moved their family there as early as 1839, for their third daughter, Octavia, was born there that year. Octavia later entered the convent of the Sacred Heart and served in St. Joseph; Marysville, Kansas; and Chicago. Suzanne died in the St. Joseph home of her nephew Julius C.[108] Another brother, Antoine, also retired to St. Joseph.

Joseph Robidoux, having led a life of considerable debauchery, donated a lot for the building of a Catholic church in 1849. Peter Sarpy did the same in Bellevue, as did Pierre Melicourt Papin in Papinsville, Missouri.[109] In short, much like the Chouteaus in Kansas City, the Robidouxs in St. Joseph had created another link in the urban chain from St. Louis. Capital provided by Pierre Chouteau and guaranteed by property in St. Louis nurtured the growth of the infant city. Transportation links were quickly established. The new place had all the birthmarks of a French Catholic child, yet clearly there would not be an adequate critical mass of Francophones necessary to sustain French culture on this evolving frontier. We should remember, however, that during this early period, Blacksnake Hills was *La Post du Serpent Noir,* and Council Bluffs was written *Ecors au Conseil.* One Anglo-American trader wrote in desperation to Pierre Chouteau in 1833: "Please observe that all communications to me must be in english as I do not read french."[110]

What we have here is not a dramatic narrative like the Lewis and Clark adventure, but rather a series of smaller stories about the founding of critical western places by shrewd French-speaking merchants. Throughout the middle decades of the antebellum period, the Chouteau companies and other French traders were consolidating their positions from Oklahoma to the Dakotas. By the 1840s and 1850s, as frontiers once again began to converge, thousands of ordinary Americans were moving west. Families searching for new homes in Oregon and forty-niners seeking gold and adventure in California were making their ways to jumping-off places for the overland trails that would take them to the West Coast. What they found along the way were ferries across the Missouri and Platte rivers operated by Frenchmen, some former Chouteau employees and others who had been independent traders. One of them, John Richard, built several bridges, including one over the Laramie River.[111] All across the first half of the trail, the emigrants found trading posts—the rest stops of their day—run by French Creoles.[112] These men, mostly from St. Louis, had spent twenty years in the western fur trade by this time and had built posts and ferries throughout the region. As the fur trade began to decline, they turned their attention to the new greenhorns. In the words of one historian, they were "canny entrepreneurs who anticipated the profit potential in catering to the many needs of overland travelers."[113]

This new western edge marked the frontier of the United States during the 1830s and 1840s, but it is best understood as the advance of an economic sphere of influence, a network of social and political connections, and a set of cultural practices emanating from Missouri—specifically, from the French Creole world of St. Louis. But to complete the picture and to gain additional perspective on this French Creole modus operandi, one must describe the activities of the French in one additional western region that occupied their attention during this same period of the 1820s to the 1840s. That is the Southwest, which included the animal-rich southern Rockies and the Spanish province of New Mexico. In that place, forty thousand New Mexicans lived at too great a distance from the political center of their world, Mexico City. From St. Louis and from their newly established base on the western border of Missouri, French merchants eyed the commercial possibilities of yet another frontier.

French merchants in Upper and Lower Louisiana had long dreamed of supplying the New Mexicans with manufactured goods in exchange for Mexican silver dollars. Two Frenchmen reached the provincial capital of Santa Fe in 1739. Then in 1792, Pierre or Pedro Vial, a native of Lyons in France employed by the Spanish governor of New Mexico, had blazed the pathway between St. Louis and New Mexico that would become known as the Santa Fe Trail. But Spanish regulations kept the trade an illegal and adventurous one for decades. As mentioned earlier, a trading venture led by A. P. Chouteau and a Chouteau in-law, Jules de Mun, from 1815 to 1817 was captured by Spanish troops, who confiscated thirty thousand dollars worth of furs and trading goods.[114]

Though Spanish imperial officials had kept French merchants from both Upper and Lower Louisiana at bay throughout the eighteenth century, they had not been able to block the influence of French traders. On the contrary, Spanish policy; the French supply of guns, cloth, and other manufactured goods; and the French demand for furs and horses had stimulated the rise of a powerful intermediary—the Comanches. Dominating the trade throughout the southern Great Plains by the mid-eighteenth century, the Comanches, in the words of historian Pekka Hämäläinen, had forged a "major trade center" on the upper Arkansas basin.[115] The center of this Comanche world filled a critical space, described by historian Ned Blackhawk as "the emerging imperial borderlands between New Spain and French Louisiana."[116] Combining trading and raiding activities, the Comanches accumulated large herds of horses—their primary export—and "ran a major redistribution point, which absorbed and sent out various commodities to all directions." The commodities included horses, mules, Indian slaves, guns, tools, produce, furs, hides, and many other items.[117] After a brief interruption in their trading power during the 1780s—caused by a more resourceful and aggressive Spanish policy, the rising power of the Osages to their east, and the declining importance of their Wichita connection to the southeast—the Comanches rebounded after a negotiated peace with the Spanish in 1786. By the early nineteenth century, the Cheyennes and Arapahoes had been drawn into this Comanche trading world, serving as intermediaries with Indian villages on the Upper Missouri.[118] West of the Comanches in present-day Colorado and Utah, the Utes also had entered the geopolitics of this borderlands complex, first as allies of the Spanish against the Comanches, and later as uneasy partners in a thriving trade in furs and Indian slaves.[119]

In short, an intricate and potentially volatile world of trade and episodic violence existed in the region between Missouri and New Mexico. The forces of change were unleashed in 1821 when Mexican independence and Missouri statehood combined to put the prospects of trade back on the agendas of Missouri merchants. After achieving independence, Mexico welcomed foreign traders. The following year—that same pivotal year of 1822—the rush of traders from Missouri began in earnest. Missouri senator Thomas Hart Benton persuaded Congress to establish a protected road between Santa Fe and St. Louis in 1825, and merchants from Missouri joined their wagons together and traveled in caravans to increase their defensive capacity against Indian raids. Trade would reorient Taos and Santa Fe away from Chihuahua and link them in an economic chain to the United States through St. Louis.[120] At the same time, New Mexicans were now burdened with providing for their own frontier defenses, and their fragile alliances with the Indian groups on their borderlands, often cemented with gift-giving, would disintegrate.[121] The fragility of the alliance system in this borderlands region would be further tested by the intensity with which American traders and trappers competed for furs, skins, and hides, exhausting the supplies to be found in the region's river valleys and "often also depleting Indian subsistence foods."[122]

Historians have long recognized the critical role traders played in advancing the cause of U.S. expansion into the Southwest, but they have paid less attention to the demographics of that advance guard. A recent study of intermarriage in New Mexico between Anglo-Americans and Hispanic New Mexicans from 1821 to 1846 includes a list of approximately 115 such marriages. Sixty-four of the so-called "Anglo" husbands were in fact French, most of them from the St. Louis region.[123]

Though it is hard to come up with exact numbers or percentages, the French became a significant presence in New Mexico during the 1820s. One was Charles Beaubien, a native of Quebec, who along with Ceran St. Vrain of St. Louis probably entered the Mexican province for the first time in 1824. In that year, the Mexican government became somewhat alarmed at the increasing number of foreign traders and trappers. Over the next several years, Americans—many of them French[124]—would spread out over the present-day states of Utah, Colorado, Arizona, and New Mexico in search of furs, and the Mexican government took several measures to control the situation. They established import duties and required foreign merchants to obtain trapping permits and *guías* or mercantile passports from the governor at Santa Fe.[125]

One way around such measures was to become a citizen of Mexico, and the Mexican congress established specific guidelines for this process in 1828. New citizens needed to have been residents for two years and were also required to be

Roman Catholics. This latter condition, of course, presented no obstacle to the French. In 1829 Charles Beaubien and Gervais Nolan became the first foreigners to be naturalized. Later that summer, brothers Antoine and Louis Robidoux followed suit. The following year, they were joined by Abraham Ledoux, Antoine Leroux, Joseph Bissonette, Pierre Laliberté, Jean Baptiste Trudeau, and a host of other Frenchmen.[126]

Did it matter that many of the Americans in New Mexico during this period were French? Given the positions of economic and political authority (or leadership) they were to occupy (as we shall see), I think it did. Moreover, by focusing briefly on the French in this region, we might understand that from their perspective, New Mexico was not so much an exceptional place, but rather one of several zones of frontier development. What I am suggesting is that the American presence in New Mexico was in part an extension of a French Creole approach to the West. Let's take a look at three family operations in New Mexico and see how they fit into the broader context, not simply of American expansion, but specifically of French expansion.

One of the most active families in this region was the Robidoux family. From his various stations on the Missouri River, Joseph channeled capital, much of it secured by mortgages on family property in the St. Louis metropolitan area, to New Mexican trading ventures. All five of his younger brothers spent a considerable amount of time in New Mexico but with varying degrees of success and commitment. The next brother in age, François, appeared on a list of foreigners "without passports" prepared by the New Mexican governor's office in 1826.[127] François appears to have gone back and forth with great regularity, spending much time during the 1820s in New Mexico, returning to the Missouri River trade during the early 1830s, and perhaps returning to New Mexico after the death of his Creole wife around 1833. François also had a common-law relationship with a New Mexican woman, Luisa Romero.[128] He apparently spent the last decade and a half of his life with his older sons, trading at Fort Laramie and at Scott's Bluff. Isadore, the next in age, also went back and forth. He managed business details in Santa Fe and may have been living in Taos after his wife in the St. Louis area, Julie Desjarlais, divorced him around 1837–1838. In a deed with their wives in Missouri, four of the Robidoux brothers (François, Isadore, Antoine, and Louis) relinquished all title to the lands of their father's estate in St. Louis in 1837.[129] The brothers were listed in the deed as "residing at present at Santa Fe in Mexico." As historian Heather Devine has observed, Julie Desjarlais had apparently "had enough of the role of faithful fur-trade wife."[130] Isadore, however, like François ended up back in the area of the North Platte between Scott's Bluff and Fort Laramie.

The next two brothers in age, Antoine and Louis, would commit to more permanent lives in New Mexico. They were there as early as 1823. Outfitted by their older brother Joseph, they established a fur-trading post, Fort Uncompahgre, on the Gunnison River in western Colorado in the mid-1820s. They then extended their intermontane fur-trading empire to the Green River area of northeastern Utah, building Fort Uintah or Fort Robidoux in the 1830s. Here in Ute territory, the Robidouxs outfitted trappers, collected furs, and after the fur resources of the southern Rockies had declined by 1840, provided supplies for overland travelers passing through the region. They also traded with the Utes, exchanging guns, metal goods, beads, and tobacco for horses, furs, and, increasingly, sheepskins.[131]

At the same time, the Robidouxs solidified their position within New Mexico. Antoine married Carmel Benavides, and Louis married Guadalupe García. Both brothers became naturalized citizens of Mexico in 1829. Antoine served as the *alcalde* of Santa Fe in 1830 and built a warehouse, store, and tannery in the town. He also speculated in various mining operations. Louis served on the town council or *ayuntamiento* of Santa Fe in 1834 and was elevated to the position of *alcalde* in 1839. Sharing the chameleonlike qualities of other French Creoles, the brothers spoke perfect Spanish and got in the habit of spelling their names in the Spanish style—Rubidú. Matt Field, a reporter for the *New Orleans Picayune* visiting Santa Fe in 1839, wrote that Louis Robidoux "shares the rule over the people almost equally with the Governor and the priests."[132] Louis constructed the first modern gristmill in Santa Fe in 1839 and also operated a *ferrería* or iron works.

In 1844, the Robidoux trading venture in Ute territory ended abruptly. That year, amidst growing hostilities between the New Mexicans and the Navajos and Utes, a Ute delegation visited the inexperienced federally appointed governor from Mexico, Mariano Martínez, at Santa Fe. A fight broke out, several Utes were killed, and the rest hurried northward, leaving a trail of destruction on their way. A period of violence ensued, and the Utes destroyed the Robidoux's Fort Uintah later that year, killing all of the New Mexican employees at the fort.[133] Louis subsequently sold his various properties in New Mexico and moved his family to California where he became a successful land developer in the San Bernardino area east of Los Angeles and lived comfortably on a flourishing farm. He served on the county board of supervisors there for years and liked to refer to himself as Don Luis. His wife Guadalupe was less pleased. Louis reported that she thought California was too spread out and that she missed the fandangos and churches of New Mexico.[134] Antoine also left New Mexico. After leading several expeditions and wagon trains to California, he retired to the Robidoux family complex in St. Joseph, Missouri.

Let us make three quick points about the Robidoux brothers. First, they were all frontier developers, moving comfortably into a variety of economic activities, with the fur trade often serving as an initial base. Second, they were uncanny in their ability to move between cultural and political contexts. They understood a variety of Indian languages and cultural practices. One might add that having multiple sexual partners clearly presented no problem. And in the Southwest as in Missouri, they operated from an urban base, linking influence in non-Indian centers with alliances in Indian country. Whereas Joseph had created a new urban center, St. Joseph, in western Missouri, brothers Louis and Antoine became prominent citizens rather quickly in a preexisting urban center, Santa Fe. Finally, the Robidouxs saw no problem becoming citizens of Mexico while retaining their status as citizens of the United States. Like their parents, who at different times had to swear loyalty oaths to several different imperial regimes and the United States, they felt that political allegiance was simply situational. Their ultimate loyalty was to family, the *maison* of Robidoux, and all of the brothers except Louis, who seems to have enjoyed his persona as a Spanish don, ultimately returned to the orbit of St. Joseph.

Another Frenchman of critical importance in the history of New Mexico during this period was Ceran St. Vrain. His uncle, Charles Dehault Delassus, had served as the last Spanish lieutenant governor of Upper Louisiana. When his own father died in 1818, St. Vrain went to live with Bernard Pratte Sr.—one of the many Chouteau cousins and partners. His niece later married a grandson of Auguste Chouteau; his brother married a Menard.[135] Connections mattered, but so did competence in the field. St. Vrain, who had already been to New Mexico, joined an 1827 expedition financed by Pratte and the Chouteaus and led by Pratte's oldest son Sylvestre. Sylvestre, who did not inspire confidence, died during the trip, and St. Vrain took over. His command of men and commerce marked him as a good credit risk in the future.

In 1831, he added a partner, Charles Bent, the son of Silas Bent, a Missouri judge and close friend of Auguste Chouteau. The new company of Bent, St. Vrain soon began taking in the lion's share of buffalo robes and furs from the southern Rockies. That same year, St. Vrain built a store and a home in Taos and became a Mexican citizen. The partners were successful from the start and had accumulated enough capital by 1833 to begin construction on what would become the centerpiece of the New Mexican trade. Bent's Fort overlooked the Arkansas River, the international boundary between Mexico and the United States. From this combination frontier hotel, fortified castle, and merchandise mart, the company of Bent, St. Vrain dominated the flow between New Mexico and Missouri of furs and robes; horses, mules, and silver; and food supplies and trade goods.[136] Many factors contributed to the company's success, including the business acumen of the two partners and their relations with a variety of tribal peoples, especially the Cheyennes because of brother William Bent's marriage to Owl Woman. William managed Bent's Fort while Charles Bent and Ceran St. Vrain lived in Taos, supervised the company's operations, and made trips to St. Louis at least once a year to buy goods. Two younger Bent brothers, George and Robert, also became partners in the company, and Marcellin St. Vrain, Ceran's brother, managed the company's outpost on the South Platte River.

In 1840, the company arranged a truce between the Cheyennes and Arapahoes, their primary Indian trading partners, and the Comanches and Kiowas. This was a major coup for the company and doubled their trade. They built a post on the South Canadian River near the Comanches and Kiowas in 1842, and Ceran St. Vrain helped establish a more permanent adobe post there in 1846. By the 1830s, buffalo robes had surpassed beaver pelts as the most marketable item of the fur trade, and the company's returns in 1842 included eleven hundred packs of buffalo robes (ten robes to a pack), almost five hundred packs of beaver (approximately eighty pelts to a pack), and more than three hundred buffalo tongues, a delicacy for the eastern market.[137] Buffalo robes alone were worth five dollars to six dollars apiece in St. Louis. At the height of their power in 1842, the company employed fifty-four traders.[138] As Pekka Hämäläinen has observed, Bent's Fort was "a most serious blow" to the trade of the Western Comanches. With an annual trade of "15,000 hides and large quantities of horses," Bent's Fort "was an American sequel to the once flourishing Western Comanche trade center" and "had put an end to their role as major traders."[139] In short, Bent, St. Vrain and Company had usurped the Comanches' role, although the latter remained important suppliers and a force to be reckoned with. Thereafter, the Comanches increasingly relied on raiding. Indeed, their population began to decrease at this point because of game depletion, drought, and increasing competition for resources from white settlers.[140]

Possibly the most important factor in the success of Bent's Fort was its connection to Pierre Chouteau Jr. and Company back in St. Louis. In 1838, Bent, St. Vrain and Company formalized an agreement to divide the fur trade in the Rockies between the two companies. From that year until the dissolution of Bent, St. Vrain ten years later, the business operated as a partnership within a partnership. The Chouteau company in St. Louis kept the books; marketed the furs and other items collected by Bent, St. Vrain; and provided the trade goods. Above all, Chouteau and Company provided a line of credit for all salaries and supplies. Bent, St. Vrain controlled its own operations, but the two companies also engaged in joint ventures and divided the profits in thirds—two-thirds for

Bent, St. Vrain and one-third for the Chouteau company. The two companies, for example, purchased a farm in Kansas City to use for pasturage for the livestock being transported between St. Louis and New Mexico. Other Santa Fe traders used the property, and it became a lucrative investment.[141] In New Mexico as in the Upper Missouri country, capital was obviously in short supply. The American Fur Company of the 1830s and 1840s (the Chouteaus) controlled the flow of information, goods, and credit throughout this region during the first phase of its commercial development. It was, indeed, the "fist in the wilderness,"[142] and that fist belonged to Pierre Chouteau Jr. and his various relations in the elite world of Creole St. Louis. Their partnership with Bent, St. Vrain—the dominant company in the New Mexican field of operations—strengthened the position of both firms.

Clearly, the economic pathway for Bent, St. Vrain and Company led back to St. Louis. For the Robidouxs, it led there through the intervening center of St. Joseph. But how did these men connect to the social and political worlds that encompassed their business activities? The Bents and St. Vrain, like the Robidouxs and many other St. Louisans—French and Anglo—mostly connected with Hispanic New Mexican women. Charles Bent had a common-law marriage with María Ignacia Jaramillo from a "good Taos family."[143] (Kit Carson married her sister, Josefa.) Ceran St. Vrain lived successively with three partners. He left the last, Luisa Branch, an annuity on the condition that their child be left in his care. Another Bent brother, George, left to his partner, María de la Cruz Padilla, his property in Taos with a similar restriction, that she allow their two children to be raised in St. Louis. William Bent also sent his métis sons (George and Charles) by Cheyenne sisters to an academy in Missouri—in Westport near Kansas City, where the family maintained a farm.[144] The partnerships with Hispanic women seem to have resembled the marriages *à la façon du pays* contracted between so many French traders and Indian women. Although many of these partnerships seem to have resulted in long-term stable relationships, the wills left by the men seem, in the words of Janet Lecompte, to "show a concern for the children, but contempt for the mothers."[145] Put a slightly different way, the objective that shaped family construction was the building of one's house—the ability to accumulate and maintain property and provide an education and orientation that would allow children to prosper in the future—and that future would include a regime change, the westward expansion of the world of St. Louis in which almost all of these traders had been raised. But whereas partnerships with Indian women provided access to the fur trade, those with Hispanic women in New Mexico cemented a trader's position in the polity and society of a place that could also provide another valuable addition to the investment portfolio of frontier entrepreneurs—land. In short, for these businessmen, the New Mexican frontier zone was a site, literally and figuratively, of translation and transition, of cultural and social adaptation and economic action and anticipation.

A third and final example of this model is provided by the activities of Charles Beaubien. Beaubien, a native not of Creole St. Louis, but of Quebec, came to New Mexico in 1824.[146] In 1827 he married a New Mexican woman from a well-to-do Taos family, María Paula Lobato, and their first child, Narciso or Narcise, was born six weeks later. Narcise attended the same school as many other French children, St. Mary's of the Barrens, south of St. Louis in Missouri. (The same school to which François and Berenice Chouteau of Kansas City sent their boys.) Charles—now Carlos—and Maria had six other children, and Beaubien became one of the most successful merchants at Taos, operating a store for Bent, St. Vrain among other activities.[147] He was naturalized in 1829 and became the *alcalde* of the town in 1834. Despite increasing opposition from native-born New Mexicans, Beaubien received several huge land grants from Governor Manuel Armijo in 1841 and 1844. The first grant included a large portion of northeastern New Mexico and was taken out in connection with a government official, Don Guadalupe Miranda. The second grant, the Sangre de Cristo grant, was patented in the name of his son Narcise and an American merchant named Stephen Lee. This grant included a large part of the San Luis Valley in southern Colorado. Anticipating future settlement, Beaubien began improving his land from 1843 to 1846. At that point, however, regime change put his plans on hold.

One might well ask how local New Mexicans reacted to the growing political influence of French and other Americans such as the Robidouxs in Santa Fe and Beaubien, the Bents, and St. Vrain in Taos. Historians have seen this period, from the mid-1820s to the outbreak of the Mexican War in 1846, as a kind of economic transition, preparing the ground for the imperial expansion of the United States. Howard Lamar, in his book *The Far Southwest*, observed that the "real conquest had been made over a thirty-year period by traders and merchant-adventurers."[148] Historian Andrés Reséndez, in a more recent book on the incorporation of Texas and New Mexico from 1800 to 1850, reaffirms Lamar's interpretation, suggesting that "two and a half decades of vigorous commercial and demographic relations" had resulted in the "Americanization of New Mexico."[149]

Several months after the Army of the West's arrival in Santa Fe in August 1846, an American on the scene wrote the following: "I have no doubt that there prevails, among many of the New Mexicans, a very bitter feeling towards our Government and people."[150] On the morning of January 19, 1847, a crowd of angry Taos Indians and New Mexicans stormed the house of Charles Bent, who had been appointed the acting U.S. governor of New Mexico. The rebels murdered Bent and other officials of the new American regime. Narcise Beaubien and his friend Pablo Jaramillo—brother of Bent's partner Ignacia Jaramillo—were stabbed to death while trying to hide in a barn. Attacks on Americans in other parts of the area followed. Eight traders heading east were killed in Mora, two died at Rio Colorado. The mill and distillery belonging to Simeon Turley at Arroyo Hondo were torched by a rebel force numbering in the hundreds. American reaction was swift: Colonel Sterling Price, stationed in Santa Fe, marched five companies of volunteer and regular army soldiers toward Taos. This group of 479 men fought three battles, the last at the Taos Pueblo. When the smoke had cleared, some 282 Mexican and Indian rebels were dead.[151]

Trials soon followed. A court martial began on February 6, 1847, and fifteen rebels were tried and hung for the crime of treason. After these trials, the Circuit Court for the Northern District of New Mexico was convened at Taos, with none other than Charles Beaubien, father of the murdered Narcise, acting as the presiding judge. Ceran St. Vrain served as the court interpreter, and a number of Frenchmen sat on the jury.[152] The lines of allegiance were clearly drawn. It should come as no surprise that the Frenchmen, who had anticipated the transition, were lined up, to a man, on the side of the new regime represented by American officials. What we are more interested in here is their activities after the dust had cleared.

Beaubien began developing his New Mexican land grants with his son-in-law Lucien Bonaparte Maxwell in the late 1840s. Maxwell was born in 1818 on the day his grandfather, Pierre Menard, became the first lieutenant governor of the new state of Illinois.[153] (He also attended school at St. Mary's of the Barrens.) His mother, Marie-Odile Menard, married an Irish storekeeper. Lucien's great-uncle, Rev. James Maxwell, was a native of Dublin who had studied for the priesthood in Spain and been appointed vicar general of Upper Louisiana during the Spanish regime. Reverend Maxwell had received a land grant from Charles Dehault Delassus—the uncle of Ceran St. Vrain. Lucien Maxwell had grown up in a world of imperial land grants and was no stranger to the process. Between 1858 and 1867, Maxwell and his wife, Luz Beaubien, inherited or purchased the entire Beaubien-Miranda grant, accumulating the largest private estate in the United States at the time of its sale (1869)—ultimately patented as having 1.7 million acres. After spending approximately fifty thousand dollars to quiet all the various heirs and claimants, Luz and Lucien—with the help of a variety of politicians and lawyers—had the famous Maxwell Land Grant confirmed by Congress in 1860. They sold the grant to an English syndicate for $1.35 million dollars.[154] Maxwell negotiated his land dealings with the aid of New Mexico's famous Santa Fe Ring. Ultimately, the deal was brokered by Jerome Chaffee, founder of the First

National Bank of Denver.[155] Maxwell himself was a major shareholder in the First National Bank of New Mexico.

The magnitude of this case should not obscure the theme. Frontier development was the family business, and the skill set that family members brought to the task included linguistic and social adaptability and an understanding of how to use imperial, national, and local politicians. Lucien's brother, Pierre Menard Maxwell, and his cousin, Michel Brindamour Menard, were the founders of Galveston, Texas. Michel had begun his career as a trader to the Shawnees in the employ of his uncle Pierre and followed the Shawnees to the country around the Trinity River in Texas in 1833. The following year he bought a huge tract of land that had been granted to Don Juan Nepomuceno Seguin and others by the State of Coahuila and Texas. This claim was confirmed in 1836 by the Congress of the Republic of Texas and later patented by President Sam Houston. It included the east end of Galveston Island. Menard organized the Galveston City Company in 1838.[156]

When Ceran St. Vrain returned to New Mexico from St. Louis in 1848, having dissolved the Bent, St. Vrain Company after the murder of Charles Bent, he followed a predictable post–fur-trade career. He built several sawmills and supplied the lumber used to build the territorial capital. He moved to Mora, New Mexico, in 1855 and erected a flour mill, later operated by his sons Vicente and Felix, that supplied much of the flour used by the military and by the Colorado gold seekers during the Pike's Peak rush of 1859.[157] He developed his Mexican land grant and speculated in land around Denver. He also dabbled in railroad and banking projects and owned a piece of the *Santa Fe Gazette*, becoming the public printer of the territory in 1858.

A pattern is clear by now. Howard Lamar has referred to such activities as "phase capitalism," making a profit "on the actual process of . . . development."[158] Beginning with extractive industries such as furs and mines, these entrepreneurs then turned to investing in land and the infrastructure of future settlement—banks and transportation. The trajectory of the activities of Beaubien, Maxwell, Menard, and St. Vrain in New Mexico and Texas was analogous to that of the Chouteaus and Robidouxs in western Missouri. What these examples suggest is that the U.S. appropriation of New Mexico in its initial phase was in part the expansion of a specific frontier community—the French Creoles of St. Louis. Though certainly not the only ones to recognize the opportunities that existed in New Mexico, the French had the resources and the experience to take advantage of them and were often the first Americans in the field. They set up a series of critical transshipment points or jumping-off places in western Missouri during the 1820s and used these bases to extend their influence in regions farther west and north. It should not surprise us that two of the lieutenants of Battery A in Kearny's Army of the West were Edmond Chouteau and John Gratiot, sons of St. Louis's French first families. In New Mexico, William Clark Kennerly, a French Creole on his mother's side, referred to his unit as the "jeunesse d'orée," the French golden youth.[159] Their parents, in the meantime, pulled the financial and political strings that made others jump. But did it really matter that they were French, or was that just an accident of history?

I would argue that being French mattered for four reasons. First, they were already Catholics. Second, the French, like the Spanish, practiced the civil law, not the common law. Third, it was often easier for the French to learn Spanish. And the fourth and most important reason was that the French Creoles were steeped in the process of middle-grounding, of occupying a cultural and social space of accommodation while pursuing an economic agenda of development and change. This is how we began the chapter, and to close we must return to this idea.

This concept, popularized by historian Richard White in his now famous book about the French and Indian world of the Great Lakes, sought to explain a world of encounters between indigenous people and colonial or European people who needed something from each other, a historical landscape characterized more by negotiation than by violence and dispossession. To this I would add that the French, experienced middle-grounders by the 1820s, had an established reper-toire for achieving their bottom line, which was, quite consistently, commercial exchange and frontier development. That repertoire included intermarriage, cul-tural flexibility, and the identification of political leaders willing to act as allies and brokers. And to this we must add a last and crucial point: the Creole French of St. Louis came from a place that had itself been the site of transition from empire to republic, Indian country to settlement frontier, French rule to Spanish rule to Anglo-American dominance. They were survivors, the sons and daughters of families who had avoided violent confrontation and marginalization and prof-ited from change. They knew what to expect.

Occupying such a middle ground in New Mexico was, in one sense, nothing more than a smart businessman's way of getting the proverbial foot in the door. By the 1840s, many such French traders had New Mexican wives and connections to political power.[160] And just as their fathers had obtained Spanish land grants in Upper and Lower Louisiana, they obtained similar grants in New Mexico. And, indeed, Mexican merchants were using their French connection as well, send-ing their sons to parochial schools in Missouri and sending their silver reserves with armed Mexican guards wearing sombreros to the banking house of L. A. Benoist in St. Louis.[161] Frederick Jackson Turner, after all, began his own dissertation with Montesquieu's remark that "the history of commerce is the history of the intercommunication of peoples."[162]

"Communication" and "accommodation" are words with positive connotations. In the end, however, the appropriation of resources, whether furs or real estate, had negative consequences for those local groups, Indian and Hispanic, whose territories the French had entered. In the New Mexico region, as in the central and Upper Missouri River valley, the trade in alcohol filled the economic niche left by the declining supply and demand for furs.[163] One of the main objectives of the rebel force of New Mexicans and Pueblos in 1847 had been Simeon Turley's distillery at Arroyo Hondo.[164] In New Mexico, the French also encountered a political force that they could not negotiate away—an evolving Mexican nationalism. Civil, military, and religious leaders were actively promoting a "sense of Mexicanness" that would bind peripheral territories such as New Mexico to the rest of the Mexican nation.[165] In Taos, its most vocal spokesman was Father Antonio José Martínez, or Padre Martínez, the opponent whom Beaubien, St. Vrain, and the Bents feared the most. As recent studies have shown, Martínez saw himself as a voice of the people, a liberal, even revolutionary priest in the tradition of Father Hidalgo.[166] French merchants, by way of contrast, preferred to deal with power relations in an old-fashioned—one might say old-regime— way, wielding influence with politicians through personal connections. In New Mexico, men such as St. Vrain and Beaubien fought to extend the territorial regime, avoiding democracy as long as possible in favor of a pliable bureaucratic hierarchy. French elites had pursued a similar course in Missouri and Michigan, using their influence to prolong the period of territorial government. Democracy was a dangerous and unpredictable playing field for merchants who belonged to an ethnic minority in New Mexico and Missouri. Martínez, on the other hand, embraced the idea of statehood with full participation for his parishioners. Ironically, the new American bishop Jean-Baptiste Lamy, appointed in 1850, was a native of France. With support from both Beaubien and St. Vrain, he excommunicated the radical Padre Martínez in 1858. Lamy later commissioned the building of a new cathedral in 1869—in the French Romanesque style with stained glass windows imported from France.[167]

In the final analysis, the middle ground was perhaps never a stable place. At least from a French perspective, cultural accommodations were linked to economic change, and the political medium in which such middle grounds seemed to flourish was usually one of clients and patrons, lobbyists and bureaucrats. Democratic elections and native resistance movements could easily upset carefully crafted private deals. The middle ground occupied by French outsiders and native and Hispanic locals may have served as a space of mediation; nevertheless, it also existed at a midpoint in the maelstrom of change. Though all peoples involved were active agents in creating a new landscape, the profits gathered in the transition flowed into the pockets of French traders and their heirs. The middle ground in New Mexico, as in western Missouri, Kansas, and Nebraska, had an American ending. A second generation of St. Louisans had extended the city's reach along the Missouri from Kansas City to Montana and into Texas and New Mexico.

Given the importance of this group of French frontier brokers and entrepreneurs, it is surprising that their historic role has gone almost unnoticed in our western narratives. Usually, the only American we hear about during this period in New Mexico is Kit Carson. But if one looks a little closer, one can easily find the French connection. The language of this phase of the American West, in fact, contained many French words: one had a *cache* of furs to elude the authorities or the Indians; trappers used the *rendezvous* system in the mountains; a thin strip of buffalo was known as *parfleche*; the fuel used by all who traveled along the unwooded plains of the West was called "bodewash"—from the French *bois de vache*, buffalo chips. This region, like the Missouri Valley, acquired French names. French trappers in Colorado referred to broad, open mountain valleys as *parcs* because they reminded them of French hunting preserves—and so we find places like South Park outside of Denver. And then there are those places named after long forgotten French westerners such as Provo, Utah—named for Etienne Provost, an employee of the Chouteau company. Provost left his name in Utah and retired to St. Louis where he purchased a tavern.[168] But the francophone culture had no staying power in the West. The French themselves comprised a relatively small group, and many of the French who stayed in places in New Mexico remained "translated" by their families and local contexts. Pierre Esperance, for example, a trapper who settled in Las Vegas, New Mexico, and built a sawmill and accumulated property, apparently forgot his native language and answered to Pedro Lesperanza. Even the nephew who came to live with him from Sorel, Quebec, changed his name from Pierre to Pedrito.[169]

But the true legacy of the French in the American West does not reside in a collection of names on our maps. Rather, it is the role they played in western expansion, in negotiating the course of American empire, that we must acknowledge. We celebrate the exploits and explorations of Lewis and Clark. They made their information public and helped establish a national vision of the West and its possibilities; as soon as they returned, French traders and merchants from the Creole world of St. Louis rushed to explore those possibilities. The western ventures of the generation that came of age around the time of Lewis and Clark are somewhat lost to us now; but from 1820 to 1850, the names Chouteau, Sarpy, Robidoux, Menard, and St. Vrain carried great weight throughout this new American domain. One might even claim that the Great West during this period was in many ways more an extension of Creole St. Louis than of Jefferson's Virginia. This story is not one of rugged individualism and heroic discoveries; rather, it is a story of private ventures and family connections. We have seen how families were shaped by economic agendas. It is now time to look at the internal evolution of the Chouteau family companies and observe how families in turn shaped the context of business.

6

Managing the Tribe of Chouteau

For the French of the Creole Corridor, kinship ties were a necessity; and community, secular and religious, a given. As a primarily urban group with commercial aspirations and genteel cultural practices, Creole merchant capitalists valued continuity and reputation more than spontaneity and democracy. In the words of one historian, they established "the regional economic and social foundations upon which subsequent settlers and entrepreneurs would build outposts of capitalist middle-class society."[1] The difficulty of finding an appropriate framework in which to place the activities of these Creole merchants is nowhere more evident than in the historiography of the fur trade. When I first began to study the fur trade, I was somewhat mystified by the application of the label "mountain man" to the likes of Pierre Chouteau Jr. and his son-in-law John F. A. Sanford. The former lived in St. Louis his entire life; the latter spent the last sixteen years of his life living on Fifth Avenue in New York City and the last six years of his life as director of the Illinois Central Railroad. Both men died millionaires.[2] I was further puzzled by the debate over the characteristics of such "mountain men"—were they romantic heroes, social outcasts, or expectant capitalists? Why debate over such a useless category that failed to distinguish between employees, small businessmen, and wealthy shareholders?[3] How could one hope to understand the actions of individuals without examining the social and economic contexts in which they operated?

North of the Canadian border, the history of the fur trade has been written differently. Multivolume histories of the North West Company and the Hudson's Bay Company exist.[4] Such efforts take as their frame of reference the structure of this vast and complex enterprise. More than forty years have passed since Dale Morgan called for "a useful history of the company which bore various names at

Sophie Amanda Benoist (born 1809) embroidered this piece in 1823 to preserve
the memory of her father, François Marie Benoist, who had died in 1819. The sampler,
with its standard representations of grief, demonstrates that the French Creole world of
St. Louis, though distinct, had much in common with other North American centers
of bourgeois life, encompassed from cradle to grave by commerce, urbanity, and
the web of affectionate family relations. Pigment, beads, and embroidery on silk.
Photograph by Cary Horton. Missouri History Museum, St. Louis.

different times but was always dominated by the Chouteaus of St. Louis," and
still we have had no progress on this front.[5] Indeed, Morgan's statement itself
indicates the difficulty historians have had in knowing how to approach the subject—do we study the career of one man such as Pierre Chouteau Jr.?; do we investigate the history of the Western Department of the American Fur Company,
which from 1827 until the dissolution of the company was run by the Chouteaus
and their relations?; or do we instead focus on that confusing collection of enterprises and partnerships that together contained the interests and investments of
this aggressive extended family?[6]

I believe that the third choice is the proper one. Unlike the Hudson's Bay
Company, the various Chouteau family businesses, with the exception of several
later industrial enterprises, were not chartered corporations with limited liability.

Rather, they were a series of multiple partnerships or family firms. In the early nineteenth century they might have been referred to as "sociétés générale" or "common-law companies."[7] Whereas some of the Chouteau companies were simply reorganizations of previous partnerships, others existed simultaneously for the purpose of handling distinct fur-trade activities such as foreign trade or the channeling of investments unrelated to the fur trade. In form, the Creole partnerships of St. Louis resembled the combinations of Scottish merchants who ran the various editions of the North West Company. Unlike the North West Company, the Chouteau firms were predominantly French from top to bottom. Moreover, unlike the North West Company partners, who viewed settlement in the West as a threat to their economic future, the Chouteau entrepreneurs made great capital, literally, out of their positions on the frontier of a nation dedicated to Indian removal. They helped to shape and facilitate the government policy of extracting Indian land cessions in exchange for annuities and migration. As we have seen, they reinvested profits from this Indian business in real estate, railroads, and other ventures. In this respect, the Chouteaus were similar to the Astors; but unlike the Astors, the Chouteaus were westerners themselves. As the business interests of the Chouteaus prospered and expanded, so did the western communities in which they lived and in which they invested. For the Chouteaus, economic prosperity and social prosperity were inextricably linked, and the foundation of both was the family.

This chapter examines the expansion of the Chouteau business enterprises and the family itself over three generations in order to provide a useable chronology of the company or companies Dale Morgan found so difficult to describe and to extract an accurate model of family structure and marriage strategy over time. Three related topics emerge: first, the education or apprenticeship of younger family members and the problem of continuity; second, the problem of profligate sons and the stress engendered by such a close relationship between family and business; and third, the role of women within the family. Finally, I would like to suggest a few ways in which focusing on families on the frontier can alter our traditional view of western expansion.

We start with Madame Chouteau's sons. By 1775, twenty-five-year-old Auguste Chouteau was shipping furs on his own account. He had gained experience in the field and in the *comptoir* as a clerk for his stepfather. He also gained experience in surveying as an assistant for Martin Duralde in 1770. Real estate, banking, and the fur trade would prove to be the sources of his fortune and that of his children and grandchildren. In 1776, Auguste began to acquire an invaluable resource: relatives. That year his sister Pelagie married Sylvestre Labbadie, a native of Béarn who had arrived in St. Louis in 1769 and had established a partnership with Joseph Marie Papin. Papin, whose father had been the royal commissary at Fort Frontenac in Canada, married Marie Louise Chouteau in 1778. Auguste and his brothers-in-law engaged in a number of short-term ventures beginning in 1777.[8] Labbadie, at his death in 1794, was said to be the richest man in St. Louis.[9] Papin inherited a sizable estate from his father in 1792 that was handled by Admyrauld and Sons, an important Protestant firm of the French seaport of La Rochelle.[10]

The next kinsman the Chouteaus acquired also had Huguenot connections. In 1781, Charles Gratiot, a native of Lausanne, Switzerland, married Auguste's youngest sister, Victoire. Although Gratiot was beset by debts for most of his life, he "eventually accumulated a fortune through land speculation."[11] Gratiot brought to the Chouteau family a willingness to travel, a perfect knowledge of English, and connections in London and eventually with John Jacob Astor in New York.

The most important kinsman Auguste Chouteau was to acquire during this period was his father-in-law, Gabriel Cerré. One year younger than Chouteau's mother, Cerré was born in a suburb of Montreal to a family of rather modest farmers. He volunteered for a militia expedition to Ohio in 1751 and settled several years later in Illinois. He moved his family to St. Louis in 1780. From 1768 to 1771, Cerré entered the fur trade in partnership with Jean Orillat, a native of Saintonge near La Rochelle, operating out of Montreal. On his own account, Cerré operated a trading post at New Madrid in Spanish territory and at present-day Nashville in Tennessee. He was respected by American, English, and Spanish officials and became by 1791 the largest slaveholder and one of the wealthiest merchants in Upper Louisiana.[12] When Auguste Chouteau married Marie Thérèse Cerré in 1786, the bride's dowry nearly doubled the couple's net worth.[13] Three years later, after the birth of the couple's first child, Chouteau purchased and renovated Pierre de Laclède's old headquarters, and this new Auguste Chouteau mansion became the centerpiece of old St. Louis.[14]

Chouteau's relationship with his new "papa" signaled the beginning of his independence in several ways. Until his marriage, Chouteau had marketed his furs and bought his goods primarily at New Orleans. During the early 1780s, a partial British blockade of the Gulf of Mexico, an unfortunate run-in with river pirates near Memphis, and increasing competition from traders operating out of Canada convinced Chouteau that he needed to deal directly with merchants in Michilimackinac, Montreal, and London. Following the suggestions of Cerré and Gratiot, Chouteau began doing business with the firms of Grant, Campion and the McGill brothers of Montreal; Bryan and Morrison of Philadelphia; and Schneider and Company and Inglis, Ellice and Company of London. In 1807,

Chouteau was invited to become a partner in the recently formed Michilimackinac Company. He refused. He also resisted the advances of John Jacob Astor.
Indeed, throughout his business career, Chouteau seems to have been intent on
avoiding any long-term commitments outside of his family.[15] In his land ventures,
he was helped immeasurably by his brother-in-law Antoine Soulard, the town
surveyor. Soulard had married Julie Cerré in 1795. At the time of his death in
1829, Auguste Chouteau was the area's largest landlord.[16]

Like his brother, Pierre Chouteau became a large landholder. Much of his
land was acquired through his first wife's grandfather, Joseph Michel dit Tayon.[17]
Unlike his brother, Pierre remained committed to the fur trade and spent much
of his time among his Indian customers.[18] François Saucier, the father of his second wife, was a valuable source of information as the commandant at Portage des
Sioux.[19]

By 1816 both Pierre and Auguste had begun to withdraw from an active role in
the fur trade. The records show that the two brothers had kept separate accounts
since 1804.[20] Although it seems obvious that the brothers had cooperated in pursuing the Osage trade, the exact nature of their business relationship is not clear
from the documents, which are rather limited for the decades before 1800. Cooperation rather than partnership seems to have been the rule. The Chouteaus
and their kin in this first generation seem to have avoided long-term associations
in favor of episodic ventures. For all the attention historians have given to the
fur trade, it seems clear that profits from other investments such as real estate,
lead, and slaves and from basic, less romantic activities such as retailing, milling,
and banking provided an important edge in the accumulation of estates. The fur
trade could be a risky business, dependent on fluctuations in a European market.
Wars in Europe had disrupted those markets during the last decade of the eighteenth century and first decade of the nineteenth.[21]

By the second decade of the nineteenth century, the estates of the first Chouteau generation were being passed on to the second generation. It is important
to note at this point the ways in which such estates were passed from the first
generation to the second. The Chouteaus and their kin followed time-honored
traditions among mercantile families. Estates were divided equally among all
children, sons and daughters. Dowries and the transfer of property to children
before the death of the parents "assured the reinvestment of funds in those . . .
commercial activities upon which the survival of the families depended."[22] The
documents in the Chouteau collections provide many examples of early transfers of property. When Marie Louise Chouteau married Gabriel Paul, a native
of St. Domingue, in 1818, her parents, Auguste and Marie Thérèse Cerré Chouteau gave her a slave and two parcels of land worth more than five thousand

dollars. Her Uncle Pierre added one thousand dollars in cash.[23] That same year Pierre Chouteau and his wife sold more than six thousand acres of land to their son Pierre Jr. and his partner, their son-in-law, Bartholomew Berthold. The elder Pierre also favored the young partners with many contracts for goods required by the Indian Department. Even Madame Chouteau got into the act by giving a number of town lots to her grandchildren before her death in 1814.[24]

As might be expected, early transfers of property and large dowries, and the rejection of primogeniture in favor of a system of partible inheritance, favored the entry of Chouteau children into commercial ventures at an early age and also encouraged the formation of many trial family partnerships, particularly between sons and sons-in-law. This is exactly what happened in the Chouteau family during the first two decades of the nineteenth century. David Herlihy has noted the same phenomenon among the mercantile families of Italy during the middle ages. According to Herlihy, "the great urban consorterie combined solidarity of spirit with policies of pronounced economic individualism." Such policies led to "the early identification and encouragement of their most talented, most energetic youth."[25] Such policies, in short, led to the formation of a new consortium in each generation. Among Chouteau kin such a reshuffling of talent and resources occurred from approximately 1808 to 1823, and occurred again during the 1840s.

The first new family firms to come of age centered around three kinsmen of approximately the same age, Bernard Pratte, Jean Pierre Cabanné, and Gregoire Sarpy. Pratte, born in 1771, came from a prominent family in Ste. Genevieve.[26] Pratte opened stores in St. Louis and Ste. Genevieve, traveled extensively in the East, and was acknowledged to be one of region's most successful merchants by 1815. Sarpy, whose brother was a commission merchant in New Orleans, entered into a partnership with Cabanné in 1800 to trade with the Kansa Indians.[27] Cabanné had arrived in St. Louis in 1798 by way of Charleston and New Orleans. Born in 1773, he married the eldest daughter of Charles Gratiot, Julie, in 1799.[28] What we should notice here is the patterns. Though it is never discussed in the documents, origins must have provided some level of trust and familiarity: Cabanné came from the same province in France as Pratte and Sarpy's father-in-law, Labbadie—Béarn, the birthplace of Pierre de Laclède, the town's founder. Business connections also mattered. Sarpy's brother provided a useful and reliable outlet in New Orleans.

Another new arrival brought a connection to a critical supplier in Italy. Bartholomew Berthold arrived in St. Louis in 1809 and married Pierre Chouteau's only daughter, Pelagie. Berthold, born Bartolomeo Bertolla in 1780 in northern Italy, entered into a partnership with his brother-in-law, Pierre Chouteau Jr., in

May 1813.[29] Berthold and Chouteau were successful from the start, beginning with a retail store, St. Louis's first brick building, and expanding into the fur trade. They were helped by Pierre's father and Berthold's connections on the East Coast and in Italy, where his brother Alessandro manufactured glass beads for the Indian trade in Murano, a suburb of Venice and the traditional site of the Italian glassmaking industry.[30]

By 1819, it was becoming clear within the family circle which kinsmen had the talent for business and which did not. The failures will be discussed later. In 1819, Cabanné and Berthold left for Indian country, where they would stay until the 1830s. Pierre Chouteau Jr. ran the store in St. Louis, and Pratte went east in search of buyers and suppliers.[31] By 1823, the four men had formed a new firm, Bernard Pratte and Company, which lasted until 1833. In December 1826, the firm signed an agreement with Astor's American Fur Company,[32] and this important business association, to be fully understood, must also be viewed from the perspective of family ties.

As early as 1816, Charles Gratiot was busy trying to negotiate a deal between the American Fur Company and the firms headed by his two sons-in-law, Cabanné and Company and Berthold & Chouteau.[33] It was not until after Ramsay Crooks, Astor's right-hand man, married Bernard Pratte's daughter Emilie in 1825 that the Creole family businessmen were persuaded to strike a deal. Unlike Astor, who remained distant and formal, Crooks soon began addressing Chouteau as "cher cousin" and in many ways undertook the responsibilities of kinship that went beyond the *comptoir*. In a revealing note to Astor in 1827, Crooks wrote: "I cannot close this letter without adverting to your remarks on the conduct of Mr. Pratte. . . . I do think you might have recollected he is my father-in-law and not have forced the subject upon me in all of your last three letters."[34] In short, much like the ties of kinship, real and fictive, that implied both social and economic obligations between French traders and Indian communities in Indian country, family connections also shaped business dealings among Americans and Europeans. This may seem obvious, but we tend to assume that the latter, unlike native people, could separate the concerns of the family sphere from the cutthroat sphere of business. No doubt, Crooks had to be concerned for the welfare of his wife's Creole relations or suffer the consequences. Moreover, as the French Creole firm was a *société générale*, a family partnership, and not a limited-liability corporation, partners were financially responsible for the company's obligations. Trust and reliability were huge considerations. Family relations at least had the potential to temper anxieties over issues of mutual welfare. Kinship mattered in St. Louis and New York as much as in Indian country.

In 1834, Pratte, Chouteau and Company bought out Astor's interest in the

Mrs. Ramsay Crooks. The marriage of Marianne Pelagie "Emilie" Pratte (1806–1863), daughter of Bernard Pratte and Emilie Labbadie, to Ramsay Crooks, right-hand man of John Jacob Astor, in 1825 facilitated the business arrangement between the French Creole family firm in St. Louis and the American Fur Company in New York City. The couple raised their family in New York. Emilie's sister Therese also lived in New York, having married a native of France, Louis Peugnet, who with his brother established a fashionable private school in the city. Photo courtesy of the Milwaukee County Historical Society.

Western Department. Crooks reincorporated the American Fur Company of New York and continued to supply goods and market furs for the St. Louis company. In 1842, when Crooks failed, the St. Louis company established its own New York office. The family firm had, in essence, swallowed up Astor's old American Fur Company. The partners were also grooming members of the next generation to assume control of the business.[35] The reshuffling increased in frequency during the years from 1838 to 1842.[36] From 1842 to 1852, the company was managed primarily by Pierre Chouteau Jr., his son Charles, and his son-in-law John F. A. Sanford. Sanford withdrew from the St. Louis–based company in 1852 to manage Chouteau's railroad interests out of the New York office.[37] Charles Chouteau ran the St. Louis firm until its sale in 1865.[38]

The consortium of second-generation cousins lasted for almost two decades and had served the family well as both a vehicle for the accumulation of wealth and a training ground for countless family members. By the 1840s, many third-generation cousins had already served their apprenticeships and were, as we saw in Chapter 5, managing outfits and departments in Kansas, present-day Oklahoma, and the Missouri River valley. Indeed, it seems that the Chouteau interests expanded as fast as the frontier itself. The West provided a vast field of opportunities in both the fur trade and land speculation. No group or family had a better position from which to view the potential investment possibilities.

While Pierre Chouteau Sr.'s sons entered the fur-trade business, Auguste—who had always shown more interest in real estate—must have encouraged several of his sons to pursue the business of land acquisition. Cerré Chouteau, Auguste's second son, returned to St. Louis from Indian country after his father's death in 1829 to manage his milling operation.[39] Cerré's younger brother Henri, who was clearly Auguste's successor, served as the county clerk and recorder for many years.[40] In 1842, he took his son-in-law, Neree Vallé, on as a partner. These partners accumulated land at sheriffs' sales all over Illinois and Missouri and entered the iron business. After Henri's death, Vallé began purchasing mining property in Colorado.[41] In the 1880s, J. Gilman Chouteau, Henri's son, was advising his nephew Azby Chouteau on the acquisition of lands in Dakota Territory. Azby, who owned a substantial amount of railroad bonds, was careful to purchase land along the planned route. He also operated a ranch near Deadwood in Dakota Territory.[42] The West, the Chouteau family, and the wealth of the latter seemed to be limitless.

How can we account for the astounding success of this family? Part of the answer surely lies with their devotion to reinvestment in their children. The correspondence of four generations of Chouteau kin includes hundreds of letters written between parents and children, uncles and nieces, aunts and nephews. The thematic continuity of these letters is striking, and the sentiments are touching. In 1800, Auguste Chouteau wrote the following to his brother-in-law, Judge Pierre-Louis Panet of Montreal, to whom he was about to entrust his oldest son:

> The education of my children is the most important thing for a father, since it concerns their happiness or unhappiness, and, finding myself living in a country where it is impossible to get a good one for mine, I finally decided to separate myself from mine, and its particular purpose was stronger than paternal love.[43]

Forty-seven years later, Henri Chouteau wrote the following to his eleven-year-old son Gilman:

> I hope my dear son that you give satisfaction to your dear and kind mother, and that you are making a good deal of progress in your education . . . the time will

come when it shall be your turn, to go into the world and work as I have been doing for many years—and without a good education, and a good moral character above all, you will perhaps find this a hard world to deal with.[44]

Children were considered the prime assets of the family. In a mercantile world, honor, a reputation for sound judgment, and compulsive attention to detail were the keys to maintaining credit, accumulating customers, and making wise investments. Over and over again, Chouteau parents stressed these virtues. They also spared no expense for formal education, sending their children to a variety of schools such as West Point, Georgetown, Bardstown, and Yale. Relatives were expected to serve as surrogate parents when required. Ramsay Crooks oversaw the progress of a number of Chouteau relatives attending the Peugnet Academy (run by in-laws of the Prattes) in New York City. In 1836 Crooks wrote the following progress report to Pierre Chouteau Jr.:

> Once a fortnight he [Charles], Berthold, and Cabanné pass the day with us, and I see them all occasionally at other times. These frequent opportunities are always made available to urge upon their attention the value of education.

Crooks then proceeds to comment quite gently:

> Charles' progress is certainly *fair* in all he undertakes, if it be not brilliant; and in music he will probably be quite successful—his deportment is I believe free from reproach, and his manners are genteel—I think you ought to be satisfied with your son, but perhaps you have the common failing of most parents—that of expecting more than is reasonable—We all desire to see our children No 1—though we all know that is impossible.[45]

Despite their efforts, not all the Chouteau children were successful. The most notable disappointment was Auguste's oldest son, Auguste Aristide. After the child had been expelled from all the schools in Montreal, his Uncle Panet pleaded with the elder Auguste to take his son back. The child grew into an incompetent adult, incapable of handling the details of fur-trade operations and managing financial accounts. He was constantly in debt to his father and wrote a number of rather sad letters begging for his parents' forgiveness.[46] Another notable failure was Bernard Pratte's eldest son, Sylvestre. Sylvestre died at the tender age of twenty-eight but not before piling up large debts that his father felt obligated to honor. Cabanné wrote to Pierre Chouteau Jr. in 1825 that the elder Pratte was "much to be pitied, for having children who, by their incapability, show themselves so little worthy of him."[47]

It is clear from such comments that kin networks that were tied to business enterprises were a two-way street. Trust, unity of purpose, shared parental responsibility, the pooling of capital, and the expansion of opportunity were the advantages. On the other hand, poor business judgment could affect both one's immediate family and a wider circle of relations. Criticism of a partner's son could prove irritating if not offered diplomatically. *This* Cabanné found out. Above all, if a partner did not live up to expectations, which were high in a dynamic family like the Chouteaus, the sense of personal failure could be devastating. Cabanné, in need of a loan in 1825, wrote Pierre Chouteau Jr. that he felt like "a burden on the shoulders of those who have generously placed me amongst them." Later in the year he wrote "I owe you my new existence."[48] Jules de Mun, in the midst of his unlucky venture with A. P. Chouteau in 1816, wrote to his wife that he found himself "in the role of a parasite for being related to the Chouteau family." The strain was too much for him; he took his family to Cuba in 1819. When they returned to St. Louis in 1831, De Mun accepted a government job and stayed clear of business.[49] A. P. Chouteau fared even worse; his younger brother Pierre sued him in 1838 to collect a debt of sixty-six thousand dollars (see Chapter 5).[50]

An additional burden for some members of the Chouteau clan was the loneliness that came with being far away from home so much of the time. Partners who traveled to New York City or Washington City (D.C.) often took their wives with them and stayed with relations. Their letters home describe art museums and operas, and receipts for cigars and sherry remain as evidence of their good times.[51] Partners in Indian country, as we have seen, either felt more isolated or turned to alternate family situations with native or métis women. Many of the men, however, seemed to have felt as did Jules de Mun when he wrote the following words to his wife, Isabelle Gratiot:

> I have now been camping here for fourteen days, sweetheart, and during this time my greatest pleasure has been to think of you; not a moment of the day passes without your being present in my mind. I love to imagine my pretty little Julie on your knees, playing with your breast and looking at you with her lovely little smile; . . . go often to Madame Cabanné's; I cannot tell you how much I love her, her and her whole family. . . . Go often to kind Emilie's too. I am, however, sorry for the contrast between our beautiful children and hers, but tell her to be consoled—perhaps she will do better next time.[52]

The importance of family life and children to the Chouteau businessmen cannot be overemphasized. Beyond practical considerations, a happy home was the true measure of a successful life.[53] Even crusty Pierre Chouteau Jr. marveled that New Yorkers seemed "to prefer money above all else."[54] Choosing a spouse, therefore, was doubly important for upon that choice depended both one's future business partners and one's potential bliss. Thomas Sarpy was said to have made an undesirable marriage while drunk. The family firm sent him to a distant post, and he died at the age of twenty-two.[55] Theodore Papin, in a letter to his brother, lamented the fate of his sister Emilie who had married a drunkard, noting that "mama predicted she would be unhappy."[56]

For the Chouteaus, women occupied a central place in a world that was modeled around the idea and the reality of family. Sociologist Elizabeth Bott has suggested that the density of the networks the spouses maintain outside the home is directly linked to the degree to which gender roles are separated; the greater the density, the more distinct the roles.[57] This certainly seems to have been true for the Chouteaus. In St. Louis, Julie Cabanné's home was known as the gathering place for women, children, grandparents, and husbands who happened to be in town.[58] The great majority of Chouteau merchants also owned farms outside of town. Here the women were charged with overseeing all operations and providing a comfortable refuge from summer heat waves and periodic epidemics.[59] Wives were also responsible for the education and socialization of children, who were expected to participate in the cosmopolitan world of international commerce. This was especially important in a town like St. Louis during the early 1800s that still lacked suitable secondary institutions.[60] It was even more important farther west where Berenice Menard Chouteau, wife of Gesseau, was described as the "mother of Kansas City."[61]

Here, then, is a very different picture of the frontier and the so-called mountain men. Here is a world of children and parents, cousins and aunts and uncles. To understand the success of the Chouteaus, it is probably more important to consider the way in which they gathered relatives than the way in which they gathered furs. Madame Chouteau began her St. Louis journey as an abandoned mother with an insolvent companion. At the time of her death, she had more than one hundred living descendants and was financially independent. For Madame and her children, success on the frontier and in pursuing the furs and other assets meant establishing connections, connections with merchants in Europe and the cities of the East Coast and connections with Indian groups. And for Creoles and Indian peoples alike, connections were best secured by marriage for that institution was sure to produce common interests. It is also important to note that the continued success of a family business, particularly a mercantile business, depended on the identification of young talent, as often as not, in-laws. The constant reshuffling that characterized the Chouteau kin companies reflected this need. Idle sons and idle capital were the devil's work. The rather traditional practices of the Chouteaus only began to change during the 1850s when they became involved with mining and manufacturing corporations.

Silhouette of Mrs. Jean Pierre Cabanné (Julie Gratiot) and grandchildren, Mary Virginia Kingsbury (Countess Armand Robert de Giverville), Adèle Louise Kingsbury (Mrs. Alfred Morgan Waterman), and Jules Cabanné Kingsbury. Julie Cabanné's home was said to be a gathering place for members of the extended family. In her youth, she was described as an attractive woman with dark hair and a "forehead built to hold a mind." Creole women were expected to oversee the education and socialization of children who would be participating in a world of international commerce and occupying positions of cultural and social authority in the increasingly complex and cosmopolitan city of St. Louis. Missouri History Museum, St. Louis.

We are still accustomed to thinking of the frontier as a temporary place without families, without children. Lumbermen, miners, and mountain men are the pioneers. Of course, we ignore Indian families. With the Chouteaus, the children literally came first, and family expansion led business expansion. And life on this frontier was not only domestic, it was downright bourgeois. When Ramsay Crooks took his new bride, Emilie Pratte, to New York City in 1825, he noted that she was "as much reconciled to her new residence as I can expect; for although we husbands think we ought to be every thing to our fair partners, still it takes some time to recover from the feelings incident to a separation from such affectionate connexions as you all are." Hoping, perhaps, to recapture the sociability of the western family circle they had left behind, Crooks described the new home they were soon to move into as "our wigwam."[62]

As fur traders, the Chouteaus became adept at calculating present costs and future returns. As bourgeois parents, the goal of all their calculations was the reputation and prosperity of their children. Their philosophy was admirably summed up by Azby Chouteau, a great-grandson of Auguste, in 1896: "I have kept my family in harmony and raised two scions to continue the propagation of the fast diminishing tribe of Chouteau — They come high, but they may become valuable in time to come."[63]

But we began this chapter with the dilemma of fur-trade historiography: how do we describe the company structure of the fur trade in the American West? The Chouteau enterprise, the dominant company in the western fur trade at its height during the 1840s, was a highly articulated business with a host of trading posts, outfits, and departments linked via steamboats and paperwork to the home office in St. Louis. It seems to provide evidence of an efficient managerial regime, a perfect example of nineteenth-century bureaucratization and rationalization as described by Max Weber and others. Surely, no one can look at the voluminous and meticulous records of this enterprise and come away thinking that the fur trade was nothing more than a couple of guys named Pierre slapping each other on the back in the wilderness.

Yet this highly structured enterprise was, throughout its history, a family business, run with a sense of familial obligation as the many letters addressed to *cher papa* and *cher cousin* attest. Departments and outfits, family and bureaucracy: where had I seen this all before? And then it hit me: the Boucicaut family of Paris and the Bon Marché. As Michael B. Miller has written in his history of that first great department store, "the managerial and family ethos are not mutually exclusive. . . . Household relationships were redesigned to build an organizational work force of managers and clerks."[64] The labor force was handled with the strong but presumably caring hand of paternalism, meant to ensure loyalty. The looming presence of the Boucicauts in the Bon Marché, the *grande famille*, also assured customers that this enormous and imposing new store was more than a machine gobbling up small shops and *ateliers*; rather, it offered a sense of family values, quite in line with their stock of household commodities.

Does such a model fit the Chouteau case? The head of each trading post, responsible for inventory and sales, was, after all, called the "bourgeois." The bourgeois was, indeed, the head of a branch of what we might visualize as a vast, decentralized department store. Though native people acted as both producers and consumers, and the bottom line of this consumer culture too often was dispossession and the dire effect of alcohol, the trade as it was organized from its St. Louis home office resembled the operation of a huge store, buying goods at wholesale prices and retailing them in the West. Though they might liken themselves to a North American tribe, the extended Chouteau family was, in the end, more like a Parisian *grande famille*. Their enterprise was informed by both traditional family relationships and nineteenth-century models of bureaucratic efficiency.

7

"AVEC BIEN DU REGRET": THE AMERICANIZATION OF CREOLE ST. LOUIS AND FRENCH DETROIT

If the francophone merchants of this bourgeois frontier played a unique and significant role in the history of American expansion, it is ironic that the cultural landscape of the region they helped establish had little room for their own distinctive culture. Overwhelmed demographically, the French by the 1840s found themselves on a small island in a sea of Anglo-American Protestants, their language and cultural practices less audible and visible in the very cities they had founded.[1] The Catholic institutions they established and supported quickly became dominated by German and Irish immigrants (although this was less true in Louisiana, where francophone culture maintained a public face[2]). In Detroit and St. Louis, francophone mercantile families became centered in the genteel enclaves of Hamtramck, Grosse Pointe, and Frenchtown (Soulard). In their family parlors and within their own circles, they kept on speaking French. Yet the French continued to exercise both political and economic power in the cities of their creation throughout the first half of the nineteenth century and beyond, and we would expect francophone culture to maintain a certain level of prestige in the urban life of these places. How then do we gauge the persistence of French or Creole culture? To what extent and how long did St. Louis and Detroit remain French towns? How significant was the French birth and infancy of these cities?

The Catholic religion, for example, certainly grew in strength throughout the nineteenth century in terms of parishioners and social influence, especially in education. But Irish and German Catholics had as much, if not more, to do with this phenomenon as the French. Yet the French interest was certainly highly visible in the growth and status of Catholicism in St. Louis and Detroit. One historian, writing in 1938, declared that Creole culture in St. Louis had been

Detroit as Seen from the Canadian Shore in 1821 (1821), by Alexander Macomb (1782–
1841). Macomb's father was a prosperous merchant, and his mother, Mary Catherine
Navarre, came from an old and well-placed French Detroit family. Macomb, awarded
a Congressional Gold Medal for his successful defense of Plattsburgh, New York,
during the War of 1812, later served as the commanding general of the U.S. Army from
1828 to 1841. Pen and ink with watercolor on paper. Gift of Ernest Newman Stanton,
Mrs. Kenneth Taylor White, and the Burton Historical Collection in memory of
Mrs. Robert Lee Stanton. Photograph © 1998 The Detroit Institute of Arts.

obliterated by 1821. He based his conclusions on the disappearance of Creole
architecture and certain household implements.[3] But no living culture can be
expected to remain static.[4]

We have seen that the initial phase of French and Anglo-American convergence was full of tension over political ideals and practices and the power to
confirm property or private land claims, that is, grants gathered before the establishment of U.S. sovereignty. There were, in addition, sources of cultural friction,
exacerbated—in French eyes—by the cultural imperialism of incoming Anglos.
Let us look first, however, at the exercise of economic and political power within
these cities.

Like the Chouteaus of St. Louis, the Campaus of Detroit—Joseph and
brothers Louis and Barnabas—began their business careers as fur traders. Louis
and Barnabas spent more time in Indian country while Joseph stayed in Detroit,
ran the store, and outfitted other traders. Also like the Chouteaus, the Campau

family at first marketed their furs through Canada but gradually switched to commission houses in New York City. The Campaus, though never as famous as their St. Louis counterparts, followed a similar path to great wealth. Joseph, who apparently spoke a number of Indian languages and welcomed natives passing through Detroit, owned and operated posts on the Huron River at Lake Erie, on the Clinton River at Lake St. Clair, and in Saginaw. Louis and later his son, Louis Jr., had posts and agents at Muskegon, Manistee, Kalamazoo, Lowell, Hastings, Eaton Rapids, and the mouth of the Grand River. As the fur trade became a business of treaty goods and land cessions, the Campaus—again like the Chouteaus—profited mightily. The key, again, was the federal government's need to dispossess the Indians. With established social and economic ties to Indian communities, both families acted as the necessary brokers. Barnabas Campau served as a witness to the treaty with the Ojibwes at Saginaw in 1819. Another treaty, signed in 1836, guaranteed a payment in silver to the Campaus to cover Indian debts. The exact profits are difficult to calculate, but Louis was said to have earned more than one hundred thousand dollars through such means.[5]

Fur-trade profits were often invested in developing urban real estate, and most of these French merchants already held potentially valuable properties. Private claims dating from the French regime were zealously defended and pursued by this mercantile elite. Joseph Campau, for example, successfully defended three separate claims in Grosse Pointe amounting to more than two hundred acres.[6] Such lands on the outskirts and in the central districts of growing cities such as Detroit were subdivided and then sold or rented. Whatever personal misgivings the French may have had about the influx of Anglo-Americans, they recognized that settlement would increase the value of their properties.

Politics and land were always connected. In St. Louis, the Chouteau family monopolized the position of city surveyor. Henri Chouteau, son of Auguste, became the clerk of the county court and recorder of St. Louis County. In Detroit, John R. Williams, nephew of Joseph Campau, served on an all-important committee to investigate private land claims, that continuing fountain of wealth for older French families. His cousin Daniel J. Campau (Joseph's son) received an appointment from President Franklin Pierce as register of the U.S. Land Office in Detroit.

Like the Chouteaus, the Campaus invested fur-trade profits in other ventures. Both families had an interest in local distilleries—alcohol being an all-too-valuable commodity in frontier places and in the Indian trade. Joseph Campau also invested in railroads, becoming a stockholder in what became the Michigan Central Railroad. Real estate, however, became the primary source of Campau's wealth. His holdings included the Normandie Hotel, Fraternity Hall, the Newberry and Campau buildings on Griswold Street, more than one thousand acres in Grosse Pointe Township, and five hundred acres in Springwells Township. In addition, he possessed lands in Macomb, St. Clair, Saginaw, Monroe, and several other Michigan counties.

The Campaus, the Morans, and other French families in Detroit with substantial landholdings tended to be cautious in their speculative ventures, preferring a steady return on individual properties to large subdivisions and wildcat ventures. This served them well during the 1830s when newcomers to Detroit such as C. C. Trowbridge served as front men for eastern capitalists such as Arthur Bronson of New York and overextended themselves as the Panic of 1837 swept over the West.[7] With a guaranteed cash flow from Indian treaties signed in 1836 (the use of federal money to cover Indian debts to traders), the Campaus were not only able to withstand the panic, they were able to increase their landholdings when others were forced to sell cheap.

Without going into the complexities of federal policies, local politics, land, and banking, I would observe that the Campaus, again like the Chouteaus and other French fur traders with means, had become private bankers to the community during the first decades of the nineteenth century. In St. Louis, Auguste Chouteau in 1816 closed most of his private accounts and helped secure a charter for the Bank of Missouri, serving as the bank's president until 1821.[8] His son Henri would pursue the family's banking interests.[9] In Detroit, Joseph Campau and his nephew John R. Williams were among the organizers and first shareholders of the Bank of Michigan in 1818, with Williams serving as the first president until 1824. In that year, he resigned because the Dwight family of Springfield, Massachusetts, had acquired two-thirds of the shares. Williams's position as a leader in the French community had by then evolved into his becoming an advocate of local control against the power of eastern outsiders. He led the fight to charter a rival bank, the Farmers' and Mechanics' Bank, in 1829, and a struggle soon developed over the issue of federal land sales deposits. In 1835, a group of Democrats led by Williams incorporated another institution, the Michigan State Bank, which a Democratic state administration used for the deposit of state funds.

Through their banking and real estate activities in their native cities, families such as the Campaus and Chouteaus not only gained additional wealth, they assured themselves of maintaining a place of prominence. Joseph Campau's death in 1863 at the age of ninety-five made the front page of the *Detroit Free Press*—the paper he had founded. The newspaper noted that "the entire city turned out for his funeral," which was conducted by the Masons. At the time of his death, Campau's estate was valued at three million dollars, making him the richest man in Michigan. In 1894, his heirs estimated his real estate empire to be worth some

Portraits of Joseph Campau and Adelaide Dequindre Campau attributed to Alvah Bradish (1806–1901). Campau (1769–1863) began his career in the fur trade, and like the various Chouteaus of St. Louis, he branched out into a variety of business ventures, including banking, railroads, and real estate. The value of his various landholdings was estimated at ten million dollars in 1894. Various chroniclers described him as being tall (six feet), spare, and typically dressed in a black broadcloth coat and vest with a white cravat. An ardent freemason, he held strong views about politics and religion, which—we may guess from her portrait—might have perturbed his wife, Adelaide. Photographs © 1988 and 1956 The Detroit Institute of Arts. Courtesy of The Detroit Historical Museum.

ten million dollars. As one French descendant wrote, referring to his ancestor Judge Charles Moran, "The steadily-growing city thus poured an ever-increasing tribute into his hands."[10]

The Chouteaus followed the same path in the city they had founded. In 1816, Auguste and his old nemesis, Judge Lucas (see Chapter 3), opened the first addition to St. Louis on the hill immediately west of the original village.[11] This addition "extended and doubled the width of the old east-west streets of the village." Chouteau and Lucas "continued the existing street pattern but donated a full block of their addition to the county for the erection of a new courthouse."[12] For the rest of the century, members of the French elite such as Julia Soulard, Bernard Pratte Jr., and Louis Labeaume—armed with a new "republican outlook" and an old ability to leverage "wealth and power"—would develop and profit from various parcels in the metropolitan area.[13] As late as 1874, when the city purchased a 1,375-acre tract west of Kingshighway that would become Forest Park, descendants of the first families, including Charles P. Chouteau (son of Pierre Jr.), would receive close to eight hundred thousand dollars for land once included in pre-American grants.[14]

In short, the French merchant elite in both places capitalized on both national expansion and urban expansion. The two stories were linked. The fur trade and the business of Indian removal produced a cash flow that served as investment capital for the development of St. Louis, Detroit, and, in the case of John Jacob Astor, New York City. Seen from the perspective of these French fur-trading families, what began as an urban venture remained an urban venture. In this sense, the Americanization of Creole St. Louis and French Detroit meant nothing more than the merging of economic interests. Successful merchants, they avoided the marginalization that was the fate of other non-Anglo communities incorporated in the course of American expansion.

Leaders of the French community in Detroit also remained politically active as the city grew. John R. Williams (son of Cecile Campau and Thomas Williams of Albany) became Detroit's first elected mayor in 1824. John R., as he was known, became an ardent spokesman for the French community, and although he spoke and wrote in English and French, he thought of himself as French. Urging his French *concitoyens* to unite, he predicted that the result would be "glorieux pour notre patrie Canadienne."[15] John R. clearly was not ambivalent about the side to which he belonged. On a business trip in Pittsburgh for his uncle Joseph Campau in 1800, he wrote home describing his "dissatisfaction to be in a foreign country of which neither the location nor the inhabitants please me."[16] (Detroit, of course, was a part of the United States at this time.)

Williams won four straight elections as mayor during the 1840s, and his cousin, Daniel J. Campau, was elected city treasurer twice during that decade. Both men, along with Judge Charles Moran, became leaders within Michigan's Democratic Party and were among the founders of Detroit's public schools, accomplished only after a compromise was reached on the reading of the Bible.[17] Ardent Jacksonian Democrats, Williams and Joseph Campau founded the *Detroit Free Press* in 1831 to serve as the voice of the party.[18]

In the contest for the political soul of the emerging state, key members of the city's elite French families supported the electoral rights of Catholic immigrants and resisted the attempts of Whigs and evangelicals to impose temperance laws. It is rather telling that in 1830, a young Whig disciple of Detroit's William Woodbridge, Munius Kenney, wrote to his patron from Washington, D.C., where he had gone to seek a government appointment. In this letter, Kenney commented

Portrait of John R. Williams (1782–1854). Born into an old and influential
French Detroit family, Williams was a Francophone in his youth and identified with
that community. John R., as he was known, clerked for his uncle, Joseph Campau,
and later became his business partner. John R. became active in politics, writing the
city's charter and serving as Detroit's first mayor during 1824–1825. He was elected
again in 1830 and served additional terms from 1844 to 1847. He also served as
chairman of the Michigan constitutional convention in 1835. Courtesy of
The Detroit Historical Museum.

about Joseph Campau's sharp business practices. Complaining about the amount
he owed Campau for an "old poney" and a rental property he described as a
"wreck, almost a stable," Kenney wrote: "I wish Shakspear had known Campau,
and he would not have fallen so far short of the insatiable sordidness of real life
as he has in his delineation of Shylock."[19] Kenney later became a Whig member
of the Michigan legislature and perhaps the leading advocate of Sabbatarian and
temperance legislation. Although Campau the staunch Democrat was undoubtedly an efficient landlord, we may also assume that political and personal differences colored Kenney's opinion. When Woodbridge ran for governor in 1839,
Whig leaders tried to attract French voters with a circular addressed "aux citoyens
français, et ancien habitans du Michigan." Despite the appeal and Woodbridge's
ability to speak French, the party's leaders later complained that there was "not
one man" on the ticket "calculated to call out any portion of the French population to our support."[20]

The French elite of St. Louis, predictably, exercised a fair amount of control in local politics in the town's first full American decade. Auguste Chouteau served as chairman of the town's first board of trustees in 1810. His half-brother Pierre Sr. held that position in 1820 and 1821. The French families and their friends dominated the board—they were, after all, the most important property owners in the town. Opposed to a new municipal charter that would expand suffrage and empower a new mayor and board of aldermen to use property assessments for urban improvements, the French lost that vote and then tried to capture the mayoralty. Two Frenchmen ran in 1822, Auguste Chouteau and Marie Philippe Leduc. They lost to a newcomer from Kentucky, William Carr Lane. Lane served six one-year terms and did much to improve the city, but he did so over the increasing opposition of the French elite, now allied with newly arrived Americans with similar class interests. Their circle became known as "the St. Louis Clique" or "the Little Junto."

The French in St. Louis certainly had learned the art of political influence under the imperial rule of the Spanish; they were nothing if not adaptable. Their candidate for Missouri's first governor, William Clark, lost in part because of his association with the privileged French circle. (The winning candidate, Alexander McNair, was married to a French Creole woman.) On the other hand, their candidate for senator, Thomas Hart Benton, was successful, and the French were perfectly content to see him appeal to the state's American electorate as a Jacksonian Democrat as long as Benton looked to their interests in Washington. The French, particularly the extended Chouteau family, in general seemed more interested in national political influence to secure the passage of profitable Indian treaties.[21] Though they never completely abandoned a more visible political role on the local scene—Bernard Pratte served two terms as mayor in 1844–1845 and Charles P. Chouteau ran unsuccessfully in 1853—the St. Louis French tended, unlike their counterparts in Detroit, to be Whigs and never made common cause with newly arrived Catholic immigrants.[22] They did occupy positions of civic leadership and seem to have been more successful than the French in Detroit in maintaining a first-family Creole presence within the city's social aristocracy. But to understand that phenomenon, we must turn to the contest between French and Anglo cultural practices.

The maintenance of economic and, to a lesser degree, political authority did not necessarily imply an equivalent ability to maintain various aspects of francophone culture. The establishment of American rule produced, from the beginning, serious cultural friction that historians of the past have tended to minimize. For Americans arriving in towns on this French-speaking western edge, language was, of course, the first obstacle. Wherever French merchants had established commercial centers in this region, the traveler would also find a French-speaking black population, not to mention a diverse group of Indian languages. John Darby, a future mayor of St. Louis, arrived in that city as a small child in 1818. In later years, he recalled his first impressions: "The first thing to be done . . . was to cross the great river. . . . The ferry consisted of a small keel-boat, which was managed entirely by Frenchmen. Their strange habilments, manner, and jabbering in the French language, had a new and striking effect upon myself and the other children, coming as we did from the plantation in the Southern country. . . . The prevailing language of the white persons on the streets was French; the Negroes of the town all spoke French."[23] John Latrobe, a young lawyer from Philadelphia and son of architect Benjamin Latrobe, captured the mood perfectly, describing New Orleans in 1834: "Last evening after tea I walked down the levee and found myself in one continued stream of people of all nations and colours. French was the language that principally met my ear. Sometimes Spanish and rarely English. Perhaps the French Men talked the loudest and the most while the americans stalked, uncommunicatively along, and thus gave an apparent preponderance to the people of their country on the Levee."[24]

Religious practices were another source of tension. It was bad enough that the French were Catholics, but they also had a different conception of the Sabbath. In Detroit, as in New Orleans and St. Louis, newly arrived Protestants were scandalized by the Creole Sabbath, which included the French habit of enjoying themselves—racing, gambling, dancing, even drinking—after church services. As Latrobe wrote from New Orleans in 1834: "on Sunday . . . brandy may be drunk, or bonbons sold, or bargains made, or soldiers drilled."[25]

In Detroit, the first board of trustees with an overwhelming Anglo majority in 1803 passed an ordinance to reduce "drunkenness, idleness, and profanity on the Sabbath day."[26] Creole members of the board of trustees of St. Louis defeated similar attempts by Clement Penrose in 1811.[27] As Baptist missionary John Mason Peck noted in 1818, "the boast was often made that the Sabbath never had crossed, and never should cross the Mississippi."[28] As late as 1857, a visitor from Pennsylvania noted his surprise on awakening in St. Louis on his first Sunday morning and discovering that it was "not a Puritan town." Thomas Rodgers went on to say that, "for me, this was quite a new feature, for in the old fashioned town of Allegheny, Pennsylvania, where I was raised, such a thing as a Sunday paper was not known. . . . Then I discovered that the saloons were all open on Sunday, and some theatres."[29]

And there were tensions over manners. While still in French Detroit, Jeffersonian bureaucrat Frederick Bates had found himself attracted to the francophone daughters of Commodore Grant and his wife, Thérèse Barthe. Bates reported to his sister that these girls had some fun at his expense during a Christmas Mass.

(They apparently kept telling him that one after another pew was soon to be occupied.) Another time at church services, Bates and an American friend carelessly spat upon the kneeling bench, and a Mlle. Navarre discovered to her horror that her dress was stained by tobacco juice. It is no wonder that Bates, in his words, was making "little progress with the french girls" of Detroit, who looked upon Americans as "a rough unpolished, brutal set of people." Bates remained unreconstructed. In a letter to his brother Richard, written in 1807 during his first stint as acting governor of Missouri, then Louisiana Territory, Bates complained of the "theatrical licence which [French Ladies] assume in their gestures." Bates wrote, "in the opinion of many they are more charming on this account, yet I must deplore the singularity of my taste when I confess, that to me, they would be more interesting with a greater show of modesty and correctness of manners."[30]

The politics of culture never made much headway in St. Louis. In their memorial to Congress of 1804, the St. Louis petitioners had requested bilingual courts and schools. These requests were summarily ignored. The Creoles of St. Louis were also unsuccessful in protecting their legal culture. A statute of 1807 was passed adopting the substance of common law in matters of successions, wills, and domestic relations. Parents could now disinherit their children, a power denied them under civil law, and the community property system of the Coutume de Paris was superseded.

That said, many traditional practices seemed to have continued in use in Creole Missouri and Illinois for some time. Creole women such as Julie Beauvais Jarrot and Thérèse Cerré Chouteau served as executrices of their "community" estates upon the deaths of their husbands. These women and others such as Julia Cerré Soulard and Clemence Coursault Chouteau managed diverse economic interests with authority and success.[31] For commercial disputes and litigation over land claims, French merchants quickly turned to Anglo lawyers. The trend, as written law replaced custom, was to establish norms that fit American procedures and substance—though this evolution was slow and painful—an "endless task," according to one American official.[32]

Detroit had suffered through a longer process of legal assimilation. After the conquest of Canada, Detroit existed in a legal vacuum until the establishment of the District of Hesse in 1788 and the appointment of a panel of three judges and other officers of the court. In the meantime, the merchants of the town had formed committees to resolve commercial disputes. This was not a solution that the merchants of Montreal found appealing, as they claimed the merchants of Detroit "owed them a quarter of a million pounds." Family law was in an even more distressed state and conflicts arose, especially when one parent in a mixed marriage (French and English) died and relatives contested the procedures for

Marie Thérèse Cerré Chouteau (1769–1842) (*left*) and Marie Julia Soulard
(1775–1845) (*right*) were both daughters of prominent merchant Gabriel Cerré.
Marie Thérèse married Auguste Chouteau and Julie married surveyor Antoine Soulard.
Marie Thérèse oversaw the management of Auguste's vast properties after his death,
and Julie Soulard laid out the initial division known as Frenchtown, which became
the center of St. Louis's Soulard District. Missouri History Museum, St. Louis.

appointing guardians.[33] While under the administration of the British, French
customs and written law in civil cases held sway because of the guarantees of the
Quebec Act. Once Detroit came under American rule, however, French legal
traditions gave way to American norms, apparently without protest from French
citizens. Only in Louisiana, with its much larger francophone population base
and a professional civilian legal class, did French legal practices survive.

The issue of language seems to have generated more heat in Detroit. The arrival of General William Hull as the first territorial governor stiffened the resolve of the French community. Among the various complaints in the petition
requesting his removal in 1809 was that he did not bother to translate his proclamations or the laws of the territory into French. Official documents were
thereafter printed in both languages until 1827, although political broadsides in
French appeared in Michigan and Indiana into the 1830s. Local politicians may
have realized that they needed to appeal to an important local constituency in

their language; however, the federal government did its best to erase the French language in the public sphere.[34]

Newspapers in French or with French sections appeared in Detroit through much of the century—in part because of successive waves of emigration from Quebec into the city, various parts of the state, and nearby Essex County, Ontario.[35] The *Detroit Gazette* printed articles in French until 1830. By the 1870s, it was clear that papers such as *L'Etoile Canadienne* had an intended audience of more recent arrivals.[36] The old families, however, continued to harbor some ill-will about the fate of their mother tongue. In his 1949 history of the Moran family of Detroit, J. Bell Moran noted with some scorn the "customary Yankee indifference" to the French language.[37]

It is safe to say that French as a dominant language in St. Louis and Detroit retreated slowly but surely during the first three decades of the nineteenth century. Above all, the leading French families in both towns groomed their sons to become businessmen. As commercial relations with New York City and Philadelphia became increasingly important, there was no question that the next generation should at least be bilingual. Auguste Chouteau had sent his son to Montreal in anticipation of the Louisiana Purchase. He expected him to learn to read and speak English. Joseph Campau insisted that his nephew John R. Williams study at night with a local English teacher, John Burrell, after minding the store during the daytime.[38] Although the lingua franca of the western fur trade remained French even longer, by the late 1830s, the prevailing language of St. Louis had become English. Virginia Sarpy was writing in French as a second language and begging her dear aunt to excuse her errors.[39]

Yet French remained an important second language at least until the Civil War. Mary Finney Barret, daughter of an Irish immigrant, recollecting her school days in St. Louis during the 1840s, noted that "my aunt desired to have me educated in the French language, so I was sent to a school kept by Madame Brazeau." She later attended a school run by Mesdames Gilbert and Bouvier, and still later, a school run by "Maman" Vitalis in Vide Poche or Carondelet. There, her classmates included Virginia Skinker, Susan Blow, Armantine Papin, Marie Soulard, and Mary Hempstead, young women from purely French, purely Anglo, and mixed marriages.[40]

This brings up a second point. Creole life in St. Louis during the nineteenth century, however we define it, was obviously no longer restricted to people of purely French extraction. Through intermarriage, friendships, snob appeal, and Catholic connections, the circle of French associations certainly increased. In Detroit, one of Pierre Desnoyer's daughters married the eminent educational reformer Henry Barnard. A granddaughter married the son of writer Orestes

Bartholomew Berthold (1780–1831) and his daughter Emilie Berthold Kennedy (1824–1893). Emilie's portrait, painted by Portuguese-born artist Manuel de França, captures the transition of St. Louis's pioneer mercantile families into a wealthy and fashionable elite by the 1840s. Her father was one of a small but significant group of Italian residents of early St. Louis. He arrived in the city in 1808 and became Pierre Chouteau Jr.'s first business partner and his brother-in-law. The Fort Berthold Reservation in North Dakota is named for him. Missouri History Museum, St. Louis.

Brownson. At the same time, two granddaughters became nuns and a grandson became the pastor of St. Aloysius in Detroit. French society, to some extent, seems also to have acquired a "first families" or high-society status.

Though the circle may have widened, the French face of St. Louis and Detroit became, by the 1830s, an increasingly private one. In St. Louis, Julia Soulard—daughter of Gabriel Cerré and widow of Antoine, the former royal surveyor—laid out an addition south of the central district.[41] There she built a twenty-room brick mansion. She also set aside two city blocks to be used for a public market. (That market—Soulard Market—still operates today. It is the St. Louis version of New Orleans' French Market, though at the time it was built, it was a country cousin to the French or Convent Market located nearby, but closer to downtown St. Louis.) Many of the French elite built lavish homes in the area during the 1840s and 1850s, and the neighborhood became known as Frenchtown. Banquets and balls were thrown with regularity. (Banquets held by the French Benevolent Society were restricted to those of French ancestry.) Here reigned the queens of St. Louis society, Sophie Labbadie Chouteau and her daughter Augustine. Another daughter, Mrs. Nicolas DeMenil, built an elaborate mansion that still stands.[42] Still another daughter, Susanne Chouteau, married an immigrant from France, Louis Cortambert. This Frenchman was an abolitionist and a socialist and published a literary newspaper, appropriately named *Le Revue de l'Ouest*, which apparently shocked its genteel readers by exhibiting an anti-Catholic bias.[43] Clearly, Frenchtown represented a next and wealthier generation of Creole culture in St. Louis.

The older part of town near the waterfront retained its original French aspect. Our best description of it comes from Charles Dickens, who visited St. Louis in 1842:

> In the old French portion of the town the thoroughfares are narrow and crooked, and some of the houses are very quaint and picturesque: being built of wood, with tumble-down galleries before the windows, approachable by stairs, or rather ladders, from the street. There are queer little barbers' shops, and drinking-houses too, in this quarter; and abundance of crazy old tenements with blinking casements, such as may be seen in Flanders. Some of these ancient habitations, with high garret gable windows perking into the roofs, have a kind of French shrug about them; and, being lop-sided with age, appear to hold their heads askew besides, as if they were grimacing in astonishment at the American Improvements.[44]

The disheveled and crowded downtown area was mostly destroyed by the great St. Louis fire of May 1849,[45] but the French elite had already moved on and had no need to "grimace." The city of their birth doubled in population from 1845 to 1850 and had almost ninety-five thousand inhabitants by 1852. Signs of economic expansion were everywhere, and their identity was now driven as much by class as ancestry.

As early as 1803, French military engineer Nicolas de Finiels had observed the increasing "pretension to fine manners, and social distinctions" of St. Louis. Said Finiels: "The women have cultivated more elegance than the men. Their finer sensibilities prompt them to adorn themselves, and they are beginning to laugh at the naive beauties of Ste. Genevieve."[46] The nineteenth century was, after all, the great bourgeois century when Paris outshone Versailles, when one learned how to talk and what to talk about in the city, not in the court. Commerce and culture went hand in hand. St. Louisans followed the Parisian model. Hardly mere *habitants*, the French Creoles patronized the arts and set the tone for respectability. A traveling Italian nobleman and friend of Louis Napoleon, Count Francesco Arese, wrote the following when visiting St. Louis in 1836: "The Saint Louis theatre is one of the best-looking I have seen in the United States, and certainly the audience is superior to those elsewhere in America. Theatrical shows are more a part of the habits of the town than in other cities, where the population, being of English or Dutch descent, cares less for such amusements than the French creoles. The performance was good; there was even a little ballet."[47] Many of the best families, French and Anglo, not only sent their daughters to one madame or another to learn French, they sent their sons to Bishop DuBourg's St. Louis Academy, run by Father François Niel. Students included the sons of Thomas Hart Benton, William Clark, and Alexander McNair. In 1828, Bishop Rosati opened a replacement for the academy, which had closed. The administrators of the new St. Louis College promised parents that "no undue influence" would be exercised on the students "in matters of religion."[48] Clearly, they expected students who were not necessarily French or Catholic. Small wonder that the Protestant organ *Home Missionary* warned its readers that "St. Louis is the seat of Romanism in the West." From this city, "the agents of Rome planned to lay siege to the region and to the nation."[49]

The city's new cathedral, the Cathedral of St. Louis of France—now known as the Old Cathedral—was dedicated in 1834. This magnificent structure, then as now, was a testament to the city's French heritage that had, in a sense, been canonized. (Yet when the new Bishop Kenrick arrived in 1843, he conducted all services in English.) Although the old Auguste Chouteau mansion was torn down in 1845, despite the eloquent pleadings of journalist Matt Field, two years later the city celebrated its founding, and old Pierre Chouteau Sr. joined in the parade, riding in a carriage with his sons Pierre Jr. and Paul Liguest and a nephew, Gabriel. The elder Chouteau spoke briefly to the crowd in French about the first inhabitants and simpler times. The city, in an expansive mood before the dark clouds of Civil War, seemed to take pride in its French origins. Said former mayor and opponent of the Chouteaus William Carr Lane to his daughters: "'I cannot say that I have seen a lady of purer good-breeding than Mrs. Cabanné or Mrs. Von-phul,' . . . though some may consider us 'poor Western devils as cannibals.'" The French Creoles of St. Louis were an American success story, and their social status could be interpreted as a sign that this western city was as polished and genteel as any city in the nation.[50]

The situation in Detroit had some parallels to that in St. Louis, though it remained a city of only about twenty thousand inhabitants in 1850 and had less to celebrate. There, the French elite moved to Hamtramck and Grosse Pointe. French citizens living to the northeast of the village (Côte du Nord-est)—described as "the most prosperous portion of the parish"—were already demanding their own church before the War of 1812. By 1834, a new parish, St. Paul's, had been dedicated at Grosse Pointe, with a church being erected in 1850.[51] Silas Farmer and Theodore Parsons Hall reported in 1886 that all sermons were given in French, "but the experiment of preaching in English is now being tried." To complete the picture of an elite francophone enclave, we can observe that the community also featured an Academy and Convent of the Sacred Heart and a country club.[52]

The social life of such communities, their private domestic habits—however elite—represented the latest evolution of francophone culture in these cities. And let us not minimize the importance of domestic culture. We might go back and reread the memoirs and reminiscences of French Creole ladies from the nineteenth century. In what ways were the French bourgeois truly different from their Anglo-American counterparts? Let us look at Adele Gratiot Washburne visiting her in-laws in Maine and noting their disapproval of her French trousseau, her lingerie with real lace and ribbons. Poor Adele spent the whole trip trying to eat boiled dinners and longing for fresh food of any kind.[53] And what did the Creoles mean by *bienséance*? What constituted proper behavior in a French family? Would it have been acceptable in an Anglo-American bourgeois family for Adele Sarpy, not yet a teenager, to have a glass of claret wine with *eau sucré*?[54] How do we determine the boundaries and meaning of this francophone culture? Did burial in Calvary Cemetery signify membership? If Creole architecture in St. Louis had ceased to be distinctive by 1820, other aspects of Creole material culture had not. One might reexamine Louis Jaccard's jewelry, M. Massot's confections, and the recipes for gumbo and croquignoles.[55]

We should also remember that francophone culture, although it occupied a smaller place within St. Louis and Detroit over the years, also maintained, even depended upon, a wider world of connections outside these cities. New Orleans, of course, was still *la ville*, and French children made friends at a variety of Catholic schools such as Bardstown (Kentucky), Georgetown, Fordham, and Notre Dame. Trips to France, of course, were de rigueur. In fact, it seems that Creole culture in St. Louis may have reemphasized connections with France during the course of the nineteenth century.

In the end, it is clear that the cultural world of the francophone elite in these two cities had become, on the one hand, nothing more than a small and somewhat precious piece of a much larger ethnic puzzle. Yet as individual citizens and business leaders, on the other hand, the French remained powerful; and as a charter group that was neither Anglo nor Protestant, their very existence mattered. In Detroit, where a number of prominent citizens played leading roles in the Democratic Party and seemed determined to make common cause with Catholic immigrants against the nativist inclinations of Anglo-American Protestants, a debate ensued over cultural values that became quite heated. During the antebellum period, however, the French identity of Detroit—perhaps already diminished by time (as it was founded more than half a century earlier than St. Louis) and a period of assimilation under British rule—seems not to have been celebrated during this first American era. In St. Louis, a period of enormous growth and prosperity that occurred within the lifetimes of some of the founding generation produced an incorporation of the French into the city's promotional sense of self. At the same time, the French Creoles of the city became a vital part of the urban social aristocracy, defined as much by class as by culture or ethnicity.

Perhaps we may simply say that the Americanization of Creole St. Louis and French Detroit was neither simple nor quick. That said, neither city—at least on the public surface—seemed overly French by mid-century and that, in the words of Pascal Cerré, speaking to his visiting nephew from Montreal in 1848, was something to be regarded "avec bien du regret."[56]

"LA CONFÉDÉRATION PERDUE": THE LEGACY OF FRANCOPHONE CULTURE IN MID-AMERICA

When Sophie Labbadie Chouteau died in St. Louis in 1862, "slaves of the various old French families carried her body from the Cathedral," apparently with great pomp and circumstance.[1] Given the bitter divisions in the city over slavery and loyalty, the funeral could easily have been regarded as a gesture of defiance. In St. Louis, a number of elite French families had already come under attack for having southern sympathies. When General Henry Halleck, the commander of the Department of the West stationed in that city, issued General Order No. 24 in December 1861 to assess prominent secessionists to provide funds for war refugees, many Creoles were on the list. Included were society matron Tullia Paul—whose brother Gabriel was a Union general in the Army of the Potomac.[2] Paul's husband, on the other hand, was a Kentuckian from an old planter family and related to Jefferson Davis, the president of the Confederacy. Her oldest son, Frederick W. Beckwith, was banished from the state by federal authorities for being a member of a pro-Confederacy group, the Broom Rangers.[3] He later died trying to return to the city in disguise.

Prominent banker L. A. Benoist, of French Canadian origin, denied the charge of being a secessionist but paid up and contributed more than forty thousand dollars to support Union volunteers and their families.[4] The Free Soil mayor of St. Louis, Oliver D. Filley, seized the occasion to try to discredit his brother Giles's powerful rival in the Missouri fur trade, Charles P. Chouteau.[5] Giles Filley had served on the committee to assess southern sympathizers in 1862, the same year he posted a bond for the opposition to Chouteau's American Fur Company in the western fur trade, La Barge, Harkness and Company. Not surprisingly, Chouteau became an early target, despite his having "filled large war material orders at cost, . . . loaned the quartermaster at St. Louis $20,000 to pay for uniforms and supplied a Minnesota regiment for months at his own expense." Chouteau, whose profits depended to some degree on federal contracts, had always maintained a pro-Union stance; nevertheless, the Indian Office denied him a trading license in 1865 for "having been reported as a rebel." That same year, Chouteau found himself arrested at Fort Rice in Dakota Territory by an overzealous commander who threatened to shoot Chouteau—"whose Southern proclivities were well understood."[6] Whether those "Southern proclivities" were real or imagined seemed not to matter. The high-society extended French families of St. Louis had owned (or continued to own) slaves—including the famous Dred Scott, owned at the time of the Supreme Court decision by Pierre Chouteau's son-in-law, John Sanford, yet defended by a French Creole lawyer, Chauvette Edmund Labeaume—and were easy prey for those on the lookout for traitors to the Union.[7]

In St. Louis, the struggle over union and slavery resonated on a personal level with the status of an elite francophone minority. The public face of French culture in that city had mostly disappeared by the Civil War. The funeral of Sophie Labbadie Chouteau in the midst of the Civil War seemed to represent the final covering of the visible veneer of St. Louis's French heritage. That was not true in New Orleans—the last city in the French bourgeois world of mid-America to have a francophone public face. In Louisiana, the battle for the survival of francophone culture was fierce and more significant—and it was intertwined with the Civil War as Francophones had come to see the invaders from the North as a new horde of vandals determined to inflict a fatal blow on their linguistic lifestyle and cultural community.

New Orleans native Dr. Alfred Mercier, living in France, captured this sentiment when he published a pamphlet in 1863, "Du Panlatinisme," urging the French government to support the Confederacy, claiming "a Southern victory would assist the survival of French in the new world."[8] In his pamphlet, Mercier posited "three forces, or elements of civilization," "Russo-Slavism, Anglo-Saxonism, and Gallo-Latinism." Although Mercier found much to admire about "Anglo-Saxonism," he argued that its North American branch was aggressive and inclined to destroy other civilizations. Describing the situation in North America, Mercier wrote:

In this enormous theater, the Anglo-Saxon element has wiped out or is headed toward wiping out all the others: the Dutch on the banks of the Hudson, the Swedes in Delaware, the French in Missouri, Michigan, Arkansas, Texas, Louisiana, Indiana, Wisconsin, and Alabama, the Spaniards in Florida, California, and New Mexico; it is on its way to absorbing all the varieties of the

white race. As for the red and black races, it has largely destroyed the former or
violently cast all of that race's remnants to the extreme frontiers of its sphere
of action; and the latter, in the North, has been pushed away with a cold, hard
caste pride that considers even living as neighbors sullying; while in the South
[the Anglo-Saxon element] has been juxtaposed with it in the more sociable
conditions of master and slave.[9]

Defending and linking the survival of francophone culture and slavery, Mercier echoed the sentiments of many of his compatriots back in Louisiana. One,
Emile Hiriart, founded a new journal in 1861, *La Renaissance Louisianaise:
Organe des Populations Franco-Américaines du Sud*, and wrote that it had simply
become impossible to "conciliate American citizenship with Louisiana patriotism."[10] The emphasis, however, was on defending francophone Louisiana, on
maintaining a political framework that would ensure their culture a permanent
status. Even French nationals living in New Orleans formed a Légion Française
to defend "leurs familles, leurs foyers, et la ville qui leur donne l'hospitalité."[11]
Across the northern border, French Canadians in Canada East (Quebec) rallied
around the cause of the Confederate raiders of St. Albans, Vermont, because
they saw southerners as an embattled minority struggling to resist the cultural
and political dominance of the Yankee North.[12]

The connection between francophone culture and the Civil War has largely
gone unnoticed. The one American historian who has explored these issues is
Joseph Tregle—who has done much to untangle the loaded myths and stereotypes of Creole New Orleans. In a 1992 essay, Tregle traced the rivalry between
the Creole and American factions in New Orleans that began as soon as the
Louisiana Purchase was consummated.[13] He concluded that the Creoles had
"clearly lost" the battle for cultural, economic, and political supremacy by the
time New Orleans—like ancient Gaul—was divided into three parts in 1836.[14] According to Tregle, the bitterness of this failure festered, especially among ardent
francophone intellectuals, until the Civil War. That war, in Tregle's words, "provided what some saw as their last chance for [the] revival of creole supremacy. . . .
But this recrudescence of Gallic nationalism almost immediately yielded precedence to a passion which swept all before it, a virulent negrophobia."[15] In short, to
quote Tregle again: "Despite the claims of so many later defenders of their cause,
it was not ruination attendant upon the Civil War which displaced creoles as the
ruling class in the community. That fate befell them long before the dislocations
of the tragic conflict."[16]

But Tregle has foreshortened his picture of francophone New Orleans to put
the very real racialization of francophone postwar attitudes in perspective. Since

we are concerned here primarily with the state of the francophone community at the time of the Civil War, it is important to revisit that community in New Orleans during the decades preceding the war. I would suggest that the francophone community had not succumbed, it had simply changed, retaining and even expanding its influence in some ways.

As we have observed in this book, far from being politically inept or naive, the French quickly adjusted to republican norms at the time of the Louisiana Purchase and learned how to manipulate the rules of the game. In Detroit and St. Louis, the French bourgeois elite maintained a position of economic and political prominence as individuals—albeit, individuals with shared values and interests. Especially in St. Louis, French Creoles realized that their minority position in the city and the state meant that they must seek power through personal connections and, on the federal level, through lobbying and influence peddling.

Of course, most of the political contests, large and small, were fought in New Orleans, for the stakes were higher. Of the three main French urban communities in the antebellum United States, only New Orleans had the opportunity, given its size, of maintaining an institutional framework adequate to sustain a vital francophone culture. The battle went well early on. The state constitution in 1812 magnified the voting strength of francophone parishes.[17] The civil law, a focal point of francophone concerns, was maintained, though blended with common-law procedures and substance.[18] Political success was partly due to the continuing emigration of French speakers from the West Indies and from France.

As historian Paul Lachance wrote: "The addition of white immigrants to the white creole population enabled French-speakers to remain a majority of the white population until almost 1830. If a substantial proportion of free persons of color and slaves had not also spoken French, however, the Gallic community would have become a minority of the total population as early as 1820."[19] In short, the addition of this new francophone element was indispensable to the maintenance of French culture in the city. Nor did the immigration of Francophones cease after 1809. Annual arrivals from 1832 until the Civil War "ranged from three thousand to over seven thousand." Although "only some" of those entering the United States through the port of New Orleans stayed in the city, the French remained "the third largest immigrant group . . . after the Irish and Germans," with the census of 1850 enumerating 7,522 natives of France and the census of 1860 listing 10,515.[20] These Foreign French kept New Orleans well supplied with francophone professionals, shopkeepers, and marriage partners.[21]

The francophone community after 1830, though no longer a majority, maintained its influence. The francophone newspapers—and there were a number of important ones, such as *L'Abeille*; *Le Louisianais et l'Ami des Lois*, which later became *L'Argus* and finally merged with *L'Abeille*; and *Le Courrier*—habitually goaded their readers into doing more to support their institutions in competition with the Anglo sector of the city.[22]

Claims of French illiteracy and ignorance are simply not borne out by the record. Citing evidence from marriage contracts signed in the city, Lachance claims that Anglo-Americans, male and female, enjoyed virtually universal literacy with white Creole and European French men at 96.5 percent, and grooms from St. Domingue at 93.7 percent. White francophone females from Louisiana and St. Domingue were also more than 90 percent literate.[23] Creole illiteracy was a myth.

As for the educational system, it is true that Anglos such as Samuel Peters took the lead, securing the passage in 1841 of a state law establishing independent school districts in the city and importing a school superintendent, teachers, and textbooks from New England for the Second Municipality or American District. The other municipalities, both francophone, quickly followed their lead. Francophone leaders Charles Gayarré in the First Municipality and Alexander Dimitry in the Third were also admirers of Horace Mann. They, too, imported teachers and texts for the English-language schools in their districts. Indeed, both men supervised the state system of public schools, Dimitry being the first to hold the position of state superintendent in 1848.[24] In the two French downtown districts, francophone schools taught English as the required "foreign" language.[25] In short, a progressive bilingual school system flourished in New Orleans, and in 1861 French newspaper editor Emile Hiriart characterized the system as "la gloire de la Nouvelle-Orléans."[26]

In addition, many private schools were available to the francophone community, and many elite Creoles sent their children to France or to such Catholic colleges as Georgetown in Washington, D.C., and St. Mary's in Maryland for higher education. The same was true in St. Louis throughout the antebellum period.[27] The French Quarter of New Orleans also boasted a substantial public library, housed on the third floor of the Cabildo (the seat of municipal government over several regimes; it now houses the Louisiana State Museum). Whereas the library of the American District featured the works of John Locke, Thomas Hobbes, and Daniel Webster, one could find books by more radical social thinkers such as Charles Fourier, Louis Blanc, and Étienne Cabet in the Cabildo.[28]

As for the dominant cultural institution of the city—its opera houses—the French community responded to the opening of James Caldwell's $325,000 St. Charles Theater (the American Theater) in 1835 by forming a new corporation with a capitalization of $600,000 the following year. The previous manager of the

French Orleans Theater, John Davis—despite the name, a French-born refugee from St. Domingue—was replaced by J. A. Durel, who in 1837 brought in a new prima donna of international repute, Mlle. Julie Calvé, and a new conductor, Eugene Prevost, who had won the grand prize in composition at the Paris Conservatoire. Though Caldwell's American opera house with an Italian opera company remained a stellar organization, the refurbished French theater took back pride of place in the eyes of the general public.[29] The Orleans Theater and its successor, the French Opera House, remained the preeminent cultural institution of the city until the latter burned down in 1919—the same year, as one historian has pointed out, that New Orleans Dixieland jazz was first taken abroad.[30] The opera was, indeed, an important institution in the city, and the French theater—as one letter writer pointed out—played a key role in preserving "the tongue and customs of our ancestors."[31] The American or Italian and the French opera houses were the pride of the city and the finest in the nation. The opera also served as a link to France, with New Orleans serving as an important provincial metropole for performers from that country throughout this period. The Franco-African community or Creoles of color had their own Philharmonic Society in the decades before the Civil War. Several individuals studied in France. One, Edmond Dédé, later became the conductor of an orchestra in Bordeaux.[32]

As for the economic position of the francophone community, it is true that the American (Anglo) upper districts during the 1840s and 1850s had pulled away from their downtown rivals. Topography played a part in this success. These were boom times for the city in general, with cotton, sugar, tobacco, pork, and other products piling up on the wharves. Merchants from the Northeast came down to the city, carved out fortunes, and built magnificent homes in the Garden District. One historian has called them "southern Yankees."[33] But as a neutral observer wrote in 1860, the Creoles could "teach a Yankee tin peddler lessons in economy."[34] In fact, the historian Robert Reinders has concluded that Creoles and Americans and immigrants could all be found on "the directorships of the city's railroads and most of the city's banks, insurance companies, and other commercial enterprises." Describing the New Orleans business community of the 1850s, Reinders notes more than forty Anglo-Creole partnerships in the directory of 1858 and suggests that the "tendency" was "toward a shared economic life."[35]

Yet the city had split into three municipalities in 1836 (with reunification in 1852), and there can be no doubt that ethnic hostility played a role. However, it is easy to overemphasize this. Many of the complaints that led to the division had to do with the city's investment in the various districts and suburbs. Starting in the 1820s, Bernard Marigny—the developer of the Third Municipality or Faubourg

Interior of the steamship *Princess/Imperial* (1861) by the French-born watercolorist
Marie Adrien Persac (1823–1873), who made his home in Louisiana. Gouache and
collage on paper; 17 by 22$^{15}/_{16}$ inches. According to H. Parrott Bacot, the former
executive director of the LSU Museum of Art and Natural Science, this "is the only
known surviving painting of the interior of one of the great pre–Civil War Mississippi
River floating palaces." The side-wheeler *Imperial*, built in 1858, "engaged in the
St. Louis–New Orleans run until 1863. The French-born artist married a Creole
woman (Odile Daigre) from Bayou Manchac near Baton Rouge in 1851. (They are
the couple pictured on the lower left. The painting was apparently an anniversary
present.) Steamboats were the primary mode of travel between the two Creole cities of
St. Louis and New Orleans. They were also a key technology in the consolidation of the
Chouteau family's control of the Upper Missouri fur trade. Various Creole companies
in St. Louis such as P. Chouteau Jr. and Company; Berthold, Tesson and Company;
and Pratte & Cabanné were shareholders in steamboats that traveled between the two
cities and bore the names of family members such as the *General Pratte* and the *Julia
Chouteau*. Pierre Chouteau Jr.'s son Charles, an acknowledged expert on the subject,
published a book in 1878 titled *The River Transportation of the West: Its Present
Condition and Probable Future*. The elegant interior of this vessel captures the gentility
and sophistication of life, at its best, enjoyed by the French inhabitants of mid-America
as they traveled between cities. LSU Museum of Art 75.8. Gift of Mrs. Mamie Persac
Lusk. Photograph by David Humphreys. LSU Museum of Art.

Marigny—complained bitterly of the favoritism shown by francophone Mayor Roffignac to the upper city. Americans complained, in turn, about the special treatment accorded Marigny's suburb.[36] Complaints such as these continued into the 1830s until the city was finally divided. A boom in real estate values ensued in all three municipalities; speculation was rampant. One Creole businessman, Nicolas Noel Destrehan, planned a new suburb in present-day Harvey, Louisiana, to be called Cosmopolite City, full of broad boulevards and public squares.[37] In fact, it was the more typically American suburban tract, the future Garden District, with its emphasis on private estates and distinctive homes, that proved most successful during the boom period that occurred after the city and state had recovered from the Panic of 1837. Its developer, Samuel J. Peters—Marigny's bitter rival—bought his land, ironically, from Marigny's sister, Madame Livaudais. In fact, many Creole landholders profited by the uptown property boom. Peters himself married a Creole woman, as did his children.[38] When the municipalities reunited in 1852, the decision to do so had broad support. All the municipalities were having credit problems, and the failure to coordinate their repairs on the levees had led to flooding in 1849.[39]

What, then, was the state of the francophone community during the 1850s? Though Francophones no longer represented a linguistic majority in the city, they had built a bilingual school system in two of the four city districts, and French continued to be an officially recognized language of the state. Despite continual calls from Anglocentric foes "to banish the French language" and complaints that "the proceedings and records, in open violation of the Act of Congress for the admission of the State of Louisiana in the Union, are kept in the French Language,"[40] the francophone community in New Orleans, far from becoming "poor losers" had in fact maintained a certain level of "institutional completeness" to ensure the *survivance* of their language and culture for at least some time.[41] That was not true, however, in Baton Rouge. There, a smaller francophone population and a more dominant Anglo business community resulted by the 1840s in the loss of an environment where French could be maintained.[42]

In New Orleans, by the 1840s, Francophones and Anglophones had reached something of a rapprochement. Intermarriage was not uncommon. If Americanization had become a fact of life, so in turn had Creolization. Especially among the Anglo elite, it had become fashionable to do things *à la française*. Harriet Martineau, writing in 1838, "witnessed with strange disgust the efforts of a young lady of Philadelphia to make herself as French as possible," not understanding, however, the proper Creole use of rouge and pearl powder.[43]

The Creole Sabbath had been attacked any number of times, often by visiting

Protestant ministers. In 1819, Benjamin Latrobe predicted that "the American majority led by such men as the Presbyterian and Episcopal preachers would so combat the pretended profanation of the Sabbath as to make that day as gloomy and [tedious], as elsewhere among us."[44] In 1831 a number of Protestant ministers supported a move to restrict the ball season. *L'Abeille* portrayed this group as men "who were ordered by God to preach to the world that the dance is a Satanic invention . . . that the Creator gave us the instinct of pleasure only so that we might procure the glory of resisting it." The ministers not only failed to restrict the pleasures of the Creole population, but in that same year, 1831, the American Theater, for the first time, gave Sunday evening performances to packed houses.[45]

Shopping, predictably, assumed a Creole and most cosmopolitan tone. At the French Market in New Orleans, female Indian vendors (referred to on occasion as "chumpa girls" from the old Mobilian trade language[46]) sold filé powder for gumbo and strings of dried grasshoppers for the mockingbirds. Black women sold chocolate bon bons, pralines, and candied oranges.[47] (Similarly, at the Soulard Market in St. Louis in the Frenchtown neighborhood, Anglos and Creoles bought wild turkeys and *mococks* of maple sugar from Indian women.[48] This sugar, mixed with water, became the popular Creole drink *eau sucré*.) And if one could not go to Paris, one could bring Paris here. Eliza Ripley, a Protestant from Uptown New Orleans, left us a vivid memoir of the social life in the city during the 1840s and 1850s. She described a day of shopping:

> Woodlief's was the leading store on Chartres Street and Barrière's on Royal, where could be found all the French nouveautés of the day, beautiful barèges, Marcelines and chinée silks, organdies stamped in gorgeous designs. . . .
>
> The first black silk dress worn on the street, and that was in '49, was proudly displayed by Miss Mathilde Eustis, who had relatives in France who kept her en rapport with the latest Parisian style. . . . Mme. Pluche's shop, on the corner of Royal and Conti, . . . dealt only in French importations. . . .
>
> The fashionable milliner was Olympe. Her specialty was imported chapeaus. . . . She met her customer at the door with "Ah, madame"—she had brought from Paris the very bonnet for you! No one had seen it; it was yours! And Mam'zelle Adèle was told to bring Mme. X's chapeau. It fit to a merveille.[49]

Upper-class American children in New Orleans, and also in St. Louis, were expected to learn French.[50] Ripley noted that many of her American friends were sent to Mesdames Granet, Delarouelle, or Desrayoux to learn French at their respective schools for girls in the Quarter. Some were also sent to Señor Marino Cubi y Soler's class on Royal Street to learn Spanish.[51] Though Spanish had ceased to be the language of state after the secret retrocession of Louisiana to France in 1800, New Orleans remained tied to the Caribbean world.

On a more official and public level, the secretary of the Louisiana senate and the clerk of the house of representatives were required by the state constitution of 1845 to be bilingual, and elected representatives were allowed to address either house in either language. The state constitution and all state laws were required to be published in both French and English. The new state constitution of 1852 continued these practices.[52] Banks issued bilingual notes, with the ten-dollar bill, or *billets de dix*, possibly popularizing the term "dixie."

I have painted this portrait to suggest that the francophone citizens in New Orleans, far from being haunted by their failure to maintain their ethnic identity and cultural integrity, were instead nervous survivors. All, of course, was not beer and skittles—or shall we say, gumbo and beignets. The biggest threat during the 1850s, as in Quebec during the 1960s, seemed to come from immigrants—anglophone immigrants, namely, the Irish, and immigrant Germans, who seemed inclined to support the looming danger of abolitionist policies. By 1860, New Orleans contained almost twenty thousand German-born residents and almost twenty-five thousand natives of Ireland. Some members of the Creole elite temporarily embraced the Know Nothing Party. Though they quarreled with the national party over their stand on Catholics, Creole supporters of the local party were themselves often at odds with the church. Known to be rather liberal in their views, Creole men who were members of the Masonic order and served as *marguilliers* (churchwardens) of St. Louis Cathedral struggled bitterly with several bishops in 1805 and again in the 1840s.[53] Some would-be Gallicans denounced the "ultramontane" inclinations of the church hierarchy and muttered about the slavish adherence of the Irish to the Pope. By 1858, however, the Creoles had left the party that in New Orleans had abandoned its anti-immigrant character and embraced all segments of the working class. The Creole and American elite, instead, united behind an independent party that nominated Major P. G. T. Beauregard for the mayoralty. Beauregard lost.[54]

On the eve of the Civil War then, the francophone citizens of New Orleans were hanging on. Perhaps the clearest statement of their feelings and hopes came in an 1856 memorial preserved in the minutes of the board of directors of the public schools of District Two—the Vieux Carré. Resisting the pressure to merge city school systems, the Creoles expressed their desire to be "one people, entirely separated from other nationalities and bound together by a community of feelings and interests." "We hope that this language [French] will never be suffered to die out amongst us; that from the two main elements of our population, in the crucible of American institutions, there will spring a people with original characteristics."[55] In short, they maintained the hope that they could continue to define themselves as both American and French. From our vantage point, such a hope may seem to have been unrealistic; nevertheless, the city's francophone community had certainly proved Lord Durham wrong when he wrote in his famous report of 1839 that "Louisianisation" would work in Quebec—that is, that economic, social, and political interests would press the elite to abandon their language and nationality.[56]

The Civil War changed everything. Creole fears that a new wave of abolitionists and Anglocentric Yankees would destroy the delicate local balance they had forged were well founded. Union general Ben Butler consolidated the public school districts of New Orleans in 1862 and "ended the use of French as a teaching language."[57] In Louisiana in 1864, a Free State convention met with few francophone delegates. When one, M. Jean P. Montamat, moved that the proceedings be printed in English and French, delegate Alfred C. Hills moved to strike the word "French." Said Hills, "I believe in a homogenous people, in one language and one system of law, and I believe that the publication of the laws of this State, or the proceedings of any convention, or any English court, in the French language, is a nuisance and ought to be abolished in this State or any other." Hills was seconded by another delegate who argued that the proceedings should be kept only "in the language in which the constitution of the United States is written. That language is my doctrine, and I never will vote for any other language but the American."[58] In fact, the convention agreed to publish the proceedings in French and English (and German), but not before one delegate sarcastically suggested that the Irish language be included.[59] Their work was not over. The convention eliminated the requirement for any state officials to be bilingual (Article 128). Most importantly, the convention struck a blow at francophone education. The original language of Article 142 read, "The English language only shall be taught in the common schools of this State." Montamat proposed a change to, "The English language shall be taught in the public schools in this State." The final wording read, "The general exercises in the common schools shall be conducted in the English language."[60] The Reconstruction constitution of 1868 went further—despite the presence of many francophone blacks at the convention—declaring that "the laws, public records, and the judicial and legislative proceedings of the State shall be promulgated, and preserved in the English language; and no law shall require judicial process to be issued in any other than the English language."[61] It was also forbidden to teach French in the elementary schools.[62]

It is telling that only a French Canadian historian, Réginald Hamel, has previously observed this dimension of cultural erasure within the policies of Louisi-

ana's Reconstruction politicians: "With peace reestablished, the occupiers imposed on Louisianians a constitution which held francophones in contempt. The
abolition of slavery and the abolition of French—in the spirit of new masters—
were inseparable. For the Yankees, it was necessary to integrate all dissidents,
cultural and biological. They imposed English on all—on the Acadians for trying
to remain neutral; on the Creoles for choosing the South; and on black francophones to render them part of the melting pot" (my translation).[63] The fate of
francophone Louisiana has not been the focus of historians, though.

Carl Brasseaux's work on the Acadian experience and the work of several historians—most recently Joseph Logsdon and Caryn Cossé Bell—on the Franco-
African or Creole black community of New Orleans are the notable and ad-
mirable exceptions.[64] Indeed, as Bell and Logsdon have shown in their various
published works on black New Orleans, the attack on francophone culture was
in part a carefully thought-out strategy for dividing the radical Franco-African
community and anglophone black Louisianians.[65] Black anglophone newcomers
to New Orleans, like their white counterparts, had little use for Franco-African
Catholicism and were offended by the Creole Sabbath and, in general, by the
city's public and private amusements. Black Anglophones viewed black Creoles as too radical and integrationist, suspiciously wealthy, and disturbingly un-
American. Conservative white Republicans, first under Butler's replacement,
General Nathaniel Banks, and then under Henry C. Warmoth, managed to iso-
late the black Creole leadership. It was not a difficult goal to achieve. As Belgian scientist Jean-Charles Houzeau, the managing editor of the *New Orleans
Tribune*—the first black newspaper published in the United States—observed
in 1868, "the so-called French colored element, the Franco-Africans" hate the
"Yankee adventurers arriving in the baggage of the federal army" for they considered "the colored race as a simple instrument . . . for profit and advancement."[66]
The paper's Creole of color owner and publisher, Dr. Louis Charles Roudanez,
was denounced by his Republican opponents as a "Napoleon," a "monarchist
who preferred France to America."[67] Logsdon and Bell suggest that "throughout
the late nineteenth century, the major division among black politicians still ran
along the Creole-American rift that had been exacerbated by the Banks leaders
in 1865."[68]

Despite the rift within the black community, Creoles of color continued to
press for what historian and professor of law Rebecca J. Scott has described as
"equal public rights."[69] Creoles of color such as Roudanez, author Rodolphe
Desdunes, and lawyer Louis A. Martinet organized the Comité des Citoyens
that "recruited Homer Plessy and supported his legal challenge" (*Plessy v. Ferguson*) to its unsuccessful conclusion before the Supreme Court in 1896.[70]

If the black francophone community had found an opportunity and a focus in the aftermath of the Civil War, the white francophone community seemed only to experience a sense of loss and defeat. Madame Louise Fortier's short story "Chronique de vieux temps: un incident de la Guerre Confédérée" captured the feeling well.[71] In between the romantic descriptions of chivalrous and charming Creoles can be found the phrase "la Confédération perdue." What exactly did this francophone author have in mind—what was her "lost cause"? In retrospect, it seems clear that it referred not only to the defeat of a southern nation, but also to the "lost cause" of francophone culture in Louisiana. The story was published in *Comptes-Rendus de l'Athénée Louisianais*, a journal founded in 1876 by our pamphleteer Alfred Mercier—now back in Louisiana. In 1879, this organization fought for the partial restoration of French language instruction.[72] Mercier himself produced several novels, including *L'Habitation Saint-Ybars, ou, Maîtres et Esclaves en Louisiane: Récit Social* in 1881. In that work, considered his masterpiece, Mercier attacks slavery and racism not only as degradations of the human spirit, but also as divisive forces between francophone groups with common goals and cultural values. It was too little and much too late. A line from Mercier's novel might have captured the spirit of his community after the Civil War: "La vie est un naufrage, sauve-qui-peut" (Life is a shipwreck. Save yourself.).[73]

Tregle was right to argue that in postbellum New Orleans, cultural concerns gave way to a "consuming preoccupation with race."[74] A few reactionary intellectuals such as Charles Gayarré spent the next few decades spinning myths and vilifying authors such as George W. Cable who dared present less flattering images of Creole life. Carl Brasseaux notes that the old Vieux Carré or French Quarter had become a "glorified slum" by the end of the Reconstruction period in 1877.[75] Ironically, the francophone communities of St. Louis and Detroit had become genteel enclaves by the Civil War. The more substantial and central francophone districts of New Orleans became impoverished after the Civil War, and their white Creole residents dispersed. Francophone poet Georges Dessommes captured the theme of exile in his poem "Un Soir au Jackson Square" (1880):

> Cependant au milieu des promeneurs joyeux,
> D'autres passaient, muets et seuls, de pauvres vieux,
> Flétris par la misère et l'exil, sans familles,
> Mal vêtus, mais gardant encor sous leurs guenilles
> La dignité des jours meilleurs . . .[76]

Before the war, the ties of language, religion, and culture had bound all Francophones across the boundaries of race. Yet white Francophones had done nothing to prevent the increasing repression of free Creoles of color during the 1850s. At war's end, white Creoles found that they themselves were threatened by a now dominant two-tier black and white racial hierarchy. Their own "negrophobia" was certainly a reaction, in part, to the tendency of Anglos increasingly to view all French people in racialized terms, as being nonwhite.

Historian Elliott West, describing the construction of "a new racial order encompassing western as well as southern people of color" during what he termed the period of "Greater Reconstruction" from the Mexican War until 1877, explained that western expansion complicated the black and white paradigm of slavery. How would the greatly enlarged United States incorporate new nonwhite peoples—racial outsiders now within the national boundaries? Turning to the Southwest, West observes that "Hispanics posed little cultural threat and played useful economic roles . . . the upshot was partly to ignore the racial issues raised by expansion and partly to turn vices into virtues. Mexican-Americans were either rendered invisible, segregated in cities and countryside, or they were reimagined as a bit of American exotica in a region we could afford to fantasize as an escape from fast-paced modern life. In the land of *poco tiempo*, these people of color became what was much tamer: people of local color."[77]

West's phrase—"local color"—seems particularly appropriate to describe that act of ordering that followed the decline of visible francophone communities in mid-America from the 1840s in St. Louis and Detroit to the 1860s and 1870s in New Orleans. But is it really appropriate to include the French as a nineteenth-century "nonwhite" group in what today is mid-America?[78] First, as West reminds us, in the nineteenth century, the words "race" and "nation" were both used to describe all ethnic groups, and each "race" was thought to have innate and immutable traits. In addition, the French in the United States were thought to be more inclined than Anglo-Saxons to racial mixing—specifically, they had liaisons with both Indians and blacks. And just as the more highly charged racial landscape after the Civil War forced white Francophones in Louisiana to contest the new racial implications of the word "Creole," the French farther north encountered similar difficulties when it came to acknowledging Indians in their family histories. But as historian Matthew Jacobson has pointed out—and as elite French families of the nineteenth century knew—whiteness in the United States was never simply about race; rather, it involved class and culture and could be fully achieved only through assimilation.[79]

The process of transforming French Creoles in Louisiana into "local color" began with the works of George W. Cable, Lafcadio Hearn, and Grace King from the 1870s onward. The creation of the French Quarter as a tourist site mostly after World War II completed the task and further obliterated the history of the cultural community, even though the effort saved historic buildings.[80]

In Michigan, the process of reimagining the French as "local color" began with the appearance of the popular *Shoepac Recollections*, written by Orlando B. Wilcox and published in 1856. Describing Detroit in the 1820s, the author wrote that one could "behold the Frenchman, riding in his two-wheeled cart to market with white fish and onions, and screaming a rascally patois."[81] Although many French families in Detroit continued to play an active role in commerce and community life throughout the nineteenth century, the local histories of these places, like the national histories, employed the same trivializing stereotypes. The French are portrayed as peasants incapable of progress, and their language is reduced to gibberish. So powerful are the stereotypes that a short historical sketch of Grosse Pointe, written by T. P. Hall and Silas Farmer in 1886, includes both descriptions of wealthy French residents and a pitiful story titled "The Habitant's Lament" written in childish Frenchified English:

> 'Waat naeu haouse eez dat,' ma waife Angelique saay toa mea h'aas weez raide hoame fraam de maarkaet de oddaire daay, whaire weez goan toa saell de leetle froag h'an beeg caatfeish . . . Daen Angelique loak saad h'an saay toa mea, 'Ah, Jean! Grosse Pointe aant laike eet waas whaen weez waar baoy h'an gaerl.' De moare h'i taink h'of dat, de moare ma maind goa baack h'on de h'oldaine taime whaen de Fraench peepale waas haappee h'on cauntaent weed de oale staile h'of doaing beesenaess. Eet make ma haeart feil toa baust whaen h'i taink haow de taime haas change.[82]

Cast as comfortably simple and close to nature, this French couple looks back to the past—frog and catfish in hand. Indeed, they seem to be characters in a French habitant minstrel show. Yet earlier in the same publication, there is a list of the members of the Grosse Pointe Club—the booklet was intended as a souvenir for that highly select circle. Grosse Pointe was already on its way to claiming a national reputation as an elite and utterly white Anglo-Saxon summer and suburban place; however, scattered in between such names as Phelps Newberry are the names of many older French elite families: Beniteau, Ducharme, several Morans, and five Campaus—one of whom had organized the club. Indeed, a number of the Anglo families also had French descendants or relatives, including one of the authors, Theodore Parsons Hall. Hall, a New York banker and Yale graduate, was married to Alexandrine Godfroy from an old and established French family—and they had children named Alexandrine Eugenie, Marie Archange, Madeleine Macomb, and Godfroy Navarre. Another member of mixed Anglo and French descent is described as speaking French fluently. To complete the picture, the booklet mentions several neighboring institutions, including the French Catholic Church of St. Paul and the Academy and Convent of the Sacred Heart.

So, what are we to make of this — the fairly painful depiction of colorful French living relics situated next to high-society elites from French founding families? One can only suggest that the latter had reached a comfortable layer of whiteness by the 1880s. Class had created enough distance to turn a wince into a wink. Yet the failure of those French elite families to contest such portrayals and the shaping of collective memory had consequences when it came to the production of history.

In 1951, *American Heritage* magazine celebrated the 250th birthday of Detroit with a series of short historical articles. The usual cast of characters made their appearance: Cadillac, Pontiac — than quickly onward to Mayor Albert E. Cobo and Walter Reuther. Raymond Miller, then chairman of the department of history at Wayne State University, wrote a brief summary of Detroit's history. Not surprisingly, he described the first Detroit as having been born in 1701 and having died in 1805. The great fire of that year cleared the air — in his words, "the old Detroit was gone." The French village now began to give way to new buildings and institutions — Miller mentions the Masonic lodge as an example (ignorant of its French members). New settlers from New York and New England swarmed in, giving the city a vital infusion of energy and leadership.[83]

Historian Melvin Holli, writing in the late 1970s, pursued such a theme in an article titled "French Detroit: The Clash of Feudal and Yankee Values" and also in his introductory essay to a documentary history of the city. Wrote Holli, "the French habitant culture [was not] able to withstand the invasion of the aggressive, literate, and institutionally mature 'cultural imperialism' of the Yankee."[84] Earlier in the century, the historian Almon Parkins stated the case bluntly: "French conservatism stood in the way of progress."[85] What all three historians were saying in slightly different ways was that the French past was irrelevant to the story of Detroit. The history of the city began with the arrival of Yankees and other Anglo-Americans.

Erasing the relevance of the fur trade as a source of capital and investment in the building of nineteenth-century Detroit and the agency of French families in the continuing story of their city, historians consigned the French to the second "prelude" chapter in their texts, the one that followed similarly irrelevant native peoples. Written to reinforce the self-congratulatory patriotism of nineteenth- and twentieth-century Americans and borrowing heavily from the racial categories established by Francis Parkman, such histories left the French to serve as mere bit players in Anglo fantasies. Not unlike the attraction of white Americans to vanishing Indian clichés and pseudo-Indian tribal names and lore, so beautifully described by historian Phil Deloria in his book *Playing Indian*,[86] French cavaliers and black-eyed Creole damsels appealed to the American imagination. From the French Quarter in New Orleans to Grosse Pointe outside Detroit, nostalgic French types at once reinforced the superiority of Anglo-American culture and provided a release from the tensions of modernity.

In St. Louis, a similar reduction of the French past occurred at almost the same time as it had in Detroit—on the eve of the Civil War. Richard Edwards and Menra Hopewell, authors of the first book-length history of St. Louis—which appeared in 1860—wrote, "The love of liberty is inherent in all men, and consequently, when the news came to St. Louis that Louisiana was purchased by the United States, the inhabitants rejoiced in the change." The incoming "race" of Anglo-Saxons, the authors continued, "possessed more industry, a superior knowledge in agricultural and mechanical pursuits, and above all, an enterprise and expansive views, which soon gave them a controlling influence" to the "mortification" and "envy" of the "native inhabitants," who were forced to "occupy only a secondary position." The authors then go on for several pages to describe the virtues of the old French, offering the usual stereotypes of "good humor, gaiety, limited education, humble fashions and cabins, love of music and dancing."[87]

This local-color trivialization had great staying power. Ernest Kirschten, in his popular history of St. Louis, *Catfish and Crystal*, published a century later in 1960, described the transfer of sovereignty in 1804: "no doubt the St. Louisans were happier to be under the American flag than under the Spanish." He goes on to state that "the American flag meant for the French of St. Louis the invasion of 'the Bostons.' That was their name for the Yankees and for all Americans from east of the Mississippi. . . . Less ambitious than the new fortune seekers, most of the French were inclined to maintain their old pace, to enjoy life, and to wonder why the newcomers did not also do so."[88] In St. Louis as in Detroit, the language and customs of the French had become a private, familial affair by the 1840s. Many of the descendants of the first families had become part of their cities' social aristocracy, and intermarriage had extended the popularity of French as a second language. Beyond the cachet of class, smaller and poorer Creole communities in Missouri—places such as Carondelet and Old Mines—were now considered local color, the homes of quaint and out-of-step folks who likely had Indian blood as well. Moreover, the history of the modern city, the history that mattered, began when Yankees and other Americans replaced the French—this despite the fact that third- and fourth-generation members of the original French families remained important members of the city's business community and occupied positions of civic leadership throughout the nineteenth century (and into the present). In short, the French legacy in mid-America by the 1870s could be found only in private attics and quaint stories about "rascally" habitants and dreamy Creoles. The past had been downplayed and disconnected from the present and the future.

One might therefore suggest that by this time, the French heritage of mid-America—especially before the preservation and transformation of the French Quarter in New Orleans as a tourist mecca—had been largely erased. There was, however, a complication in northern states such as Michigan and Wisconsin. Starting primarily in the 1840s, a new wave of French Canadian immigrants began arriving in the United States. The French Canadian population of New England almost doubled during that decade, reaching close to twenty thousand. Immigrants, especially from the Montreal region, also came in substantial numbers to midwestern states such as Michigan, which by 1850 also boasted a French population of about twenty thousand. More than two-thirds of those were recent arrivals from Canada, the remainder being "first-wave" Francophones, the charter or founding group of colonists who remained centered around older towns such as Detroit and Frenchtown or Monroe.[89]

The lack of land and rise of rural workers (*journaliers* or *emplacitaires*) seeking seasonal employment as farmhands or lumberjacks drove the movement of French Canadians south of the border, especially as the production of wheat in Quebec and timber in the Ottawa Valley declined during the 1840s. Political instability in Canada also played a role in the migration. The failed rebellions of 1837–1838 and the Act of Union of 1840, which threatened to establish a new Anglicizing regime, generated much uncertainty about the future in Quebec and talk of annexation (of Canada by the United States) as a means of protecting the language and religion of the French Canadian homeland. After the Civil War, the movement of French Canadians to the United States became "a veritable exodus,"[90] with more than 325,000 emigrants arriving in New England from 1860 to 1900, the peak being the last two decades of the century. Michigan and other midwestern states also received their fair share of French Canadian immigrants during these decades, though the movement there paled in comparison to New England. Michigan, the primary midwestern magnet, drew French Canadians to the lumber mill towns of the Saginaw Valley and the copper and iron regions of the Upper Peninsula. Little Canadas soon dotted the map. According to the 1900 census, Michigan's population of foreign-born French Canadians (32,483) ranked behind that of Massachusetts and New Hampshire but ahead of Rhode Island and Maine.[91] The question for us, however, is how did this new influx of Francophones connect to the "first wave" of Francophones, especially those who had founded Detroit?

There seems to have been some connection, at least early on. A newspaper, *Le Citoyen*, was founded in Detroit in the early 1850s but had a short life. A mutual aid society was founded with a Canadian orientation, but the French Canadian leaders turned to a member of the older French first families, Daniel J. Campau, for help. Campau promptly changed the Canadian name—Société Saint-Jean-Baptiste—to one with American resonance: the Société Lafayette. By the 1860s, a variety of francophone organizations had emerged, but a division occurred at the end of the decade ostensibly over the issue of annexation. More likely, those groups outside of Detroit whose members were recent French Canadian immigrants were less concerned with promoting the legacy of Michigan's French birth and more concerned with helping their immigrant constituency, maintaining ties to Quebec, and celebrating the Canadian holiday of Saint-Jean-Baptiste on June 24.[92]

It is hard to know whether the relations between the first or founding generation of Francophones and the second wave of French Canadian immigrants resembled that of German and Russian Jews in cities such as New York, but one suspects there were similar aspects. The first-wave French were established and considered themselves not only Americans but first families in every sense. The second wave maintained their connections to Canada and properly belonged to an immigrant and working-class narrative. The second wave produced several short-lived newspapers, many of them edited by Télésphore Saint-Pierre, who became a well-respected journalist and historian. But we may safely conclude that in general the two groups had "little interaction."[93] The various chapters of the Société Saint-Jean-Baptiste around the state—twelve at the turn of the twentieth century—were connected with the headquarters in Montreal and protested the execution of Louis Riel, an event that rocked French Canada, in 1885.[94] The old-line elite francophone families in places like Grosse Pointe may have permitted the publication of grotesque stereotypes of French Canadian habitants the following year in 1886 in part to distance themselves from contemporary working-class French Canadian immigrants. Neither group seems to have done much to contest the characterization of Michigan's French legacy as noble but irrelevant and French town builders as illiterate fur traders. Rather, the lone voice to do so in the nineteenth century belonged to a French historian and sociologist, François-Edme Rameau de Saint-Père, who became interested in France outre-mer, traveled in North America, and published a number of volumes on French North America with a special focus on Acadia. He delivered a lecture to an audience in Windsor, Ontario—across from Detroit—in 1861. That lecture was published the same year in Montreal. The Frenchman did not mince words:

Quels étaient alors vos pères? . . . combien de fois ne les avez vous pas enten-
due dire que c'étaient de braves gens, mais ignorants, incapables, arriérés. . . .
A croire certaines gens aujourd'huy, il semblerait vraiment que l'art d'ecrire
soit une innovation merveilleuse que l'invasion anglaise aurait importé en ce
pays;—mais avant cette époque un grand nombre de vos aïeux lisaient et écri-
vaient fort bien, et je dois dire qu'en parcourant les vieux papiers . . . j'ai été
étonné souvent de trouver dans l'ancienne population du Détroit une si forte
proportion de personnes sachant lire et écrire. [Who, then, were your fathers?
. . . how many times have you heard that they were brave men, but ignorant,
incompetent, backwards. . . . To believe some men today, it would truly seem
that the art of writing was a marvelous innovation imported to this country by
the English invasion; but before this era a large number of your ancestors read
and wrote very well, and I have to say that in browsing old papers, I was often
astonished to find among the former population of Detroit such a strong proportion of people who could read and write.]⁹⁵

If the two waves of francophone settlement barely connected in Michigan in
the nineteenth century, the overlap was more consequential in the midwestern
state with the second highest concentration of Francophones in the 1900 census,
Minnesota. The commercial hub of early Minnesota had formed around Fort
Snelling and the settlements of Mendota and St. Paul—which would become
the capital of the territory in 1849 and the state in 1858. J. Fletcher Williams,
in his *History of the City of Saint Paul*, first published in 1876, quoted St. Paul's
pioneer newspaper publisher James Goodhue as suggesting that "a knowledge of
the French language was indispensable to a trader." Williams went on to observe
that St. Paul's early stores often bore the sign, "Ici on parle Français [French spoken here]."⁹⁶ Who were the French in Minnesota during the 1840s? The LaBis-
sonières were refugees from the Selkirk Colony in the Red River valley. Joseph
LaBissonière and his son Isaac helped build the Chapel of St. Paul in 1841.
Joseph had been educated in Canada; Isaac, a stonemason by trade who grew
up in the West, never learned to read or write. Isaac's great-grandson, William
LaBissonière, became the University of Minnesota librarian.⁹⁷ Other francophone settlers served as clerks for the American Fur Company; some, such as
Alexis Bailly and Joseph Renville, operated as semi-independent traders. Still
others such as Joseph Rolette Sr. were partners who owned a piece of the action.
Rolette's son, "Jolly" Joe Jr., is often the subject of "colorful" anecdotes, but he
also grew up in a household with a piano—that symbol of bourgeois status—and
was sent to New York for an education.⁹⁸

Francophone settlers occupied different rungs of the economic ladder; they
also came from a variety of places. Many came to Minnesota from the mixed

French-Indian communities of Pembina on the Red River and Prairie du Chien in Wisconsin—although not all of those who came from these places were métis themselves. Charles Bazille, for example, was born near Montreal and came to St. Paul by way of Prairie du Chien. He married a daughter of Abraham Perry, a francophone watchmaker born in Switzerland and another refugee from the Selkirk Colony. Benjamin Gervais was born in Rivière-du-Loup in Quebec but arrived in Minnesota via Red River. He married Genevieve Larans, a native of Berthier, Quebec. The well-known trader Jean-Baptiste Faribault also came from Berthier. Still others came to St. Paul from the Creole communities of St. Louis, among them Louis Robert, a successful businessman and steamboat captain born in Carondelet, and his brother-in-law Louis Desnoyer. Auguste Louis Larpenteur, one of St. Paul's most respected citizens, came west from Baltimore following in the footsteps of his uncle Charles, a clerk for the American Fur Company. After spending two years in St. Louis, Larpenteur removed to St. Paul in 1843 as a clerk—his most valuable skill being his ability to speak French. The Larpenteur family had come to North America in 1816 after Waterloo to escape the Bourbon Restoration. Although the majority of Francophones in Minnesota in 1850 were born in Quebec, the Great Lakes region, or St. Louis, the census of 1850 listed twenty-nine natives of France and the census of 1860 more than eight hundred. In short, like their confreres in francophone communities from Belleville, Illinois, to New Orleans, the Francophones of the St. Paul–Mendota hub occupied a variety of economic niches and came from a variety of places.[99]

They also came from mixed ethnic and cultural backgrounds. Pierre Bottineau was the son of a French trader and an Ojibwe mother. The sons of Jean-Baptiste Faribault were one-quarter Mdewakanton through their métis mother, Pélagie Ainsé. Given this variety, how can we characterize the francophone community of St. Paul and its environs? One Quebecois scholar, Jean Morisset, has written that the "distinguishing trait" of French America is "the color of our language."[100] But the ability to speak French was not simply the unifying characteristic of a diverse collection of people of French extraction, it was a feature of Minnesota society in general. Make no mistake about that sign in the store; the preferred language of business in Minnesota during its territorial and early statehood period was often French. As Judge Charles Flandrau noted, "nearly all the people were French, and that language was quite as usually spoken as English. The town of Mendota was almost exclusively French and half-breed Sioux, the latter speaking French if they deviated from their native tongue."[101] Flandrau goes on to tell a story about a court case in Minnesota from the mid-1850s featuring two lawyers originally from New York. Major Jacob Noah, the son of a Jewish Jacksonian Democrat, allied himself with prominent Democrat and former fur trader Henry H. Sibley. Flandrau notes that Noah "spoke French like a native." The other lawyer, Yale graduate John Brisbin, was a newcomer to town. Brisbin presented his case first with "an exhaustive argument . . . fortified with numerous citations from English and New York cases, all of which he read to the court." Then, according to Flandrau, Major Noah

> opened his case to the court in French, and had hardly begun before Mr. Brisbin interposed an objection, that he did not understand French, and that legal proceedings in this country had to be conducted in English. The major answered by saying: "I am only interpreting to the court what you have been saying." Mr. Brisbin indignantly replied: "I don't want any interpretation of my argument; I made myself perfectly clear in what I said." "Oh yes," said the major, "you made a very clear and strong argument; but his honor, the judge, does not understand a single word of English," which was literally true.[102]

And so the ability to speak French was expected, even of the Anglos in St. Paul. Sibley, Minnesota's first governor, had been born in the then bilingual city of Detroit in 1811 and spoke French fluently.[103] The Sibley papers, for example, include a pamphlet he wrote in French in 1877 to promote the sale of railroad bonds, *Les Bons de Chemin de Fer de l'Etat*.[104] Sibley business associates, William Forbes and Norman Kittson, although of Scottish extraction, also spoke and wrote French fluently, having grown up in Montreal and Sorel, Quebec, respectively.[105] Flandrau tells a story about another Minnesota pioneer, George McLeod, with whom he served in the territorial assembly in 1856. McLeod was a tall red-headed Scotsman from Quebec whose brother was a Presbyterian preacher. Nevertheless, McLeod considered French his first language. After an altercation, McLeod was attended to by a Doctor Le Boutillier, the delegate from St. Anthony. The doctor said, "Georges, mon ami; ne bouge pas, tu a le bras cassé [George, my friend; don't budge, you have a broken arm]." McLeod responded, "Fiche-Moi la paix, on peut courber le bras à un Ecossais; on ne peut pas le lui casser [Leave me alone, you can bend the arm of a Scotchman; but you can't break it]."[106] (There is something humorous about this reply being made in McLeod's mother tongue of French.)

If the use of the French language was a general characteristic of Minnesota society at this time, adherence to Catholicism was not. The church was a clearer marker of social boundaries—a national trait, if you will. Catholicism in Minnesota was established within a francophone cultural context, and that context continued to predominate until the Civil War. The church sent Bishop Loras of Dubuque to assess the situation in Minnesota in 1839. Two missionary priests born in France, Fathers Lucien Galtier and Augustin Ravoux, served the region during the 1840s, and the Right Reverend Joseph Cretin arrived in 1851 as the first bishop of St. Paul—an outward sign of that community's emergence as a settlement of importance and permanence.[107] The Sisters of St. Joseph of Carondelet opened a school and a hospital in St. Paul during the 1850s—a sign of the city's link with Creole St. Louis.[108]

But the most important link between St. Paul and St. Louis came in the person of Pierre Chouteau Jr., whose involvement in Minnesota affairs began in 1842. That year, Ramsay Crooks—on the verge of bankruptcy—sold his interest in the American Fur Company's Western Outfit to Chouteau. The fur trade in 1842 was quickly becoming a business dependent on treaties and annuity payments. Chouteau and his field representative, Joseph Sire—a former steamboat captain and a junior partner—encouraged their Minnesota agents to diversify their investments and begin speculating in town lots, farms, and other ventures. Properties were registered jointly in Chouteau's name and the name of his agent. By 1848, when the Minnesota division was reorganized as the Northern Outfit, with Chouteau holding a half interest and Sibley and Vermonter Henry M. Rice each holding a sixth, the outfit had essentially become an investment firm. If one reads the letterbooks and ledgers of Pierre Chouteau and Company for the 1850s, in between the Upper Missouri fur-trade accounts and railroad bonds, one will find the personal and business accounts of Dr. Charles W. Borup (a native of Denmark who married a French métis woman), future senator Henry M. Rice, future governor Henry H. Sibley, and John S. Prince, the future five-term mayor of St. Paul during the 1860s.[109] (Prince had become a Chouteau employee in 1842, continuing as his agent after moving to St. Paul in 1854.) Although none of these Minnesota politicians seemed publicly to have a French connection, all received advances and salaries from Chouteau and handled his Minnesota investments.

And so Chouteau held a substantial interest in a variety of Minnesota ventures, including Kittson's addition; the Central House and Ramsey House buildings in St. Paul; properties in St. Anthony, Mendota, Lac qui Parle, and Hastings; and the Minnesota Packet Company, which controlled the steamboats linking St. Paul and St. Louis.[110] In exchange, Chouteau contributed two hundred dollars toward the completion of St. Paul's new Catholic cathedral in 1857.[111]

This first wave of francophone Minnesotans and the powerful absentee presence of Pierre Chouteau Jr. resembled the charter or founding generations in Detroit and St. Louis with their connections to native peoples and the fur trade and their investments in an emerging American regime of property and network of transportation links. They were also deeply involved in the treaties of dispossessions, treaties such as Mendota and Traverse des Sioux, signed in 1851, which provided capital for such investments and poured profits into the coffers of the Chouteau home office in St. Louis. But in Minnesota, with its later nonnative timeline, the first wave was quickly reinforced by a second wave.

Immigrants from Canada were attracted to settlements established by members of the earliest francophone communities. Alexander Faribault, the métis son of fur trader Jean Baptiste Faribault, founded a French Canadian colony in 1844 in what is now the city of Faribault in Rice County, Minnesota. He brought Edmund and Nicholas La Croix from Montreal to Minnesota to oversee his flour mill, and they developed a middlings purifier that made it possible to produce white flour from the spring wheat grown in the region. A more substantial French Canadian colony was established by the retired métis engagé Pierre Bottineau, his son Jean Baptiste, and a francophone merchant from St. Paul named Louis Fontaine. Bottineau and his son purchased nine thousand acres of land in Polk and Red Lake counties in 1877–1878 using so-called half-breed scrip. Fontaine and another partner, Rémi Fortier, served as chief promoters—inducing French Canadians headed to Manitoba to purchase farmland south of the border, placing ads in the French-language press, and distributing pamphlets in Quebec and New England. Their efforts were quite successful, and towns such as Gentilly and Crookston emerged as new centers of francophone life. Closer to St. Paul, another Red River pioneer, Benjamin Gervais, built a gristmill and attracted settlers to new towns such as Little Canada, Vadnais Heights, and Centerville—now all within the suburban orbit of the Twin Cities.[112]

The link between old and new francophone settlements aside, these stories also suggest that métis ethnicity and Red River origins were no impediment to economic success. Bottineau, Faribault, and Gervais—like Antoine LeClaire, the French-Potawatomi developer of Davenport, Iowa—were all careful businessmen. The careers of such men also seem to imply that capital—the color of money—was a potent factor in determining the future of a métis family.[113] Perhaps we should also consider the possibility that many métis families settled in French Canadian communities like those of Minnesota during the 1870s and 1880s.[114]

In Minnesota as in Michigan, francophone life was clearly perpetuated by the arrival of French Canadian immigrants after the Civil War. A number of factors were involved: the growth of lumbering, the métis troubles in Manitoba, the opening of the Great Northern and Soo Line railroads (which expanded farming opportunities), and finally, the Canadian efforts to repatriate French Canadians who had moved to New England. Francophone settlers moved to Minnesota from Quebec, New England, and Michigan. Indeed, francophone consciousness reached a high water mark around the turn of the twentieth century, with

French-language newspapers being published in the Twin Cities and Duluth, notably the *Echo de l'Ouest* in Minneapolis and *Le Canadien* in St. Paul. Fraternal organizations, political clubs such as the Club Democratie Franco-Americaine and the Lafayette-Papineau Republican League, literary and theater clubs: all flourished for a time.[115]

Although the first and second waves of francophone settlement came one upon the other in relatively rapid succession, their narratives—though not without connection—seem rather distinct. Issues of class seem less salient than in Detroit, but the all-important nexus of the Indian business and the transition to American hegemony characterizes the first and not the second francophone wave. The very inclusion of the name Papineau in a later francophone political club certainly suggests that the second wave is best contextualized by a French Canadian narrative that highlights events in nineteenth-century Quebec, not a fur-trade narrative that begins much earlier in the Great Lakes and Mississippi Valley. In short, Minnesota, like Michigan, experienced what we might call a re-Canadianization during the second half of the nineteenth century.

At the same time, the role of the French in the histories of both Michigan and Minnesota underwent the same type of erasure and trivialization. The complex story of cultural fluidity and, in the words of historian Maria Montoya, property translation never appears. Likewise, serious historical agents such as Pierre Chouteau Jr., Charles Larpenteur, Judge Charles Flandrau, and a host of others are never mentioned in accounts of St. Paul's founding era. Instead, always mentioned in any popular account of the city's beginnings, Pierre Parrant became the perfect comic representative of a historical phase characterized as being "colorful." Not to be taken very seriously, poor Pierre was the ubiquitous voyageur—a purveyor of whiskey, a thorn in the side of Major Lawrence Taliaferro, the representative of legitimate authority at Fort Snelling. Blind in one eye, a member of the fur-trade proletariat who had served in St. Louis, Prairie du Chien, and Sault Ste. Marie before arriving in Minnesota, Pig's Eye Parrant was described in 1876 by J. Fletcher Williams, St. Paul's first chronicler, as having "intemperate and licentious" habits, speaking "execrable English," and as being "the Romulus of our future city."[116] Today is he pictured on the beer cans produced by a local brewery.

And so, by the end of the nineteenth century in mid-America, the legacy, the historical importance of the French in the region's and the nation's past seemed to have been erased or at least reduced to that of colorful and irrelevant prelude. In northern states such as Michigan and Minnesota, the Canadian connection and context had been reinforced, but the once vital francophone worlds of New Orleans and St. Louis were fading from memory.[117] Back in St. Louis, however, the death of that legacy would be contested by a number of Chouteau descendants, chief among them Pierre Chouteau, the grandson of Pierre Chouteau Jr.

His father Charles P. Chouteau, born in 1819, had begun working for the family business at the age of eighteen. He closed the books of the great fur-trading company in 1870 to focus on railroads and his iron business. His son, Pierre, was born the year his great-grandfather, Pierre Sr., died—1849. Born into wealth, the young Pierre went to school at Seton Hall and in Belgium, where he received training as a civil engineer. He retired from business early and married late. His wife, Manette Chauvin, was apparently a descendant of Nicolas Chauvin de Lafreniere, one of the leaders of the French revolt against Spanish rule in New Orleans in 1768.

Pierre's father Charles had known the fur-trade business intimately and was considered a national authority on steamboats. As a young man, Pierre had witnessed the passing of generations. The last of those who had grown up in the Creole town and been acquainted with the founders were buried—and it seemed the memory of that place and the significance of the French past might be buried as well.

Pierre and a number of his cousins were determined not to let that happen. In 1893, the Missouri Historical Society in St. Louis opened its doors to the public. Founded in 1866—Pierre's father Charles had been a charter member—the society had operated much like a private club, and membership had dwindled by the early 1890s. Now in 1893, the society chose a university historian to be its president and hired its first librarian and curator. During this same decade, Pierre Chouteau took an active role in transmitting what had become a fragmented and very private collection of memories and stories, documents and objects, to newer, more publicly accessible contexts.[118]

In March 1898, Chouteau read a paper at an afternoon meeting of the society on his favorite topic, old St. Louis. The paper, a collection of anecdotes and details of Creole material culture, also contained several striking passages that contested the strain of Anglo-Saxonism that prevailed in the nation's politics and histories at the time.[119] Indeed, his portrait of the Creole community of early St. Louis anticipated the more nuanced rendering of a cosmopolitan and commercial people presented by historian John Francis McDermott in the twentieth century.

Perhaps more importantly, Chouteau, along with his first cousin Pierre Chouteau Maffitt, began to collect and prepare historical documents in the family's private possession. Chouteau may have been pushed in this direction by Hiram Chittenden, an officer in the Army Corps of Engineers. Chittenden found himself stationed in St. Louis in 1896 and decided to study the fur trade. With Chou-

Pierre Chouteau.

Oct. 10, 1758.   July 10, 1849.

teau's help, Chittenden in 1902 published the three-volume study *The American Fur Trade of the Far West*, the first scholarly work on the subject and still considered a fundamental text.[120]

Three years before his death in 1910, Chouteau's vast collection of documents came to the Missouri Historical Society. Those papers, along with a collection amassed by his cousin and several later additions, form the pivotal Chouteau Collections, whose richness as an archival source has provided a foundation for countless scholarly studies and a new understanding not only of the fur trade and Indian relations, but also of the French in the Mississippi Valley. Even in his own day, Chouteau encouraged historians such as Chittenden and Louis Houck to get the story right. The legacy preserved, the challenge—I hope—has been at least partially met.

Four generations of Chouteaus. *Top left*: Pierre Chouteau Sr. (1758–1849) cultivated good relations with native clients, especially the Osages. He and his half brother Auguste were acknowledged as the first citizens of St. Louis. *Top right*: Pierre Chouteau Jr. (1789–1865), also know as "Cadet," or the younger son. Under his leadership, the family business achieved the pinnacle of its success, dominating the flow of goods and information in the expanding American western empire. *Bottom left*: Charles P. Chouteau (1819–1901). Educated in New York City, he returned to St. Louis to work in the family business. Like his grandfather, Pierre Sr., he ran unsuccessfully for mayor of the city; nevertheless, he remained active in St. Louis affairs and had a passionate interest in science and steamboats. *Bottom right*: Pierre Chouteau III (1849–1910). Educated at Seton Hall and trained in Belgium as a civil engineer, he also returned to St. Louis to help manage the family's business affairs. He is credited with initiating the plans that led to the St. Louis World's Fair of 1904. An enthusiastic supporter of the Missouri Historical Society, he began the process of collecting the family papers and making them accessible to historians. All images courtesy of the Missouri Historical Society Photograph and Print Collection, Missouri History Museum, St. Louis.

CONCLUSION

Anyone with even a passing interest in the history of the American West has almost certainly come across a historical character with a French name. When I first became interested in western history, the more I read, the more French people I seemed to come across—running a store along the Oregon Trail or trading furs and goods with a seemingly infinite number of Indian communities. At the same time, one can easily look at a map of the nation, especially at the middle third of the nation, and see a variety of towns with French names or names that suggest a French presence: St. Louis, Prairie du Chien, Detroit, Ste. Genevieve, Des Moines, New Orleans, Terre Haute, Vincennes, Baton Rouge—the list goes on. And when one digs a little deeper, it turns out that there were many more American places founded by the French: Mobile, Milwaukee, Chicago, Peoria, Grand Rapids, Kansas City, Galveston—again, the list goes on.

It seems natural to want to connect the dots. So many French people in the West, so many towns with French names in mid-America—were the towns all founded during the period of French rule, which ended formally in 1763? The answer, it turns out, is "no." St. Louis, the most important of these places from the perspective of a historian of the American West, was founded in 1764 on the basis of a trading grant received from the last French governor of Louisiana after the territory had been transferred to Spain. Milwaukee was founded years later during the 1830s. This is clearly not a story about the French empire in North America. So is this then a story about French fur traders who might have been on the scene temporarily—traders of little consequence who lent their names to these infant towns and then left like so many absentee fathers?

Consider Milwaukee and its founder, Solomon Juneau. On a trip to Milwaukee, my family and I had dinner with a former student and his father. Out of curiosity, I asked them about Solomon Juneau, and they replied that he was just an illiterate fur trader. But I didn't think so. After all, fur traders who ran their own operations, even if connected to a larger company, had to keep the books and handle a great deal of correspondence. It was unlikely that he was illiterate. So we went to the Milwaukee County Historical Society, which had a collection of Juneau's papers, photographs of his family, and even one of his old coats. And his letters—some written in French, some in English. Not only had he mastered those two languages, but he probably knew at least one or two Indian languages as well—certainly Menominee, the language of the local native community. Obviously, he was not the supposedly illiterate fur trader. And there was a touching letter that his wife, Josette Vieau Juneau, wrote—in English—in 1838 that opened as follows:

> My dear daughters:
>
> I received your estimable and affectionate letter last Friday, which pleased me much to hear from you and Henrietta, and also to hear that you was both learning the French and Music. The French language, if you can learn grammatically, will please me above all other branch of education and I live in hopes that you will be able in a few months to write me a letter in the French language, as you know very well I do not understand the English. Tho I do wish in the same time that your English education should not be neglected and hope to see you both well educated in both languages. This is what I and your father wishes to see, all of you dear children well educated, which is the best Fortune we can leave you all after we are dead and gone.[1]

I had seen letters expressing such sentiments before. French traders and their families prized education, and letters between family members were at once respectful and full of warmth and affection. Such families were indeed bourgeois—and I mean that in the positive sense of the word. They sought a comfortable material existence, education, and respectability. And they were—as the etymology of "bourgeois" reminds us—citizens of the town. Indeed, they might well be founders of the town. Juneau's nephew Joe was the cofounder of Juneau, Alaska.

Solomon Juneau was a determined town founder. After a typical American land craze from 1835 to 1837—with land he purchased for $1.25 an acre reaching prices of $2,000 an acre—the Panic of 1837 hit and the bubble burst. Juneau weathered the storm and did what any solid developer would do: he improved transportation and communication links, founded the *Milwaukee Sentinel* in 1837 to promote the place, and served as the infant city's first postmaster and mayor. He was praised on his death in 1856 for his "generosity and public spirit."[2]

The life and career of Solomon Juneau
(1793–1856) exemplified the transition
from fur trader to town founder.
Photo courtesy of the Milwaukee
County Historical Society.

The fur trade, of course, had brought Juneau to the area in the first place. (He had been born in Repitigny, Quebec.) He had first established his trading post in Milwaukee in 1818. The previous trader there had been his father-in-law, Jacques Vieau. His connection to the fur trade and to the Menominees who lived nearby served him well later on—when cash ran short—in his efforts to develop the town. His correspondence, for example, contains a note from William Brewer at the Indian subagency in Green Bay. In the note, Brewer relates the approval of a claim of Juneau's to the tune of five thousand dollars.[3] The claim for debts owed by the Menominees had been endorsed by commissioners approved by the tribe. On frontiers strapped for capital, such payments—made in cash by the federal government—made a difference and were invaluable for western developers.

Juneau's story is not exceptional. With variations, it resembles the story of Alexis Coquillard in South Bend, Indiana; Joseph Campau in Detroit, Michigan; Louis Campau in Grand Rapids, Michigan; Antoine LeClaire in Davenport, Iowa; Hyacinthe Lasselle in Terre Haute and Logansport, Indiana; and all the extended Chouteau kin in St. Louis and Kansas City, Missouri. The dots have proved hard to connect for a variety of reasons. First, we have not wanted to connect the story of the fur trade with that of town-building. The former is full of adventure, Indians, and challenges that call for physical bravery and cunning; whereas the latter is a bit dull and prosaic and provides little room for fantasy. But the connections are there, and both stories are stories ultimately about business.

It is also hard to connect the dots because the dots are located, more or less, on a north-south axis—from the Great Lakes region to Lower Louisiana—and the usual story of American frontiers moves from east to west. This axis deserves a name, and I have called it the Creole Corridor, even though the term "Creole" has shifted meaning with time. It is the term that the French in New Orleans and St. Louis used for themselves, but not the French in Detroit. There, they simply used "French" or "Canadien." That last term would not do for Louisiana, a place with such a large and varied group of Francophones that separate categories arose during the nineteenth century: the old Creoles, *Gens de couleur* or Creoles of color, Acadians, the new Creoles from St. Domingue, the Foreign French (those who recently emigrated from France).

In addition, the stories of these places, each with its own set of actors, have meaningful parallels but specific differences. For example, the French inhabitants of these different places came under the sovereignty of the United States at different times: New Orleans and St. Louis after the Louisiana Purchase in 1803, the Illinois Country after the Treaty of Paris in 1783 (though arguably a few years earlier), Detroit in 1796, Natchez in 1798. Still, when we look at the stories in this book, the francophone actors from different places had certain characteristics in common: a dedication to commerce and the pursuit of profit; a Catholicism that was often tempered with a receptivity to enlightenment philosophers, freemasonry, and other modernizing forces; an understanding that doing business with native peoples meant learning their languages and maintaining their goodwill; an acceptance of slavery but also the possibility of marriages or liaisons across ethnic and racial lines; a dedication to family as the cornerstone of both business and society; and, above all for our purposes, a willingness to use the political culture of any regime, imperial or republican, to their own advantage. They were loyal to family and business; their political allegiance was situational.

It seems clear that there is a coherent story worth telling, but the problem is how to situate that story. There is a frontier story, a story of the role of French traders in the transformation of Indian lands into American private property. This story, I have argued, properly begins after the Seven Years War. It is during the era between the end of that war and the War of 1812 that the French begin to understand that the middle ground of the fur trade can become a negotiable instrument, a profitable position from which to broker the transition to an

American regime of settlement—that is, to facilitate the dispossession of native peoples. The French, in this story, become the advance guard of American empire. It is a national story that moves from Illinois to New Mexico, a story of frontiers in motion.

But there is also a regional story of town-building. This is a story of politics, culture, race, and urban development. It begins, at different times in different places, when American settlers and bureaucrats arrive. In each place, from New Orleans to Detroit, St. Louis to St. Joseph, francophone inhabitants moderated their incorporation, avoided marginalization, and capitalized on their priority. They did so with varying degrees of success, but the challenge produced francophone "first families" throughout mid-America. The local stories of these individual communities deserve to be seen as a whole, thereby revealing a mid-America that has, from the start, been urban, cosmopolitan, connected, and diverse. Once we acknowledge the significance of the French, not simply in a distant and irrelevant past, but into the American period of growth, we see that Catholicism and languages other than English are deeply embedded in our national narrative and are not just more recent phenomena.

But how do we connect these two stories—the regional story about place and the national story about process? It seems to be the old Turnerian dilemma— the frontier, place or process—most recently revisited in the thesis of Jeremy Adelman and Stephen Aron.[4] It is clear that French families such as the Chouteaus, Campaus, and Coquillards invested their profits from the fur trade and the Indian business of annuity goods and treaty debts into urban real estate, transportation ventures, banks, and other enterprises. The problem with Turner, however, was that his use of process to create place was weak on history. History existed only on one side of his frontier line—Indian agency was erased. This book has focused on the French, their roles as traders and negotiators, but Indians were the other party in this business—albeit often a party with unequal power. By restoring the French as historical actors and connecting the region-building and nation-building contexts of their activities, we remind ourselves that the development of mid-American places cannot be understood apart from the story of native communities—and that aspect of midwestern history is rarely told.[5] To understand the map of both region and nation and how it evolved, we must see both native and nonnative places on it. It is my hope that seeing this story of transition, of the brokering of frontiers, will remind us that native people, their pain and their survival, are deeply involved in every phase of the process. Turner's concept of a frontier line of settlement placed native people on the side without agency and without history. Understanding the critical role the French brokers played reminds us that there never was a simple line that came to life as a magic wand creating a new American landscape. Nor are these stories only about noble or tragic combatants whose victories or defeats are recorded on the scorecards of history. On the contrary, these messy and complex frontiers involve families, business transactions, and treaties—actions that are familiar and hard to romanticize. The consequences linger.

For me, the intersection of place and process resides in urban history, and I have always thought of this book as an urban history of the first phase of the American Midwest and its port city, New Orleans. For the French merchants who played a critical role in this region for arguably three-quarters of a century *after* the fall of the French empire in North America, the learned experience of social and cultural accommodation and situational political allegiance allowed them to build and expand a network of urban places. The history of cities, after all, combines a place-based story of community and a process-oriented story of commerce and investment. In the end, this is a story about the private sector, about merchants using social and economic capital (including federal funding of Indian treaty provisions) to develop their home bases such as Detroit and St. Louis and expand outward to new urban links such as Grand Rapids and St. Paul, Kansas City and St. Joseph. But these merchants and their families were also French, and as I have argued, it mattered that they were French for a variety of reasons, such as their past experience with native peoples, their priority and land claims, and even their Catholicism.

The activities and the towns of the French in mid-America provided a bridge between the era of colonies and empires and the era of nation-making. Historian Peter Kastor, in his book *The Nation's Crucible: The Louisiana Purchase and the Creation of America*, argues that the incorporation of that seemingly un-American place, Louisiana, was central to the formation of national identity and the political process of nation-making.[6] I hope that this book has shown that French mid-America was equally important in providing a model for the pursuit of American empire.

Ironically, the French themselves, perhaps more aware than others that the cities of their making were built on Indian lands, also understood the process of historical erasure. As one French descendant—remembering the anti-French attitude of incoming Anglos a century and a half earlier—observed in a talk given in St. Louis in 1953: "Woe to the conquered, woe to the absorbed."[7] The standard meta-narrative of the American frontier privileges individuals, often explorers or adventure-seekers, clearing a pathway for humble settlers. All, of course, speak English. This is a story of French-speaking traders, embedded in families (sometimes with native partners), exhibiting not so much "undaunted courage" but a careful and clear business sense and the ability to balance risk and return.

Walnut brass-bound writing box belonging to Jules de Mun (circa 1815). Perhaps no other artifact can more effectively counter the well-worn stereotype of self-sufficient mountain men seeking rugged adventures far from the constraints of family and home. De Mun likely dragged this portable writing desk with him during his ill-fated trading and trapping journey to the southern Rockies between 1815 and 1817. During the expedition, he wrote long and touching letters to his wife, Isabelle Gratiot. Photograph by Cary Horton. Missouri History Museum, St. Louis.

"Mountain men" may have reveled in their isolation, but French traders in the field wrote letters back home to their loved ones.

It is high time we understood the central importance of this francophone world in the story of national expansion and the urban history of mid-America. Frontier history was, until recently, Anglocentric and simplistic. The past two decades have seen attempts to restore the Indian side of that history, but the French have remained invisible, in part because their story demands that we accept a frontier past that transcends our old dichotomies of heroes and villains, settlers and Indians.

The title of this book was meant to startle with the juxtaposition of "bourgeois" and "frontier." We end with another such juxtaposition: "French" *and* "American." It may be hard to acknowledge that these frontier actors were both, but we must recognize this side of our national ancestry. Move over Uncle Sam and make room for *Oncle Auguste*.

NOTES

INTRODUCTION

1. Keating, *Narrative of an Expedition*, 75.
2. Throughout this book the term "Creole" will refer to French-speaking individuals in the region from St. Louis to New Orleans, their culture and their society. To be sure, the term is problematic. It was not a word the Creoles themselves used with great frequency until the 1820s, but it is still the term of self-description used by the descendants of the first French settlers in these cities today. Only in Louisiana did the term seem to take on a highly charged sociopolitical meaning in the process of community formation—although political, social, and cultural battles were fought throughout this region between French-speakers and English-speakers. Why not use the term "French-speakers" or "Francophones?" "Creole" is shorter; moreover, it conveys accurately, I believe, the sensibility of a people—individuals, families, social groups—who could not identify themselves as "Americans," "Canadians," or "Europeans." As the struggle over the elaboration of a definitive linguistic and political order is gradually decided in favor of the Anglo-American, "Creole" becomes more and more a label of ethnicity, bound to ancestry. Race then becomes a new battleground. For an intriguing and enlightening history and analysis of Creole identity in Louisiana, see Domínguez, *White by Definition*. Domínguez argues that ethnicity and racial classification are shaped by legal and social forces—in short, are creatures of history. She shows that the application of the term "Creole" was broadest when the struggle over the elaboration of community in Louisiana was at its height.
3. A number of books and articles have been written on "la survivance," the survival of French culture in Louisiana. See Roland Breton, *Géographie du français et de la francité en Louisiane* (Quebec: Centre International de Recherche sur le Bilinguisme, 1979); Jerah Johnson, "The Louisiana French," *Contemporary French Civilization*, I (Fall 1976); Larbi Oukada, "The Territory and Population of French-speaking Louisiana," *Revue de Louisiane/Louisiana Review*, 7 (Summer 1978); Baker, "Les Acadiens en Louisiane avant la Guerre de Sécession; and Lachance, "Intermarriage." Tinker,

Bibliography of the French Newspapers and Periodicals of Louisiana, provides information on French-language journalism, which flourished in the 1840s in Louisiana. Nineteenth-century short stories from French Louisiana were collected recently in St. Martin and Voorhies, eds., *Ecrits Louisianais du Dix-Neuvième Siècle*. For a general picture of Creole society in Louisiana during the antebellum period, see Crété, *Daily Life in Louisiana*. For the establishment of Acadian communities in Louisiana, see Brasseaux, *The Founding of New Acadia*. Dargo, *Jefferson's Louisiana*; Haas, ed., *Louisiana's Legal Heritage*; Tregle, "Political Reinforcement"; and Kmen, *Music in New Orleans*, all discuss the struggle for cultural dominance in Louisiana during the first few decades of the American regime. The literature on the survival of French language and culture in the other centers of the Creole corridor is not nearly as rich. For Missouri, see Dorrance, "The Survival of French"; Smelser, "Folkways in Creole St. Louis"; and Hoffhaus, *Chez les Canses*. For Michigan, see the somewhat suspect reminiscences of Hubbard, *Memorials of a Half-Century*. My general estimate of the gradual decline of the use of the French language is based on an acquaintance with the correspondence of French men, women, and children during the 1830s and 1840s.

4. James Axtell, "Europeans, Indians, and the Age of Discovery in American History Textbooks," *American Historical Review*, 92:3 (June 1987), 627.

5. Francis Jennings, "Francis Parkman: A Brahmin among Untouchables," *William and Mary Quarterly*, 42:3 (July 1985), 328.

6. Francis Parkman, *The Old Regime in Canada* (Boston: Little, Brown, 1874), 464–465.

7. Pierre Chouteau and Co. also arranged for Chatillon to be Parkman's guide. The passport and line of credit issued by John Clapp, an employee of P. Chouteau and Co. is reproduced in Wade, ed., *The Journals of Francis Parkman*, II, facing page 438. See also pp. 494–495 in vol. 2. For a fresh and brilliant analysis of the representations of French frontier or colonial culture in the American literary discourse of the nineteenth century, see Watts, *In This Remote Country*.

8. Francis Parkman, *The Conspiracy of Pontiac and the Indian War after the Conquest of Canada* (Boston, 1882), 251.

9. Nelson Vance Russell, "The French and British at Play in the Old Northwest, 1760–1796" (1938), reprinted in Clyde C. Walton, ed., *An Illinois Reader* (DeKalb: Northern Illinois University Press, 1970), 62.

10. This is the last line of Maurice Thompson's classic Hoosier novel *Alice of Old Vincennes* (Indianapolis, Ind.: Bowen-Merrill, 1900). Another wonderful example of a romantic historical novel with quaint midwestern Creoles as its central characters is Mary Hartwell Catherwood, *Old Kaskaskia* (Boston: Houghton Mifflin, 1893). Louisiana Creoles have, of course, "inspired" a large number of "moonlight and magnolia" novels. Ross Phares, *Cavalier in the Wilderness: The Story of the Explorer and Trader Louis Juchereau de St. Denis* (Baton Rouge: Louisiana State University Press, 1952) is a good example of a very romantic work of nonfiction. A more scholarly and still useful work, J. H. Schlarman's *From Quebec to New Orleans* (Belleville, Ill.: Buechler, 1929), exhibits the power exerted by Parkman's narrative.

11. Turner, "The Character and Influence." The dissertation was reprinted by the University of Oklahoma Press in 1977. My discussion of Turner has benefited greatly from William Cronon, "Revisiting the Vanishing Frontier: The Legacy of Frederick Jackson Turner," *Western Historical Quarterly*, 18:2 (April 1987).

12. For an elegant refutation of this aspect of Turner's thinking see Cronon, *Nature's Metropolis*, esp. ch. 1, "Dreaming the Metropolis."

13. Turner, "The Rise and Fall of New France," reprinted in *Minnesota History*, 18:4 (December 1937), 384.

14. Ibid., 392.

15. Ibid., 393.

16. Peterson, "Prelude to Red River," 51–53. See also Peterson, "The People In Between."

17. Augustin Grignon, "Seventy-Two Years' Recollections of Wisconsin," 284.

18. Peterson, "'Wild' Chicago," 64–71.

19. Snyder, "Antoine LeClaire"; Matson, *Pioneers of Illinois*, 262–272; see also "Antoine Le Clair's Statement," in *Collections of the State Historical Society of Wisconsin*, 11 (Madison, 1888). LeClaire's house in Davenport is presently being restored. To raise money for the project, a pamphlet/coloring book reprinting several items of interest has been produced by grade school students and published by the school system. LeClaire deserves a biography.

20. Anson, *The Miami Indians*. See also Anson's richly detailed dissertation, "The Fur Traders," and Robertson and Riker, eds., *The John Tipton Papers*.

21. John E. Foster, "Some Questions and Perspectives on the Problem of Métis Roots," in Peterson and Brown, eds., *The New Peoples*.

22. R. David Edmunds, "'Unacquainted with the laws of the civilized world': American Attitudes toward the Métis Communities in the Old Northwest," in Peterson and Brown, eds., *The New Peoples*, 190.

23. *Collections of the Pioneer and Historical Society of Michigan* (Lansing, 1886), VIII:587–592.

24. For Lucas, see *Letters of J. B. C. Lucas from 1815 to 1836* (St. Louis, 1905); Gates, *History of Public Land Law Development*, ch. 6; and Primm, *Lion of the Valley*, ch. 4. For Cass, see Woodford, *Lewis Cass*; and Haeger, *The Investment Frontier*.

25. Keating, *Narrative of an Expedition*, 76.

26. For more on the diversity of origins in early St. Louis, see Chapter 2. The numbers come from Jay Gitlin, "Trading Posts and Suburbs: The Urban Context of Creole Society and Commercial Expansion on the Missouri Frontier," paper read at the Western History Association annual meeting, Kansas City, Missouri, 1980. Sources: O. W. Collet, "Index to St. Louis Register, Baptisms, Marriages and Burials, 1766–1781," manuscript in Missouri Historical Society, St. Louis; Billon, *Annals of St. Louis*; Houck, *A History of Missouri*; Beckwith, *Creoles of St. Louis*; Cunningham and Blythe, *The Founding Family*. For Detroit, see genealogy compiled by Father Christian Denissen in the Burton Historical Collection, Detroit Public Library.

27. Very little has been done on this topic. See Ekberg, *Colonial Ste. Genevieve*, ch. 7. Many excellent books have appeared in the past decade or so on Afro-Creole culture and life in Lower Louisiana. See Gwendolyn Midlo Hall, *Africans in Colonial*

Louisiana: The Development of Afro-Creole Culture in the Eighteenth Century (Baton
Rouge: Louisiana State University Press, 1992); Thomas N. Ingersoll, *Mammon and
Manon in Early New Orleans: The First Slave Society in the Deep South, 1718–1819*
(Knoxville: University of Tennessee Press, 1999); Kimberly S. Hanger, *Bounded Lives,
Bounded Places: Free Black Society in Colonial New Orleans, 1769–1803* (Durham,
N.C.: Duke University Press, 1997); and Bell, *Revolution, Romanticism*. Carl J. Ek-
berg, *Stealing Indian Women: Native Slavery in the Illinois Country* (Urbana: Univer-
sity of Illinois Press, 2007), explores native slavery in French Illinois in greater depth,
and a forthcoming book by Brett Rushforth, *Savage Bonds: Indigenous and Atlantic
Slaveries in New France*, promises to completely revise our understanding of race and
slavery in francophone North America.

28. For examples of this, see Thomas James's account of the Missouri Fur Company expedition of 1809 led by Manuel Lisa, Pierre Menard, and Pierre Chouteau, *Three Years
among the Indians and Mexicans* (1846), and Charles Larpenteur's description of life
at Fort Union, *Forty Years a Fur Trader on the Upper Missouri*, 2 vols. (1898).

29. John Francis McDermott's essay "Cultural Conditions on the Confines of a Wilderness," in his *Private Libraries in Creole St. Louis* (Baltimore: Johns Hopkins University
Press for the Institut Français de Washington, 1938), is still the essential starting point
for understanding the lives of these French merchants. With a wonderful command
of the sources, McDermott finally dispelled previous notions of the unambitious, isolated Creole trader.

30. For a preliminary investigation of this phenomenon, see Kenneth Haltman, "Sober
and Obedient: Preliminary Notes to a Biographical Index of Interpreters in the American West," unpublished paper, Yale University, 1984.

31. Quoted in John Francis McDermott, "The Frontier Re-examined," in McDermott,
ed., *The Frontier Re-examined* (Urbana: University of Illinois Press, 1967), 6.

32. White, *The Middle Ground*, x.

33. Ibid., 316.

34. Faribault-Beauregard, ed., *La vie aux Illinois*, 15.

CHAPTER 1. CONSTRUCTING THE
HOUSE OF CHOUTEAU

1. Most of the information about the founding of St. Louis is taken from John Francis
McDermott, "Myths and Realities Concerning the Founding of St. Louis," in Mc-
Dermott, ed., *The French in the Mississippi Valley*. John Francis McDermott, ed.,
The Early Histories of St. Louis (St. Louis: St. Louis Historical Documents Founda-
tion, 1952) contains Chouteau's narrative and other important early writings about the
town.

2. For more on Maxent and the affairs of the partnership, see James Julian Coleman Jr.,
Gilbert Antoine de St. Maxent: The Spanish-Frenchman of New Orleans (Gretna, La.:
Pelican, 1980).

3. My thanks to colleague and friend Fred Fausz (associate professor of history, University of Missouri–St. Louis) for graciously sharing his intimate knowledge of the manu-

script with me. A new edition of the manuscript is in preparation: J. Frederick Fausz, ed., *First City of the West: Auguste Chouteau and the Founding of St. Louis* (St. Louis: St. Louis Mercantile Library at the University of Missouri–St. Louis, 2010). According to Fausz, the Chouteau manuscript was most likely written in the winter of 1804 — between Meriwether Lewis's arrival in early December 1803 and before he and Clark departed on their expedition in May 1804. Captain (later Major) Amos Stoddard, who took possession of the city for the United States after the Louisiana Purchase, had already copied key portions of the manuscript by the time he left St. Louis in October 1804.

4. McDermott, ed., *Early Histories of St. Louis*, 48.

5. For more on this earliest phase of St. Louis's history, see Primm, *Lion of the Valley*; and Peterson, *Colonial St. Louis*. Another very useful book for this period that should not be overlooked is Musick, *St. Louis as a Fortified Town*. Van Ravensdaay, *Saint Louis*, provides an invaluable anecdotal history in a well-illustrated volume. Foley and Rice, *The First Chouteaus*, is the definitive study of the first generation of this family, placing their activities in their local, regional, and national contexts.

6. W. J. Eccles, *The Canadian Frontier, 1534–1760* (New York: Holt, Rinehart and Winston, 1969), 3.

7. J. Frederick Fausz, "Becoming 'A Nation of Quakers': The Removal of the Osage Indians from Missouri," *Gateway Heritage*, 21:1 (Summer 2000), 30.

8. Quoted in McDermott, "Myths and Realities," 14.

9. Journal of Captain Harry Gordon, August 1766, in Alvord and Carter, eds., *The New Régime*, 300.

10. McDermott, "Myths and Realities," 15.

11. Coleman, *Maxent*, 50.

12. McDermott, "Myths and Realities," 11–13.

13. John Francis McDermott, "Auguste Chouteau: First Citizen of Upper Louisiana," in McDermott, ed., *Frenchmen and French Ways*, 10–11; and Van Ravensdaay, *Saint Louis*, 101.

14. Tanis Chapman Thorne, "People of the River: Mixed-Blood Families on the Lower Missouri" (PhD diss., University of California–Los Angeles, 1987), 85–86.

15. For more on these satellite communities and the population distribution of early St. Louis, see Primm, *Lion of the Valley*, 65–68; and Thorne, "People of the River," ch. 2.

16. Coeur qui Brule to Delassus, 1800, Box 3, Chouteau Collections, Missouri Historical Society, St. Louis, hereafter cited as CCMO.

17. Billon, "Annals of St. Louis," 158.

18. Darby, *Personal Recollections*, 13.

19. For more on this attack, see John Francis McDermott, "The Myth of the 'Imbecile Governor' — Captain Fernando de Leyba and the Defense of St. Louis in 1780," in McDermott, ed., *The Spanish in the Mississippi Valley*; Hodes, *Beyond the Frontier*, ch. 6; and Musick, *St. Louis as a Fortified Town*, ch. 6.

20. Corbett, "Veuve Chouteau," provides the most complete portrait of the founding mother. See also, Van Ravensdaay, *Saint Louis*, ch. 1 ("Monsieur Laclède and Madame Chouteau") and ch. 6 ("The Royal Family of the Wilderness").

21. Van Ravenswaay, *Saint Louis*, 23.
22. Foley and Rice, *The First Chouteaus*, 22.
23. Van Ravenswaay, *Saint Louis*, 25. The descendant was Alexander DeMenil.
24. Foley and Rice, *The First Chouteaus*, 24.
25. Van Ravenswaay, *Saint Louis*, 35.
26. For more on the interplay between family and business, see Chapter 6.
27. Timothy Flint, *Recollections of the Last Ten Years* (Boston, 1826), 110; quoted in George R. Brooks, "St. Louis in 1818," in Harriet Lane Cates Hardaway and Dorothy Garesché Holland, eds., *Philippine Duchesne and Her Times* (St. Louis: Maryville College, 1968), 1.
28. One might think of Chouteau's American Fur Company, in its heyday, as a kind of decentralized Bon Marché in Indian country. Not surprisingly, the Hudson's Bay Company ultimately became exactly that, a department store chain. Of course, the fur trade also had a dark side — game depletion, alcoholism, and dispossession.
29. Van Ravenswaay, *Saint Louis*, 95.
30. Corbett, "Veuve Chouteau."

CHAPTER 2. "WE ARE WELL OFF THAT THERE ARE NO VIRGINIANS IN THIS QUARTER"

1. Foley and Rice, *The First Chouteaus*, 16.
2. Calloway, *The Scratch of a Pen*, 112.
3. J. F. Bosher, "Government and Private Interests in New France," *Canadian Public Administration/Administration publique du Canada*, X (1967), 257.
4. Phillips, *Fur Trade*, I:604.
5. I use this term in part because I rather like the sound of it. The term "Creole" to describe Francophones born in the New World became more popular in Louisiana during the late eighteenth century and the antebellum period as Creoles sought to distinguish themselves from the Foreign French (francophone Louisianians born in France) and Acadians or Cajuns. The term seems to have become popular in St. Louis during the Spanish regime as well. It remains the term of choice to describe those of French ancestry in the St. Louis region. It was not used as a self-identifying term in places like Detroit, where "French" or "French Canadian" remained the norm. (Francophone John R. Williams of Detroit tellingly scratched out the word "Canadiens" in a letter dated July 6, 1808, and replaced it with "natives of this country." My thanks to Mara Harwel for bringing this to my attention.) That said, I think this francophone zone as it emerged after 1763, being anchored by St. Louis, fits the term "Creole Corridor," if a bit uncomfortably. See Carl A. Brasseaux, *French, Cajun, Creole, Houma: A Primer on Francophone Louisiana* (Baton Rouge: Louisiana State University Press, 2005). Several groups such as Les Amis in the St. Louis region are now promoting the establishment of a national heritage district using the terms "Creole Colonial District" and "Creole Colonial Corridor" in their literature.
6. Norman Gelb, ed., *Jonathan Carver's Travels through America, 1766–1768* (New York: John Wiley & Sons, 1993), 76.

7. For Pond's full description, see "Memoir of Peter Pond [1773]," in Charles M. Gates, ed., *Five Fur Traders of the Northwest* (St. Paul: Minnesota Historical Society, 1965). See also Scanlan, *Prairie du Chien*, and Mary Antoine de Julio, "Prairie du Chien and the Rediscovery of Its French Log Houses," in Michael Roark, ed., *French and Germans in the Mississippi Valley: Landscape and Cultural Traditions* (Cape Girardeau, Mo.: Center for Regional History and Cultural Heritage, Southeast Missouri State University, 1988), 98–110.

8. Murphy, *A Gathering of Rivers*, 50. See also, Peterson, "The People In Between."

9. Quoted in Phillips, *Fur Trade*, I:589.

10. Quoted in Keith R. Widder, "The French Connection: The Interior French and Their Role in French-British Relations in the Western Great Lakes Region, 1760–1775," in David Curtis Skaggs and Larry L. Nelson, eds., *The Sixty Years' War for the Great Lakes, 1754–1814* (East Lansing: Michigan State University Press, 2001), 137.

11. Archibald, "From 'La Louisiane' to 'Luisiana,'" 30–32; Nasatir, "Government Employees"; Bannon, "The Spaniards and the Illinois Country," 113–114.

12. Banner, *Legal Systems in Conflict*, 17–22. For more on the constructive role of Spanish government in Lower Louisiana, see Gilbert C. Din and John E. Harkins, *The New Orleans Cabildo: Colonial Louisiana's First City Government, 1769–1803* (Baton Rouge: Louisiana State University Press, 1996). On the role of the Chouteaus in maintaining Indian relations during the Spanish regime, see Foley and Rice, *The First Chouteaus*, ch. 3.

13. Quoted in Rea, *Major Robert Farmar*, 37.

14. Morris, *Journal of Captain Thomas Morris*.

15. My rather condensed analysis draws heavily upon the considerable number of brilliant overviews of this period: White, *The Middle Ground*; Hinderaker, *Elusive Empires*; Calloway, *The Scratch of a Pen*; Anderson, *Crucible of War: The Seven Years' War and the Fate of Empire in British North America, 1754–1766* (New York: Alfred Knopf, 2000); Michael N. McConnell, *A Country Between: The Upper Ohio Valley and Its Peoples, 1724–1774* (Lincoln: University of Nebraska Press, 1992); Jane T. Merritt, *At the Crossroads: Indians and Empires on a Mid-Atlantic Frontier, 1700–1763* (Chapel Hill: University of North Carolina Press, 2003); Merrell, *Into the American Woods*; and Gregory E. Dowd, *War under Heaven: Pontiac, the Indian Nations, and the British Empire* (Baltimore: Johns Hopkins University Press, 2002).

16. Hinderaker, *Elusive Empires*, 160, 162.

17. Calloway, *The Scratch of a Pen*, 168. As Calloway notes, to finish the quotation: "They [then—after the American Revolution] turned to the kind of empire they did best—an ocean-based commercial empire." At that point, their position in the fur trade increased considerably.

18. Quoted in Susan Sleeper-Smith, "'Ignorant bigots and busy rebels': The American Revolution in the Western Great Lakes," in Skaggs and Nelson, eds., *The Sixty Years' War*, 159.

19. There was some truth to this. For a neglected aspect of this story, see Carl A. Brasseaux and Michael J. Leblanc, "Franco-Indian Diplomacy in the Mississippi Valley, 1754–1763: Prelude to Pontiac's Uprising?," *Journal de la Société des Américanistes*,

LXVIII (1982), 59–71. See also David Dixon, *Never Come to Peace Again: Pontiac's Uprising and the Fate of the British Empire in North America* (Norman: University of Oklahoma Press, 2005).

20. Sosin, "The French Settlements in British Policy," summarizes with great clarity the attitudes and policies of British officials vis-à-vis the French during this period. Documentation can be found in Carter, ed., *Correspondence of General Thomas Gage*; Clarence W. Alvord and Clarence E. Carter, eds., *The Critical Period, 1763–1765* (Springfield: Illinois State Historical Library, 1915); Alvord and Carter, eds., *The New Régime*; Alvord and Carter, eds., *Trade and Politics*. These volumes constitute vols. 10, 11, and 16 of the Collections of the Illinois State Historical Library, British Series, vols. 1–3. Tousignant, "The Integration of the Province of Quebec," provides a wonderful overview of the period, and Lawson, *The Imperial Challenge*, throws a whole new light on British imperial philosophy and policy during this period, reexamining the issues that governing Quebec engendered. In the process, Lawson not only clarifies the discourse that surrounded the Quebec Act of 1774, he also broadens our understanding of minor issues affecting western policy. On the curious absence of civil jurisdiction in the British portion of the Creole Corridor in the West, see Neatby, *The Administration of Justice*.

21. Quoted in Widder, "The French Connection," 128.

22. For the clearest history of British fur-trade policy during this period, see Phillips, *Fur Trade*, I, chs. 27 and 28.

23. Quoted in Calloway, *The Scratch of a Pen*, 127.

24. Ibid., 125.

25. Quoted in Phillips, *Fur Trade*, I:598.

26. For the story of Baynton, Wharton, and Morgan's efforts in the Illinois country and their role in the larger contexts of British policy and the imperial economy, see Marjorie G. Reid, "The Quebec Fur-Traders and Western Policy, 1763–1774," *Canadian Historical Review*, 6:1 (March 1925), 15–32; Charles M. Thomas, "Successful and Unsuccessful Merchants in the Illinois Country," *Journal of the Illinois State Historical Society*, 30:4 (January 1938), 429–440; Dunn, *The New Imperial Economy*; and Hinderaker, *Elusive Empires*, 163–170.

27. Widder, "The French Connection," 133.

28. Quoted in Cayton, *Frontier Indiana*, 62–63.

29. Faragher, *A Great and Noble Scheme*. It is interesting to note that one officer, Captain George Turnbull, described the French as people who "have adopted the very Principles and Ideas of Indians, and Differ from them only a Little in Colour." Quoted in Widder, "The French Connection," 134.

30. Ibid., 63–64.

31. Reid, "Quebec Fur-Traders and Western Policy," 30–31.

32. Alvord and Carter, eds., *Invitation Serieuse*.

33. The best overview of British-Indian relations during this period is Calloway, *Crown and Calumet*. Calloway's article "Foundations of Sand: The Fur Trade and British-Indian Relations, 1783–1815" and Peter Marshall, "The Government of the Quebec Fur Trade: An Imperial Dilemma, 1761–1775," in Trigger et al., eds., *Le Castor Fait*

Tout, offer convenient summaries of the politics of British fur trade policy. Stevens, *The Northwest Fur Trade*, written as a doctoral dissertation under Clarence Alvord, remains the most complete study of the fur trade in this region during this period.

34. Shelburne to Board of Trade, October 5, 1767, quoted in Phillips, *Fur Trade*, I:583.

35. On this point, see Nicolas de Finiels, *An Account of Upper Louisiana*, 53.

36. Hinderaker, *Elusive Empires*, 172.

37. Ibid., 184, 175.

38. Sosin, *The Revolutionary Frontier*, 60.

39. Foley and Rice, *The First Chouteaus*, 37.

40. Great Britain had entertained the notion of seizing New Orleans in 1771 when war with Spain over the Falkland Islands seemed imminent. See Alvord, *The Mississippi Valley in British Politics*, 50. On British war aims and efforts in the West during the American Revolution, see, in addition to Alvord, Horsman, "Great Britain and the Illinois Country; Armour and Widder, *At the Crossroads*; Stevens, *Northwest Fur Trade*. On the contraband trade, see Carter, *Great Britain and the Illinois Country*; and Phillips, *Fur Trade*. Documents concerned with this trade can be found throughout the three volumes edited by Alvord and Carter (see esp. the Gage-Shelburne, Gage-Hillsborough correspondences in *Trade and Politics*) cited above and in Kinnaird, ed., *Spain in the Mississippi Valley*. For Spanish policy, see Nasatir, "The Anglo-Spanish Frontier; Nasatir, *Borderland in Retreat*; and Nasatir, *Spanish War Vessels*.

41. For a much more accurate and believable local reading of the event, see Brown, *History as They Lived It*, 170–172. On the British situation in Illinois at that time, see Paul L. Stevens, "'To Keep the Indians of the Wabache in His Majesty's Interest': The Indian Diplomacy of Edward Abbott, British Lieutenant Governor of Vincennes, 1776–1778," *Indiana Magazine of History*, 83:2 (June 1987), 141–172.

42. Evans, ed., *Detroit to Fort Sackville*, 108–111. See also James, ed., *George Rogers Clark Papers*; Barnhart, *Henry Hamilton*; and Seineke, ed., *The George Rogers Clark Adventure*.

43. Paul L. Stevens, ed., *Louis Lorimier in the American Revolution, 1777–1782: A Mémoire by an Ohio Indian Trader and British Partisan* (Naperville, Ill.: Center for French Colonial Studies, Extended Publications Series, No. 2, 1997), 5.

44. Lernoult to Haldimand, March 26, 1779, *Michigan Pioneer and Historical Collections*, X (Lansing, Mich., 1888), 328, quoted in Philip P. Mason, *Detroit, Fort Lernoult, and the American Revolution* (Detroit: Wayne State University Press, 1964), and Sleeper-Smith, "'Ignorant bigots and busy rebels,'" 155.

45. Wyman, *The Wisconsin Frontier*, 94.

46. White, *The Middle Ground*, 377.

47. Ibid., 375.

48. Ibid., 371.

49. Quoted in Calloway, *The Scratch of a Pen*, 125.

50. Barnhart, ed., "The Letterbooks," 75, 250.

51. John Francis McDermott, "The Myth of the 'Imbecile Governor': Captain Fernando de Leyba and the Defense of St. Louis in 1780," in McDermott, ed., *The Spanish in the Mississippi Valley*, 339; Hodes, *Beyond the Frontier*, 185.

52. Sleeper-Smith, "'Ignorant bigots and busy rebels'"; Musick, *St. Louis as a Fortified Town*, ch. 9. There is an interesting and significant complication regarding the second attack on St. Joseph led by Pourré in February 1781. The Milwaukee band of Potawatomis led by a chief named Siggenauk or Blackbird (known as Le Tourneau to the French, El Heturno to the Spanish) most probably instigated this attack, which—from a native perspective—was an assault on a rival Potawatomi band led by Le Petit Bled or Little Corn. Siggenauk had supported the Americans and the Spanish during the British attack on St. Louis in 1780. He apparently proposed the second St. Joseph attack to Francisco Cruzat, the Spanish lieutenant governor at St. Louis. Cruzat felt obligated to honor the request and organized the expedition. In short, the events in this region at this time were shaped by tribal rivalries as well as by the competing interests of French traders, nations, and empires. I am indebted to Carolyn Gilman, special projects historian at the Missouri History Museum of St. Louis, for pointing this out and sharing her research with me.
53. Quaife, ed., *The Siege of Detroit*, 96.
54. Widder, "The French Connection," 127.
55. For more on both men, see Ekberg, *Colonial Ste. Genevieve*.
56. For more on Cerré, see Faribault-Beauregard, ed., *La vie aux Illinois*, and Douglas, "Jean Gabriel Cerré." On Papin, see Cunningham and Blythe, *The Founding Family*, and Admyrauld and Sons to Joseph Marie Papin, February 3, 1792, CCMO. On Menard, see Seineke, ed., *Guide to the Microfilm Edition*, 1–17.
57. See Miquelon, ed., *Society and Conquest*, and Igartua, "The Merchants of Montreal." The list of merchants of Montreal that Igartua profiles reads like a Who's Who of the American fur trade during the first half of the nineteenth century: Charles Réaume, Louis Blondeau, François Berthelet, Nicholas Marchesseau, Antoine Reihle, Simon Sanguinet, Pierre Hurtebise, Antoine Janisse, Hyacinthe Lasselle, etc. These merchants and their descendants settled all over the French Midwest—in Missouri, Michigan, Wisconsin, Indiana, and the like. Because of a variety of factors, some of their descendants wound up in Indian country in a marginal economic situation; others prospered and became town founders and/or privileged bourgeois. Their relationships with Indian women do not seem to offer a reliable basis for predicting their success as businessmen and American citizens.
58. See footnote 26 in the introduction for sources.
59. See Stevens, *Northwest Fur Trade*, and Anson, "The Fur Traders."
60. See Foley and Rice, *The First Chouteaus*, ch. 3.
61. Clark, *New Orleans*, 356–357.
62. Bradley J. Birzer, "French Imperial Remnants on the Middle Ground: The Strange Case of August de la Balme and Charles Beaubien," *Journal of the Illinois State Historical Society* (Summer 2000).
63. Barnhart, ed. "The Letterbooks," 67–70.
64. Hinderaker, *Elusive Empires*, 186.
65. White, *The Middle Ground*, 421–433.
66. Stevens, *Lorimier*, 6. As Stevens points out, some of the French supported the British

regime. They often did so for personal reasons—and not only economic ones. In addition to having Shawnee connections and being dependent on British trade, Lorimier had three brothers who took commissions in His Majesty's service back in Quebec. In Detroit in 1777, Lieutenant Governor Hamilton commissioned a dozen Canadien gentry as departmental officers, including Fontenoy de Quindre. These Frenchmen may well have been following a time-honored tradition of the *Canadien noblesse*. See Stevens, *Lorimier*, 10.

67. White, *The Middle Ground*, 431.
68. Quoted in Bald, *Detroit's First American Decade*, 12.
69. Ibid., 11.
70. Ibid., 11–15.
71. Barnhart, ed., "The Letterbooks," 106.
72. P.-L. Panet to Auguste Chouteau, May 18, 1804, CCMO.

CHAPTER 3. SURVIVING THE TRANSITION TO AMERICAN RULE

1. Auguste Chouteau to Baron de Carondelet, December 8, 1796, CCMO.
2. Chouteau to Gayoso, June 24, 1797, CCMO.
3. Foley and Rice, *The First Chouteaus*, 53.
4. Ibid., 198; Billon, *Annals of St. Louis*, 72.
5. Lecompte, "Pierre Chouteau, Jr.," 46.
6. Trudeau to Vallé, December 1792, Vallé Papers, Ste. Genevieve Archives, Missouri Historical Society, St. Louis. The French in Upper Louisiana had ample opportunity to observe Anglo-Americans. A generous Spanish land policy attracted immigrants from the states. By 1804, three-fifths of the ten thousand inhabitants of Upper Louisiana were Americans. The French still occupied most leadership positions and dominated the fur trade and commerce of the region.
7. Tardiveau to Gratiot, March 21, 1799, CCMO.
8.

> Welcome here, dear son of sodomy
> Welcome man of Romish habits
> And you detestable whore whose cunt disgusts us
> Go to the homes of the Americans,
> There you will find people who will fuck you.

Misc. manuscripts, recorded in Ste. Genevieve in the 1790s, attributed to the Bolduc family, Music Collection, Box 3, Missouri Historical Society, St. Louis. According to David Barry, professor of modern languages at the University of Louisiana–Lafayette, the use of the plural *les* in the first line may be an oblique reference to "money or goods"—a nod to the church practice of selling dispensations, which was a Jacobin target. *Milieux* in the second line can also be translated as "from the middle of"—another possible reference to sodomy. Carl Brasseaux, professor of history at the University of Louisiana–Lafayette, suspects the poem might have been written by Henri Peyroux de la Coudreniere. I thank them both for their help with this unusual and rare glimpse into the feelings of the French in this region at this time.

9. Dargo, *Jefferson's Louisiana*, 10.

10. See chs. 2 and 3 in Foley and Rice, *The First Chouteaus*; also McDermott, ed., *The Spanish in the Mississippi Valley*; Kinnaird, ed., *Spain in the Mississippi Valley, 1765–94*; Nasatir, ed., *Before Lewis and Clark*.

11. Kmen, *Music in New Orleans*, 27–29.

12. Quoted in Dargo, *Jefferson's Louisiana*, 82.

13. Kettner, *The Development of American Citizenship*, 251.

14. One could add, of course, that the French seemed too closely allied to the many Indian groups in the region.

15. Frederick Bates to Richard Bates, December 17, 1807, in Marshall, ed., *The Life and Papers of Frederick Bates*, I:237–247.

16. Gallatin to Jefferson, August 20, 1804, in Henry Adams, ed., *Writings of Albert Gallatin*, 3 vols. (Philadelphia, 1870), I:202.

17. Quoted in Dargo, *Jefferson's Louisiana*, 182.

18. Ibid., 182, and Fossier, *New Orleans*, 94. Ironically, Eustis's nephew George moved to New Orleans and ultimately became the attorney general of Louisiana. George's son—also George Eustis—went to Harvard Law School, was elected to Congress from Louisiana, went to France as secretary of the Confederate legation, and died there in 1872. The New Englanders had been transformed.

19. Berthold, *Glimpses of Creole Life*.

20. Gallatin to Jefferson, August 20, 1804, in Adams, ed., *Writings of Albert Gallatin*, I:202–203.

21. See Hammes, "Land Transactions," 110–111.

22. Much of this information comes from Paul F. Lachance, "The Foreign French," in Hirsch and Logsdon, eds., *Creole New Orleans*, 101–130.

23. Tregle, *Louisiana in the Age of Jackson*, 100.

24. See Holli, "French Detroit," 81–90. For more on Campau and this characterization, see Chapter 7. Campau died in 1863, and his estate was valued at three million dollars.

25. Bald, *Detroit's First American Decade*, 205.

26. See Bell, *Revolution, Romanticism*, ch. 5, "French Freemasonry and the Republican Heritage."

27. Meneray, ed., *The Rebellion of 1768*, 103.

28. Quoted in de Lagrave, *Voltaire's Man in America*, 55–56.

29. Ibid.

30. Quoted in Houck, *A History of Missouri*, II:391.

31. *Collections of the Pioneer and Historical Society of Michigan*, vol. VIII (Lansing, Mich., 1886), 587–592.

32. John R. Williams to François Navarre, August 31, 1819, Navarre Family Papers, Burton Historical Collection, Detroit Public Library, Detroit, Michigan. The French reads: "Je vous exhorte mon cher colonel, ainçi que tous nos amis & concitoyens, de tenir

ferme—soyez assuré que la conteste est veritablement entre nous, les natifs du pays, & les Etrangers qui voudroient deja insolémment nous ravir nos droits & nos priviléges naturels."

33. "Memoire of Bernard Marigny Resident of Louisiana addressed to His Fellow-Citizens," (Paris, 1822), trans. Olivia Blanchard, in New Orleans Municipal Papers, Howard-Tilton Memorial Library, Tulane University, 20–21.

34. Fossier, *New Orleans*, 95.

35. Primm, *Lion of the Valley*, 80.

36. Louis Nicholas Fortin to Antoine Marechal, July 25, 1803, Lasselle Papers, Indiana State Library, Indiana Division, Indianapolis; hereafter cited as LIND.

37. Banner, *Legal Systems in Conflict*, 94.

38. Dargo, *Jefferson's Louisiana*, 13–17; see also Arnold, *Unequal Laws*.

39. For more on this and the pro-francophone state constitution of 1812, see Chapter 8. On the legal history of Louisiana and Canada, see Billings and Fernandez, eds., *A Law unto Itself?*; Fernandez, *From Chaos to Continuity*; Greenwood, *Legacies of Fear*; Dargo, *Jefferson's Louisiana*; Haas, ed., *Louisiana's Legal Heritage*; and Young, *The Politics of Codification*. In Missouri, as Stuart Banner points out, the unwritten legal norms of the French were replaced by imported Anglo-American written law that served the needs of an increasingly diverse public. See Banner, *Legal Systems in Conflict*, ch. 7.

40. Primm, *Lion of the Valley*, 80.

41. See Alvord, ed., *Kaskaskia Records*; also McDermott, ed., *Old Cahokia*. For a good recent discussion of the slavery problem, see Finkelman, "Slavery and the Northwest Ordinance; also J. P. Dunn Jr., *Indiana: A Redemption from Slavery* (Boston, 1888).

42. Myer, "Charles Gratiot's Land Claim Problems."

43. See, for example, Documents 26, 300, 410, 426, and 511, Vigo Papers, Indiana Historical Society, Indianapolis.

44. Foley, "The Lewis and Clark Expedition's Silent Partners"; Foley and Rice, *The First Chouteaus*, 89–93.

45. Houck, *A History of Missouri*, II:381; on Lorimier, see Usner, "An American Indian Gateway."

46. Foley and Rice, *The First Chouteaus*, 91. The Spanish official, Charles Dehault Delassus (the uncle of Ceran St. Vrain), finally returned to St. Louis in 1836 on a visit to see old friends and arrange for the sale of lands that had recently been confirmed to him by a decision of the Supreme Court. See Gates, *History of Public Land Law Development*, ch. 6, on private land claims; and McDermott, ed., "Diary of Charles Dehault Delassus."

47. This grant was the subject of much controversy. After a long history of attempts to have this huge claim confirmed, it was finally rejected by the Supreme Court in 1853. Dubuque had sold the claim to satisfy his debts to Auguste Chouteau and John Mullanphy. Mullanphy, an occasional business associate of the Chouteaus, was born in Ireland in 1758, served in the Irish Brigade of the French Army until 1789, and sailed for America in 1792. He spent six years in Philadelphia and Baltimore where he became a fast friend Bishop John Carroll. According to Carroll, Mullanphy was dis-

turbed by the "profaness [*sic*] of the numerous French democrats." Nevertheless, Mullanphy maintained good relations with the St. Louis Creoles, most of whom were at least lukewarm supporters of Catholic institutions. Mullanphy was the second largest taxpayer in St. Louis in 1820 after Auguste Chouteau. His wealth was assured when he cornered the cotton market in Louisiana right before the Battle of New Orleans in 1815. See Alice L. Cochran, "The Mullanphys at Mid-Century: The First and Second Generations," in Russell M. Magnaghi, ed., *From the Mississippi to the Pacific: Essays in Honor of John Francis Bannon, SJ* (Marquette: Northern Michigan University Press, 1982).

48. Primm, *Lion of the Valley*, 80; Foley and Rice, *The First Chouteaus*, 100–101; Houck, *A History of Missouri*, II:400–401.

49. For more on this story, see Gates, *History of Public Land Law*, ch. 6; Primm, *Lion of the Valley*, 80–88; Billon, *Annals*; and *Missouri Land Claims*. For more on Bates, see Gitlin, "Avec bien du regret": The Americanization of Creole St. Louis," *Gateway Heritage*, 9:4 (Spring 1989), 2–11, and Marshall, ed., *The Life and Papers of Frederick Bates*.

50. Davis, "Community and Conflict," 341.

51. Foley and Rice, *The First Chouteaus*, 112–126.

52. Edward Hempstead to Stephen Hempstead, March 11, 1805, Hempstead Papers, Missouri Historical Society, St. Louis.

53. Foley and Rice, *The First Chouteaus*, 126.

54. Gratiot and his family often took the lead in making alliances with the Americans. Gratiot, married to Victoire Chouteau, was born in Lausanne, Switzerland. His ancestors were Huguenots, and he learned the mercantile trade by serving apprenticeships with two uncles, one in London and one in Montreal. He supported the American Revolution while a resident in the Illinois country and was one of the few Frenchmen to welcome with enthusiasm the new regime at the time of the transfer.

55. Charless to P. Chouteau, October 7, 1810, CCMO.

56. David Diggs to Auguste Chouteau, October 25, 1822; August 25, 1823; September 8, 1826, CCMO.

57. Mullanphy to A. Chouteau, November, 25, 1807, CCMO.

58. Lecompte, "Pierre Chouteau, Jr.," 26–27.

59. Gracy, *Moses Austin*, 126.

60. For more on the Gratiots' activities, see Mahoney, *Provincial Lives*, ch. 2, and Susan Burdick Davis, *Old Forts and Real Folks*, 184–198.

61. Boilvin to Julien Dubuque, May 22, 1809; Saucier to P. Chouteau, June 19, 1811, CCMO.

62. Ray H. Mattison, "John Pierre Cabanné, Sr.," in LeRoy R. Hafen, ed., *Fur Traders, Trappers, and Mountain Men of the Upper Missouri* (Lincoln: University of Nebraska Press, 1995), 16.

63. Bent to A. Chouteau, February 21, 1813, CCMO.

64. Owens to Gratiot, December 11, 1814, CCMO.

65. See Kastor, *The Nation's Crucible*, 160–163. He points out that the constitution writers in Louisiana (in 1811–1812) and in Philadelphia (in 1787) had paid little attention to

the "relation between state and federal citizenship." See also Kettner, *The Development of American Citizenship*, 252–253.

66. Reports, December 23, 1812, and December 20, 1813, Forsyth Papers, Missouri Historical Society, St. Louis. See also Matson, *Pioneers of Illinois*, 239–273.

67. *Collections of the Pioneer and Historical Society of Michigan*, vol. 8, 642–652; see also, Stagg, *Mr. Madison's War*, 225; C. Glenn Clift, *Remember the Raisin* (Frankfort: Kentucky Historical Society, 1961); and Fabre-Surveyer, "From Montreal to Michigan and Indiana," 72–73. The situation in Detroit was complicated by the fire of 1805, which dictated that the entire town be rebuilt. Despite some animosity, the French seemed to have adjusted quite well to American rule during its first decade. The second decade opened less auspiciously with the great fire and the arrival soon thereafter of the first governor of the newly created Territory of Michigan, General William Hull. Hull quickly alienated the French majority. They grew so exasperated by 1809 that they sent a petition to President Madison requesting that Hull be removed. Among their many complaints were the following: that Hull encouraged runaway slaves—indeed, had formed them into a military company and appointed a black man to be their commander; that Hull seemed deficient in military judgment, an opinion that was to be confirmed in only three years; that Hull did not bother to translate his proclamations or the laws of the territory into French; and finally, that Hull was essentially a pompous ass. The outbreak of hostilities in the Old Northwest in 1811 found the French citizens of Michigan in a less-than-patriotic mood.

68. Grignon, "Seventy-two Years' Recollections of Wisconsin." For more on the War of 1812 in Wisconsin, see Wyman, *The Wisconsin Frontier*, 120–126.

69. Foley and Rice, *The First Chouteaus*, ch. 8.

70. William Burnett in 1791, quoted in Anson, "The Fur Traders," 29.

71. James L. Clayton, "The Growth and Economic Significance of the American Fur Trade, 1790–1890," in Morgan et al., eds., *Aspects of the Fur Trade*, 68. More on this practice in footnote 1 of Chapter 4.

72. Anson, "The Fur Traders," 170.

CHAPTER 4. HOW THE WEST WAS SOLD

1. James L. Clayton, "The Impact of Traders' Claims in the American Fur Trade," in Ellis, ed., *The Frontier in American Development*, 301–302. Clayton credits William Clark and Auguste Chouteau as being the innovators, but it seems that the practice had begun earlier in treaties signed with the Choctaws and Chickasaws in 1805. In both of these cases, the Indians were heavily indebted to Panton, Leslie and Company, the trading powerhouse of the Southeast (actually operating as John Forbes and Company at this point). See Prucha, *American Indian Treaties*, 105–110; and Coker and Watson, *Indian Traders*, ch. 12. However, Prucha himself, on page 140, credits the 1825 Osage treaty as initiating the practice of paying "specific debts owed by the tribe." Whatever the distinctions, it is fair to claim that the Chouteaus became the masters of this practice and that the 1825 treaty led directly to an expansion of this aspect of treaty-making.

2. For a detailed account of Benton's first years, see Primm, *Lion of the Valley*, 114–117. Edward Hempstead died suddenly in 1817 at the age of thirty-eight. Benton quickly became the most prominent public face of "the Little Junto." That same year, he killed Charles Lucas, son of Judge Lucas, in a duel.

3. See Gates, *History of Public Land Law Development*, ch. 6, "Private Land Claims."

4. Thomas Hart Benton to Bernard Pratte, January 23, 1824, CCMO.

5. Lecompte, "Pierre Chouteau, Jr.," 46.

6. See Steffen, *William Clark*; Beers, *The Western Military Frontier*, 107–108; and Trennert, *Alternative to Extinction*, 18.

7. See Sunder, *Joshua Pilcher*, 151.

8. Still the best accounts of the American Fur Company and Astor are Porter, *John Jacob Astor*, and Lavender, *The Fist in the Wilderness*. Haeger, *John Jacob Astor: Business and Finance in the Early Republic*, provides excellent coverage of Astor's financial and real estate dealings.

9. For more details, see Wishart, *The Fur Trade*; Sunder, *The Fur Trade*; Lecompte, "Pierre Chouteau, Jr."; and Michel, "The St. Louis Fur Trade." The details of this company expansion are overwhelming, as anyone who has looked at the Chouteau Collections will agree. A definitive monograph, not surprisingly, has not been written.

10. See CCMO, November 19, 1850, and February 27, 1851 (Chouteau-Maffitt Papers).

11. See, for examples, December 29 and 31, 1830, and October 14, 1831, CCMO; also, James L. Clayton, "The Growth and Economic Significance of the American Fur Trade, 1790–1890," in Morgan et al., eds., *Aspects of the Fur Trade*, 65.

12. Trennert, *Indian Traders*, 99.

13. For the hotel receipt, see CCMO (Chouteau-Maffitt Papers), May 25, 1837; for the itemized claim, see the same collection, September 1837.

14. Trennert, *Indian Traders*, 110–111.

15. For some representative documents, see April 9, 1831; July 1838; September 10, 1839; February 1840; November 15, 1840; December 21, 1840; June 17, 1846; January 28, 1847; May 8, 1847; January 1, 1848; and December 5, 1849, CCMO.

16. For the Traverse des Sioux Treaty, see Trennert, *Indian Traders*, ch. 7, and Gilman, *Henry Hastings Sibley*, ch. 9. Gilman's account and figures differ somewhat from Trennert's. For the transportation contract, see Lass, *A History of Steamboating*, 24–25.

17. For a fuller look at Richardville and the process of treaty-making in Indiana, see Jay Gitlin, "Private Diplomacy to Private Property: States, Tribes, and Nations in the Early National Period," *Diplomatic History*, 22:1 (Winter 1998), 85–99.

18. Isabel F. Dolch, "Calendar of Pierre Chouteau-Maffitt Papers regarding the Fur Trade" (1922), in Missouri Historical Society, St. Louis, 192.

19. Trennert, *Indian Traders*, 202–203.

20. Clayton, "Growth and Economic Significance," 68.

21. Quoted in Hagan, *American Indians*, 121.

22. Adler, *British Investment*, 176.

23. Primm, *Lion of the Valley*, 210.

24. For information on the activities of Pierre Chouteau Jr. and John F. A. Sanford, see

CCMO for the years 1834–1890. A convenient summary is Lecompte, "Pierre Chouteau, Jr.," and "John F. A. Sanford."

25. Lecompte, "Pierre Chouteau, Jr.," 52.

26. Sunder, *The Fur Trade*, 169.

27. Ibid.

28. John Mullan to Charles P. Chouteau, March 11, 1861, CCMO.

29. Sunder, *The Fur Trade*, 261.

30. For information on the Ewings, see Trennert, *Indian Traders*.

31. Miami chief Richardville was also reported, at the time of his death, to be the richest man in Indiana—though one historian has suggested that his people expected him "to be generous." Richardville's son-in-law, Francis Lafontaine, succeeded him and later helped found the town of Kokomo, Indiana. See Gitlin, "Private Diplomacy to Private Property."

32. The best summary of these relations and schemes is Anson, "The Fur Traders." For more on kinship ties, see Fabre-Surveyer, "From Montreal to Michigan and Indiana."

33. Anson, "The Fur Traders," 143.

34. McKee, ed., *The Trail of Death*, 102–103.

35. Quoted in Mahoney, *Provincial Lives*, 57.

36. See Anson, "The Fur Traders," 170–200.

37. See McKee, *The Trail of Death*.

38. Until the rush of settlement became overwhelming, not only French traders, but also Anglo-American settlers might enjoy cooperative and neighborly relations with local native communities. We should also observe that the removal process in states such as Michigan and Indiana was complex and did not replicate the experience of tribal groups in the South. See, for example, Gray, *The Yankee West*, ch. 3; and John Mack Faragher, "'More Motley than Mackinaw': From Ethnic Mixing to Ethnic Cleansing on the Frontier of the Lower Missouri, 1783–1833," in Cayton and Teute, eds., *Contact Points*, 304–326; and Bethel Saler, *A Settlers' Empire: State Formation and Colonialism in America's Old Northwest, 1783–1854* (Philadelphia: University of Pennsylvania Press, forthcoming).

39. Frederick Buhl to Antoine Campau, June 4, 1867, Campau Family Collection, Grand Rapids History and Special Collections Center, Grand Rapids Public Library, Grand Rapids, Michigan.

40. John H. Thompson (on behalf of Pierre Chouteau Jr. and Company) to Antoine Campau, September 8, 1858, and Frederick Buhl to Antoine Campau, September 10, 1858, Campau Family Collection, Grand Rapids History and Special Collections Center, Grand Rapids Public Library, Grand Rapids, Michigan. The collection also includes a variety of newspaper clippings relating to Louis Campau. One clipping from 1964 describes Campau as "A Friend of the Indians." A later article describes him as "the man who sold the firewater to the Indians." Both articles use the same photograph of Louis and his wife, Sophie de Marsac Campau. The emphasis clearly changed with the times, but the historical reality undoubtedly justified both conclusions. It is not

clear from the records exactly why Chouteau felt compelled to present Antoine Campau with a gold watch, but I suspect from the timing that it had to do with the windfall profits generated by the cash payments allowed in the treaty of 1855 with the Ottawas and Chippewas.

41. This was less true in Indiana than in St. Louis and New Orleans. See Lachance, "Intermarriage."

42. Fabre-Surveyer, "From Montreal to Michigan and Indiana," 74.

43. Lasselle and Pierre St. Germain, agreement to manage distillery, November 21, 1810, LIND; Peter Jones to Lasselle, account, 1810–1813, LIND.

44. See invitation of February, 10, 1824, LIND.

45. Bullitt to Lasselle, May 29, 1817; deed transfer from Louizon to Lasselle, October 28, 1832; Coquillard to Lasselle, June 16, 1835, LIND; see also Fabre-Surveyer, "From Montreal to Michigan and Indiana."

46. For more on Tipton, see Gitlin, "Private Diplomacy to Private Property."

47. See correspondence for April 1820, LIND.

48. See Finkelman, "Slavery and the Northwest Ordinance"; *Lasselle v. Polly*, negress, July 27, 1820, LIND.

49. Fraser to Lasselle, October 14, 1823, and Chambers to Lasselle, July 23, 1831, LIND.

50. Subscription notice, August 26, 1830, LIND.

51. See, for example, Bruté to Lasselle, March 13, 1835, LIND.

52. One might also observe that in Montana, as in other frontier areas, native individuals and communities also participated in a whole range of economic activities, sometimes in connection with French and métis neighbors. The success of such activities may have spurred the establishment of reservation boundaries and restrictions on native endeavors to benefit incoming entrepreneurs. The economic history of tribal communities has yet to be fully explored and may well reveal some interesting revisions to our standard accounts.

CHAPTER 5. BEYOND ST. LOUIS

1. For an excellent discussion of the somewhat anomalous nature of this vast, unincorporated, and complex company—capitalized in 1839 at five hundred thousand dollars yet operating as a family business—see Sunder, *The Fur Trade*, ch. 1. As Sunder observes: "The Company reorganized almost yearly during the forties. The bookkeepers, harassed and overworked, simply numbered each reorganization as if it were a new French Republic! 'Company 3' followed 'Company 2' and was, in turn, succeeded by 'Company 4'" (p. 7).

2. Ronda, *Finding the West*, 79.

3. For Lisa's activities, see Oglesby, *Manuel Lisa*. For the Chouteau activities during this period, see Foley and Rice, *The First Chouteaus*, and Lecompte, "Pierre Chouteau, Jr." 25. The Lecompte entry is from the Bison Book reprint edition.

4. Foley and Rice, *The First Chouteaus*, 135.

5. Thorne, *The Many Hands of My Relations*, 137–140. Thorne's book traces the incredibly complex history of French and Indian relations and métis families and commu-

nities in this region from the founding of St. Louis until the 1880s. Though the story I
tell is a different one, it should be read along with the one in Thorne's book. For Côte
Sans Dessein, also see Bell, *Côte Sans Dessein*, and Schake, *La Charrette*.

6. Garraghan, *Catholic Beginnings*, 68, 121.

7. As Tanis Thorne points out, the move away from St. Charles was also due to a variety
   of "push" factors, including indebtedness, taxes, and the rise in land values caused by
   the influx of Anglo-American farmers. Add alcoholism to this, and the result was an
   increase in properties being sold for back taxes and acquired through merchants' liens.
   See Thorne, *The Many Hands of My Relations*, 124–125.

8. Stephen Warren points out that French was the "most commonly spoken European
   language" among the Shawnees. See Warren, *The Shawnees and Their Neighbors*,
   76.

9. Ibid., 89. See also Aron, *American Confluence*, 203–216, and Prucha, *American Indian
   Policy*, 229–273.

10. Sunder, *The Fur Trade*, 19.

11. William B. Astor to Pierre Chouteau Jr., May 18, 1833, CCMO.

12. Frederick Jackson Turner, *The Character and Influence of the Indian Trade in Wis-
    consin: A Study of the Trading Post as an Institution*, ed. David Harry Miller and
    William W. Savage, Jr. (Norman: University of Oklahoma Press, 1977), 75–79.

13. Franklin G. Adams, compiler, "Reminiscences of Frederick Chouteau," *Transactions
    of the Kansas State Historical Society*, vol. 8 (1903–1904), 425, 431.

14. Ibid., 423.

15. McDermott, ed., *Tixier's Travels*, 87.

16. For more on A. P. Chouteau's life and career, see Janet Lecompte, "Auguste Pierre
    Chouteau," in *French Fur Traders and Voyageurs in the American West*, ed. LeRoy R.
    Hafen (Spokane, Wash.: Arthur H. Clark, 1995), 96–123, and the famous description
    of A. P. Chouteau's home in McDermott, ed., *The Western Journals of Washington
    Irving*, 108–112.

17. Lecompte, "Auguste Pierre Chouteau," 105.

18. Pierre Chouteau Jr. to Gabriel Sylvestre Chouteau, July 19, 1822, CCMO.

19. McDermott, ed., "Diary of Charles Dehault Delassus," 379.

20. Berthold & Chouteau had added Bernard Pratte as a partner. For more on the organi-
    zation of the St. Louis firm, see Chapter 6.

21. For more on the exact timing and location of the first post, see David Boutros, "Con-
    fluence of People and Place: The Chouteau Posts on the Missouri and Kansas Rivers,"
    in Marra, Pal, and Boutros, *Cher Oncle, Cher Papa*.

22. Marra, Pal, and Boutros, *Cher Oncle, Cher Papa*, 228.

23. Thorne, *The Many Hands of My Relations*, 150.

24. François Chouteau to Pierre Chouteau Jr., August 25, 1829, CCMO, and Marra, Pal,
    and Boutros, *Cher Oncle, Cher Papa*, 61.

25. McDermott, ed., *Tixier's Travels*, 130.

26. Thorne, *The Many Hands of My Relations*, 148.

27. McDermott, ed., *Tixier's Travels*, 148.

28. Lecompte, "Auguste Pierre Chouteau," 107. According to historian J. Frederick Fausz,

"Clermont's group was a faction of the Grand Osages that moved to the Three Forks region. After a 1794 Chickasaw ambush killed three important Osage chiefs at one time, the Chouteaus manipulated the succession by installing a compliant Paw-Hiu-Skah (Pawhuska/'Cheveux Blanc'/'White Hair') as the principal chief of the Grand Osages in Missouri, despite his lack of essential hereditary qualifications. In apparent protest, the rightful claimant, the young Gra-to-moh-se (Clermont II/'Iron Hawk'), led a large band of supporters south to the Verdigris River near present-day Clare-more, Oklahoma, joining, and giving legitimacy to, an earlier breakaway band under Cash-e-se-gra ('La Grande Piste'/'Makes Tracks Far Away'). There they found other Osages—Cheniers or 'Shainers'—who had long exploited the Arkansas territory to the south, which provided abundant game; huge salt deposits for fur preparation and food preservation; protection from raiding northern tribes; and the freedom for young men to pursue war honors with minimal scrutiny by Spanish officials and less interference from St. Louis merchants" (correspondence with the author, March 2, 2009). See also Thorne, *Many Hands of My Relations*, 105–106.

29. Thorne, *The Many Hands of My Relations*, ch. 2, and Tanis C. Thorne, "The Chou-teau Family and the Osage Trade: A Generational Study," in Thomas C. Buckley, ed., *Rendezvous: Selected Papers of the Fourth North American Fur Trade Conference, 1981* (St. Paul: n.p., 1984).

30. Thorne, *The Many Hands of My Relations*, 125.

31. Ibid., n. 42.

32. Lecompte, "Auguste Pierre Chouteau," 116–117.

33. Ibid., 107–122.

34. Lecompte, "Pierre Chouteau, Jr.," 56, and Pierre Chouteau Jr. Will, Wills Collection, Missouri Historical Society Archives, St. Louis.

35. The child's uncle, Pierre Louis Panet of Montreal, sent many frustrated letters to the elder Chouteau. A.A. lived with his aunt and uncle for four years and was dismissed from all the best schools in the city before returning home to St. Louis. See Foley and Rice, *The First Chouteaus*, 187–188.

36. Auguste A. Chouteau to Auguste Chouteau, August 19, 1828, CCMO.

37. McDermott, ed., "Diary of Charles Dehault Delassus," 385.

38. On the issue of polygyny, a standard practice among leading men of the Osage, see Thorne, *The Many Hands of My Relations*, 146.

39. McDermott, ed., *Tixier's Travels*, 151–152.

40. Theodore Papin to P. M. Papin, September 2, 1833, CCMO.

41. Thorne, *The Many Hands of My Relations*, 162, 167, 169.

42. Cunningham and Blythe, *The Founding Family*, 202.

43. Theodore Papin to P. M. Papin, September 2, 1833, CCMO.

44. Thorne, *The Many Hands of My Relations*, 163.

45. Ibid., 139, and Cunningham and Blythe, *The Founding Family*, 60–65.

46. Rodabaugh, *Frenchtown*, 18–21.

47. Lecompte, "Auguste Pierre Chouteau," 118.

48. Copy of 1835 treaty, dated March 14, 1835, in CCMO; also see Lecompte, "Auguste Pierre Chouteau," 122.

49. Thorne, "The Chouteau Family," 113, 118–119.
50. Marra, Pal, and Boutros, *Cher Oncle, Cher Papa*, 77–78.
51. Ibid., 15.
52. Ibid., 226.
53. Ibid., 100, 102, 104, 221.
54. Ibid., 123.
55. Ibid., 232–233.
56. Ibid., 128.
57. Ibid., 183.
58. Ibid., 185, 232.
59. Westport, a jumping-off place for the various overland trails, was four miles south of the settlements at Kawsmouth or Chouteau's Town and was annexed by Kansas City in 1897.
60. Thorne, *The Many Hands of My Relations*, 163, and McDermott, ed., *Tixier's Travels*, 98.
61. This interview was apparently retyped from the original article in the *St. Louis Post-Dispatch*. No date was given. It is one of a collection of notes and articles collected by Sophie's granddaughter, Sophie Little Bear Dahlberg, *Those Illustrious Frenchmen: The Chouteaus and the Osage Indians* (n.p., 2000), 21.
62. Lecompte, "Auguste Pierre Chouteau," 123.
63. Shelby M. Fly, *The Saga of the Chouteaus of Oklahoma* (Norman, Okla.: Levite of Apache, 1988), 27.
64. Lewis, *Robidoux Chronicles*, 44.
65. For more on Cabanné, see Ray H. Mattison, "John Pierre Cabanné Sr.," in LeRoy R. Hafen, ed., *Fur Traders, Trappers, and Mountain Men of the Upper Missouri* (Lincoln: University of Nebraska Press, 1995), n. 2.
66. Adèle Cabanné Sarpy to Jean Pierre Cabanné, September 1, 1823, Peugnet Collection, Missouri Historical Society, St. Louis.
67. J. P. Cabanné to Pierre Chouteau Jr., April 28, 1825, CCMO.
68. J. P. Cabanné to Pierre Chouteau Jr., February 2, 1831, CCMO.
69. J. P. Cabanné to Pierre Chouteau Jr., February 21, 1831, CCMO.
70. See, for example, the letters of April 28, 1825, and February 21, 1831, CCMO.
71. Lecompte, "Pierre Chouteau, Jr.," 31–37.
72. J. P. Cabanné to Pierre Chouteau Jr., April 28, 1825, CCMO.
73. J. P. Cabanné to Pierre Chouteau Jr., October 23, 1827, CCMO. See also Thorne, *The Many Hands of My Relations*, 189–193.
74. J. P. Cabanné to Pierre Chouteau Jr., January 6, 1828, CCMO.
75. J. P. Cabanné to Pierre Chouteau Jr., June 5, 1828, CCMO. See also Lewis, *Robidoux Chronicles*, 45–49.
76. For a more complete account of these conditions, see Thorne, *The Many Hands of My Relations*, 182–205.
77. Lecompte, "Pierre Chouteau, Jr.," 40–41, and Thorne, *The Many Hands of My Relations*, 196–197.
78. J. P. Cabanné to Pierre Chouteau Jr., April 28, 1825, CCMO.

79. J. A. MacMurphy, "Some Frenchmen of Early Days on the Missouri River," *Transactions and Reports of the Nebraska State Historical Society*, vol. V (Lincoln, 1893), 52.

80. P. A. Sarpy to Mimi Sarpy, March 8, 1847, Peugnet Collection, Missouri Historical Society, St. Louis.

81. Peter A. Sarpy, Last Will and Testament, April 7, 1845, Peugnet Collection, Missouri Historical Society, St. Louis.

82. John E. Wickman, "Peter A. Sarpy," in Hafen, ed., *French Fur Traders and Voyageurs*, 291–297.

83. Thorne, *The Many Hands of My Relations*, 204.

84. Sunder, *The Fur Trade*, 11–14.

85. Thorne, *The Many Hands of My Relations*, 194–195.

86. U.S. Indian Department account with Peter A. Sarpy, Council Bluffs, April 22, 1851; copy of Sac and Foxes Indian obligation, certified statement of the agent, October 18, 1851; copy of national obligation of Pottowattamies, November, 3, 1851, CCMO.

87. Thorne, *The Many Hands of My Relations*, 203–204.

88. Settlers found Decatur, located at the southern boundary of the new Omaha reservation, to be quite an attractive site. Sarpy had a branch store there as well. See Wishart, *An Unspeakable Sadness*, 118.

89. For more on Sarpy, see Edward F. Sterba, "Peter Sarpy, 1805–1865," in Jerold L. Simmons, ed., *"La Belle Vue": Studies in the History of Bellevue, Nebraska* (Marceline, Mo.: Walsworth, for the Mayor's Advisory Committee [of Bellevue, Nebraska] on the Bicentennial, 1976), 87–106. See also Thorne, *The Many Hands of My Relations*, 155–164.

90. Thorne, *The Many Hands of My Relations*, 229–230.

91. Unrau, *The Kansa Indians*, 148–161.

92. Gabriel Franchere to Pierre Chouteau Jr. and Company, January 28, 1847, Cherokee Nation Beaties Prairie, CCMO.

93. Wickman, "Peter A. Sarpy," 300.

94. One story about the founding of St. Joseph contained the following anecdote: "Mr. Robidoux was now in a quandary as to the names to be given the streets. He had determined on the names of the streets running parallel with the river, and when he intimated that he was undecided as to the streets running back from the river, [an] old gentleman suggested that it was an easy matter, and said, 'Why not name them after your children. You have about seventy, and that number is quite sufficient for the present.'" This story comes from W. A. Goulder, *Reminiscences of a Pioneer* (Boise, Idaho: Timothy Regan, 1909), 87–88. It is given in full in Lewis, *Robidoux Chronicles*, 236, n. 170.

95. Thorne, *The Many Hands of My Relations*, 155–156.

96. Lewis, *Robidoux Chronicles*, 229; Jh. Robidoux to Pierre Chouteau Jr., December 28, 1833, CCMO.

97. Thorne, *The Many Hands of My Relations*, 127. Thorne suggests that Robidoux had been operating in this vicinity as early as 1803.

98. Angelique was his second wife. His first wife, Eugenie Delisle dit Bienvenue, had died after giving birth to a son in 1810.

99. Joseph and Angelique mortgaged more of their property to Chouteau in 1841 to build a water gristmill. They took out another substantial loan from Chouteau in 1847. See Lewis, *Robidoux Chronicles*, 53–58, n. 154 and n. 172.

100. Aron, *American Confluence*, 230–232.

101. Lewis, *Robidoux Chronicles*, 54.

102. Ibid., 232–233, n. 157.

103. Ibid., 56, and Sheridan A. Logan, *Old Saint Jo: Gateway to the West, 1799–1932* (n.p.: John Sublett Logan Foundation, 1979), 24.

104. Lewis, *Robidoux Chronicles*, 58.

105. Ibid., 56.

106. Logan, *Old Saint Jo*, 18–44. For a look at some of Joseph Robidoux's other activities, see Thorne, *The Many Hands of My Relations*, 155–156.

107. Lewis, *Robidoux Chronicles*, 223, n. 118.

108. Ibid., 130.

109. Thorne, *The Many Hands of My Relations*, 206; Lewis, *Robidoux Chronicles*, 238, n. 178.

110. Joshua Pilcher to Pierre Chouteau Jr., June 16, 1833, CCMO.

111. John D. Unruh Jr., *The Plains Across: The Overland Emigrants and the Trans-Mississippi West, 1840–60* (Urbana: University of Illinois Press, 1979), 229, 242, 247.

112. Ibid., chs. 7 and 8 passim.

113. Ibid., 198.

114. For more on this incident, see Lecompte, "Pierre Chouteau, Jr.," 29–30.

115. Pekka Hämäläinen, "The Western Comanche Trade Center: Rethinking the Plains Indian Trade System," *Western Historical Quarterly*, 29 (Winter 1998), 485–513. For more on the early French role in this borderlands region, see John, *Storms Brewed*, and Folmer, *Franco-Spanish Rivalry*.

116. Blackhawk, *Violence over the Land*, 61.

117. Hämäläinen, "The Western Comanche Trade Center."

118. Ibid., 506.

119. Blackhawk, *Violence over the Land*, chs. 2 and 3.

120. Ibid., 117.

121. Ibid., 114–121, and see David J. Weber, *The Mexican Frontier, 1821–1846* (Albuquerque: University of New Mexico Press, 1982), 11.

122. Blackhawk, *Violence over the Land*, 120.

123. Rebecca McDowell Craver, *The Impact of Intimacy: Mexican-Anglo Intermarriage in New Mexico, 1821–1846*, University of Texas at El Paso, Southwestern Studies: Monograph No. 66 (El Paso: Texas Western Press, 1982).

124. This includes some whose ethnicity is hard to know at first glance. For example, the Leitensdorfer brothers, Eugene and Thomas, were important American merchants in New Mexico for many years. Their father was an Italian soldier who changed his name, came to the United States, and married a French Creole woman named Gamache in Carondelet, just south of St. Louis. One brother married a Creole woman named Michaud; the other married Solidad Abreu, daughter of a governor of New Mexico. See Stella M. Drumm, ed., *Down the Santa Fé Trail and into Mexico: The Diary of*

Susan Shelby Magoffin, 1846–1847 (New Haven, Conn.: Yale University Press, 1926), 62, n. 23.

125. Weber, *Taos Trappers*, ch. 7. This book remains by far the best book on the subject. See also ch. 6 on the French.

126. Weber, *Taos Trappers*, ch. 11.

127. Lewis, *Robidoux Chronicles*, 67.

128. See Weber, *Taos Trappers*, 88.

129. Lewis, *Robidoux Chronicles*, 74, and Devine, *The People Who Own Themselves*, 71, 258.

130. Devine, *The People Who Own Themselves*, 71.

131. Blackhawk, *Violence over the Land*, 127–128.

132. Sunder, ed., *Matt Field*, 213. See also David J. Weber, "Louis Robidoux," in LeRoy R. Hafen, ed., *Trappers of the Far West* (Lincoln: University of Nebraska Press, 1983), 40. The information about the Robidoux family's activities in the Far West comes from Weber; Lewis, *Robidoux Chronicles*; Orral M. Robidoux, *Memorial to the Robidoux Brothers* (Kansas City: Smith-Greaves, 1924); and Wallace, *Antoine Robidoux*.

133. Blackhawk, *Violence over the Land*, 132.

134. Weber, "Louis Robidoux," 48.

135. The information on St. Vrain comes from a variety of sources, including Lavender, *Bent's Fort*; Harold H. Dunham, "Ceran St. Vrain," in Hafen, ed., *Mountain Men and Fur Traders*; Samuel P. Arnold, "William W. Bent," in Hafen, ed., *Trappers of the Far West*; Seineke, ed., *Guide to the Microfilm Edition*; and Ranie Hotis, "Ceran St. Vrain and the Santa Fe Trade: Forging the St. Louis Connection" (senior essay, Yale College, 1996).

136. The most complete account and description of the company can be found in Lavender, *Bent's Fort*. I have also benefited from the encyclopedic knowledge of the late Sam Arnold.

137. Wishart, *The Fur Trade*, 59; Lecompte, *Pueblo, Hardscrabble, Greenhorn*, 23. Chapter 2 of Lecompte's book contains an excellent summary of the company's activities and Bent's Fort.

138. Lecompte, *Pueblo, Hardscrabble, Greenhorn*, 23.

139. Hämäläinen, "The Western Comanche Trade Center," 512.

140. Pekka Hämäläinen, "The Rise and Fall of Plains Indian Horse Cultures," *Journal of American History*, 90:3 (December 2003), 9 (electronic version).

141. The insights and information about the relationship between the two companies come from Hotis, "Ceran St. Vrain," who conducted exhaustive research at the Missouri Historical Society in St. Louis. Her work on this subject is by far the most thorough, careful, and perceptive that I have seen. I am grateful for her efforts. On the farm in Kansas City, see Hotis, 33.

142. The phrase is taken from the title of David Lavender's book on the fur trade, first published in 1964 by Doubleday.

143. Lecompte, *Pueblo, Hardscrabble, Greenhorn*, 72, 288.

144. George E. Hyde, *Life of George Bent Written from His Letters*, ed. Savoie Lottinville (Norman: University of Oklahoma Press, 1968), 94.

145. Lecompte, *Pueblo, Hardscrabble, Greenhorn*, 72.
146. The information on Beaubien comes primarily from Lawrence R. Murphy, "Charles H. Beaubien," in Hafen, ed., *French Fur Traders and Voyageurs*, 29–41.
147. Lecompte, *Pueblo, Hardscrabble, Greenhorn*, 17.
148. Lamar, *The Far Southwest*, 66.
149. Reséndez, *Changing National Identities*, 248–249. See also David Weber, *The Mexican Frontier, 1821–1846: The American Southwest under Mexico* (Albuquerque: University of New Mexico Press, 1982), chs. 2, 7, 10, 12. Reséndez, building upon the insights of Weber's foundational work, fully acknowledges the gravitational pull and "transformative power" of the "expanding American economy" on New Mexico, but he also gives us a fuller picture of the complexities of Mexican politics during this period and the countervailing force of Mexican nationalism upon *nuevomexicanos*. Shortly after reentering New Mexican politics for a third term as governor, Armijo learned that a coup had occurred in Mexico City, bringing to power a man from a rival political party. To make matters worse, Armijo had to deal with a variety of political factions within New Mexico itself, a full spectrum of divided opinions over issues of localism versus centralization, foreign trade, and national identity. With religious monarchists and liberal free-traders barking at his heels and no help in sight from Mexico City, it is small wonder that Armijo threw up his hands at the sight of Kearny's army. Painting a far different picture than that of passive New Mexican peasants welcoming the conquering heroes, Reséndez quotes the acting governor Vigil y Alarid who sadly turned over control to Kearny and observed that "internal strife had been the 'damned venom' that had brought down one of the greatest nations ever created on the face of the earth" (referring to Mexico), 247–248.
150. Stephen G. Hyslop, *Bound for Santa Fe: The Road to New Mexico and the American Conquest, 1806–1848* (Norman: University of Oklahoma Press, 2002), 368.
151. Alvin R. Sunseri, "Revolt in Taos, 1846–47: Resistance to U.S. Occupation," *El Palacio*, 96 (Fall 1990), 42.
152. Ibid., 45. See also Cheetham, "The First Term of the American Court in Taos, New Mexico," *New Mexico Historical Review*, 1:1 (January 1926), 23–41.
153. The information on Maxwell comes from the biography written by Murphy, *Lucien Bonaparte Maxwell*.
154. See Montoya, *Translating Property*, ch. 2, and Murphy, *Lucien Bonaparte Maxwell*, ch. 8.
155. Lamar, *The Far Southwest*, 276.
156. This brief summary was compiled from various materials in the Wade biography of Michel B. Menard Collection, Woodson Research Center, Fondren Library, Rice University, Houston, Texas.
157. Lamar, *The Far Southwest*, 46, 90.
158. Ibid., 277.
159. Kennerly, *Persimmon Hill*, 185, 191.
160. This brings up the intriguing issue of marriage and social status. Partnerships with Indian and métis women were often the main source of cultural knowledge and social and political connection in Indian country for French traders. The permanence

of such relationships varied, but many Frenchmen also had nonnative wives in places such as St. Louis. The ultimate goal for many—though certainly not all—French traders, it seems to me, was literally the building of one's "house" in town. In the end, that depended on wives who could provide the required socialization and education for the next generation. Catholicism, inheritance practices, and connections to capital of all kinds also mattered. In short, such homes were built, not in Indian villages, but in Euro-American towns that privileged such values and practices and rules of property. Hispanic women in New Mexican towns satisfied such needs. For more on this complicated issue, see Thorne, *The Many Hands of My Relations*, passim. Needless to say, as more Anglo-Americans entered a region, racial categorization also became an issue.

161. Lamar, *The Far Southwest*, 48, and Kennerly, *Persimmon Hill*, 172.

162. Frederick Jackson Turner, *The Character and Influence of the Indian Trade in Wisconsin: A Study of the Trading Post as an Institution*, ed. David Harry Miller and William W. Savage, Jr. (Norman: University of Oklahoma Press, 1977), 2.

163. Blackhawk, *Violence over the Land*, 186–188.

164. Reséndez, *Changing National Identities*, 116; see also Hyslop, *Bound for Santa Fe*, 382–386.

165. Reséndez, *Changing National Identities*, 265–266.

166. See Lynn Bridgers, *Death's Deceiver: The Life of Joseph P. Machebeuf* (Albuquerque: University of New Mexico Press, 1997), 138; E. A. Mares, ed., *Padre Martínez: New Perspectives from Taos* (Taos, N.Mex.: Millicent Rogers Museum, 1988); and David J. Weber, *On the Edge of Empire: The Taos Hacienda of Los Martínez* (Santa Fe: Museum of New Mexico Press, in cooperation with the William P. Clements Center for Southwest Studies, Southern Methodist University, 1996), ch. 7.

167. For a very readable version of the story, see Paul Horgan, *Lamy of Santa Fe* (New York: Farrar, Straus and Giroux, 1975).

168. See LeRoy R. Hafen, "Etienne Provost," in Hafen, ed., *Trappers of the Far West*, and Jack B. Tykal, *Etienne Provost: Man of the Mountains* (Liberty, Utah: Eagle's View, 1989).

169. Janet Lecompte, "Pierre Lesperance," in Hafen, ed., *French Fur Traders and Voyageurs in the American West*, 194.

CHAPTER 6. MANAGING THE TRIBE OF CHOUTEAU

1. Mahoney, *Provincial Lives*, 13. See chs. 2 and 4 for a discussion of the Gratiot-Hempstead clan and the evolving genteel practices of this region.

2. Lecompte, "John F. A. Sanford."

3. Carter and Spencer, "Stereotypes of the Mountain Man."

4. E. E. Rich, *Hudson's Bay Company, 1670–1870*, 3 vols. (London: Hudson's Bay Record Society, 1958–1960); L. R. Masson, *Les Bourgeois de la compagnie du Nord-Ouest*, 2 vols. (1889–1890; reprint, New York: Antiquarian Press, 1960); M. W. Campbell, *The North West Company* (Toronto: Macmillan, 1957).

5. Dale L. Morgan, "The Fur Trade and Its Historians," in Gilman, ed., *Aspects of the Fur Trade*, 7.

6. This task may be easier now that the ledgers of the various companies are available on microfilm from the Missouri Historical Society.

7. Clark, *La Rochelle*, 68; E. E. Rich, *The Fur Trade and the Northwest to 1857* (Toronto: McClelland and Stewart, 1967), 173. See also Rich, *Montreal and the Fur Trade*, ch. 3.

8. Foley and Rice, *The First Chouteaus*, 20.

9. McDermott, *Private Libraries in Creole St. Louis*.

10. Admyrauld and Sons to Joseph Marie Papin, February 3, 1792, Box 1, CCMO. See Clark, *La Rochelle*, 50, 98–99.

11. Primm, *Lion of the Valley*, 54. Also see Barnhart, ed., "The Letterbooks."

12. For Cerré see Faribault-Beauregard, ed., *La vie aux Illinois*; Douglas, "Jean Gabriel Cerré"; Primm, *Lion of the Valley*, 50–51. On Orillat, see Igartua, "The Merchants of Montreal."

13. Marriage contract of Auguste Chouteau and Marie Thérèse Cerré, September 21, 1786, CCMO.

14. Foley and Rice, *The First Chouteaus*, 45.

15. See Boxes 3–10, CCMO.

16. For examples of Auguste's land dealings, see October 29, 1817; July 6, 1818; and August 25, 1823, CCMO. Also see Foley and Rice, *The First Chouteaus*, 82, 176–177.

17. See land survey of Antoine Soulard for Pierre Chouteau, March 20, 1804, CCMO; list of unconfirmed lands, October 20, 1824, CCMO; Foley and Rice, *The First Chouteaus*, 44.

18. It is hard to know why this is the case. Pierre may have simply assumed the traditional role of the younger son, seeking opportunity beyond the home circle. He may also have enjoyed his native clients. Whatever the reason, it was Pierre Sr. who had the closest relations with native communities, and several of his sons followed in his footsteps. See Chapter 5.

19. See, for example, the letter from Saucier to Chouteau, June 19, 1811, CCMO.

20. Foley and Rice, *The First Chouteaus*, 167.

21. Ibid., ch. 4.

22. Clark, *La Rochelle*, 66.

23. Marriage contract of Gabriel Paul and Marie Louise Chouteau, March 28, 1818, Soulard Papers, Box 1, Missouri Historical Society, St. Louis.

24. Pierre Chouteau and Sauciér Chouteau to Bartholomew Berthold and Pierre Chouteau Jr., June 19, 1818, CCMO; Pierre Chouteau letterbook, expenses incurred, Indian Department, Drafts 141 and 142, May 21, 1813, CCMO; Veuve Chouteau to Bartholomew Berthold, April 4, 1811, CCMO.

25. Herlihy, *Medieval Households*, 91.

26. In 1794, Pratte married Emilie, the oldest daughter of Sylvestre Labbadie. Sarpy, born in the Gascony region of France in 1764, married the next oldest Labbadie daughter, Pelagie, in 1797.

27. Unrau, *The Kansa Indians*, 78.

28. Cunningham and Blythe, *The Founding Family*; Beckwith, *Creoles of St. Louis*; Billon, *Annals of St. Louis in Its Territorial Days*; Pratte, "Reminiscences of General Bernard Pratte, Jr."; and Ray H. Mattison, "John Pierre Cabanné, Sr.," in Hafen, ed., *Mountain Men*.

29. Berthold had come to the United States in 1798 as secretary to General Willet. He settled first in Philadelphia and then Baltimore, forming a partnership with several French émigrés in those cities: F. A. Junel, Gabriel and René Paul, and Theotime Générelly. The Paul brothers were born in St. Domingue and had fled to Philadelphia. René moved to St. Louis in 1808 and married Eulalie Chouteau, daughter of Auguste, in 1812. Gabriel came to St. Louis in 1817 and married Eulalie's sister Louise in 1818, as previously noted. Générelly had married the Pauls' sister Sophie and established himself in New Orleans. The partnership between the various émigrés was dissolved with some rancor in 1812. Junel, the Baltimore connection, wrote an angry letter to Berthold that year which chided the latter for not using his Chouteau connections to further the interests of the firm and pitied Berthold for having to deal with Paul, a "man of easy temper." Berthold responded by dissolving his connection with the Pauls and forming a partnership with Pierre Chouteau Jr., his brother-in-law. See F. A. Junel to Berthold, June 12, 1812, CCMO. Also see Cunningham and Blythe, *The Founding Family*, and Beckwith, *Creoles of St. Louis*, for biographical information. For more on the French émigrés to Baltimore and Philadelphia, see Frances Sergeant Childs, *French Refugee Life in the United States, 1790–1800* (Baltimore: Johns Hopkins University Press, 1940).

30. Lecompte, "Pierre Chouteau, Jr.," and references in Nute, *Calendar*.

31. Cabanné went to Council Bluffs; Berthold traded in opposition to Manuel Lisa, whom he referred to as "l'escargot," on the Upper Missouri. Berthold thought Lisa was "very boastful" and "the least able of all the traders." Lisa has always been celebrated as one of the great entrepreneurs in the fur trade. It is interesting to read this assessment by a fellow merchant, who obviously did not share the opinion of later historians. Perhaps the historians have been more interested in adventure and risk-taking; Lisa's fellow traders may have judged him more on the basis of financial acumen. Berthold to Chouteau, August 20, 1819, CCMO.

32. The two companies, which were and remained separate companies, agreed to become equal partners in the Western Department of the American Fur Company. Astor's corporation would furnish all supplies for the trade for a fee. Astor would also market all the furs, robes, and skins that accrued to his account and those belonging to Pratte and Company, the latter at a commission of 2.5 percent if Astor did not choose to buy them on the corporation's account. In essence, Astor and Pratte and Company jointly owned this division or franchise. Chouteau received a salary of two thousand dollars as the agent of the American Fur Company. Cabanné and Berthold remained in the field at salaries of twelve hundred dollars each. After salaries, expenses, and fees, the profits were to be divided between the two companies.

33. Porter, *John Jacob Astor*, II:692–693.

34. Quoted in ibid., II:764.

35. In the reorganization of 1834, two new partners were added, Jean-Baptiste (Jean Berald) Sarpy and the firm of Menard and Vallé. Sarpy, the son of Cabanné's original partner, Gregoire, had married Cabanné's daughter Adele, his second cousin, in 1820. Sarpy had handled the books for the family business since dissolving his first partnership with A. P. Chouteau. Menard and Vallé, a family firm operating out of Kaskaskia and Ste. Genevieve, had been started by Pierre Menard and Jean-Baptiste Vallé. Their sons, Edmond and Felix, respectively, were running the business by the late 1830s. Needless to say, there were various family connections. The Vallés were related to the Prattes, and the Menards to the Chouteaus.

36. Bernard Pratte died in 1836; Berthold had died in 1831. Pratte's son withdrew from the company in 1838 to serve in the Missouri legislature. His place in the firm was taken by Joseph Sire. Sire, born in 1799 in La Rochelle, came to St. Louis in 1821 by way of Philadelphia. Cabanné, whose letters from Council Bluffs to the partners in St. Louis were always full of gossip, had noted Sire's abilities as early as 1825. Sire became a master of various company steamboats and a partner in 1838. He had ensured himself a position of importance by marrying Virginia Labbadie, Bernard Pratte's niece, in 1827. The other new partner in 1838 was John F. A. Sanford, a native of Virginia. In 1832, Sanford had married Pierre Chouteau Jr.'s daughter, Emilie. He began working for the firm in 1835 and moved to New York in 1841 to manage the company's new import-export office. Even in this third generation of family partners, in-laws played a most important role. It is also worth noting that the great majority of in-laws who became partners over three generations were born in southwestern France or St. Domingue. It was clear by 1839 that the old consortium was a thing of the past. That year the company was reorganized once more and renamed Pierre Chouteau Jr. and Company. Cabanné, whose lack of discretion had become an irritant to Chouteau, withdrew with some hard feelings. He formed a partnership the following year with Bernard Pratte Jr. but died in 1841.

37. Railroad construction and mining had by now replaced the fur trade as the focal point of Chouteau's investments.

38. Lecompte, "Pierre Chouteau, Jr.," and "John F. A. Sanford"; and Michel, "The St. Louis Fur Trade." Even the St. Louis office during these later years served primarily as an investment brokerage, often dealing in railroads and mining property. See Pierre Chouteau Jr. to Charles P. Chouteau, April 11, 1855; April 13, 1855; August 22, 1857; August 26, 1857; September 5, 1857; January 12, 1860; and January 16, 1860; John H. Thompson to Charles Chouteau, December 29, 1859, CCMO.

39. Berthold, Chouteau, and Pratte to G. S. Chouteau, July 19, 1822, CCMO; Cunningham and Blythe, *The Founding Family*, 7.

40. He married Clemence Coursault, a niece of Henri's brothers-in-law, René and Gabriel Paul. Henri, his cousins Antoine and Gustave Soulard, and René Paul, who was the city surveyor until 1838, spent most of their careers dealing in real estate. Rodabaugh, *Frenchtown*, 12–13.

41. Inventory of Auguste Chouteau estate, May, 13, 1829, CCMO; Henri Chouteau be-

comes administrator of estate, September 22, 1842, CCMO; see Boxes 40–42, CCMO, for Henri's real estate transactions. Henri also ran interference for his cousin Pierre's real estate interests. See Crooks to Pierre Chouteau Jr., January 24, 1836, CCMO.

42. Azby Chouteau to J. Gilman Chouteau, October 2, 1871; February 15, 1881; December 21, 1887, CCMO.

43. Auguste Chouteau to P.-L. Panet, October 5, 1800, CCMO.

44. Henri Chouteau to Guilmain Chouteau, December 8, 1847, CCMO.

45. Crooks to Chouteau, January 24, 1836, CCMO.

46. Panet to Chouteau, February 2, 1797; May 18, 1804; December 7, 1804; May 18, 1805; December 28, 1805; A. A. Chouteau to Auguste Chouteau, April 3, 1816, August 19, 1828, CCMO.

47. Cabanné to Chouteau, September 16, 1825, CCMO, quoted in David J. Weber, "Sylvestre S. Pratte," in Hafen, ed., *Mountain Men.*

48. Cabanné to Chouteau, April 28, 1825; November 6, 1825, CCMO.

49. "Journals of Jules DeMun," Collections, Missouri Historical Society, 5:2 (February 1928).

50. Lecompte, "August Pierre Chouteau."

51. Receipts, May 25, 1837, CCMO.

52. Jules to Isabelle de Mun, July 24, 1816, quoted in Janet Lecompte, "Jules and Isabelle DeMun," *Bulletin*, Missouri Historical Society (October 1969).

53. For more on French Creole family life and codes of behavior in St. Louis, see Saxton, *Being Good.*

54. Pierre Chouteau Jr. to Emilie Chouteau, July 25, 1854, CCMO.

55. George M. Platt, "Thomas L. Sarpy," in Hafen, ed., *Mountain Men.*

56. Theodore Papin to Pierre Melicourt Papin, September 2, 1833, CCMO.

57. Segalen, *Historical Anthropology*, 223.

58. Berthold, *Glimpses of Creole Life.*

59. Bartholomew Berthold to Bernard Pratte, October 17, 1823; Jean Pierre Cabanné to Pierre Chouteau Jr., August 2, 1824; Pierre Chouteau to Pierre Chouteau Jr., September 21, 1824; Ramsay Crooks to Pierre Chouteau Jr., March 23, 1836, CCMO.

60. Hall, "Family Structure."

61. Garraghan, *Catholic Beginnings*, 117, and see Marra, Pal, and Boutros, *Cher Oncle, Cher Papa.*

62. Crooks to Pierre Chouteau Jr., April 21, 1825, CCMO.

63. Azby Chouteau to Gilman Chouteau, May 26, 1896, CCMO.

64. Michael B. Miller, *The Bon Marché: Bourgeois Culture and the Department Store, 1869–1920* (Princeton, N.J.: Princeton University Press, 1981), 15. See esp. the introduction and chs. 1 and 6.

CHAPTER 7. "AVEC BIEN DU REGRET"

1. It is also fair to suggest that the size of the francophone population in such cities might have been greater if the social economy of the fur trade had not siphoned off substantial numbers of métis employees and their families over the years. Both the St. Louis

and Detroit metropolitan areas contained outlying villages populated in part by such families.

2. That story will be explored in greater depth in Chapter 8.

3. Smelser, "Housing in Creole St. Louis." This article is rather strange. It contains a brief description of Creole material culture, followed by what can only be described as an unrelated interpretation having to do with the rise of class consciousness in St. Louis in the early years of American rule. He seems to be arguing that Creole St. Louis was a classless society and that the emergence of a bourgeois class and an incipient consumer culture marked the end of Creole "folkways." Such an argument, such as it is, ignores the dominant role that the Creole merchant elite played from the very beginning of St. Louis's history.

4. Timothy Mahoney notes that the Creole elite in St. Louis were showing a marked preference for "Federal or Greek Revival houses built in the 'French manner'" by the 1830s. See Mahoney, *Provincial Lives*, 131.

5. See Johnson, *The Michigan Fur Trade*, 129, 135; and Kappler, ed., *Indian Affairs*, II:185–187.

6. The information on the Campau landholdings comes from Denis J. Campau, Rent Book, 1863–1880, and Denis J. Campau, Cash Book Commencing June 9th, 1863 of Denis J. Campau, Receiver of the Estate of Joseph Campau, Esq., Campau Family Papers, Burton Historical Collection, Detroit Public Library, Detroit, Michigan; Robert B. Ross, "Detroit in 1837: Reminiscences of Joseph and Daniel J. Campau," *Detroit Sunday News Tribune*, November 4, 1894; Farmer, *The History of Detroit and Michigan*, 977–982; Donald W. Voelker, "Joseph Campau: Detroit's 'Big Shot,'" *Michigan History*, 75:4 (July/August 1991); and S. Heath Ackley, "Understanding Joseph Campau" (senior essay, Yale University, 1997). I am especially indebted to Mr. Ackley, who gathered many of the documents I have used for this chapter.

7. For a fuller account, see Kilfoil, *C. C. Trowbridge*; and Formisano, *The Birth of Mass Political Parties*, 42.

8. Primm, *Lion of the Valley*, 108–110; Foley and Rice, *The First Chouteaus*, 178–179.

9. For some representative documents on Henri's activities, see March, 26, 1836; June 28, 1837; and April 16, 1846, CCMO.

10. Moran, *The Moran Family*, 56.

11. Foley and Rice, *The First Chouteaus*, 176.

12. Sandweiss, *St Louis*, 35–36. This book not only covers the activities of various developers in St. Louis, it provides a unique model for historians of how to describe and analyze the patterns of urban growth.

13. Ibid., 45–46.

14. Primm, *Lion of the Valley*, 306.

15. John R. Williams to François Navarre, August 31, 1819, Navarre Family Papers, Burton Historical Collection, Detroit Public Library, Detroit, Michigan.

16. John R. Williams to Jacques Campau, August 30, 1800, trans. Max Lehucher, John R. Williams Papers, Burton Historical Collection, Detroit Public Library, Detroit, Michigan. Thanks to Mara Harwel for bringing this letter to my attention.

17. The French and other Catholics felt that Protestants, many of them New Englanders,

wanted to use Bible reading in public schools to proselytize. They were not wrong about this. The second Michigan superintendent of public instruction, Franklin Sawyer, edited the anti-Catholic *Detroit Daily Advertiser*. The superintendent in 1845—with the telling name Oliver Cromwell Comstock—recommended daily readings from the Bible. Four women from important French families in Detroit, Elizabeth Williams (sister of John R.), Elizabeth Lyons (a Chene on her mother's side), Angelique Campau, and Monique Labadie Beaubien, took the lead in providing education for young women. They established the Academy of the Ladies of the Sacred Heart and later the French Female Charity School for girls from families without means. For a full discussion of these issues, see Vinyard, *For Faith and Fortune*, ch. 1.

18. For two representative documents, see Daniel J. Campau, Letter to the Delegates of the Detroit City Democratic Convention, February 19, 1853, Campau Family Papers; and John R. Williams, "To the Free and Independent Electors of Michigan," August 30, 1823, Williams Family Papers; both in the Burton Historical Collection, Detroit Public Library, Detroit, Michigan. The best overview of politics in Michigan during this period is Formisano, *The Birth of Mass Political Parties*.

19. Munius Kenney to William Woodbridge, William Woodbridge Correspondence and Papers, Burton Historical Collection, Detroit Public Library, Detroit, Michigan.

20. Formisano, *The Birth of Mass Political Parties*, 200.

21. For more on this, see Primm, *Lion of the Valley*, and Davis, "Community and Conflict."

22. See Primm, *Lion of the Valley*, 165, 183.

23. Darby, *Personal Recollections*, 8–9.

24. Wilson Jr., ed., *Southern Travels*, 45.

25. Ibid., 43.

26. Corporation of the Town of Detroit, *Act of Incorporation*, 40–41.

27. Primm, *Lion of the Valley*, 102.

28. Babcock, ed., *Forty Years of Pioneer Life*, 87.

29. Rodgers, "Recollections of St. Louis," 112.

30. Frederick Bates to Sally Bates, May 5, 1799, in Marshall, ed., *The Life and Papers of Frederick Bates*, I:17; Frederick Bates to Richard Bates, December 17, 1807, in ibid., I:237–247.

31. A study of Creole marriage contracts, wills, and probate files during the American period would shed much light on the continuity of legal traditions and the economic role of French women. (See the various papers relating to the estates of Auguste Chouteau and Henri Chouteau in CCMO and the marriage contract between Gabriel Paul and Marie Louise Chouteau, March 28, 1818, Soulard Papers, Missouri Historical Society, St. Louis; also McDermott, ed., *Old Cahokia*, and Snyder, "The Old French Towns." Useful studies of the "clash of legal traditions" on this frontier and others are Dargo, *Jefferson's Louisiana*; David J. Langum, *Law and Community on the Mexican California Frontier* (Norman: University of Oklahoma Press, 1987); and Arnold, *Unequal Laws*. On the legal rights and economic maneuverability of women in Creole communities, see Winstanley Briggs, "The Enhanced Economic Position of Women

in French Colonial Illinois," in Glasrud, ed., *L'Heritage Tranquille*, and Boyle, "Did She Generally Decide?"

32. See Banner, *Legal Systems in Conflict*, 96–97.

33. Neatby, *The Administration of Justice*, 292–293, 328–329.

34. On this and various other bones of contention between the French and the incoming Anglos in Detroit and its hinterland, see Bidlack, *The Yankee Meets the Frenchman*; Bald, *Detroit's First American Decade*; and Kadler, "The French in Detroit."

35. This topic will be covered in Chapter 8. The pattern in Michigan can also be seen in Minnesota, where by the end of the nineteenth century the older francophone population had merged with newer arrivals from Quebec and could sustain newspapers in the Twin Cities such as *Echo de l'Ouest* and *Le Canadien*. Political clubs included the Club Democratie Franco-Americaine and the Lafayette-Papineau Republican League. For more, see Rubinstein, "The French Canadians and the French," and Scholberg, *The French Pioneers*.

36. Farmer, *The History of Detroit*, 672–680; and D. Aidan McQuillan, "French-Canadian Communities in the Upper Midwest during the Nineteenth Century," in Louder and Waddell, eds., *French America*.

37. Moran, *The Moran Family*, xxi.

38. Mara Harwel, "La Justice Mon Devoir" (unpublished paper, December 2007), 4.

39. Virginia L. Sarpy to "ma chere tante" [Emilie Gratiot Chouteau], n.d. [but sometime in the late 1830s], CCMO.

40. Barret, "Recollections of Mary Finney Barret," 122–123.

41. Rodabaugh, *Frenchtown*, 9–21.

42. It is interesting to note that Sophie Chouteau's husband was A. P. Chouteau, the same "Col. Choteau" described by Washington Irving in *A Tour of the Prairies*. This Chouteau spent most of his time in Indian country at his agency, which resembled a frontier plantation (see Chapter 5). A.P. rarely returned home—certainly in part to avoid his creditors. The high-society predilections of his wife and daughters may have been an additional reason. See Irving, *A Tour of the Prairies*, 21.

43. Van Ravenswaay, *Saint Louis*, 375.

44. Charles Dickens, *American Notes* (Gloucester, Mass.: Peter Smith, 1968), 201.

45. Thomas M. Easterly captured the devastation caused by this fire in his daguerreotypes. Easterly also recorded, thankfully, some of the last remaining Creole homes in St. Louis. See Dolores A. Kilgo, *Likeness and Landscape: Thomas M. Easterly and the Art of the Daguerreotype* (St. Louis: Missouri Historical Society Press, 1994), 162–167.

46. de Finiels, *An Account of Upper Louisiana*, 67.

47. Count Francesco Arese, *A Trip to the Prairies and in the Interior of North America (1837–1838)*, trans. Andrew Evans, reprint edition (New York: Cooper Square, 1975), 58–59.

48. Richard C. Wade, *The Urban Frontier: The Rise of Western Cities, 1790–1830* (Cambridge: Harvard University Press, 1959), 248, and Primm, *Lion of the Valley*, 90.

49. These and other wonderful quotations are collected in Jeffrey S. Adler, *Yankee Mer-*

chants and the Making of the Urban West: The Rise and Fall of Antebellum St. Louis (New York: Cambridge University Press, 1991), 52.

50. Van Ravenswaay, *St. Louis*, 300–301, 355–356, 364–365.

51. Paré, *The Catholic Church in Detroit*, 302, 485.

52. Hall and Farmer, *Grosse Pointe*, 35.

53. Fowler, *Reminiscences*, 17–18.

54. Morrison, *Memoirs*, 3.

55. For more information on the Jaccards, Joseph Bouju, and other craftsmen, see Ruth H. Roach's delightful little book, *St. Louis Silversmiths*; a brief description of M. Massot's confectionary shop can be found in Kennerly, *Persimmon Hill*, 29–30; Frémont, *Souvenirs of My Time* also contains several descriptive chapters on Creole St. Louis during this early American period; the letters of Christian Wilt, excerpted in Jennings, *A Pioneer Merchant*, contain interesting comments on the preferences in shoes and soap of Creole customers (163, 176).

56. Quoted in Faribault-Beauregard, ed., *La vie aux Illinois*, 119.

CHAPTER 8. "LA CONFÉDÉRATION PERDUE"

1. Rodabaugh, *Frenchtown*, 20.

2. For a fuller understanding of the confusion and conflict in war-torn Missouri, see William E. Parrish, *A History of Missouri, Volume III, 1860 to 1875* (Columbia: University of Missouri Press, 1973). For the situation in St. Louis, see Primm, *Lion of the Valley*, ch. 7, esp. 260–263. Gabriel Paul (1813–1886) graduated from West Point in 1834. He fought in the Seminole War in 1842 and in the Mexican War. As a Union general, he led a brigade at the battles of Fredericksburg, Chancellorsville, and Gettysburg. During this last campaign, he was wounded and ultimately lost his sight as a result. He held the rank of brigadier general at his death. His son, Auguste Chouteau Paul, named after his great-grandfather, enlisted in the Union Army in 1861 and fought in the Battle of the Wilderness. He was confined in a southern prison for almost a year during the war and later served in the regular army with General Crooks in various Indian campaigns. See Beckwith, *Creoles of St. Louis*, 26–31, and Cunningham and Blythe, *The Founding Family*, 10–18. For more on Tullia Paul, see Rodabaugh, *Frenchtown*, 14–20. Tullia Paul, the "Queen of St. Louis Society," undoubtedly had little use for parvenus like Mayor O. D. Filley, a Free-Soiler and stove manufacturer. Nevertheless, the family had personal and economic reasons to support the Union cause. Of course, it was certainly possible for family members to be divided on the issues of slavery and allegiance. Such was the case for the Garesché family of St. Louis; see William B. Faherty, SJ, *Dream by the River: Two Centuries of Saint Louis Catholicism, 1766–1980*, rev. ed. (St. Louis: River City, 1981).

3. Beckwith, *Creoles of St. Louis*, 39.

4. Primm, *Lion of the Valley*, 248.

5. Ibid., 263. President Lincoln later ordered an end to the assessment and the collections. See also Sunder, *The Fur Trade*, 235.

6. Sunder, *The Fur Trade*, 262–264.

7. Van Ravenswaay, *Saint Louis*, 409.

8. George Reinecke, "Alfred Mercier, French Novelist of New Orleans," in Kenneth W. Holditch, ed., *In Old New Orleans* (Jackson: University Press of Mississippi, 1983), 161.

9. Roger, *The American Enemy*, 88–89.

10. Joseph G. Tregle Jr., "Creoles and Americans," in Hirsch and Logsdon, eds., *Creole New Orleans*, 168.

11. *Réglements de la Légion Française Formée a la Nouvelle-Orléans le 26 Avril 1861* (Nouvelle-Orléans: J. Lamarre, 1861) in Beinecke Rare Book and Manuscript Library, Yale University, New Haven, Connecticut.

12. Stephen Butler, "The St. Albans Raid of 1864: A Confederate Attack on Vermont and Its Impact on the Confederation Debate in Canada" (senior thesis, Yale College, 2006). Several years after the St. Albans Raid of October 1864, a French Canadian delegation expressed its sympathy with the slaves, visiting Mrs. Lincoln and declaring, "You, Madam, mourn your noble husband; we mourn the liberator!" (*New York Times*, 10 May 1867). I am grateful to Ryan Brasseaux for bringing this article to my attention.

13. Tregle, "Creoles and Americans," 131–185. Tregle's more recent book, *Louisiana in the Age of Jackson*, repeats the same argument and focuses on the 1820s and 1830s (see chs. 2 and 12). See also Tregle's influential essay "Early New Orleans Society: A Reappraisal," *Journal of Southern History*, 18 (1952), 21–36. A final note on the term "Creole." Virginia R. Domínguez in her book *White by Definition* demonstrates clearly that the meaning of the term has shifted over time in response to changing conditions in Louisiana. As Tregle and Domínguez both show, the use of the term became more widespread after 1803 "to establish a primacy of native identity against the newcomer," that is, "incoming Americans" (Tregle, "Creoles and Americans," 138). That the term, used primarily in the sense of "native-born," took so long to become popular does, indeed, as Tregle notes, "[reveal] much about the area's colonial relationship to both France and Spain" (134). Tregle also makes it clear that "Creole" could simply mean any thing or person "native" to Louisiana during the antebellum period or could be used, especially as "the Creoles," to refer to that *ancienne population*—"the indigenous Latin inhabitants" (141). The term would not necessarily be applied to francophone individuals born outside the state, and Domínguez has been rightly criticized for not making enough of the distinction between the so-called Foreign French and the *ancienne population*. On the other hand, the term became increasingly politicized during the antebellum period, and Paul F. Lachance—in his review of the Domínguez book (*Louisiana History*, 29 [1988], 190–192)—noted that "language became the crucial criterion distinguishing the *ancienne population* from the non-French and non-Creole immigrants, mainly Anglo-Americans." Therefore, while I have tried in this chapter to use the clearer term—"Francophone"—I think it is safe to say that in the context of antebellum Louisiana cultural politics, "Creoles" more often than not implies Francophones.

14. Tregle, "Creoles and Americans," 157. By the legislative act of incorporation, the First Municipality—the French Quarter or *vieux carré*—covered the area between Espla-

nade and Canal; the Second Municipality or American District—also known as Faubourg St. Mary or Ste. Marie—covered the area above Canal; the Third Municipality—or Faubourg Marigny—covered the area below (downriver of) Esplanade. The first and third municipalities were primarily francophone. The city reunited in 1852.

15. Ibid., 168.
16. Ibid., 159.
17. See Tregle, "Political Reinforcement."
18. This story is well told by Dargo, *Jefferson's Louisiana*. More recently, Mark F. Fernandez has contributed a nuanced look at the legal system that emerged in antebellum Louisiana, a blend of civilian and common law traditions that, in the end, relied on a common law style of judicature. Nevertheless, the Code of 1825 provided a legal comfort zone for the *ancienne population*. See Fernandez, *From Chaos to Continuity*.
19. Paul F. Lachance, "The Foreign French," in Hirsch and Logsdon, eds., *Creole New Orleans*, 117. See also Lachance, "The 1809 Immigration of Saint-Domingue Refugees to New Orleans: Reception, Integration and Impact," *Louisiana History*, 29:2 (Spring 1988), 109–141.
20. Lachance, "Foreign French," 112.
21. Ibid., 113–114, and S. Frederick Starr, *Southern Comfort: The Garden District of New Orleans, 1800–1900* (Cambridge, Mass.: MIT Press, 1989), 22.
22. Tinker, *Bibliography*.
23. Lachance, "Foreign French," 123.
24. Reinders, *End of an Era*, 132.
25. Ibid., 149, n. 8.
26. Emile Hiriart, "Guerre aux Écoles Publiques," *La Renaissance Louisianaise*, May 19, 1861, quoted in ibid., 137.
27. Reinders, *End of an Era*, 143; Tregle, "Creoles and Americans," 160; and see Chapter 7 of this book. For a Detroit example, see Moran, *The Moran Family*, 60, 68. On the values and goals of higher education, the Creole elite and their Yankee counterparts were not in disagreement. On at least one occasion, the two streams met: Henry Barnard, a famous early educator from New England, married a woman from an old Detroit Creole family, Josephine DesNoyers. Barnard's son married a young woman from another distinguished Detroit Creole family, Catherine Elizabeth Moran.
28. Reinders, *End of an Era*, 147.
29. Kmen, *Music in New Orleans*, 149–166.
30. Ibid., 200.
31. Ibid., 102.
32. Ibid., 234–236; Lester Sullivan, "Composers of Color of Nineteenth-Century New Orleans: The History behind the Music," *Black Music Research Journal*, 8:1 (1988), 51–82.
33. Roger G. Kennedy, *Architecture, Men, Women and Money in America, 1600–1860* (New York: Random House, 1985), 402; and see Starr, *Southern Comfort*, chs. 1 and 2.
34. James Creecy, *Scenes in the South and Other Miscellaneous Pieces* (1860), quoted in Reinders, *End of an Era*, 11.

35. Reinders, *End of an Era*, 14.

36. Some of Marigny's complaints can be found in *Mémoire de Bernard Marigny, Habitant de la Louisiane: Addressee à ses concitoyens* (Paris: C. J. Trouvé, 1822; trans. Olivia Blanchard, typescript, Special Collections Division, Howard-Tilton Memorial Library, Tulane University, New Orleans), 25–27. For the bickering on both sides—a tangle of ethnic hostility and competing demands for capital improvements—see Fossier, *New Orleans*, ch. 9.

37. Starr, *Southern Comfort*, 22–26.

38. Ibid., 21–26; Reinders, *End of an Era*, 62, n. 3.

39. Residents of the Third Municipality below Esplanade, home to many immigrants and Creoles, were opposed to the annexation of Lafayette, an Anglo-American suburb full of southern Democrats. They were afraid this addition would upset the city's delicate balance of power. On this and the drive for reunification, see Reinders, *End of an Era*, ch. 4.

40. Letter of "Civius" to *Louisiana Gazette*, June 30, 1825, quoted in Fossier, *New Orleans*, 124; see also p. 292.

41. See Brasseaux, *Acadian to Cajun*, 90.

42. Audisio, "Crisis in Baton Rouge."

43. Quoted in Fossier, *New Orleans*, 277; see also Reinders, *End of an Era*, 12–13.

44. Newton, "Creoles and Anglo-Americans," 39.

45. Ibid.

46. James M. Crawford, *The Mobilian Trade Language* (Knoxville: University of Tennessee Press, 1978), 82.

47. Ripley, *Social Life*, 25–27.

48. Morrison, *Memoirs*.

49. Ibid.

50. Ripley, *Social Life*, 7–13, and Frémont, *Souvenirs of My Time*, 155–160.

51. Ripley, *Social Life*, 9–11.

52. *Journal of the Proceedings of the Convention of the State of Louisiana* (New Orleans: Besançon, Ferguson, 1845), Articles 104 and 132 (Articles 101 and 129 cover the same ground in the 1852 constitution); John Smith-Thibodeaux, *Les Francophones de Louisiane* (Paris: Editions Entente, 1977), 33; Hamel, *La Louisiane créole*, 1:126; see also, Kloss, *Les droits linguistiques des Franco-Américains aux Etats-Unis* (Quebec: Presses de l'Université Laval par le Centre International de Recherches sur le Bilinguisme, 1970).

53. Bell, *Revolution, Romanticism*, ch. 5.

54. See Reinders, *End of an Era*, chs. 2 and 4.

55. Quoted in editors' introduction to "Part II, The American Challenge," in Hirsch and Logsdon, eds., *Creole New Orleans*, 96.

56. On the Louisiana-Quebec comparison, see Eric Waddell, "French Louisiana: An Outpost of *l'Amérique Française* or Another Country and Another Culture?," in Louder and Waddell, eds., *French America*, 246–247; and Hero Jr., *Louisiana and Quebec*.

57. Joseph Logsdon and Caryn Cossé Bell, "The Americanization of Black New Orleans, 1850–1900," in Hirsch and Logsdon, eds., *Creole New Orleans*, 242.

58. *Debates in the Convention for the Revision and Amendment of the Constitution of the State of Louisiana, Assembled at Liberty Hall, New Orleans, April 6, 1864* (New Orleans: W. R. Fish, 1864), 47.

59. Ibid., 49.

60. Ibid., 478, 642.

61. *Official Journal of the Proceedings of the Convention, for Framing a Constitution for the State of Louisiana* (New Orleans: J. B. Roudanez, 1867–1868), 305.

62. Caulfield, *French Literature*, 63.

63. Hamel, *La Louisiane créole*, 1:44.

64. Brasseaux, *Acadian to Cajun*; Caryn Cossé Bell and Joseph Logsdon, "The Impact of Revolutionary Upheaval in France and the French Caribbean on Nineteenth-Century Black Leadership in New Orleans," in Patricia Galloway and Philip P. Boucher, eds., *Proceedings of the Fifteenth Meeting of the French Colonial Historical Society Martinique and Guadeloupe, May 1989* (Lantham, Md.: University Press of America, 1992), 130–141; Logsdon and Bell, "The Americanization of Black New Orleans," 201–261; and Bell, *Revolution, Romanticism*.

65. See Logsdon and Bell, "The Americanization of Black New Orleans," esp. 232–251.

66. Jean-Charles Houzeau, *My Passage at the New Orleans Tribune*, ed. David C. Rankin (Baton Rouge: Louisiana State University Press, 1984), 48.

67. Ibid., 51–52.

68. Logsdon and Bell, "The Americanization of Black New Orleans," 245.

69. For more on the Caribbean context of this struggle, see Rebecca J. Scott, "The Atlantic World and the Road to *Plessy v. Ferguson*," *Journal of American History*, 94 (December 2007).

70. Arnold R. Hirsch, "Fade to Black: Hurricane Katrina and the Disappearance of Creole New Orleans," *Journal of American History*, 94 (December 2007), 758.

71. Louise Augustin Fortier, "Chronique du vieux temps: Un Incident de la Guerre Confédérée," in Gerard Labarre St. Martin and Jacqueline K. Voorhies, eds., *Ecrits Louisianais du Dix-Neuvième Siècle* (Baton Rouge: Louisiana University Press, 1979), 71–81. The story was originally published in the magazine *Comptes-Rendus de l'Athénée Louisianais* in April 1905. See Caulfield, *French Literature*.

72. Caulfield, *French Literature*, 63–64.

73. Alfred Mercier, *L'Habitation Saint-Ybars, ou, Maîtres et Esclaves en Louisiane: Récit Social*, ed. Réginald Hamel, trans. Richard Lanoie (Montreal: Guérin, 1989), 29. I am grateful to James (Beau) Babst for this reference and translation.

74. Tregle, "Creoles and Americans," 171.

75. Carl A. Brasseaux, *French, Cajun, Creole, Houma: A Primer on Francophone Louisiana* (Baton Rouge: Louisiana State University Press, 2005), 100. Indeed, very little work has been done on the white Creole community after the Civil War. By way of contrast, the study of the black community, francophone and anglophone, has blossomed. For a sampling of recent work, see Sybil Kein, ed., *Creole: The History and Legacy of Louisiana's Free People of Color* (Baton Rouge: Louisiana State University Press, 2000). The only book on the former remains the anecdotal and rather nostalgic

compendium by Leonard V. Huber, *Creole Collage: Reflections on the Colorful Customs of Latter-Day New Orleans Creoles* (Lafayette: Center for Louisiana Studies, University of Southwestern Louisiana, 1980).

76. The entire poem can be found in Shapiro, trans., and Weiss, ed., *Creole Echoes*, 55. Shapiro's translation of this passage is:

> But others, too, passed by—pathetic, mute—
> Family-less, unloved, poor, destitute
> Exiles among the strollers gay: and, though
> Tattered their dress and worn, still do they show
> The dignity of far-off, fairer days.

I thought of this poem after Hurricane Katrina, but it is here to convey the sense of loss and exile some Francophones clearly felt in the postbellum world of Louisiana. It might be read with the deeply engaging essay by Hubert Aquin, which explores, among other things, the theme of exile: "The Cultural Fatigue of French Canada" (1962), in Anthony Purdy, ed., *Writing Quebec: Selected Essays by Hubert Aquin* (Edmonton: University of Alberta Press, 1988).

77. Elliott West, "Reconstructing Race," *Western Historical Quarterly*, 34:1 (Spring 2003), 1, 35.

78. A fuller story of racial prejudice and even violence directed against the French could be told. Such a history would find much evidence throughout the first half of the nineteenth century, and we are not far removed from an era when the words "Cajun" and "coonass" were hurled at Francophones in Louisiana as racial epithets. I have also met ethnically French residents of the Old Mines and Ste. Genevieve area in Missouri who confirmed that the terms "coonass," "frog," and the more local "pawpaw" were commonly used to insult members of their communities and were meant to have a racial dimension. In Canada, where Francophones constitute a significant segment of the population, the struggle over economic and cultural place remains fresh and combustible. A mere forty years ago, Pierre Vallieres (1968) wrote his famous manifesto for the independence of Quebec, describing French Canadians, significantly, as "the white niggers of Canada."

79. Matthew Frye Jacobson, *Whiteness of a Different Color: European Immigrants and the Alchemy of Race* (Cambridge: Harvard University Press, 1998).

80. The literature on the authors themselves and the creation of the modern French Quarter has been growing. See for example S. Frederick Starr, ed., *Inventing New Orleans: Writings of Lafcadio Hearn* (Jackson: University Press of Mississippi, 2001); Thomas J. Richardson, ed., *The Grandissimes: Centennial Essays* (Jackson: University Press of Mississippi, 1981); Anthony J. Stanonis, *Creating the Big Easy: New Orleans and the Emergence of Modern Tourism, 1918–1945* (Athens: University of Georgia Press, 2006); Alecia P. Long, *The Great Southern Babylon: Sex, Race, and Respectability in New Orleans, 1865–1920* (Baton Rouge: Louisiana State University Press, 2004); and J. Mark Souther, *New Orleans on Parade: Tourism and the Transformation of the Crescent City* (Baton Rouge: Louisiana State University Press, 2006).

81. March, *Shoepac Recollections*, 11.
82. The words are almost impossible to read, and apparently French is nothing more than English with some extra vowels. Hall and Farmer, *Grosse Pointe*, 99.
83. Raymond C. Miller, "Detroit—Old and New," *American Heritage*, 2:4 (Summer 1951).
84. Holli, "French Detroit," 95; and Holli, *Detroit*, 5.
85. Parkins, *The Historical Geography of Detroit*, 146.
86. Philip J. Deloria, *Playing Indian* (New Haven, Conn.: Yale University Press, 1998).
87. Richard Edwards and Menra Hopewell, *The Great West and Her Commercial Metropolis* (St. Louis, 1860), 278.
88. Ernest Kirschten, *Catfish and Crystal* (Garden City, N.Y.: Doubleday, 1960), 79–80.
89. Lamarre, *French Canadians of Michigan*, 19, 25. See also D. Aidan McQuillan, "French-Canadian Communities in the Upper Midwest during the Nineteenth Century," in Louder and Waddell, eds., *French America*, and DuLong, *French Canadians in Michigan*.
90. Roby, *The Franco-Americans*, 11–12.
91. DuLong, *French Canadians in Michigan*, 23.
92. Lamarre, *The French Canadians of Michigan*, 88–94.
93. DuLong, *French Canadians in Michigan*, 3.
94. Ibid., 27.
95. François-Edme Rameau de Saint-Père, *Notes historiques sur la colonie canadienne de Détroit: Lecture prononcée par Mr. Rameau à Windsor sur le Détroit Comté d'Essex, C. W. le lundi Ier avril 1861* (Montreal: J. B. Rolland, 1861), 41. I am indebted to Mara Harwel for finding and translating this quotation in her seminar paper, "'La Justice Mon Devoir': John R. Williams' Path from Clerk to Mayor of Detroit" (December 2007).
96. Williams, *A History of the City of Saint Paul*, 271.
97. Scholberg, *French Pioneers*, 40–41.
98. Ibid.; White, "The Power of Whiteness." For evidence of the Rolette family's musical education, see March 30, 1824, CCMO.
99. This information has been compiled from three sources: Scholberg, *French Pioneers*; Williams, *A History of the City of St. Paul*; and Rubinstein, "The French Canadians and the French."
100. Jean Morisset, "An America That Knows No Name: Postscript to a Quincentenary Celebration," in Louder and Waddell, eds., *French America*, 342.
101. Flandrau, *The History of Minnesota*, 400–401.
102. Ibid.
103. Sibley had been a member of the American Fur Company since 1829 when he moved to Mackinac as a company clerk at the age of eighteen. He had been a partner in the trade in Minnesota since 1834. Sibley had a daughter named Helen, or Muzzahwa-konwin, by a Wahpekute woman. Although little is known about this daughter, we do know that Sibley assumed financial responsibility for her. At the age of twelve, Helen received one thousand dollars in the Mendota Treaty of 1851 that Sibley had facilitated. Sibley invested the money in an Iron Mountain Railroad bond. This rail-

road was a Chouteau company. (Sibley Papers, Minnesota Historical Society, St. Paul, Roll 29, Volume 89.) As we might expect, the biography of Sibley published in 1889 by Nathaniel West never mentions his métis daughter. The author, of course, does spend almost fifty pages on Sibley's English ancestry and the accomplishments of his Massachusetts forebears. Sibley's political and military accomplishments are lauded and his place of honor in Minnesota history secured. (Nathaniel West, "The Ancestry, Life, and Times of Hon. Henry Hastings Sibley, LL.D." [St. Paul, 1889].) The dated and rather worthless accounts of Sibley have finally been replaced by a biography that captures beautifully a complex man in a context much more complicated than we have imagined: Rhoda R. Gilman, *Henry Hastings Sibley: Divided Heart* (St. Paul: Minnesota Historical Society Press, 2004).

104. Pamphlet, Henry Hastings Sibley Papers, Minnesota Historical Society, St. Paul.
105. Williams, *A History of the City of St. Paul*, 47–56.
106. Flandrau, *History of Minnesota*, 382.
107. Although the Catholic Church helped define and perpetuate the French heritage of Minnesota, ultimately it proved to be more a francophone bequest to other Catholics, not an effective tool of *survivance*, or cultural survival. In St. Paul, as in St. Louis and New Orleans, the strong presence of the church was a factor in attracting Catholic settlers, especially the Irish, whose numbers quickly overwhelmed the francophone character of the early church. By 1868, the Francophones of St. Paul had abandoned the cathedral parish and were ready to establish their own national parish, the Church of St. Louis. A parish school, the École St. Louis, provided instruction in French from its founding in 1873 until the 1960s. In Minneapolis a French national parish, Notre Dame de Lourdes, was established in 1877 with a parish school operating from 1888 to 1959. Although the Catholic Church has long been involved in the struggle for French Canadian cultural survival and the evolution of Quebecois nationalism, outside Quebec the church has not always been seen as an ally in that struggle. The French Creoles of New Orleans labeled English-speaking Irish immigrants "ultramontanists" during the 1850s and threatened to join the Know-Nothing Party in an effort to maintain "gallican" privileges. Four decades later in 1893, the French-language newspaper of Minneapolis, *Echo de l'Ouest*, complained bitterly of the influence of Irish Catholics in Minnesota, urging their readers to stem the tide of linguistic assimilation. See Rubinstein, "The French Canadians and the French," 45–50.
108. Williams, *A History of the City of St. Paul*, 108–116, 311–313.
109. Part 1, Reel 34; Part 2, Reel 16, Volumes TT–WW, CCMO.
110. William L. Ames to Charles Chouteau, May 25, 1872, CCMO.
111. Reel 16, March 1857, CCMO.
112. These details have been compiled from Rubinstein, "The French Canadians and the French," and Scholberg, *French Pioneers*.
113. The work of Gerhard Ens on the Red River métis also concludes that many métis people made a successful transition to market capitalism and that the Riel Rebellion of 1869–1870 was as much a class struggle as a "national" or ethnic uprising. See Ens, *Homeland to Hinterland*.
114. Indeed, Minnesota offers an interesting case study of the fate of the métis. When the

Lake Pepin half-breed tract was opened up in 1854 in exchange for certificates or scrip, how many of the métis were defrauded of their property? Was Bottineau's success an isolated case? We should also take a closer look at the influence of party politics, as Howard Lamar did many years ago in his study of Dakota Territory. In Dakota, Republican governor William Jayne urged the passage of a bill that would abolish slavery in the territory. The Democratic Assembly instead passed a bill prohibiting negroes from living in Dakota. The Republicans, on the other hand, fearful that the mixed-blood residents of the territory would keep the so-called Moccasin Democrats in power, killed a bill that would grant the métis any political rights. (See Lamar, *Dakota Territory*, 86–88.) In Minnesota, however, the Democrats in control of the convention to frame the state constitution in 1857 managed to extend the franchise to the métis. It was a wise move as historians and contemporaries alike attributed the election of Henry H. Sibley as the state's first governor to the late returns from the Pembina region. See Shortridge, *The Transition of a Typical Frontier*, 129–130.

115. Shortridge, *The Transition of a Typical Frontier*, passim.
116. Williams, *A History of the City of St. Paul*, 64–84.
117. The erasure of this important francophone world of mid-America from memory and history has had a number of consequences. It has reinforced the notion that French America resembles an archipelago (see Louder and Waddell, eds., *French America*). It has reinforced the dominant position of Quebec as the arbiter of francophone culture and historical production. Above all, it has allowed the American general public to assume that francophone culture occupies only a quaint space of no real significance in Louisiana and an occasionally troublesome space in the Canadian periphery. Without the connecting link of a francophone world in mid-America, the textbooks that shape our East-to-West national narrative can proceed without ascribing a meaningful role to the French.
118. For a more complete telling of Pierre Chouteau's story, see Jay Gitlin, "From Private Stories to Public Memory: The Chouteau Descendants of St. Louis and the Production of History," St. Louis Mercantile Library, forthcoming.
119. The notes from this lecture were collected and published by another French descendant, Chouteau's brother-in-law, Edward Villeré Papin, as "The Village under the Hill: A Sketch of Early St. Louis," in *Missouri Historical Society Collections* (October 1927), V:1. For a nice summary of the Anglo-Saxonism of this period, see Edward P. Kohn, *This Kindred People: Canadian-American Relations and the Anglo-Saxon Idea, 1895–1903* (Montreal: McGill–Queen's University Press, 2004), ch. 3.
120. Hiram M. Chittenden, *The American Fur Trade of the Far West*, 3 vols. (New York: Francis P. Harper, 1902). For Chouteau's contribution, see the preface, xxxiv–xxxv.

CONCLUSION

1. Josette Vieau Juneau to daughters, September 12, 1838, Solomon Juneau Papers, Milwaukee County Historical Society, Milwaukee, Wisconsin.
2. Barbara Whalen, "The Lawyer and the Fur Trader: Morgan Martin and Solomon

Juneau," *Milwaukee History*, 11:1 (Spring–Summer 1988), 31. See also Anderson, "Solomon Juneau," 109–112.

3. William Brewer to Solomon Juneau, March 22, 1851, Solomon Juneau Papers, Milwaukee County Historical Society, Milwaukee, Wisconsin.

4. Jeremy Adelman and Stephen Aron, "From Borderlands to Borders: Empires, Nation-States, and the Peoples in Between in North American History," *American Historical Review*, 104:3 (June 1999). See also the responses to this article in the following issue (October 1999).

5. For more on this midwestern story of removal, see for example Jay Gitlin, "Private Diplomacy to Private Property: States, Tribes, and Nations in the Early National Period," *Diplomatic History*, 22:1 (Winter 1998), 85–99.

6. Kastor, *The Nation's Crucible*.

7. Eugenia Berthold, "Notes on the Early French Families of St. Louis" manuscript for talk given in February 1953, Missouri Historical Society, St. Louis.

Selected Bibliography

MANUSCRIPT COLLECTIONS

Missouri Historical Society, St. Louis
    Chouteau Collections
    Fur Trade Papers
    Stephen Hempstead Diaries
    William Carr Lane Papers
    J. B. C. Lucas Collection
    Mullanphy Papers
    Papin Family Papers
    Peugnet Family Papers
    St. Louis Court House Papers
    Sibley Papers
    Soulard Papers
    Vallé Papers
    Wills Collection
Burton Historical Collection, Detroit Public Library, Detroit, Michigan
    Henry Berthelet Papers
    Campau Family Papers
    Campau, Barnabas Papers
    Campau, Daniel J. Papers
    Campau, Joseph Papers
    Campau, Louis P. Papers
    Charles Moran Papers
    John R. Williams Papers
    William Woodbridge Papers
Indiana Historical Society, Indianapolis
    Vigo Papers

Indiana State Library, Indiana Division, Indianapolis
  Lasselle Papers
Minnesota Historical Society, St. Paul
  Henry Hastings Sibley Papers
Howard-Tilton Memorial Library, Tulane University, New Orleans, Louisiana
  Favrot Family Papers
  Grima Family Papers
  New Orleans Municipal Papers
Grand Rapids History and Special Collections Center, Grand Rapids Public Library, Grand Rapids, Michigan
  Louis Moran Account Journal, 1796–1819
  Campau Family Collection
Woodson Research Center, Fondren Library, Rice University, Houston, Texas
  Wade Biography of Michel B. Menard Collection (MS 189)
Illinois Historic Preservation Agency, Abraham Lincoln Presidential Library, Springfield, Illinois
  Pierre Menard Collection
Milwaukee County Historical Society, Milwaukee, Wisconsin
  Solomon Juneau Papers

PRIMARY SOURCES

Alvord, Clarence W., ed. *Kaskaskia Records, 1778–1790*. Collections of the Illinois State Historical Library, vol. V. Springfield, 1909.

Alvord, Clarence W., and Clarence E. Carter, eds. *The Critical Period, 1763–1765*. Springfield: Illinois State Historical Library, 1915.

———, eds. *Invitation Serieuse aux Habitants des Illinois par un Habitant des Kaskaskias* (1772). 1908. Reprint, New York: Burt Franklin, 1968.

———, eds. *The New Régime, 1765–1767*. Springfield: Illinois State Historical Library, 1916.

———, eds. *Trade and Politics, 1767–1769*. Springfield: Illinois State Historical Library, 1921.

Babcock, Rufus, ed. *Forty Years of Pioneer Life: Memoir of John Mason Peck*. 1864. Reprint, Carbondale: Southern Illinois University Press, 1965.

Barnhart, John D. *Henry Hamilton and George Rogers Clark in the American Revolution, with the Unpublished Journal of Lieutenant Governor Henry Hamilton*. Crawfordsville, Ind.: R. E. Banta, 1951.

Barnhart, Warren L., ed. "The Letterbooks of Charles Gratiot, Fur Trader: The Nomadic Years, 1769–1797." PhD diss., St. Louis University, 1971.

Barret, Mary Finney. "Recollections of Mary Finney Barret." In *Glimpses of the Past* 9:4. St. Louis: Missouri Historical Society, 1942.

Berthold, Eugénie. *Glimpses of Creole Life in Old St. Louis*. Address published by the Missouri Historical Society, St. Louis, 1933.

Carter, Clarence E., ed. *Correspondence of General Thomas Gage.* 2 vols. New Haven, Conn.: Yale University Press, 1931–1933.

———. *The Territorial Papers of the United States.* Vols. 13 and 14, *The Territory of Louisiana-Missouri, 1803–1806 and 1806–1814.* 28 vols. Washington, D.C.: U.S. Government Printing Office, 1948 and 1949.

Corporation of the Town of Detroit. *Act of Incorporation and Journal of the Board of Trustees, 1802–1805.* Detroit: Burton Historical Collection, Detroit Public Library, 1922.

Darby, John F. *Personal Recollections.* St. Louis: G. I. Jones, 1880.

de Finiels, Nicolas. *An Account of Upper Louisiana.* 1803. Edited by Carl Ekberg and William E. Foley. Columbia: University of Missouri Press, 1989.

Evans, William A., ed. *Detroit to Fort Sackville, 1778–1779: The Journal of Normand Mac-Leod.* Detroit: Wayne State University Press, 1978.

Faribault-Beauregard, Marthe, ed. *La vie aux Illinois au XVIIIe siècle: Souvenirs inedits de Marie-Anne Cerré.* Montreal: Société de Recherche Historique Archiv-Histo, 1987.

Fowler, Marie Washburne. *Reminiscences: My Mother and I.* New Haven, Conn.: n.p., 1927.

Frémont, Jessie Benton. *Souvenirs of My Time.* Boston: D. Lothrop, 1887.

Grignon, Augustin. "Seventy-two Years' Recollections of Wisconsin." *Collections of the State Historical Society of Wisconsin.* Vol. 3. Madison, 1857.

Irving, Washington. *A Tour of the Prairies.* Edited by John Francis McDermott. Norman: University of Oklahoma Press, 1956.

James, James Alton, ed. *George Rogers Clark Papers.* 2 vols. Collections of the Illinois State Historical Library, vols. 3, 19 (Virginia series, vols. 3–4). Springfield: Illinois State Historical Library, 1912, 1926.

Jennings, Sister Marietta. *A Pioneer Merchant of St. Louis, 1810–1820.* New York: Columbia University Press, 1939.

Kappler, Charles J., ed. *Indian Affairs: Laws and Treaties.* Vol.2. *Treaties.* 1904. Reprint, Mattituck, N.Y.: Amereon, 1972.

Keating, William H. *Narrative of an Expedition to the Source of St. Peter's River.* 1825. Reprint, Minneapolis: Ross and Haines, 1959.

Kennerly, William Clark. *Persimmon Hill: A Narrative of Old St. Louis and the Far West.* Norman: University of Oklahoma Press, 1948.

Kinnaird, Lawrence, ed. *Spain in the Mississippi Valley, 1765–94.* Annual Report of the American Historical Association, vols. 2–4. Washington, D.C.: U.S. Government Printing Office, 1946–1949.

March, Walter (Orlando B. Wilcox). *Shoepac Recollections: A Way Side Glimpse of American Life.* New York: 1856.

Marra, Dorothy Brandt; Marie-Laure Dionne Pal, trans.; and David Boutros, ed. *Cher Oncle, Cher Papa: The Letters of François and Berenice Chouteau.* Kansas City: Western Historical Manuscript Collection–Kansas City, University of Missouri–Kansas City, 2001.

Marshall, Thomas M., ed. *The Life and Papers of Frederick Bates.* 2 vols. St. Louis: Missouri Historical Society, 1926.

Matson, Nehemiah. *Pioneers of Illinois*. Chicago: privately printed, 1882.

McDermott, John Francis, ed. "Diary of Charles Dehault Delassus from New Orleans to St. Louis, 1836." *Louisiana Historical Quarterly* 30:2 (April 1947), 359–438.

———, ed. *Old Cahokia*. St. Louis: St. Louis Historical Documents Foundation, 1949.

———, ed. *Tixier's Travels on the Osage Prairies*. Norman: University of Oklahoma Press, 1940.

———, ed. *The Western Journals of Washington Irving*. Norman: University of Oklahoma Press, 1944.

McKee, Irving, ed. *The Trail of Death: Letters of Benjamin Marie Petit*. Indiana Historical Publications, vol. 14. Indianapolis, 1944.

Meneray, Wilbur E., ed. *The Rebellion of 1768: Documents from the Favrot Family Papers and the Rosamonde E. and Emile Kuntz Collection*. New Orleans: Howard-Tilton Memorial Library of Tulane University, 1995.

Missouri Land Claims (Report from the Commissioner of the General Land Office, 1835). New Orleans: Polyanthos, 1976.

Morris, Thomas. *Journal of Captain Thomas Morris*. 1791. Reprint, New York: Readex, 1966.

Morrison, Adele Sarpy. *Memoirs*. St. Louis: Woodward & Tiernan, 1911.

Nasatir, Abraham P., ed. *Before Lewis and Clark: Documents Illustrating the History of Missouri, 1785–1804*. St. Louis: St. Louis Historical Documents Foundation, 1952.

Nute, Grace Lee, ed. *Calendar of the American Fur Company's Papers, volumes 2 and 3 of the Annual Report of the American Historical Association, 1944*. Washington, D.C.: U.S. Government Printing Office, 1945.

Pratte, Bernard, Jr. "Reminiscences of General Bernard Pratte, Jr." *Bulletin*, Missouri Historical Society, 6:1 (October 1949), 59–71.

Quaife, Milo Milton, ed. *The Siege of Detroit in 1763: The Journal of Pontiac's Conspiracy and John Rutherford's Narrative of a Captivity*. Chicago: R. R. Donnelley & Sons, 1958.

Ripley, Eliza. *Social Life in Old New Orleans*. New York: D. Appleton, 1912.

Robertson, Nellie Armstrong, and Dorothy Riker, eds. *The John Tipton Papers*. 3 vols. Indianapolis: Indiana Historical Bureau, 1942.

Rodgers, Thomas L. "Recollections of St. Louis—1857–1860." In *Glimpses of the Past* 9:4. St. Louis: Missouri Historical Society, 1942.

St. Martin, Gérard Labarre, and Jacqueline K. Voorhies, eds. *Ecrits Louisianais du Dix-Neuvième Siècle*. Baton Rouge: Louisiana State University Press, 1979.

Seineke, Kathrine W., ed. *The George Rogers Clark Adventure in the Illinois*. New Orleans: Polyanthos, 1981.

Shapiro, Norman R., trans., and M. Lynn Weiss, ed. *Creole Echoes: The Francophone Poetry of Nineteenth-Century Louisiana*. Urbana: University of Illinois Press, 2004.

Sibley, H. H. "Reminiscences of the Early Days of Minnesota." In *Collections of the Minnesota Historical Society*. Vol. 3. St. Paul: Minnesota Historical Society, 1880.

Sunder, John E., ed. *Matt Field on the Santa Fe Trail*. Norman: University of Oklahoma Press, 1960.

Wade, Mason, ed. *The Journals of Francis Parkman*. 2 vols. New York: Harper and Brothers, 1947.

Williams, J. Fletcher. A *History of the City of Saint Paul to 1875*. 1876. Reprint, St. Paul: Minnesota Historical Society Press, 1983.

Wilson, Samuel, Jr., ed. *Southern Travels: Journal of John H. B. Latrobe, 1834*. New Orleans: Historic New Orleans Collection, 1986.

SECONDARY SOURCES

Adler, Dorothy R. *British Investment in American Railways, 1834–1898*. Charlottesville: University Press of Virginia, 1970.

Alvord, Clarence W. *The Illinois Country, 1673–1818*. Edited by John Francis Bannon, SJ. Chicago: Loyola University Press, 1965.

———. *The Mississippi Valley in British Politics*. 2 vols. 1916. Reprint, New York: Russell and Russell, 1959.

Anderson, Gary Clayton. *Kinsmen of Another Kind: Dakota-White Relations in the Upper Mississippi Valley, 1650–1862*. Lincoln: University of Nebraska Press, 1984.

Anderson, Harry H. "Solomon Juneau: Fur Trader as Newspaper Publisher." *Milwaukee History* 17 (Autumn-Winter 1994), 109–112.

Anson, Bert. "The Fur Traders in Northern Indiana, 1796–1850." PhD diss., Indiana University, 1953.

———. *The Miami Indians*. Norman: University of Oklahoma Press, 1970.

Archibald, Robert R. "From 'La Louisiane' to 'Luisiana': The Imposition of Spanish Administration in the Upper Mississippi Valley." *Gateway Heritage* 11:1 (Summer 1990), 24–37.

Armour, David A., and Keith R. Widder. *At the Crossroads: Michilimackinac during the American Revolution*. Mackinac Island, Mich.: Mackinac Island State Park Commission, 1978.

Arnold, Morris S. *Unequal Laws unto a Savage Race: European Legal Traditions in Arkansas, 1686–1836*. Fayetteville: University of Arkansas Press, 1985.

Aron, Stephen. *American Confluence: The Missouri Frontier from Borderland to Border State*. Bloomington: Indiana University Press, 2006.

Audisio, Gabriel. "Crisis in Baton Rouge, 1840–1860: Foreshadowing the Demise of Louisiana's French Language?" *Louisiana History* 29:4 (Fall 1988), 343–363.

Baker, Vaughan. "Les Acadiens en Louisiane avant la Guerre de Secession: Etude d'assimilation culturelle." *Revue de Louisiane/Louisiana Review* 8 (Winter 1979), 101–115.

Bald, F. Clever. *Detroit's First American Decade, 1796 to 1805*. Ann Arbor: University of Michigan Press, 1948.

Banner, Stuart. *Legal Systems in Conflict: Property and Sovereignty in Missouri, 1750–1860*. Norman: University of Oklahoma Press, 2000.

Bannon, John Francis, SJ. "The Spaniards and the Illinois Country, 1762–1800." *Journal of the Illinois State Historical Society* 69:2 (May 1976), 110–118.

Beckert, Sven. *The Monied Metropolis: New York City and the Consolidation of the American Bourgeoisie, 1850–1896*. New York: Cambridge University Press, 2001.

Beckwith, Paul. *Creoles of St. Louis*. St. Louis: Nixon-Jones, 1893.

Beers, Henry P. *The Western Military Frontier, 1815–1846*. 1935. Reprint, Philadelphia: Porcupine Press, 1975.

Bell, Caryn Cossé. *Revolution, Romanticism, and the Afro-Creole Protest Tradition in Louisiana, 1718–1868*. Baton Rouge: Louisiana State University Press, 1997.

Bell, Ovid. *Côte Sans Dessein: A History*. Fulton, Mo.: n.p., 1930.

Belting, Natalia. *Kaskaskia under the French Regime*. Urbana: University of Illinois Press, 1948.

Bidlack, Russell E. *The Yankee Meets the Frenchman: River Raisin 1817–1830*. Ann Arbor: Historical Society of Michigan Occasional Publications No. 2, 1965.

Billings, Warren M., and Mark F. Fernandez, eds. *A Law unto Itself? Essays in the New Louisiana Legal History*. Baton Rouge: Louisiana State University Press, 2001.

Billon, Frederic. *Annals of St. Louis in Its Territorial Days from 1804 to 1821*. St. Louis: privately printed, 1888.

———. *Annals of St. Louis under the French and Spanish Dominations*. St. Louis: privately printed, 1886.

Blackhawk, Ned. *Violence over the Land: Indians and Empires in the Early American West*. Cambridge: Harvard University Press, 2006.

Bowes, John P. *Exiles and Pioneers: Eastern Indians in the Trans-Mississippi West*. New York: Cambridge University Press, 2007.

Boyle, Susan C. "Did She Generally Decide? Women in Ste. Genevieve, 1750–1805." *William and Mary Quarterly* 44:4 (October 1987), 775–789.

Brasseaux, Carl A. *Acadian to Cajun: Transformation of a People, 1803–1877*. Jackson: University Press of Mississippi, 1992.

———. *The Founding of New Acadia: The Beginnings of Acadian Life in Louisiana, 1765–1803*. Baton Rouge: Louisiana State University Press 1987.

Brown, Jennifer S. H. *Strangers in Blood: Fur Trade Company Families in Indian Country*. Vancouver: University of British Columbia Press, 1980.

Brown, Jennifer S. H., W. J. Eccles, and Donald P. Heldman, eds. *The Fur Trade Revisited: Selected Papers of the Sixth North American Fur Trade Conference, Mackinac Island, Michigan, 1991*. East Lansing: Michigan State University Press, 1994.

Brown, Margaret Kimball. *History As They Lived It: A Social History of Prairie du Rocher, Illinois*. Tucson, Ariz.: Patrice Press, 2005.

Buckley, Jay H. *William Clark: Indian Diplomat*. Norman: University of Oklahoma Press, 2008.

Burns, Louis F. *A History of the Osage People*. Tuscaloosa: University of Alabama Press, 2004.

Calloway, Colin G. *Crown and Calumet: British-Indian Relations, 1783–1815*. Norman: University of Oklahoma Press, 1987.

———. *The Scratch of a Pen: 1763 and the Transformation of North America*. New York: Oxford University Press, 2006.

Carter, Clarence E. *Great Britain and the Illinois Country, 1763–1774*. Washington, D.C.: American Historical Association, 1910.

Carter, Harvey L., and Marcia C. Spencer. "Stereotypes of the Mountain Man." *Western Historical Quarterly* 6:1 (January 1975), 17–32.

Caulfield, Ruby Van Allen. *The French Literature of Louisiana.* New York: Institute of French Studies, Columbia University, 1929.

Cayton, Andrew R. L. *Frontier Indiana.* Bloomington: Indiana University Press, 1996.

Cayton, Andrew R. L., and Fredrika J. Teute, eds. *Contact Points: American Frontiers from the Mohawk Valley to the Mississippi, 1750–1830.* Chapel Hill: University of North Carolina Press, 1998.

Chaput, Donald. "The Family of Drouet de Richerville: Merchants, Soldiers, and Chiefs of Indiana." *Indiana Magazine of History* 74 (June 1978), 103–116.

Clark, John G. *La Rochelle and the Atlantic Economy during the Eighteenth Century.* Baltimore: Johns Hopkins University Press, 1981.

———. *New Orleans, 1718–1812: An Economic History.* Baton Rouge: Louisiana State University Press, 1970.

Coker, William S., and Thomas D. Watson. *Indian Traders of the Southeastern Spanish Borderlands: Panton, Leslie & Company and John Forbes & Company, 1783–1847.* Pensacola: University of West Florida Press, 1986.

Corbett, Katharine T. "Veuve Chouteau: A 250th Anniversary." *Gateway Heritage* 3:4 (Spring 1983), 42–48.

Crété, Liliane. *Daily Life in Louisiana, 1815–1830.* Baton Rouge: Louisiana State University Press, 1981.

Cronon, William. *Nature's Metropolis: Chicago and the Great West.* New York: W. W. Norton, 1991.

Cunningham, Mary B., and Jeanne C. Blythe. *The Founding Family of St. Louis.* St. Louis: Midwest Technical Publications, 1977.

Cunningham, Wilbur M. *Land of Four Flags: An Early History of the St. Joseph Valley.* Berrien Springs, Mich.: Hardscrabble Books, 1973.

Dargo, George. *Jefferson's Louisiana: Politics and the Clash of Legal Traditions.* Cambridge: Harvard University Press, 1975.

Davis, Ronald L. F. "Community and Conflict in Pioneer St. Louis, Missouri." *Western Historical Quarterly* 10:3 (July 1979), 337–355.

Davis, Susan Burdick. *Old Forts and Real Folks.* Madison, Wisc.: Zoe Bayliss and Susan Davis, 1939.

Dawdy, Shannon Lee. *Building the Devil's Empire: French Colonial New Orleans.* Chicago: University of Chicago Press, 2008.

de Lagrave, Jean-Paul. *Voltaire's Man in America.* Montreal: Robert Davies, 1997.

Devine, Heather. *The People Who Own Themselves: Aboriginal Ethnogenesis in a Canadian Family, 1660–1900.* Calgary: University of Calgary Press, 2004.

Domínguez, Virginia R. *White by Definition: Social Classification in Creole Louisiana.* New Brunswick, N.J.: Rutgers University Press, 1986.

Dorrance, Ward. "The Survival of French in the Old District of Sainte Genevieve." *University of Missouri Studies* 10:2 (April 1935).

Douglas, Walter B. "Jean Gabriel Cerre: A Sketch." *Missouri Historical Collections* II, No. 2 (St. Louis, 1900–1906), 58–76.

DuLong, John P. *French Canadians in Michigan.* East Lansing: Michigan State University Press, 2001.

Dunn, Walter S., Jr. *Choosing Sides on the Frontier in the American Revolution.* Westport, Conn.: Praeger, 2007.

————. *The New Imperial Economy: The British Army and the American Frontier, 1764–1768.* Westport, Conn.: Praeger, 2001.

Dunnigan, Brian Leigh. *Frontier Metropolis: Picturing Early Detroit, 1701–1838.* Detroit: Wayne State University Press, 2001.

Du Terrage, Marc de Villiers. *The Last Years of French Louisiana.* Translated by Hosea Phillips and edited by Carl A. Brasseaux and Glenn R. Conrad. 1904. English edition, Lafayette: Center for Louisiana Studies, University of Southwestern Louisiana, 1982.

DuVal, Kathleen. *The Native Ground: Indians and Colonists in the Heart of the Continent.* Philadelphia: University of Pennsylvania Press, 2006.

Eblen, Jack Ericson. *The First and Second United States Empires: Governors and Territorial Government, 1784–1912.* Pittsburgh: University of Pittsburgh Press, 1968.

Eccles, W. J. *Canadian Society during the French Regime.* Montreal: Harvest House, 1968.

Edmunds, R. David. "George Winter: Mirror of Acculturation." In *Indians and a Changing Frontier: The Art of George Winter.* Compiled by Sarah E. Cooke and Rachel B. Ramadhyani. Indianapolis: Indiana Historical Society, 1993.

————. "'Nothing Has Been Effected': The Vincennes Treaty of 1792." *Indiana Magazine of History* 74 (March 1978), 23–35.

Ekberg, Carl J. *Colonial Ste. Genevieve.* Gerald, Mo.: Patrice Press, 1985.

————. *François Vallé and His World: Upper Louisiana before Lewis and Clark.* Columbia: University of Missouri Press, 2002.

————. *French Roots in the Illinois Country: The Mississippi Frontier in Colonial Times.* Urbana: University of Illinois Press, 1998.

————. *Louis Bolduc: His Family and His House.* Tucson, Ariz.: Patrice Press, 2002.

Ellis, David M., ed. *The Frontier in American Development: Essays in Honor of Paul Wallace Gates.* Ithaca, N.Y.: Cornell University Press, 1969.

Ens, Gerhard J. *Homeland to Hinterland: The Changing Worlds of the Red River Metis in the Nineteenth Century.* Toronto: University of Toronto Press, 1996.

Fabre-Surveyer, E. "From Montreal to Michigan and Indiana." *Proceedings and Transactions of the Royal Society of Canada, Third Series.* Ottawa, 1945.

Faragher, John Mack. *A Great and Noble Scheme: The Tragic Story of the Expulsion of the French Acadians from Their American Homeland.* New York: W. W. Norton, 2005.

Farmer, Silas. *The History of Detroit and Michigan.* Detroit: Silas Farmer, 1884.

Fernandez, Mark F. *From Chaos to Continuity: The Evolution of Louisiana's Judicial System, 1712–1862.* Baton Rouge: Louisiana State University Press, 2001.

Finkelman, Paul. "Slavery and the Northwest Ordinance: A Study in Ambiguity." *Journal of the Early Republic* 6:4 (Winter 1986), 343–370.

Flandrau, Charles E. *The History of Minnesota and Tales of the Frontier.* St. Paul: E. W. Porter, 1900.

Foley, William E. "The Lewis and Clark Expedition's Silent Partners: The Chouteau Brothers of St. Louis." *Missouri Historical Review* 77:2 (January 1983), 131–146.

————. *Wilderness Journey: The Life of William Clark.* Columbia: University of Missouri Press, 2004.

Foley, William E., and C. David Rice. *The First Chouteaus: River Barons of Early St. Louis.* Urbana: University of Illinois Press, 1983.

Folmer, Henry. *Franco-Spanish Rivalry in North America, 1524–1763.* Glendale, Calif.: Arthur H. Clark, 1953.

Formisano, Ronald P. *The Birth of Mass Political Parties: Michigan, 1827–1861.* Princeton, N.J.: Princeton University Press, 1971.

Fossier, Albert A. *New Orleans: The Glamour Period, 1800–1840.* New Orleans: Pelican, 1957.

Garraghan, Gilbert J., SJ. *Catholic Beginnings in Kansas City, Missouri.* Chicago: Loyola University Press, 1920.

———. *Saint Ferdinand de Florissant.* Chicago: Loyola University Press, 1923.

Gates, Paul Wallace. *History of Public Land Law Development.* Washington, D.C.: U.S. Government Printing Office, 1968.

———. "Indian Allotments Preceding the Dawes Act." In *The Frontier Challenge: Responses to the Trans-Mississippi West,* edited by John G. Clark. Lawrence: University of Kansas Press, 1971.

Gilbert, Arthur N. "The American Indian and United States Diplomatic History." *History Teacher* 8 (February 1975), 229–241.

Gilman, Rhoda, ed. *Aspects of the Fur Trade.* St. Paul: Minnesota Historical Society Press, 1967.

———. *Henry Hastings Sibley: Divided Heart.* St. Paul: Minnesota Historical Society Press, 2004.

Glasrud, Clarence A., ed. *L'Heritage Tranquille: The Quiet Heritage.* Moorhead, Minn.: Concordia College, 1987.

Gracy, David B., II. *Moses Austin: His Life.* San Antonio: Trinity University Press, 1987.

Gray, Susan E. *The Yankee West: Community Life on the Michigan Frontier.* Chapel Hill: University of North Carolina Press, 1996.

Greenwood, F. Murray. *Legacies of Fear: Law and Politics in Quebec in the Era of the French Revolution.* Toronto: University of Toronto Press, 1993.

Haas, Edward F., ed. *Louisiana's Legal Heritage.* Pensacola, Fla.: Louisiana State Museum, 1983.

Haeger, John D. *The Investment Frontier: New York Businessmen and the Economic Development of the Old Northwest.* Albany, N.Y.: SUNY Press, 1981.

———. *John Jacob Astor: Business and Finance in the Early Republic.* Detroit: Wayne State University Press, 1991.

Hafen, LeRoy, ed. *Mountain Men and the Fur Trade of the Far West.* 10 vols. Glendale, Calif.: Arthur H. Clark, 1965–1972.

Hagan, William T. *American Indians.* Chicago: University of Chicago Press, 1961.

Hall, Peter Dobkin. "Family Structure and Economic Organization: Massachusetts Merchants, 1700–1850." In *Family and Kin in Urban Communities, 1700–1930,* edited by Tamara K. Hareven. New York: Franklin Watts, 1977.

Hall, Theodore Parsons, and Silas Farmer. *Grosse Pointe on Lake Sainte Claire.* Detroit: Silas Farmer, 1886.

Hämäläinen, Pekka. *The Comanche Empire.* New Haven, Conn.: Yale University Press, 2008.

Hamel, Reginald. *La Louisiane creole: Litteraire, politique et sociale, 1762–1900.* 2 vols. Ottawa: Les Editions Lemeac avec la collaboration du Conseil de la langue française, 1984.

Hammes, Raymond H. "Land Transactions in Illinois prior to the Sale of Public Domain." *Journal of the Illinois State Historical Society* LXXVII (Summer 1984), 110–111.

Herlihy, David. *Medieval Households.* Cambridge: Harvard University Press, 1985.

Hero, Alfred Olivier, Jr. *Louisiana and Quebec: Bilateral Relations and Comparative Socio-political Evolution, 1673–1993.* Lanham, Md.: University Press of America and Tulane Studies in Political Science, 1995.

Hinderaker, Eric. *Elusive Empires: Constructing Colonialism in the Ohio Valley, 1673–1800.* Cambridge: Cambridge University Press, 1997.

Hine, Robert V. *Community on the American Frontier.* Norman: University of Oklahoma Press, 1980.

Hirsch, Arnold R., and Joseph Logsdon, eds. *Creole New Orleans.* Baton Rouge: Louisiana State University Press, 1992.

Hodes, Frederick A. *Beyond the Frontier: A History of St. Louis to 1821.* Tucson, Ariz.: Patrice Press, 2004.

Hoffhaus, Charles E. *Chez les Canses: Three Centuries at Kawsmouth: The French Foundations of Metropolitan Kansas City.* Kansas City: Lowell Press, 1984.

Holli, Melvin G. *Detroit.* New York: Franklin Watts, 1976.

———. "French Detroit: The Clash of Feudal and Yankee Values." In *The Ethnic Frontier: Group Survival in Chicago and the Midwest,* edited by Melvin G. Holli and Peter d'A. Jones. Grand Rapids, Mich.: Eerdmans, 1977.

Horsman, Reginald. "Great Britain and the Illinois Country in the Era of the American Revolution." *Journal of the Illinois State Historical Society* 69:2 (May 1976), 100–109.

Houck, Louis. *A History of Missouri.* 3 vols. Chicago: R. R. Donnelley & Sons, 1908.

———. *The Spanish Regime in Missouri.* 2 vols. Chicago: R. R. Donnelley & Sons, 1909.

Hubbard, Bela. *Memorials of a Half-Century in Michigan and the Lake Region.* New York: G. P. Putnam's Sons, 1888.

Hunter, Juanita. "The Indians and the Michigan Road." *Indiana Magazine of History* 83 (September 1987), 244–266.

Igartua, Jose E. "The Merchants of Montreal at the Conquest: Socio-Economic Profile." *Histoire Sociale—Social History* 8:16 (November 1975), 275–293.

Jaenen, Cornelius. *Friend and Foe: Aspects of French-Amerindian Cultural Contact in the Sixteenth and Seventeenth Centuries.* New York: Columbia University Press, 1976.

John, Elizabeth A. H. *Storms Brewed in Other Men's Worlds: The Confrontation of Indians, Spanish, and French in the Southwest, 1540–1795.* College Station: Texas A&M University Press, 1975.

Johnson, Ida Amanda. *The Michigan Fur Trade.* Lansing: Michigan Historical Commission, 1919.

Jorstad, Erling. "Personal Politics in the Origin of Minnesota's Democratic Party." *Minnesota History* 36 (September 1959), 259–271.

Kadler, Eric H. "The French in Detroit, 1701–1880." *French-American Review* 6:2 (Fall 1982), 296–309.

Kastor, Peter J. *The Nation's Crucible: The Louisiana Purchase and the Creation of America.* New Haven, Conn.: Yale University Press, 2004.

Kettner, James H. *The Development of American Citizenship, 1608–1807.* Chapel Hill: University of North Carolina Press, 1978.

Kilfoil, Jack F. *C. C. Trowbridge, Detroit Banker and Michigan Land Speculator.* 1969. Reprint, New York: Arno Press, 1979.

Kmen, Henry A. *Music in New Orleans: The Formative Years, 1791–1841.* Baton Rouge: Louisiana State University Press, 1966.

Lachance, Paul. "Intermarriage and French Cultural Persistence in Late Spanish and Early American New Orleans." *Histoire sociale — Social History* XV, no. 29 (May 1982), 47–81.

Lamar, Howard. *Dakota Territory, 1861–1889.* New Haven, Conn.: Yale University Press, 1956.

———. *The Far Southwest, 1846–1912: A Territorial History.* New Haven, Conn.: Yale University Press, 1966.

———. *The Trader on the American Frontier: Myth's Victim.* College Station: Texas A&M University Press, 1977.

Lamarre, Jean. *The French Canadians of Michigan: Their Contribution to the Development of the Saginaw Valley and the Keweenaw Peninsula, 1840–1914.* Detroit: Wayne State University Press, 2003.

Lass, William E. *A History of Steamboating on the Upper Missouri River.* Lincoln: University of Nebraska Press, 1962.

Lavender, David. *Bent's Fort.* Garden City, N.Y.: Doubleday, 1954.

———. *The Fist in the Wilderness.* Garden City, N.Y.: Doubleday, 1964.

Lawson, Philip. *The Imperial Challenge: Quebec and Britain in the Age of the American Revolution.* Montreal: McGill–Queen's University Press, 1989.

Lecompte, Janet. "Auguste Pierre Chouteau." In *French Fur Traders and Voyageurs in the American West*, edited by LeRoy R. Hafen, 96–123. Spokane, Wash.: Arthur H. Clark, 1995.

———. "John F. A. Sanford." In *The Mountain Men and the Fur Trade of the Far West*, 10 vols., edited by LeRoy R. Hafen, IX:351–359. Glendale, Calif.: Arthur H. Clark, 1972.

———. "Pierre Chouteau, Jr." In *Mountain Men and Fur Traders of the Far West*, edited by LeRoy R. Hafen, 24–56 (Lincoln: University of Nebraska Press, 1982).

———. *Pueblo, Hardscrabble, Greenhorn: The Upper Arkansas, 1832–1856.* Norman: University of Oklahoma Press, 1978.

Lewis, Hugh M. *Robidoux Chronicles: French-Indian Ethnoculture of the Trans-Mississippi West.* Victoria, BC: Trafford, 2004.

Louder, Dean R., and Eric Waddell, eds. *French America: Mobility, Identity, and Minority Experience across the Continent.* Baton Rouge: Louisiana State University Press, 1983.

Mahoney, Timothy R. *Provincial Lives: Middle-Class Experience in the Ante-Bellum Middle West.* New York: Cambridge University Press, 1999.

Mabie, Christopher. *Uncle Louis: The Biography of Louis Campau, founder of Saginaw and Grand Rapids.* Walker, Mich.: Van Naerden, 2007.

McAvoy, Thomas T. *The Catholic Church in Indiana, 1789–1834.* New York: Columbia University Press, 1940.

McDermott, John Francis. *A Glossary of Mississippi Valley French, 1673–1850.* Washington University Studies New Series: Language and Literature No. 12. St. Louis: Washington University Press, 1941.

———. *Private Libraries in Creole St. Louis.* Baltimore: Johns Hopkins University Press, 1938.

———, ed. *The Spanish in the Mississippi Valley, 1762–1804.* Urbana: University of Illinois Press, 1974.

———, ed. *The French in the Mississippi Valley.* Urbana: University of Illinois Press, 1965.

———, ed. *Frenchmen and French Ways in the Mississippi Valley.* Urbana: University of Illinois Press, 1969.

Merrell, James H. *Into the American Woods: Negotiators on the Pennsylvania Frontier.* New York: W. W. Norton, 1999.

Michel, Peter. "The St. Louis Fur Trade: Fur Company Ledgers and Account Books in the Archives of the Missouri Historical Society." *Gateway Heritage* 6:2 (Fall 1985), 10–17.

Middleton, Richard. *Pontiac's War: Its Causes, Course and Consequences.* New York: Routledge, 2007.

Miller, Irma R. *French-Indian Families in America's West: Lessert (aka Claymore), Roy, Chatillon, Delor, Royer,* 2nd ed. Victoria, BC: Trafford, 2005.

Miquelon, Dale, ed. *Society and Conquest: the Debate on the Bourgeoisie and Social Change in French Canada, 1700–1850.* Toronto: Copp Clark, 1977.

Montoya, María E. *Translating Property: The Maxwell Land Grant and the Conflict over Land in the American West, 1840–1900.* Berkeley: University of California Press, 2002.

Moran, J. Bell. *The Moran Family: 200 Years in Detroit.* Detroit: Alved, 1949.

Morgan, Dale L. et al., eds. *Aspects of the Fur Trade: Selected Papers of the 1965 North American Fur Trade Conference.* St. Paul: Minnesota Historical Society, 1967.

Murphy, Lawrence R. *Lucien Bonaparte Maxwell: Napoleon of the Southwest.* Norman: University of Oklahoma Press, 1983.

Murphy, Lucy Eldersveld. *A Gathering of Rivers: Indians, Métis, and Mining in the Western Great Lakes, 1737–1832.* Lincoln: University of Nebraska Press, 2000.

Musick, James B. *St. Louis as a Fortified Town: A Narrative and Critical Essay of the Period of Struggle for the Fur Trade of the Mississippi Valley and Its Influence upon St. Louis.* St. Louis: R. F. Miller, 1941.

Myer, Mrs. Max. "Charles Gratiot's Land Claim Problems." *Bulletin of the Missouri Historical Society* XXI (April 1965), 237–244.

Nasatir, Abraham P. "The Anglo-Spanish Frontier in the Illinois Country during the American Revolution." *Journal of the Illinois State Historical Society* 21:3 (October 1928), 343–350.

———. *Borderland in Retreat.* Albuquerque: University of New Mexico Press, 1976.

———. "Government Employees and Salaries in Spanish Louisiana." *Louisiana Historical Quarterly* 29 (1946), 885–1040.

———. *Spanish War Vessels on the Mississippi, 1792–1796.* New Haven, Conn.: Yale University Press, 1968.

Neatby, Hilda. *The Administration of Justice under the Quebec Act.* Minneapolis: University of Minnesota Press, 1937.

Newton, Lewis W. "Creoles and Anglo-Americans in Old Louisiana: A Study in Cultural Conflicts." *Southwestern Social Science Quarterly* 14:1 (June 1933), 31–48.

Oglesby, Richard. *Manuel Lisa and the Opening of the Missouri Fur Trade of the Far West.* Norman: University of Oklahoma Press, 1963.

Paré, George. *The Catholic Church in Detroit, 1701–1888.* Detroit: Gabriel Richard, 1951.

Parkins, Almon E. *The Historical Geography of Detroit.* Lansing: Michigan Historical Commission, 1918.

Peterson, Charles. *Colonial St. Louis: Building a Creole Capital.* St. Louis: Missouri Historical Society, 1949.

Peterson, Jacqueline. "The People in Between: Indian-White Marriage and the Genesis of a Métis Society and Culture n the Great Lakes Region, 1680–1830." PhD diss., University of Illinois at Chicago Circle, 1981.

———. "Prelude to Red River: A Social Portrait of the Great Lakes Metis." *Ethnohistory* 25:1 (Winter 1978), 41–67.

———. "'Wild' Chicago: The Formation and Destruction of a Multiracial Community on the Midwestern Frontier, 1816–1837." In *The Ethnic Frontier,* edited by Melvin G. Holli and Peter d'A. Jones. Grand Rapids: Eerdmans, 1977.

Peterson, Jacqueline, and Jennifer S. H. Brown, eds. *The New Peoples: Being and Becoming Metis in North America.* Manitoba Studies in Native History. Lincoln: University of Nebraska Press, 1985.

Phillips, Paul C. *The Fur Trade.* 2 vols. Norman: University of Oklahoma Press, 1961.

Poinsatte, Charles. *Outpost in the Wilderness: Fort Wayne, 1706–1828.* Fort Wayne, Ind.: Allen County, Fort Wayne Historical Society, 1976.

Porter, Kenneth W. *John Jacob Astor, Business Man.* 2 vols. Cambridge: Harvard University Press, 1931.

Primm, James N. *Lion of the Valley: St. Louis, Missouri.* Boulder, Colo.: Pruett, 1981.

Prucha, Francis Paul. *American Indian Policy in the Formative Years: The Indian Trade and Intercourse Acts, 1790–1834.* Cambridge: Harvard University Press, 1962.

———. *American Indian Treaties: The History of a Political Anomaly.* Berkeley: University of California Press, 1994.

Rea, Robert R. *Major Robert Farmar of Mobile.* Tuscaloosa: University of Alabama Press, 1990.

Reinders, Robert C. *End of an Era: New Orleans, 1850–1860.* Gretna, La.: Pelican, 1964.

Reséndez, Andrés. *Changing National Identities at the Frontier: Texas and New Mexico, 1800–1850.* New York: Cambridge University Press, 2005.

Rich, E. E. *Montreal and the Fur Trade.* Montreal: McGill University Press, 1966.

Roach, Ruth H. *St. Louis Silversmiths.* St. Louis: Eden, 1967.

Roby, Yves. *The Franco-Americans of New-England: Dreams and Realities,* translated by Mary Ricard. Quebec: Septentrion, 2004.

Rodabaugh, John. *Frenchtown.* St. Louis: Sunrise, 1980.

Roger, Philippe. *The American Enemy: The History of French Anti-Americanism.* Chicago: University of Chicago Press, 2005.

Ronda, James P. *Finding the West: Explorations with Lewis and Clark.* Albuquerque: University of New Mexico Press, 2001.

Rubinstein, Sarah P. "The French Canadians and the French." In *They Chose Minnesota: A Survey of the State's Ethnic Groups,* edited by June D. Holmquist. St. Paul: Minnesota Historical Society Press, 1981.

Sandweiss, Eric. *St. Louis: The Evolution of an American Urban Landscape.* Philadelphia: Temple University Press, 2001.

Satz, Ronald N. "Indian Policy in the Jacksonian Era: The Old Northwest as a Test Case." *Michigan History* 60 (Spring 1976), 71–93.

Savage, Sister Mary Ludida. *The Congregation of Saint Joseph of Carondelet: A Brief Account of Its Origin and Its Work in the United States (1650–1922).* St. Louis: B. Herder, 1923.

Saxton, Martha. *Being Good: Women's Moral Values in Early America.* New York: Hill and Wang, 2003.

Sayad, Elizabeth Gentry. *A Yankee in Creole Country: The Unfinished Vision of Justus Post in Frontier St. Louis.* St. Louis: Virginia Publishing Company, 2004.

Scanlan, Peter L. *Prairie du Chien: French-British-American.* Menasha, Wisc.: Collegiate Press, 1937.

Schake, Lowell M. *La Charrette.* Lincoln: iUniverse Star, 2006.

Scharf, J. Thomas. *History of St. Louis, City and County.* 2 vols. Philadelphia: Louis H. Evarts, 1883.

Scholberg, Henry. *The French Pioneers of Minnesota/Les Pionniers Français du Minnesota.* Eau Claire, Wisc.: NorthStar, 1996.

Schroeder, Walter A. *Opening the Ozarks: A Historical Geography of Missouri's Ste. Genevieve District, 1760–1830.* Columbia: University of Missouri Press, 2002.

Segalen, Martine. *Historical Anthropology of the Family.* Cambridge: Cambridge University Press, 1986.

Seineke, Kathrine W., ed. *Guide to the Microfilm Edition of the Pierre Menard Collection.* Springfield: Illinois State Historical Society, 1972.

Shortridge, Wilson P. *The Transition of a Typical Frontier: The Life of Henry Hastings Sibley.* Menasha, Wisc.: George Banta, 1919.

Skinner, Claiborne A. *The Upper Country: French Enterprise in the Colonial Great Lakes.* Baltimore: Johns Hopkins University Press, 2008.

Sleeper-Smith, Susan. *Indian Women and French Men: Rethinking Cultural Encounter in the Western Great Lakes.* Amherst: University of Massachusetts Press, 2001.

Smelser, Marshall. "Folkways in Creole St. Louis: The Transition from Creole to American Customs." Master's thesis, St. Louis University, 1938.

———. "Housing in Creole St. Louis, 1764–1821: An Example of Cultural Change." *Louisiana Historical Quarterly* 21:2 (April 1938), 337–348.

Snyder, Charles. "Antoine LeClaire, the First Proprietor of Davenport." *Annals of Iowa.* 3rd series, 23 (1941–1942), 77–117.

Snyder, J. F. "The Old French Towns of Illinois in 1839: A Reminiscence." *Journal of the Illinois State Historical Society* 36:4 (December 1943), 345–367.

Sosin, Jack M. "The French Settlements in British Policy for the North American Interior, 1760–1774." *Canadian Historical Review* 39:3 (September 1958), 185–208.

———. *The Revolutionary Frontier, 1763–1783.* New York: Holt, Rinehart and Winston, 1967.

Stagg, J. C. A. *Mr. Madison's War.* Princeton, N.J.: Princeton University Press, 1983.

Steffen, Jerome O. *William Clark: Jeffersonian Man on the Frontier.* Norman: University of Oklahoma Press, 1977.

Stepenoff, Bonnie. *From French Community to Missouri Town: Ste. Genevieve in the Nineteenth Century.* Columbia: University of Missouri Press, 2006.

Stevens, Wayne E. *The Northwest Fur Trade, 1763–1800.* Urbana: University of Illinois Studies in the Social Sciences, 1928.

Sunder, John E. *The Fur Trade on the Upper Missouri, 1840–1865.* Norman: University of Oklahoma Press, 1965.

———. *Joshua Pilcher: Fur Trader and Indian Agent.* Norman: University of Oklahoma Press, 1968.

Tousignant, Pierre. "The Integration of the Province of Quebec into the British Empire, 1763–91." *Dictionary of Canadian Biography.* Vol. IV, 1771–1800. Toronto: University of Toronto Press and les Presses de l'Université Laval, 1979.

Thorne, Tanis C. *The Many Hands of My Relations: French and Indians on the Lower Missouri.* Columbia: University of Missouri Press, 1996.

Tinker, Edward Larocque. *Bibliography of the French Newspapers and Periodicals of Louisiana.* Worcester, Mass.: American Antiquarian Society, 1933.

Tregle, Joseph G., Jr. *Louisiana in the Age of Jackson: A Clash of Cultures and Personalities.* Baton Rouge: Louisiana State University Press, 1999.

———. "Political Reinforcement of Ethnic Dominance in Louisiana, 1812–1845." In *The Americanization of the Gulf Coast, 1803–1850,* edited by L. F. Ellsworth. Proceedings of the Gulf Coast History and Humanities Conference, Pensacola, Fla. 3 (1971).

Trennert, Robert A., Jr. *Alternative to Extinction: Federal Indian Policy and the Beginnings of the Reservation System, 1846–51.* Philadelphia: Temple University Press, 1975.

———. "The Fur Trader as Indian Administrator: Conflict of Interest or Wise Policy?" *South Dakota History* 5 (Winter 1974), 1–19.

———. *Indian Traders on the Middle Border: The House of Ewing, 1822–1854.* Lincoln: University of Nebraska Press, 1981.

Trigger, Bruce G. et al., eds. *Le Castor Fait Tout: Selected Papers of the Fifth North American Fur Trade Conference, 1985* Montreal: Lake St. Louis Historical Society, 1987.

Turner, Frederick Jackson. "The Character and Influence of the Indian Trade in Wisconsin." Edited by Herbert Baxter Adams. *Johns Hopkins University Studies in Historical and Political Science,* Ninth Series, Vols. XI–XII (November and December 1891), 547–615.

———. "The Rise and Fall of New France." *Chautauquan* 24 (October, December, 1896).

Unrau, William E. *The Kansa Indians.* Norman: University of Oklahoma Press, 1971.

Usner, Daniel H., Jr. "An American Indian Gateway." *Gateway Heritage* 11:3 (Winter 1990–1991), 42–51.

———. "The Frontier Exchange Economy of the Lower Mississippi Valley in the Eighteenth Century." *William and Mary Quarterly* 44:2 (April 1987), 165–192.

Van Kirk, Sylvia. *"Many Tender Ties": Women in Fur-Trade Society, 1670–1870.* Winnipeg: Watson & Dwyer, 1980.

Van Ravenswaay, Charles. *Saint Louis: An Informal History of the City and Its People, 1764–1865.* St. Louis: Missouri Historical Society Press, 1991.

Vinyard, JoEllen McNergney. *For Faith and Fortune: The Education of Catholic Immigrants in Detroit, 1805–1925.* Urbana: University of Illinois Press, 1998.

Wallace, William S. *Antoine Robidoux, 1794–1860: A Biography of a Western Venturer.* Los Angeles: Glen Dawson, 1953.

Warren, Stephen. *The Shawnees and Their Neighbors, 1795–1870.* Urbana: University of Illinois Press, 2005.

Watts, Edward. *In This Remote Country: French Colonial Culture in the Anglo-American Imagination, 1780–1860.* Chapel Hill: University of North Carolina Press, 2006.

Weber, David J. *The Taos Trappers: The Fur Trade, 1540–1846.* Norman: University of Oklahoma Press, 1970.

White, Bruce M. "The Power of Whiteness, or the Life and Times of Joseph Rolette Jr." In *Making Minnesota Territory, 1849–1858*, edited by Anne R. Kaplan and Marilyn Ziebarth. St. Paul: Minnesota Historical Society Press, 1999.

White, Richard. *The Middle Ground: Indians, Empires, and Republics in the Great Lakes Region, 1650–1815.* New York: Cambridge University Press, 1991.

Wishart, David J. *The Fur Trade of the American West, 1807–1840: A Geographical Synthesis.* Lincoln: University of Nebraska Press, 1979.

———. *An Unspeakable Sadness: The Dispossession of the Nebraska Indians.* Lincoln: University of Nebraska Press, 1994.

Woodford, Frank B. *Lewis Cass: The Last Jeffersonian.* New Brunswick, N.J.: Rutgers University Press, 1950.

Wyman, Mark. *The Wisconsin Frontier.* Bloomington: Indiana University Press, 1998.

Young, Brian. *The Politics of Codification: The Lower Canadian Civil Code of 1866.* Montreal: McGill–Queen's University Press, 1994.

INDEX

Page numbers in italics indicate illustrations.